YEARS TO GROW

BY MARTA H. YEMM

Publishers
T.S. DENISON and COMPANY, INC.
Minneapolis, Minnesota

T.S. DENISON & COMPANY, INC.

Standard Book Number: 513-01724-0
Library of Congress Number 81-68369

Minneapolis, Minn. 55431

This book is dedicated to the Marys everywhere who truly love children and can radiate the excitement and enthusiasm that spark the learning process

and

to a certain lady who as a small child insisted that the only way to spell JANE was JPNOA.

FOREWARD

This book is comprised of ten chapters named for school months. Each chapter presents basic abstract units (colors, shapes, numbers, alphabet) and specific social studies units that may be used in daily pre-primary teaching.

It is expected that the teachers will provide additional stimuli to their students, for these study units are only a guide and outline of subjects for daily classroom activities. Various supplies will be needed to implement this course, including: scissors, paste, crayons, waterbase paints, tape, elementary pencils, record player and suitable records, puppets, models, blocks, and craft items listed for individual special projects.

The drawings included in this book have been tested in a day care facility for one year and have proven effective in teaching pre-primary children. They are presented at the end of each chapter and are aimed at specific ages and capabilities. The suggested age group for each picture may be found in the upper right corner of the page. The circled number immediately following is the day number in the monthly series. Many of these drawings are ideal for flannel-board use. All drawings may be reproduced for student use as color, cut, and paste activities.

Appendix I is a booklet to be made by the children about colors. Appendix II is a booklet of alphabet review pages. Because holidays occur throughout the year on different days, a special holiday section is presented in Appendix III, to be referred to when the holiday approaches.

CONTENTS

SEPTEMBER UNITS:

I. Community Helpers
   A. This unit is designed for the use of pre-school children aged 2-4 years.
   B. The time period involved to present the entire unit is four weeks.

II. Summary of key ideas (general overview)
   A. A community can be defined as a number of people living in the same locality who share common benefits and responsibilities.
      1. Many things can be accomplished cooperatively that are difficult to do as an individual.
      2. The use of good manners facilitates group living.
   B. What can be learned about people who protect us?
      1. Police Officer
      2. Fire Fighter
   C. What is the work of people in various stores?
      1. Clerks
      2. Stock personnel
   D. Other helpers
      1. Mail Carrier
      2. Librarian
   E. The community must have rules
      1. For protection
      2. Consequences

III. Objectives
   A. General
      1. Develop an understanding of ho community helpers are.
      2. Develop a positive attitude toward community helpers.
      3. Give children a positive attitude from related experiences which help develop an awareness of their place in a well-balanced school program.
      4. Provide opportunities for group interaction.
      5. Develop a sense of individual responsibility.
   B. Specific
      1. Recognition
         a. Police Officer
         b. Fire Fighter
         c. Electrical Worker
         d. Mail Carrier
         e. Librarian
      2. Help children understand and appreciate the services and work of people in the community.
      3. Understand the importance of the rules and regulations that govern a community.
      4. Make the children aware of ways that they can help make the community a better place to live.
      5. Make the children aware of how to use the various facilities available in the community.

IV. Initiation of the unit
  A. Experiences
    1. Displays of movable objects
      a. Trucks and cars
      b. Equipment used by community helpers
    2. Environment
      a. Display attractive pictures of community helpers doing their jobs.
      b. Have illustrated books on hand.
      c. Supply blocks for building.
      d. Have wooden or pipe cleaner dolls for role playing.
      e. Collect boxes of various sizes for buildings.
  B. Discussions
    1. Where do Mommy and Daddy work?
    2. Where does the child go in the neighborhood, and beyond the neighborhood? Why?

PROBLEM/CONCEPT	SUGGESTED ACTIVITIES
COMMUNITY HELPERS: A community may be defined as a number of people living in the same locality who **share** common benefits and responsibilities.	Make a bulletin board map of the community, noting things we share such as: 1. Streets 2. Sidewalks 3. Stores 4. Libraries Talk about what is in the neighborhood and discuss sharing: 1. Swings 2. Parks 3. Trees On the map locate children's homes and landmarks.
Many things can be done cooperatively that are difficult to do as an individual.	Show filmstrip of community helpers working together. Start a scrapbook of magazine pictures of community helpers. For older children (4) if a park is close by, take a class trip to see how it is kept for everyone to use. 1. Trash containers 2. Grass cutters 3. Sprinklers

	Use paper plates to make masks of community helpers for role playing. Make hand puppets from paper bags or construction paper on sticks.
What can we learn about buying and selling in stores? 1. Courtesy 2. How to carry money The use of manners facilitates living in any kind of group.	Discuss what you do in a store and who helps you. Discuss manners and why they are used. 1. Don't push in line 2. Use "excuse me" 3. Use "thank you" 4. Use "please" 5. Sharing
Learn about people who protect us: Police Officer How can we help him/her? What does his/her uniform look like? How do we call him/her? Fire Fighter How does he/she help us?	Ask local force to send speaker to the school. Learn the rules for 1. Crossing the street 2. Riding in a car or on a bus 3. Rules for strangers 4. Staying out of the way 5. Reporting something Check color of local force uniform. 1. Hat is like a stop sign 2. Badge is either a star or a shield. Method: 1. Tell an adult 2. If alone, dial 911 Bring a toy telephone to class and practice calling for help. Dramatize: 1. Fighting a fire 2. Fire fighter caring for equipment Explain fire drill procedures and practice. If school holds regular drills, stress rules once per week.
The community must have rules concerning the use of its facilities, such as: 1. Traffic laws 2. Rules for parks 3. Rules for behavior 4. Special dispensations	Discuss ways we share consideration for neighbors. 1. Toys kept out of street 2. Keeping noise down Dramatic representations of community laws, i.e., cross at corner.

Rules protect individuals and ensure health and safety.	Make miniature stop signs and traffic lights and use them in the room.
What can we learn about the people who take care of a community? 1. Street repair 2. Gas company 3. Electric company 4. Telephone company	What are their duties? What are their uniforms like? What tools do they use? Color pictures of helpers at work
What can we learn about people who help us have fun? 1. Playground director 2. Park employees 3. Librarian	Emphasize having a personal library. Learn how to take care of books so that they will last. 1. Clean hands 2. No tearing 3. No marking in book Organize a room library, a special corner with books to be kept in the room.
A community is only as good as the people who live in it.	Discuss infractions of laws and rules: 1. Hurting others by fighting 2. Speeding 3. Taking things that don't belong to us 4. Destroying public property
COLORS: Distinguish	Point out objects in the room that are the color of the day. Give out crayons of only that color. Cut construction paper in different shapes and have the class help match the colors in piles. Have people with the color of the day stand up in their places. Name another color and have others stand. Try to think of objects not in the room that are the color of the day. Review constantly from story books and other materials.

September

MONTH: SEPT

(1) Calendar	(2) Bus Safety	(3) Police visibility (car)	(4) Introduce colors: RED	(5) Stop sign RED
(6) Police Officer as friend	(7) RED cherries	(8) Introduce YELLOW	(9) Feelings and Manners	(10) Please and thank you
(11) YELLOW (bees)	(12) YELLOW (lemons)	(13) Fire Fighter visibility (hat)	(14) Fire truck	(15) Fire Fighter in uniform
(16) Review RED (fire hydrant)	(17) YELLOW (bananas)	(18) Electric Co. visibility (truck)	(19) Mail Carrier service	(20) Introduce ORANGE
(21) Library Service (books)			Craft items: 1. popsicle sticks 2. yarn	

SEPTEMBER

SUN.	MON.	TUES.	WED.	THURS.	FRI.	SAT.

3. ②

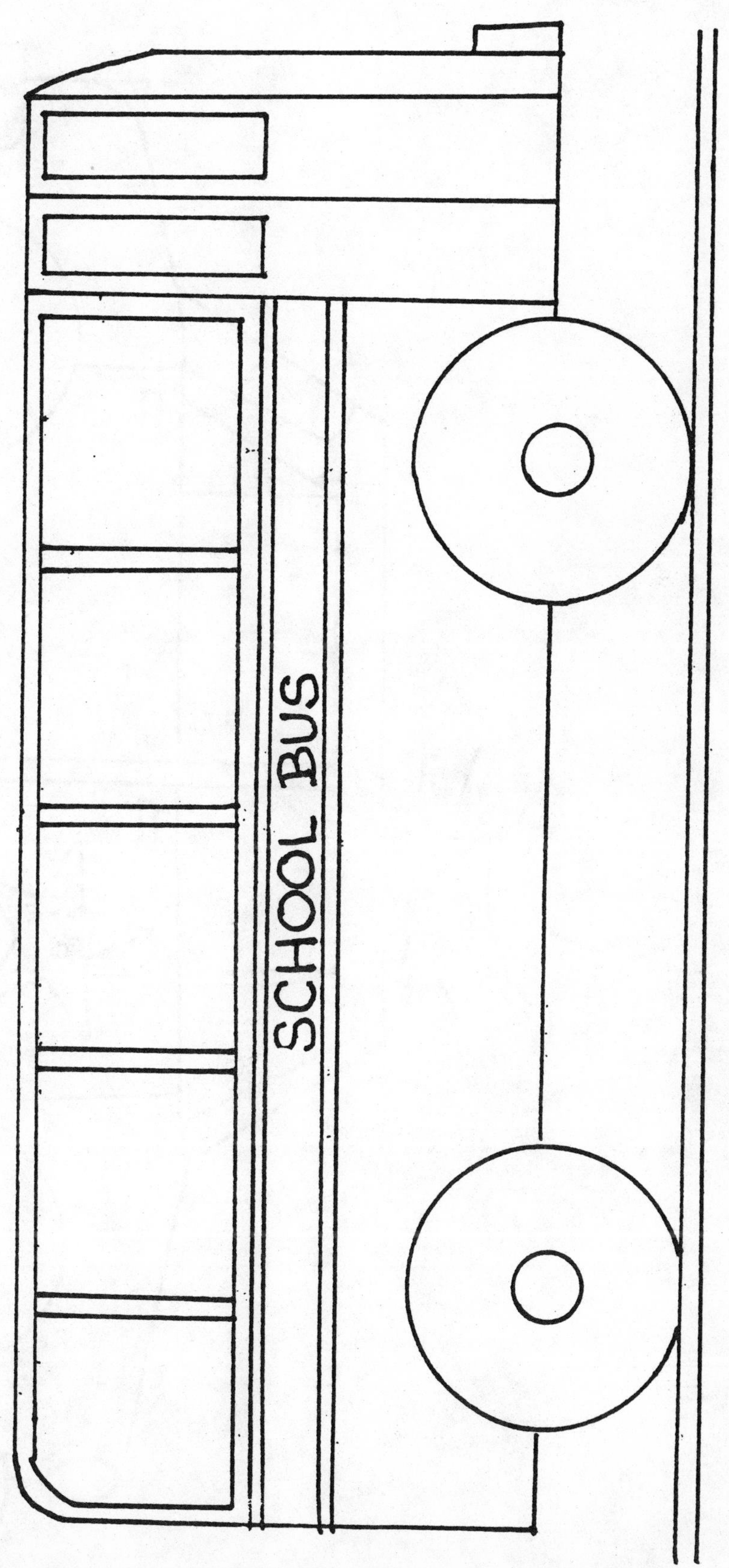
SCHOOL BUS

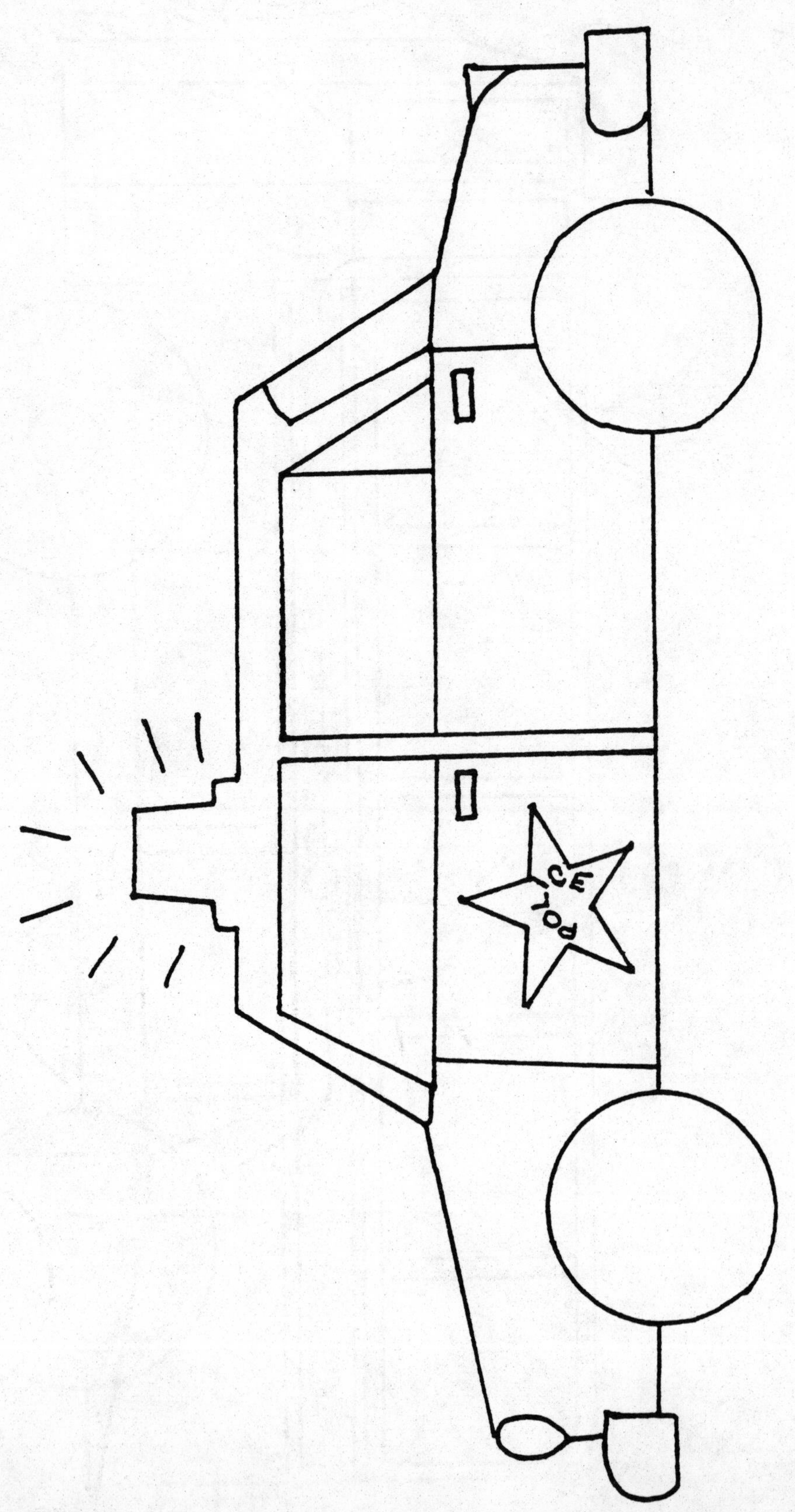
POLICE

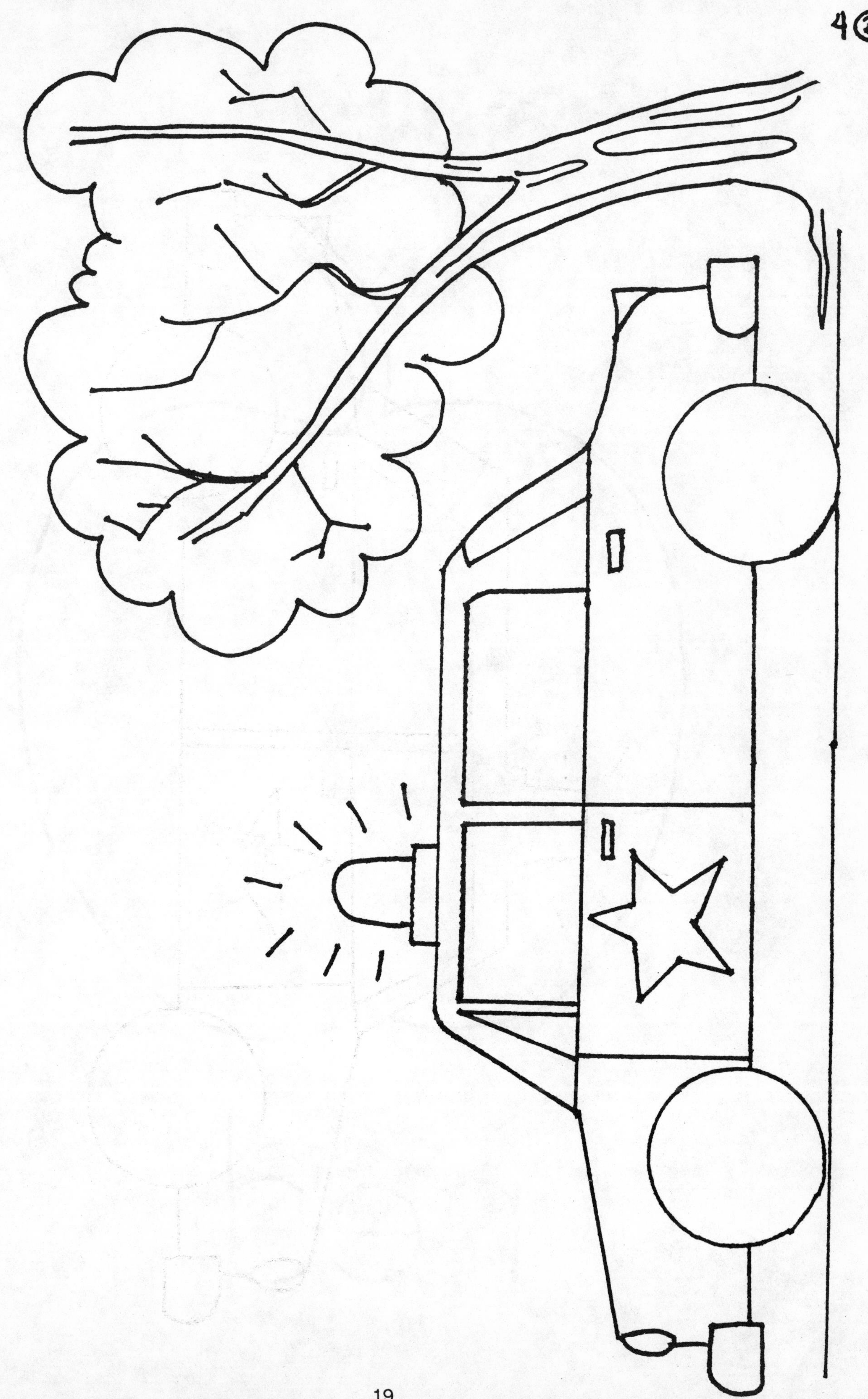

red

red

Age 3: paint, paste on craft stick

Age 4: reproduce on red paper, cut out, paste to craft stick.

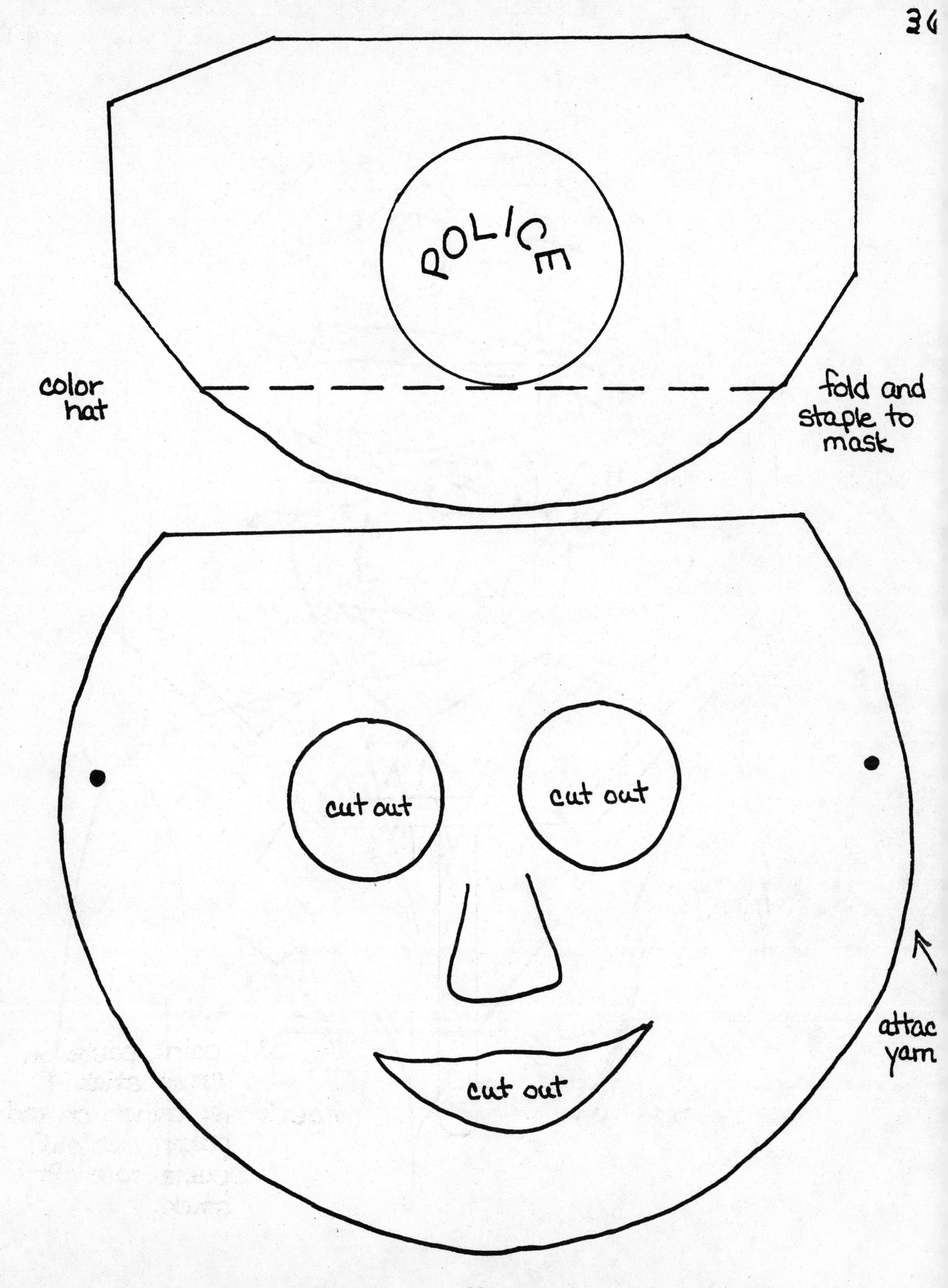
POLICE
color hat
fold and staple to mask
cut out
cut out
cut out
attac
yarn

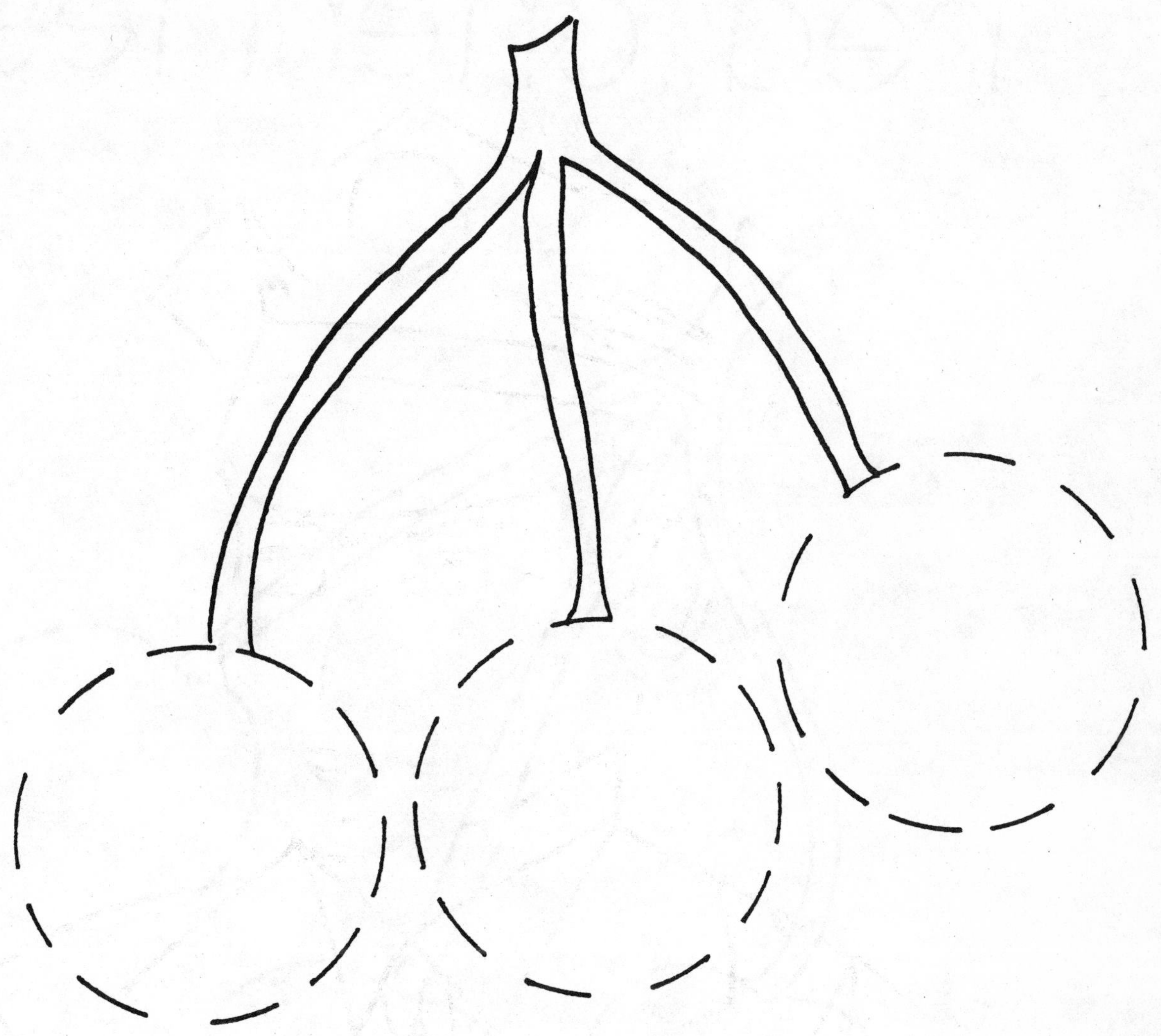

Cut out red circles: child pastes in place.

red cherries

red cherries

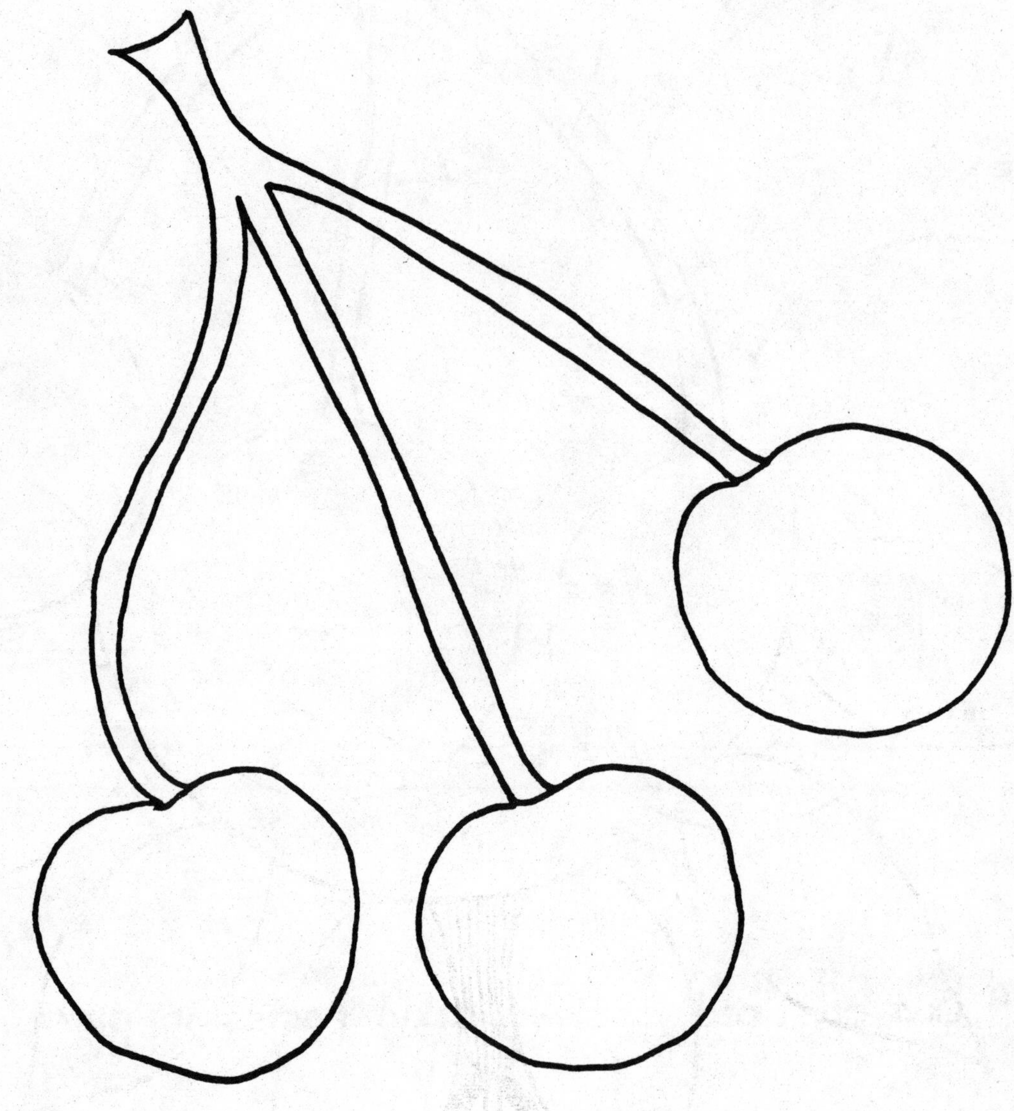

Age 3: color
Age 4: paint

yellow

Make the sun shine bright; paste yellow rays in place.

yellow

Finish the sad face

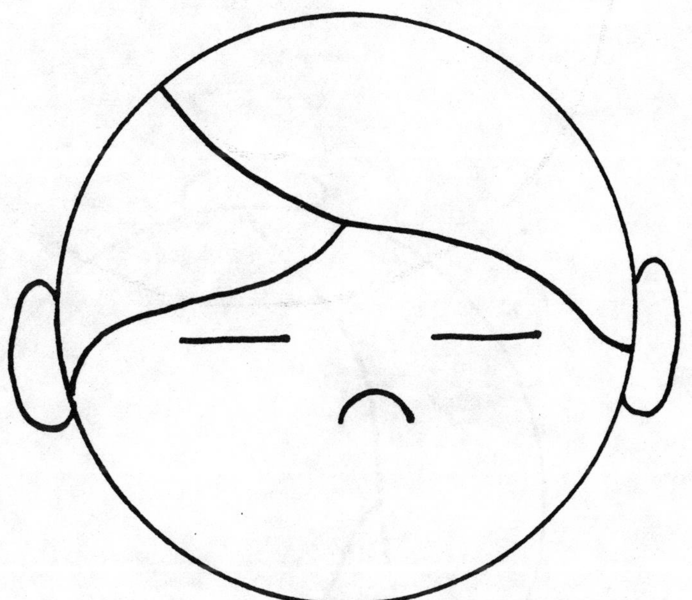

Make this face happy

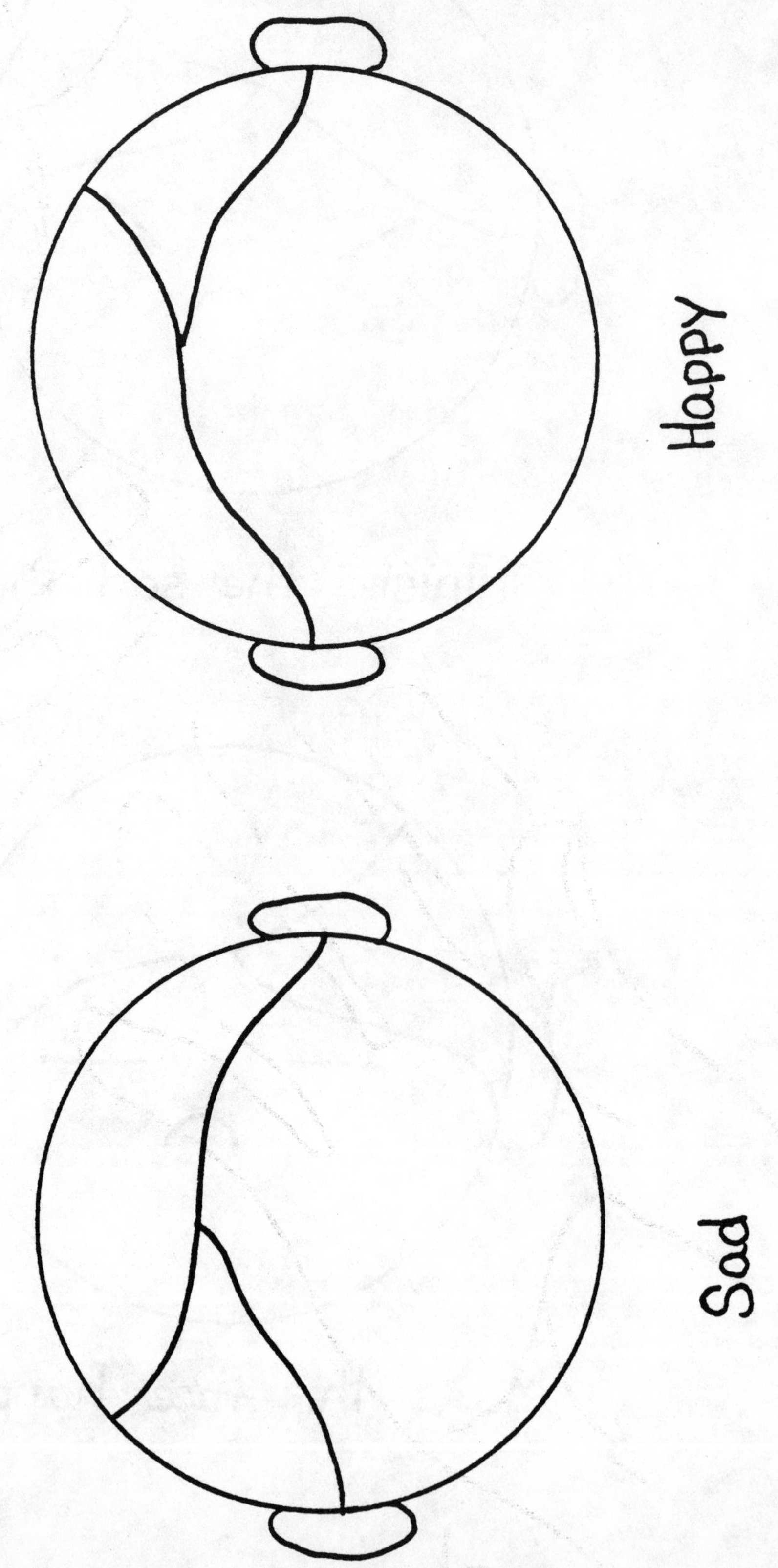
Happy
Sad

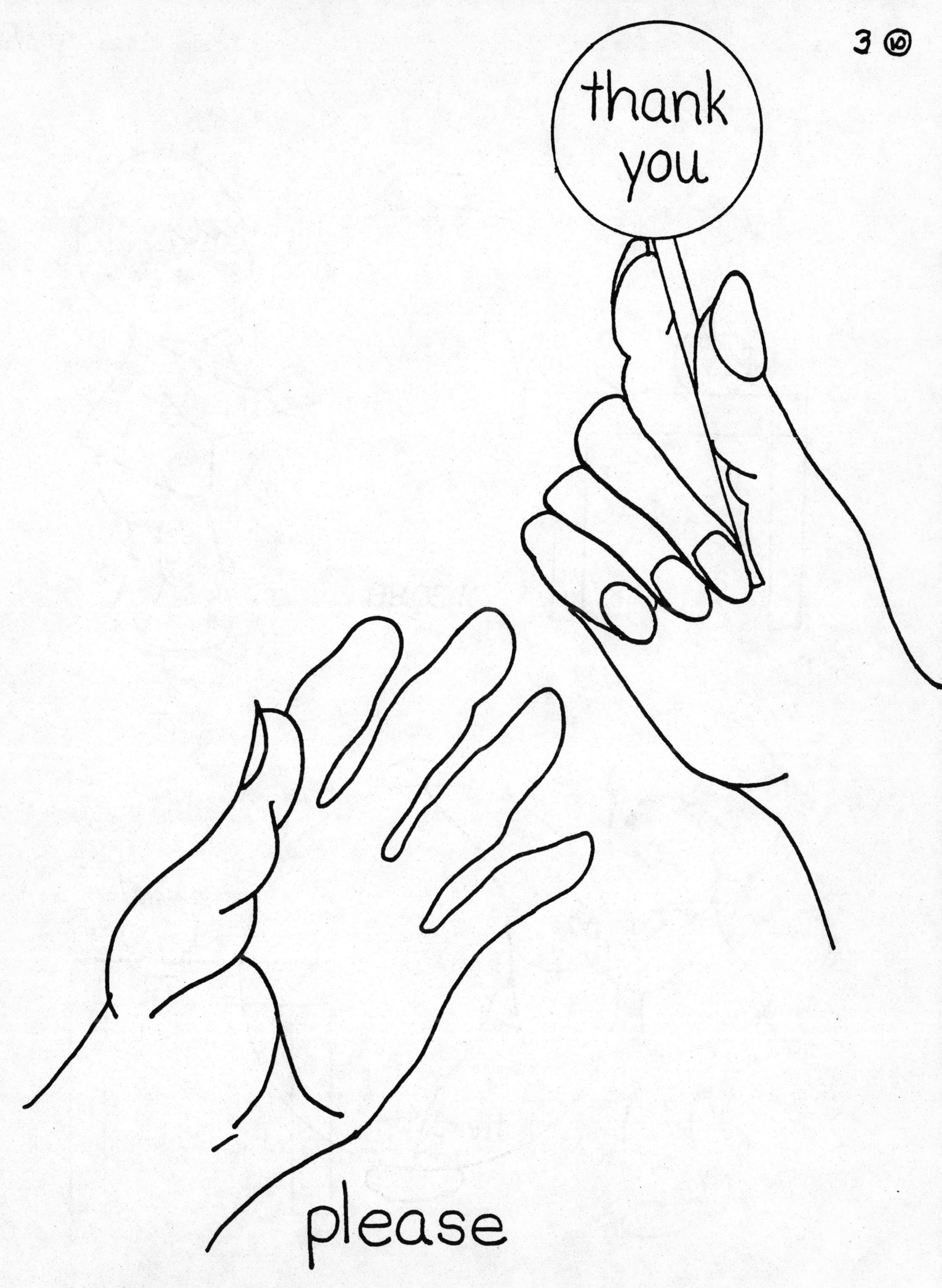
thank you
please

please
thank you

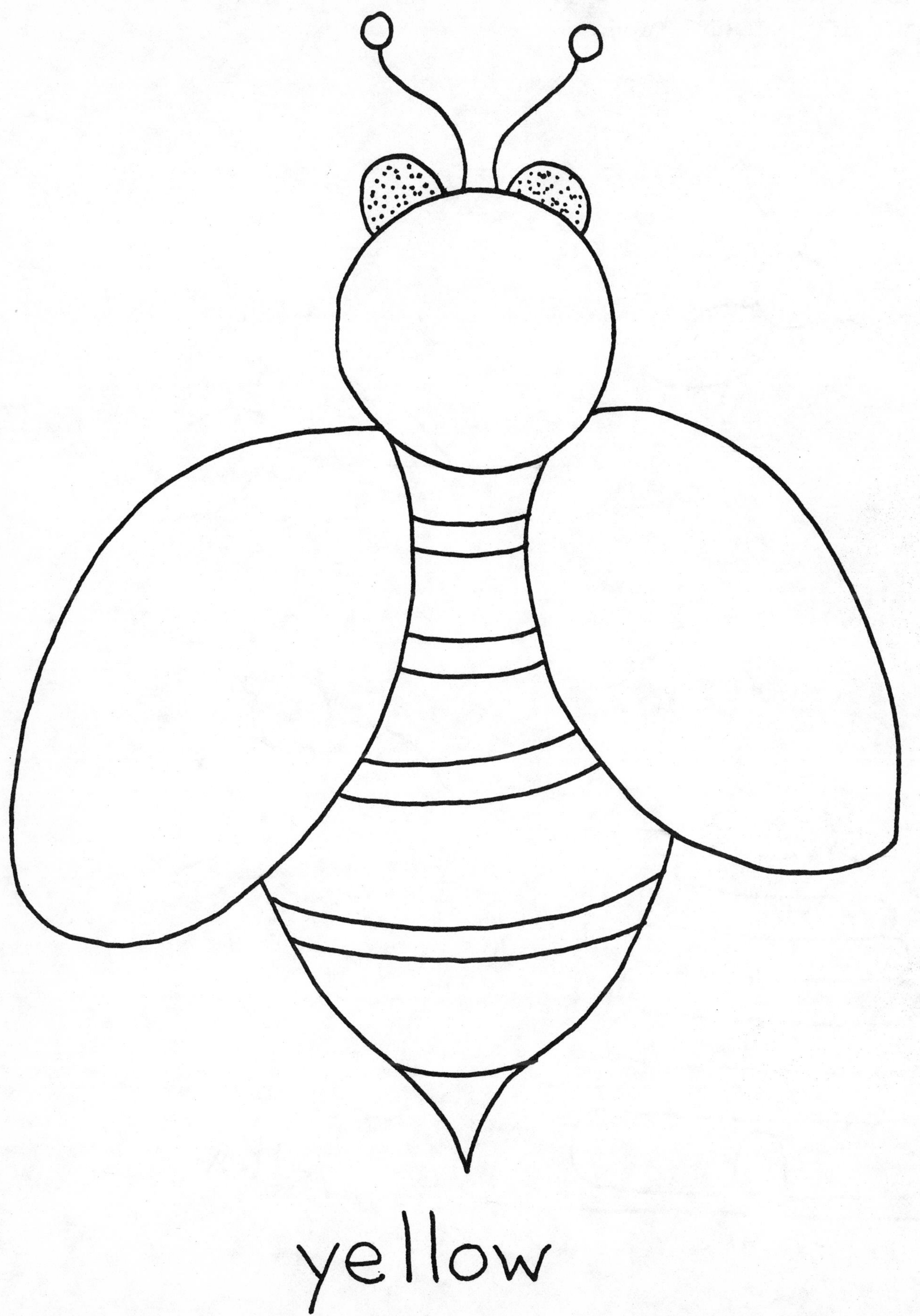
yellow

Cut out yellow construction paper bodies; paste to picture; color hive.

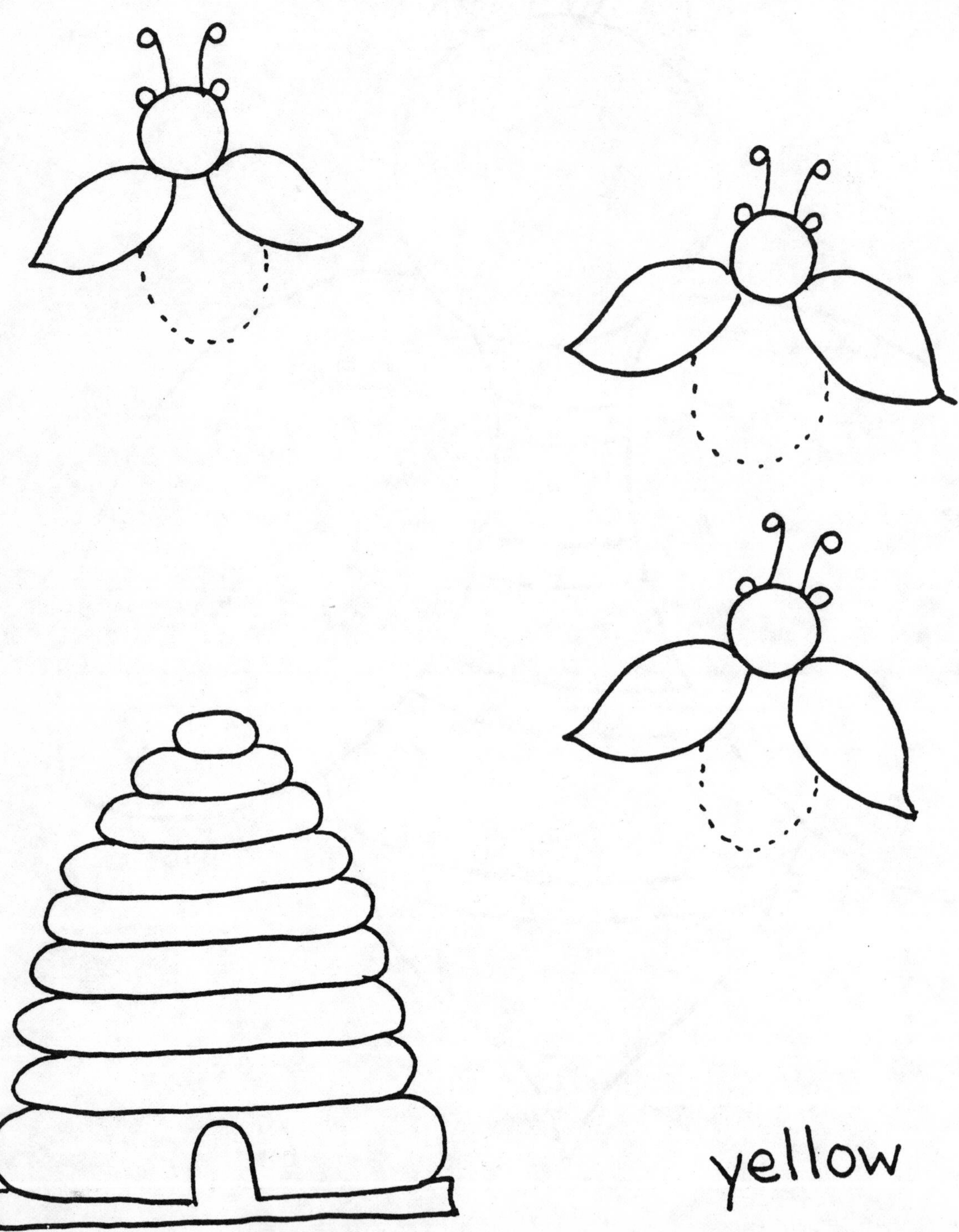

yellow

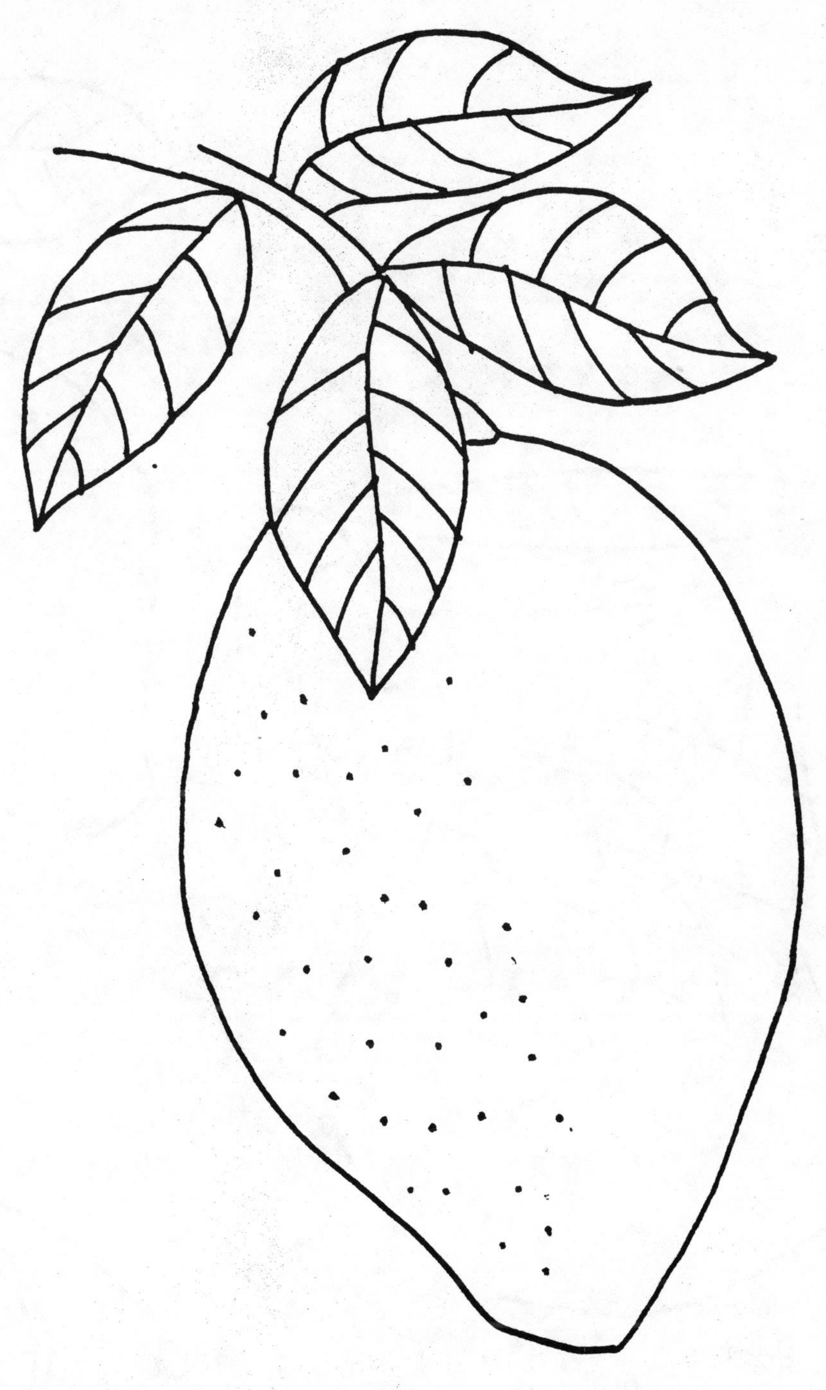

yellow lemon

yellow lemons

3 (13)

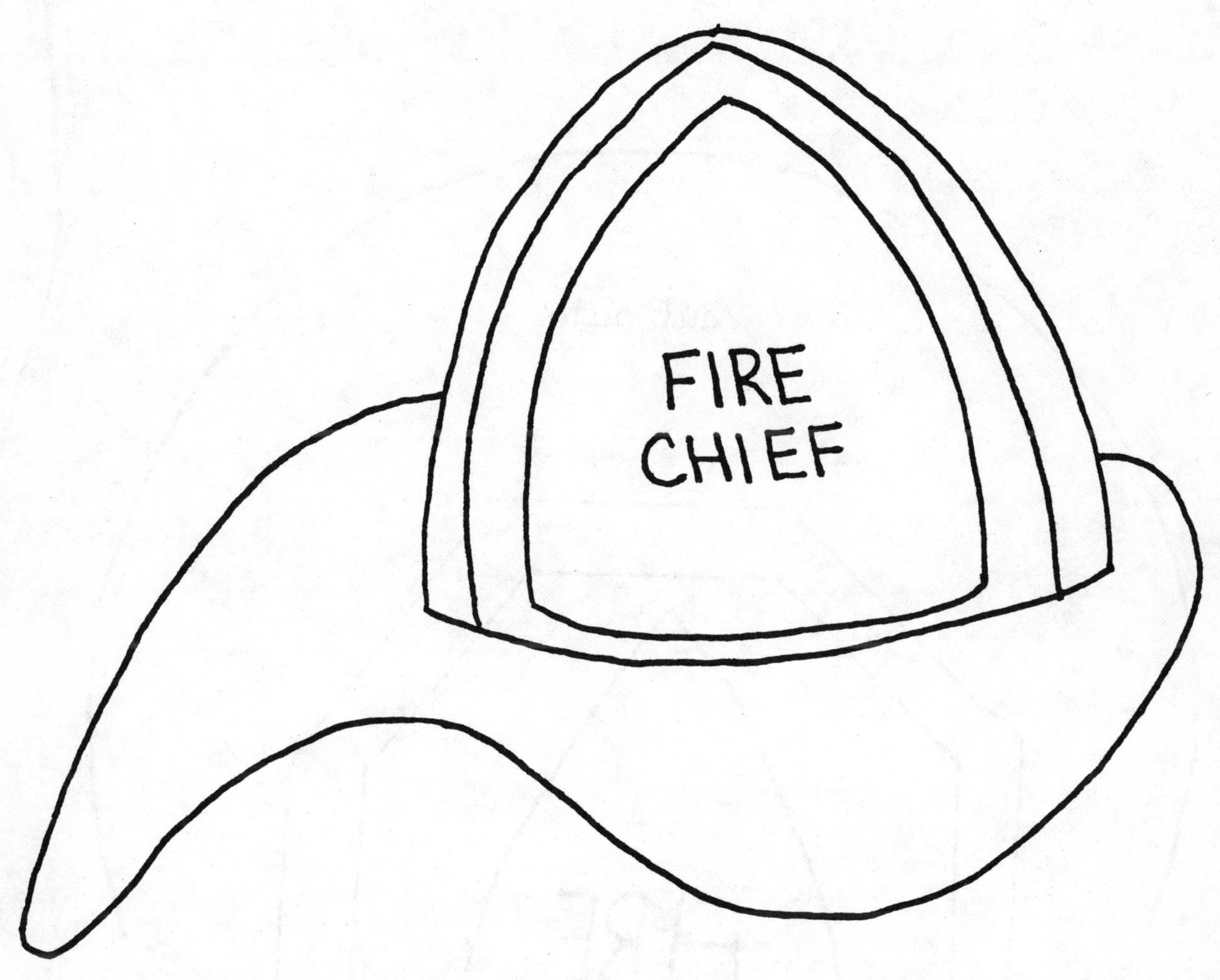

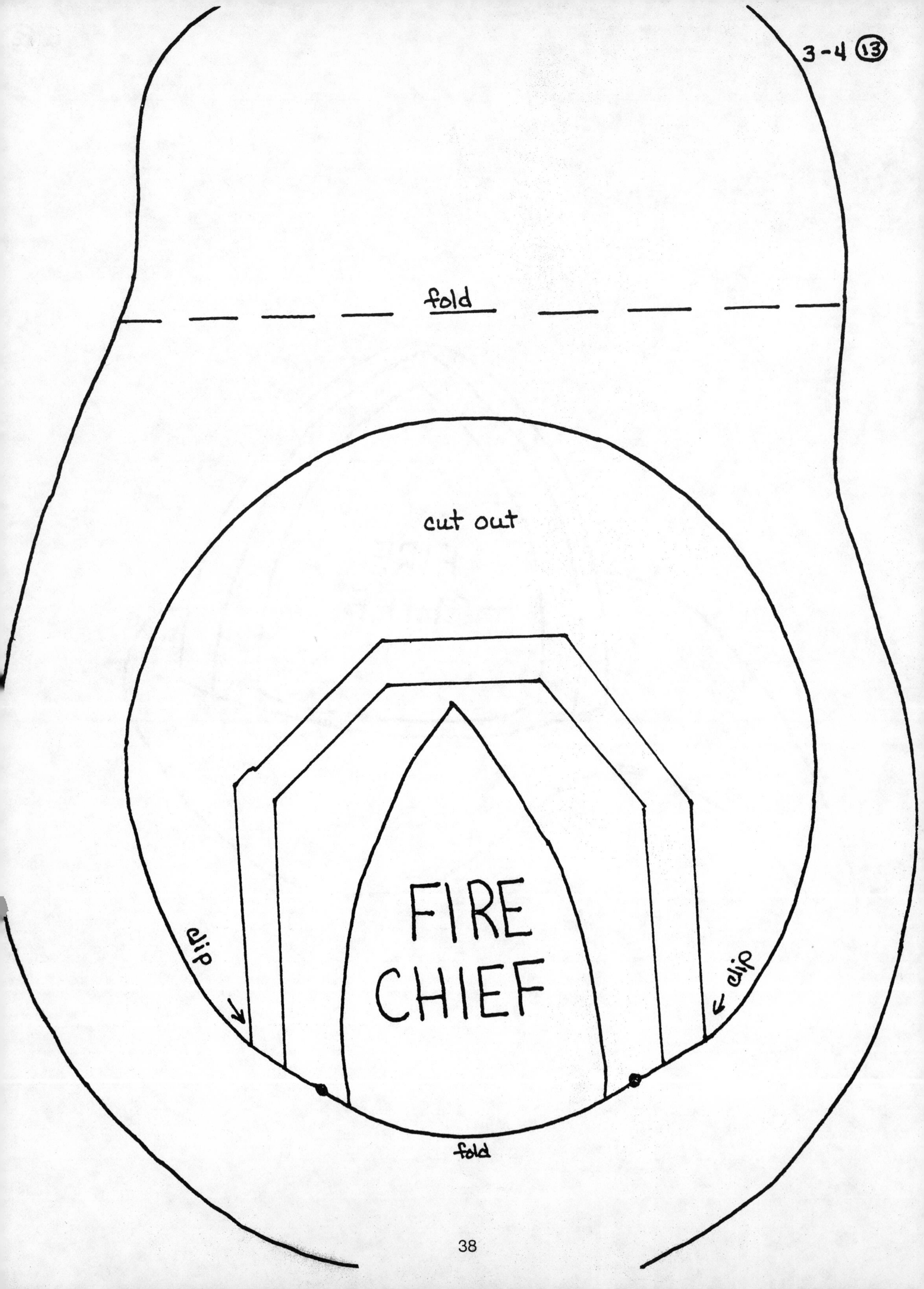
fold
cut out
FIRE
CHIEF
clip
clip
fold

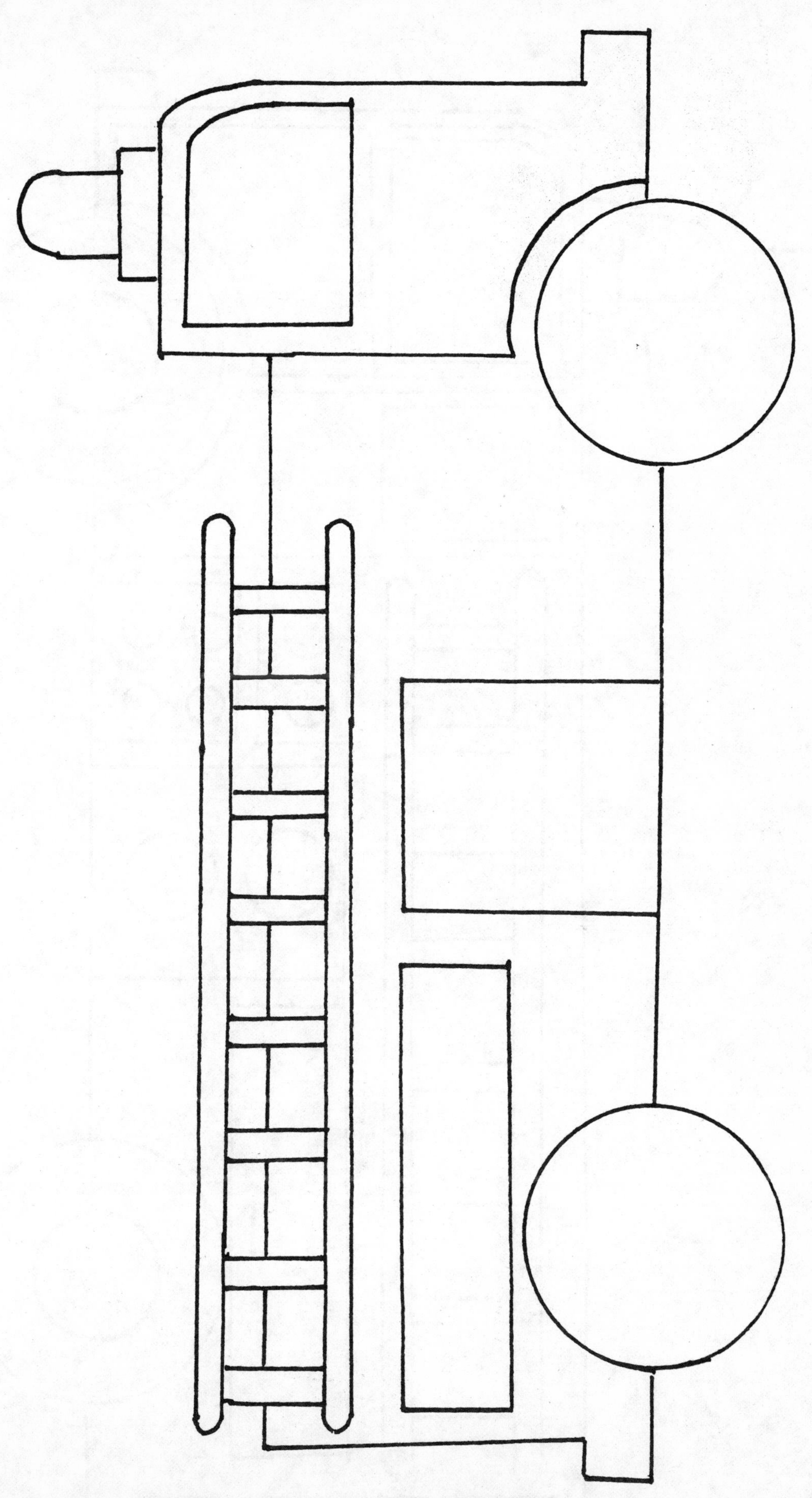

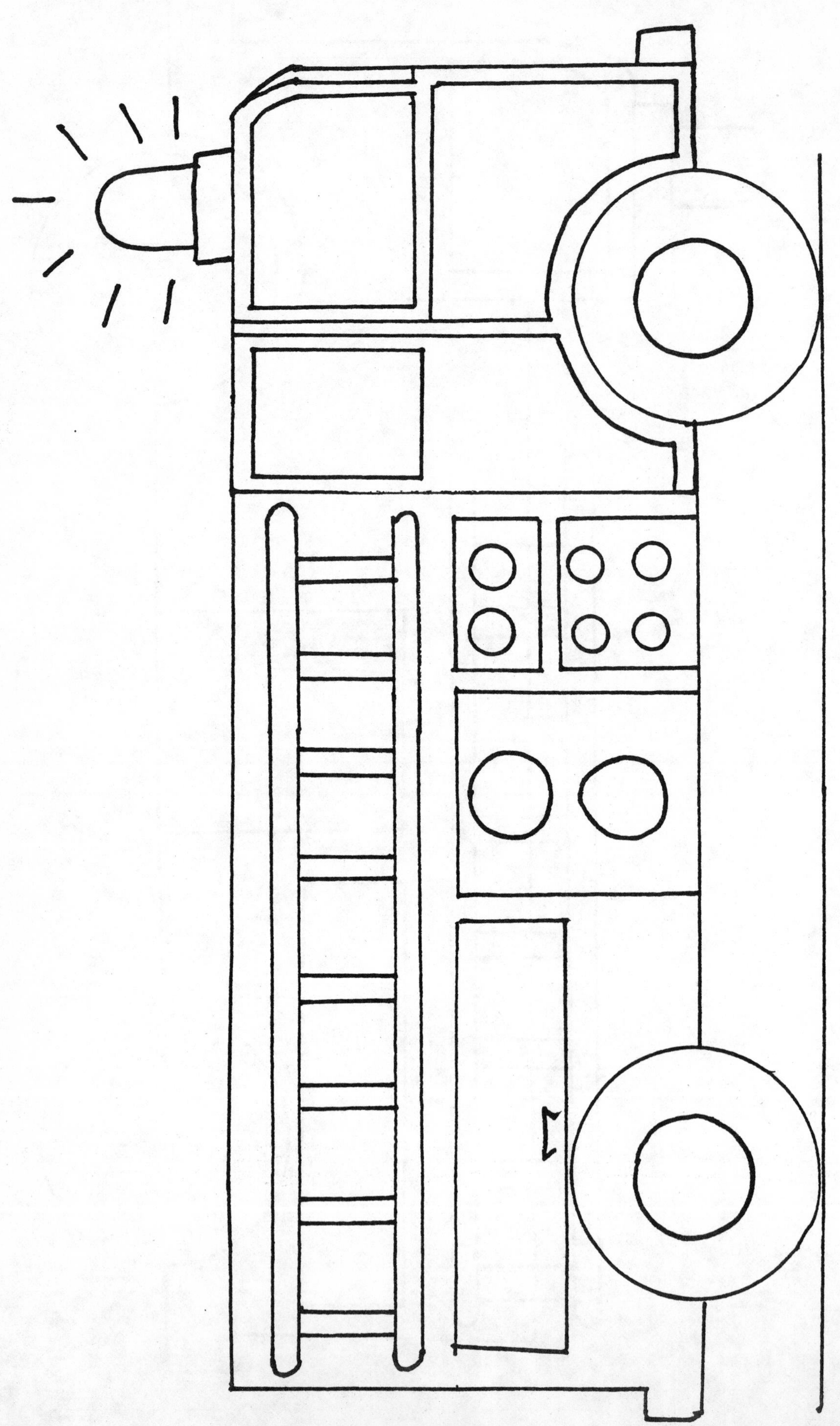

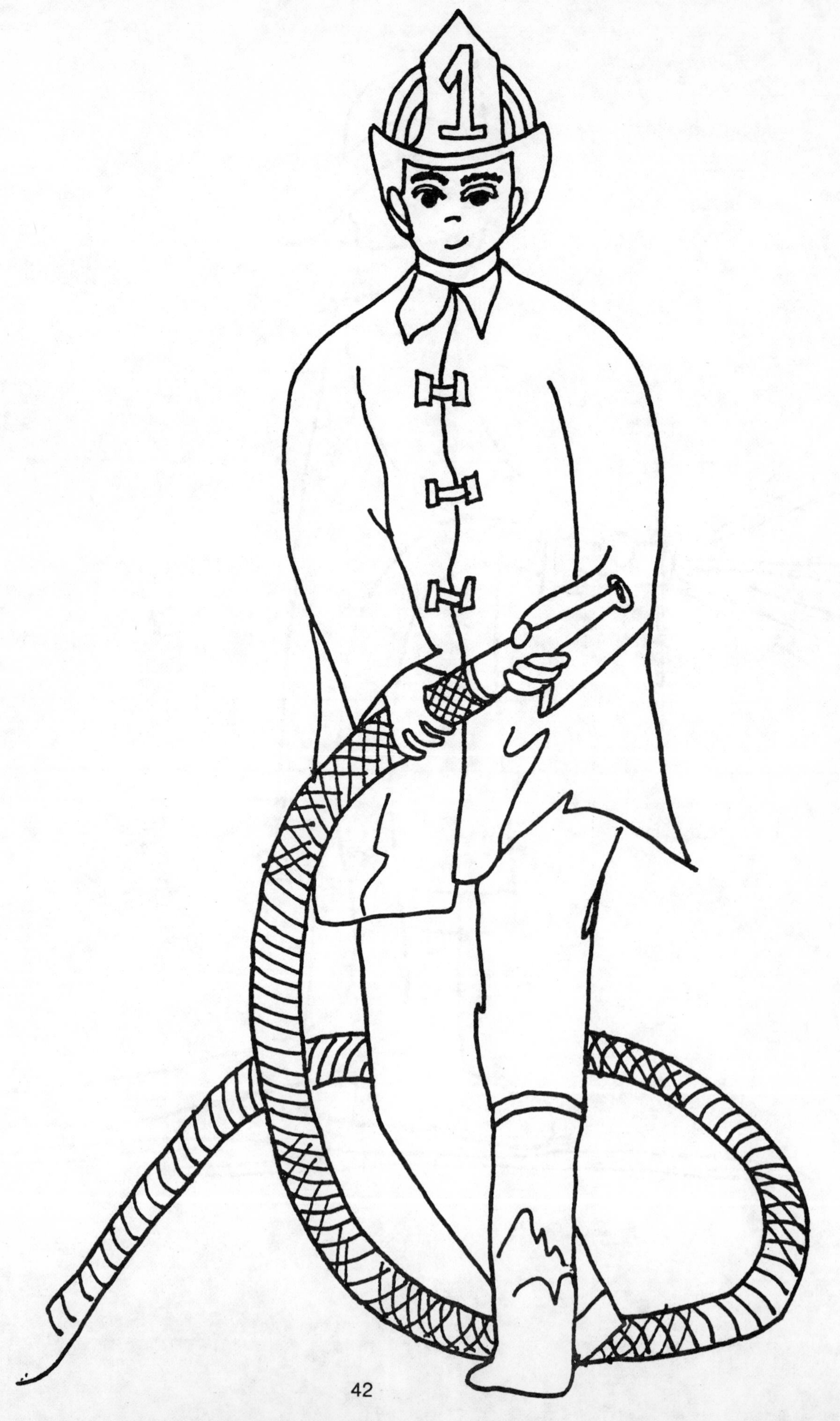
1

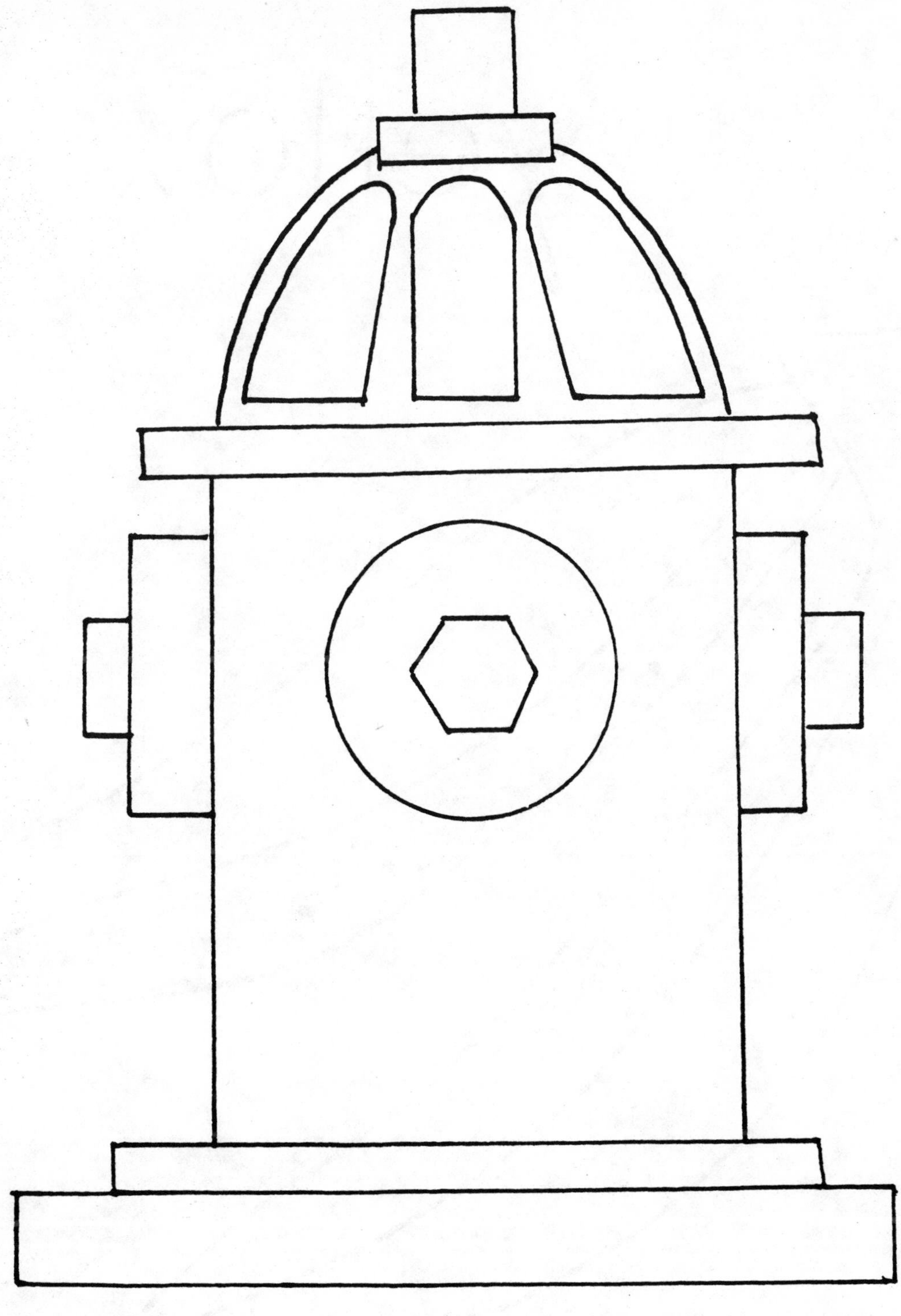

Age 3 - color, cut out
4 - paint

yellow

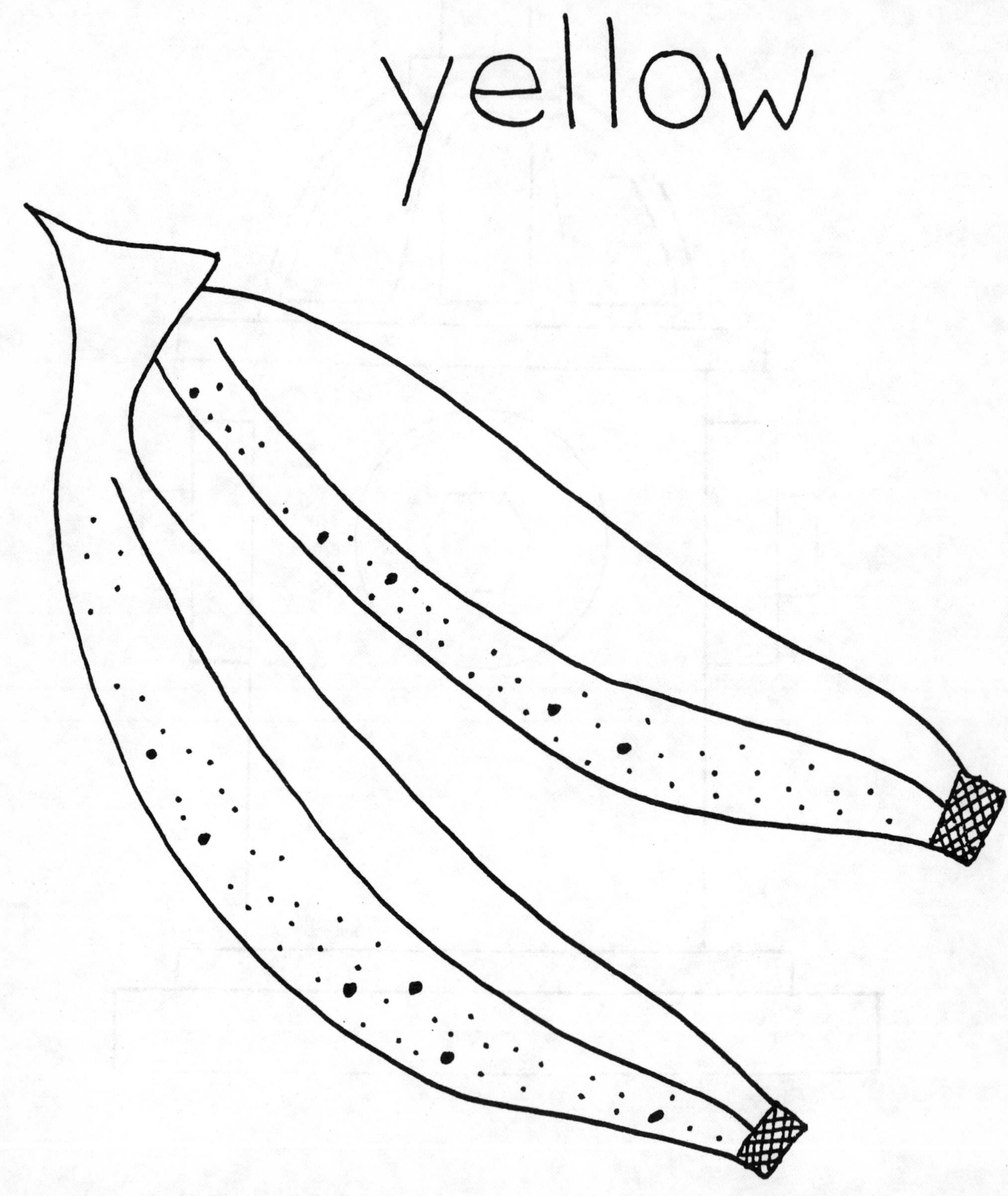

yellow bananas

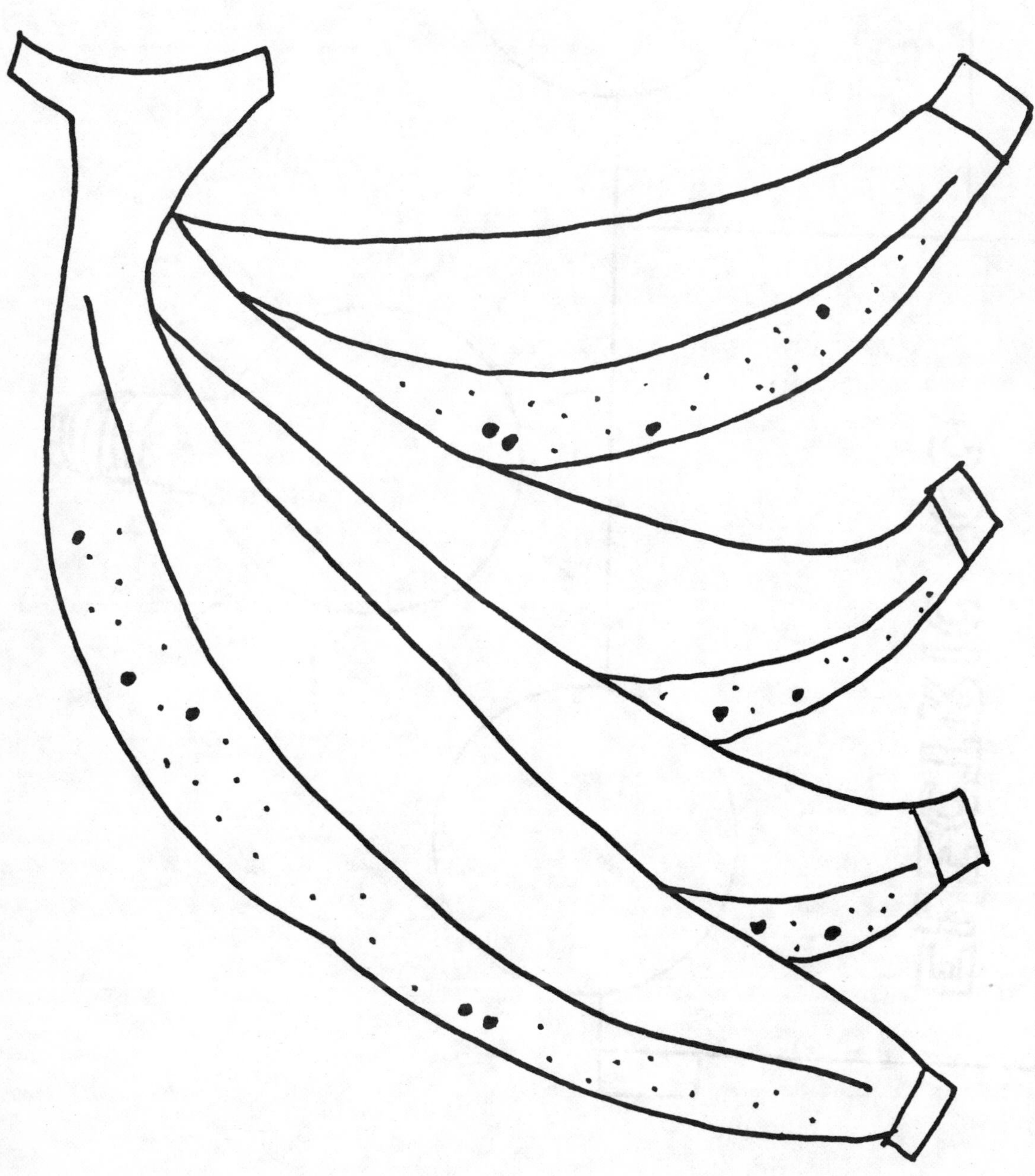

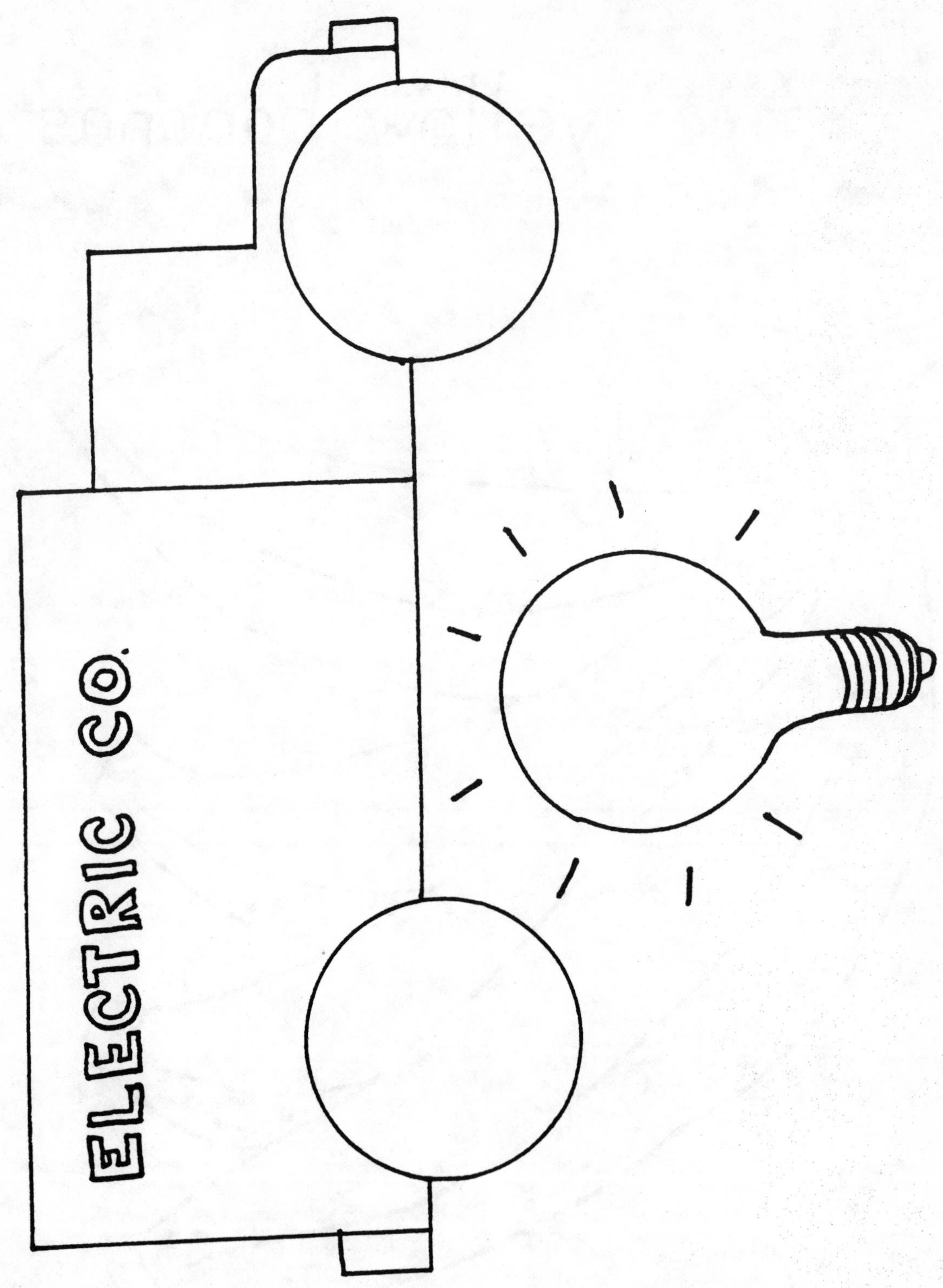
ELECTRIC CO.

4 (18)

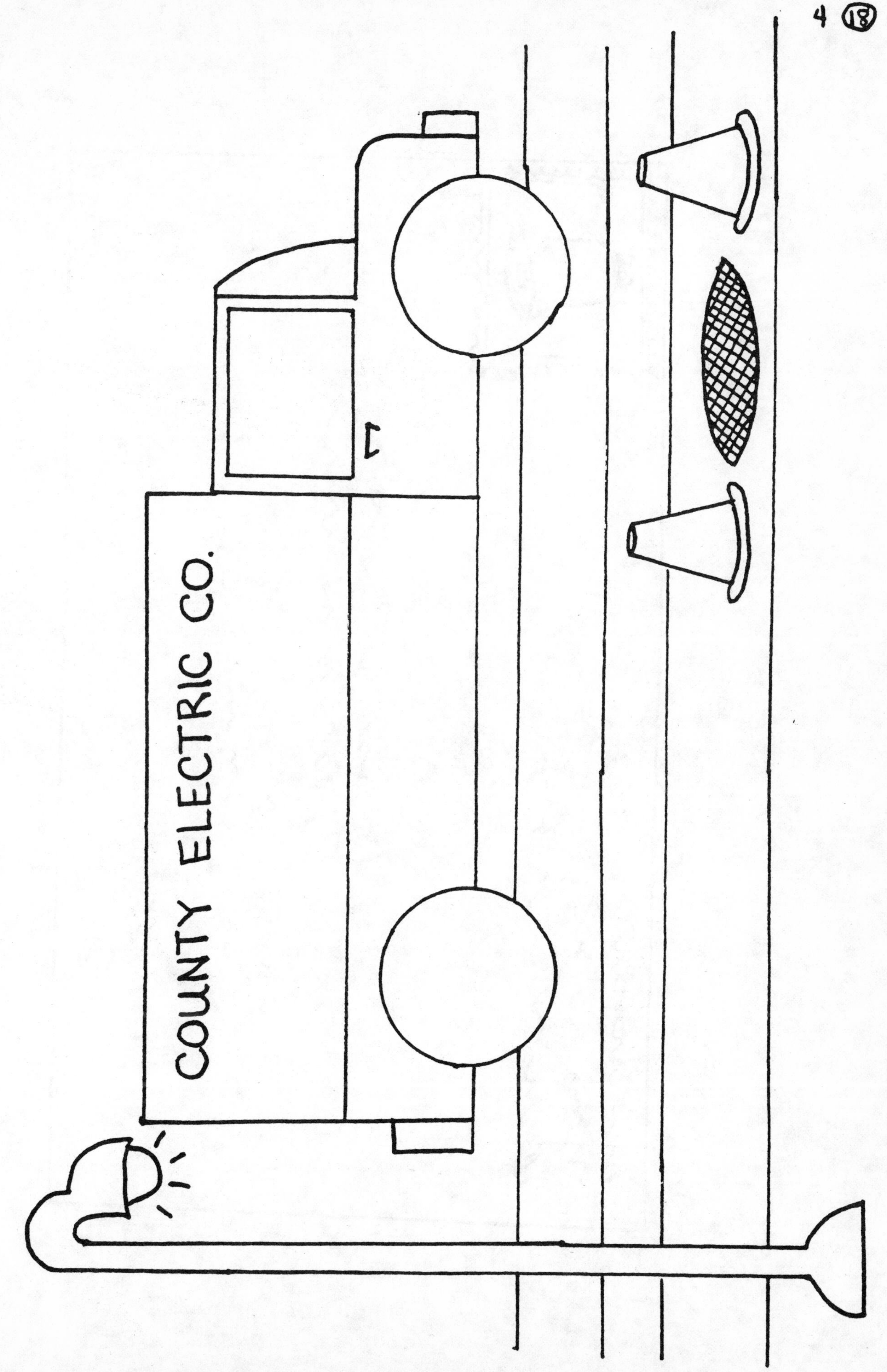

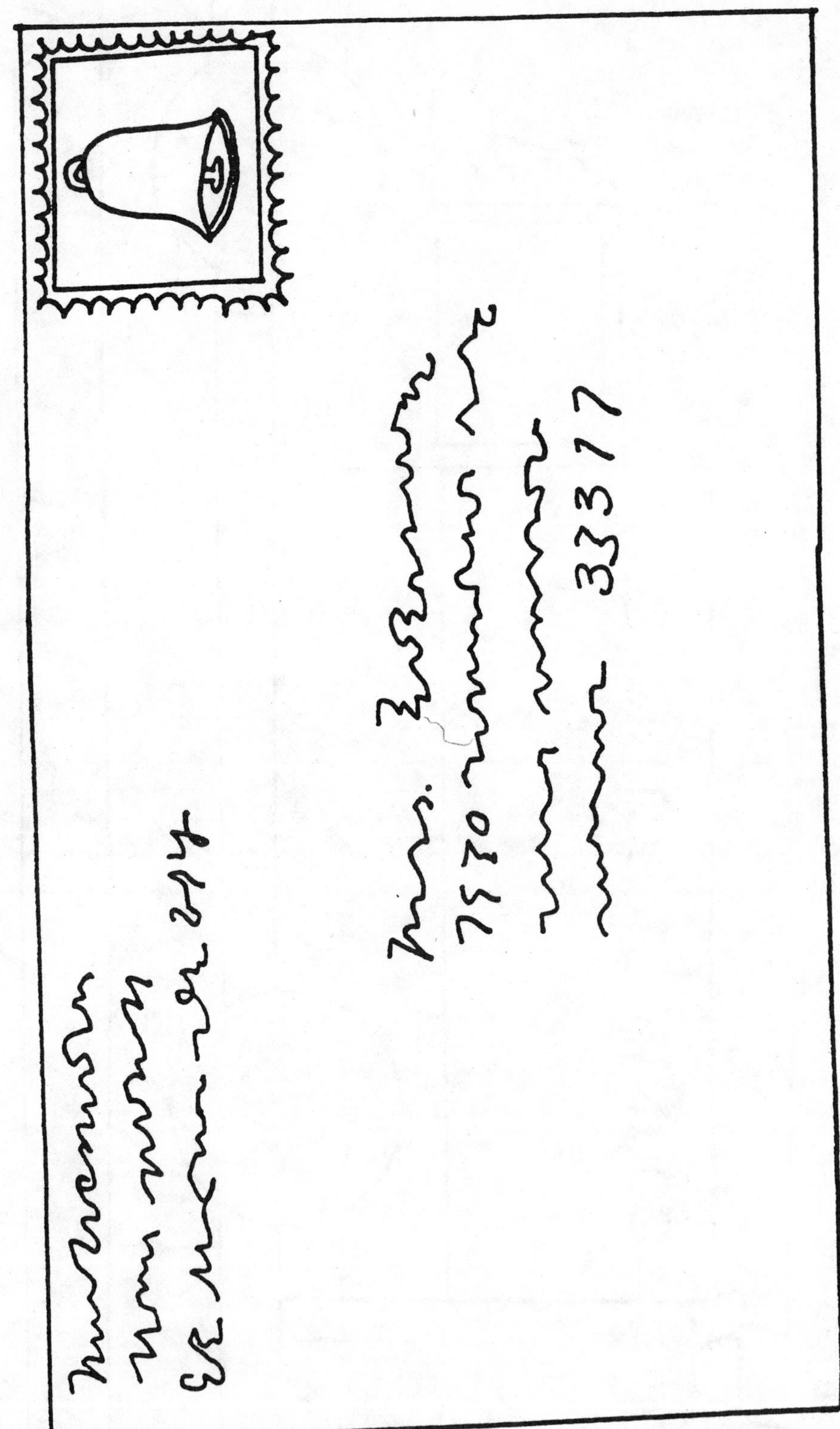

U.S. MAIL

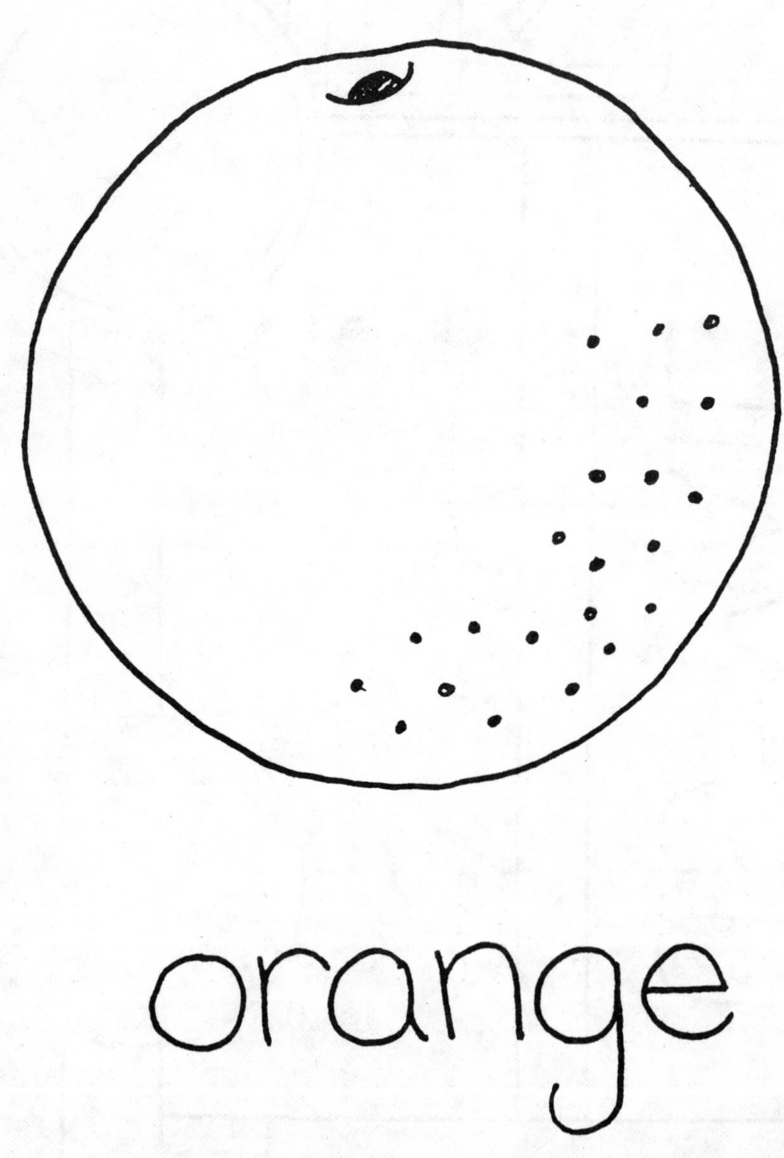
orange

orange

Visit the library; Visit the books.

3 (21)

Visit Friends at the Library

OCTOBER UNITS:

I. Nursery Rhymes

- **A.** This unit is designed for ages 3-4 years.
- **B.** The time period involved is three weeks.
- **C.** Key Ideas
  1. Establish oral activity
  2. Reinforce ideas that have begun at home, thereby involving the parents with their child's work at school.
- **D.** Rhymes used
  1. Hickory, Dickory Dock
  2. Little Bo-Peep
  3. Mary, Mary, Quite Contrary
  4. Jack Be Nimble
  5. Humpty Dumpty
  6. Four and Twenty Blackbirds
  7. Little Jack Horner

II. Colors

- **A.** Continuation from September
- **B.** Review
  1. Red
  2. Yellow
  3. Orange
- **C.** Introduce
  1. Blue
  2. Black
  3. Green

III. Holidays - Explain "special day"

- **A.** Columbus Day
  1. Tell the story of Columbus.
  2. Color picture of three ships.
- **B.** Halloween
  1. Emphasize the day as a fun experience, not scary.
  2. Integrate color unit with this one
  3. Projects: mask and tissue ghost

Explanation of GHOST PROJECT:
Materials needed: Kleenex (white)
String
Black magic marker

Method:
1. Roll one tissue into a ball
2. Cover with second tissue
3. Tie string around neck
4. Mark face

PROBLEM/CONCEPT	SUGGESTED ACTIVITIES
NURSERY RHYMES: Nursery rhymes are almost songs. Some have been set to music.	Listen to records of nursery rhymes. Sing along with the children. Explain what the words say. Try to avoid rote memorization by the class. Show what the story says. Use various craft items on the drawings to make collages. Use cotton balls on the sheep, egg shell pieces on the egg, etc.
COLORS: Reviewing Colors: Red, Yellow, Orange	This is a family of warm colors; they relate to fire, heat, and the sun. Use blocks of the same size and shape to show only the difference in color. Crayons may be used too, but a change of example is helpful. Point out different colors in the classroom. Have the child eat the color. Use life savers, oranges, jelly on crackers, icing on cookies (blue), apples, lemon drops, make instant chocolate pudding in class.
Introducing Colors: Blue, Black, Green	This is a family of cool colors like ice, grass, and sea water. Determine which children can already differentiate colors. Use blocks and food as in review above. Color, paint and cut out pictures provided.
HALLOWEEN:	See outline suggestions. Emphasize the "fun" aspect.

	Explain safety for trick or treating. 1. Go with an adult, never alone. 2. Think about attending a community party instead. 3. Take only wrapped treats. 4. Go to the homes of friends only, never to strangers. Costumes: a trick on people 1. Think of a safe costume. 2. Keep mask off until you get to the door. 3. Don't run. 4. Stay on sidewalk if possible. 5. Carry a light of some kind.
Halloween symbols: Witches	They can be scary, but are also supposed to be just people. There are good witches and bad witches. They usually have a cat for a pet.
Pumpkins	Correlate with the color orange. Jack-O-Lanterns have funny faces to keep witches and ghosts away.
Ghosts	A way to explain pranks Described as mischievious

Hickory, dickory dock,
The mouse ran up the clock
The clock struck one
The mouse ran down,
Hickory, dickory, dock.

Mistress Mary, quite contrary
How does your garden grow?
With silver bells and cockle shells
And pretty maids all in a row.

Little Bo-Peep has lost her sheep
And can't tell where to find them;
Leave them alone and they'll come home,
Wagging their tails behind them.

Jack be nimble,
Jack be quick,
Jack jump over the candlestick.

Humpty Dumpty sat on a wall,
Humpty Dumpty had a great fall;
All the king's horses, and all the king's men
Couldn't put Humpty Dumpty together again.

Sing a song of six pence, pocket full of rye,
Four and twenty blackbirds baked in a pie.
When the pie was opened, the birds began to sing,
Wasn't that a dainty dish to set before the king?

Little Jack Horner
Sat in a corner
Eating a Christmas pie.
He put in his thumb
And pulled out a plum
And said, "What a good boy am I."

October

MONTH: OCTOBER

1 Calendar	2 Begin nursery rhymes. "Hickory, dickory, dock..." Review RED	3 Review rhyme RED (wagon)	4 "Mary, Mary" Review: YELLOW (butter)	5 "Little Bo-Peep" Review YELLOW
6 "Jack Be Nimble" Review fire safety Review: ORANGE	7 Review: RED YELLOW ORANGE	8 "Humpty-Dumpty" Begin: BLUE (bird)	9 Review: BLUE (flower)	10 Begin: BLACK "Four and 20 Blackbirds"
11 Continue: BLACK (house with black driveway)	12 "Little Jack Horner" Review: Previous rhymes	13 Begin: GREEN (frog)	14 Continue: GREEN (turtle)	15 Continue GREEN (tree)
16 Begin Halloween Safety (witch)	17 Make tissue ghost (pumpkin)	18 Review: ORANGE BLACK Paste shapes to sheet	19 Cat face—use as picture or as mask	20 Teacher carves small pumpkin. Discuss safety (cat)
21 Party Take home treats		Craft items: tissue string markers cotton balls egg shells green egg cartons		22 Insert Columbus Day Project at appropriate time.

OCTOBER

SUN.	MON.	TUES.	WED.	THURS.	FRI.	SAT.

3 ②

Hickory, Dickory, Dock

4 ②

Hickory, Dickory, Dock

3 ②

red

red
red
red
red

red wagon

red wagon

3 ④

Mary, Mary

Mary, Mary

yellow butter

Bo-Peep's Sheep

Little Bo-Peep

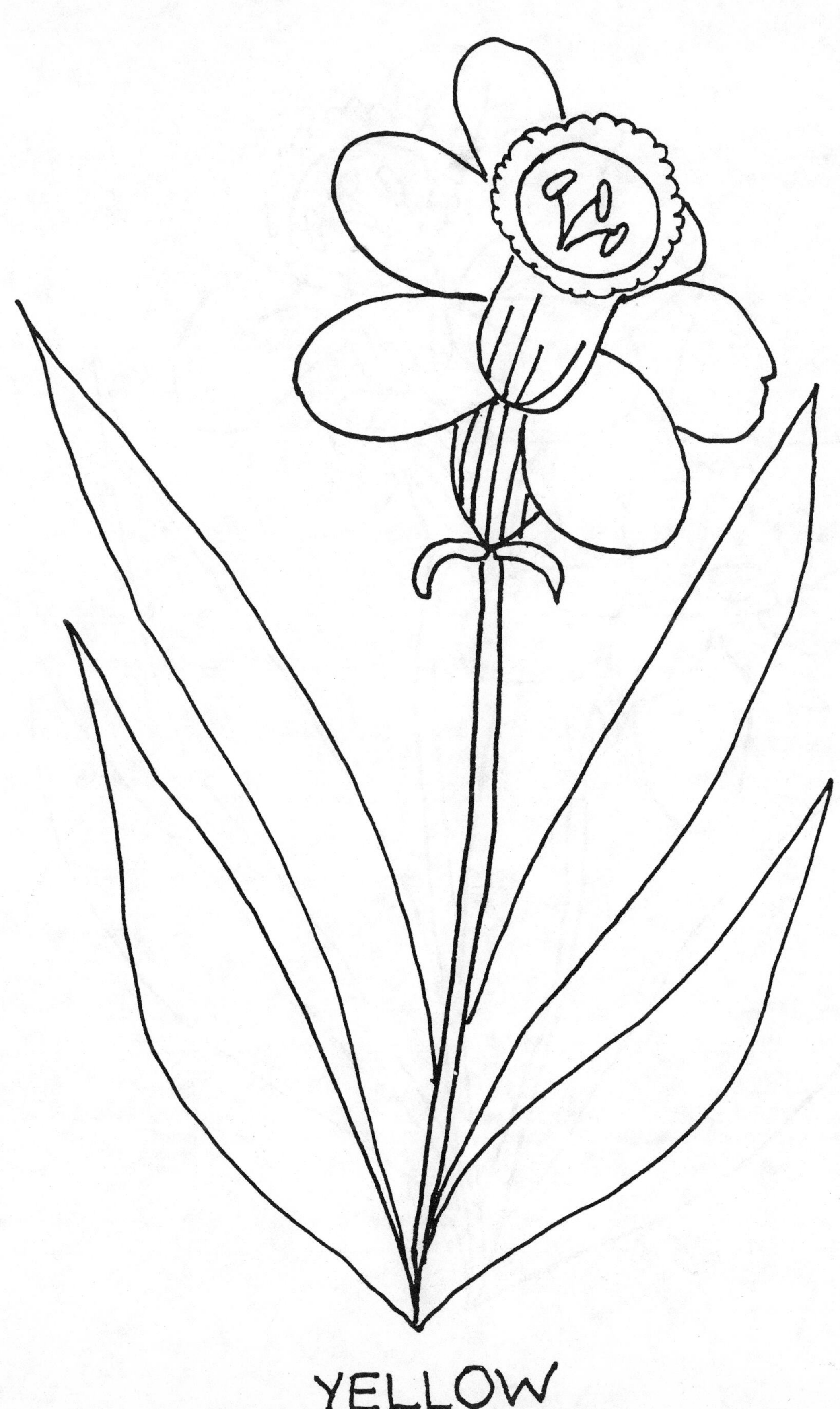

YELLOW

YELLOW

Jack-be-nimble

Jack-be-nimble

* may paste birthday candle to paper for 3-D effect

2-4 ⑥

orange

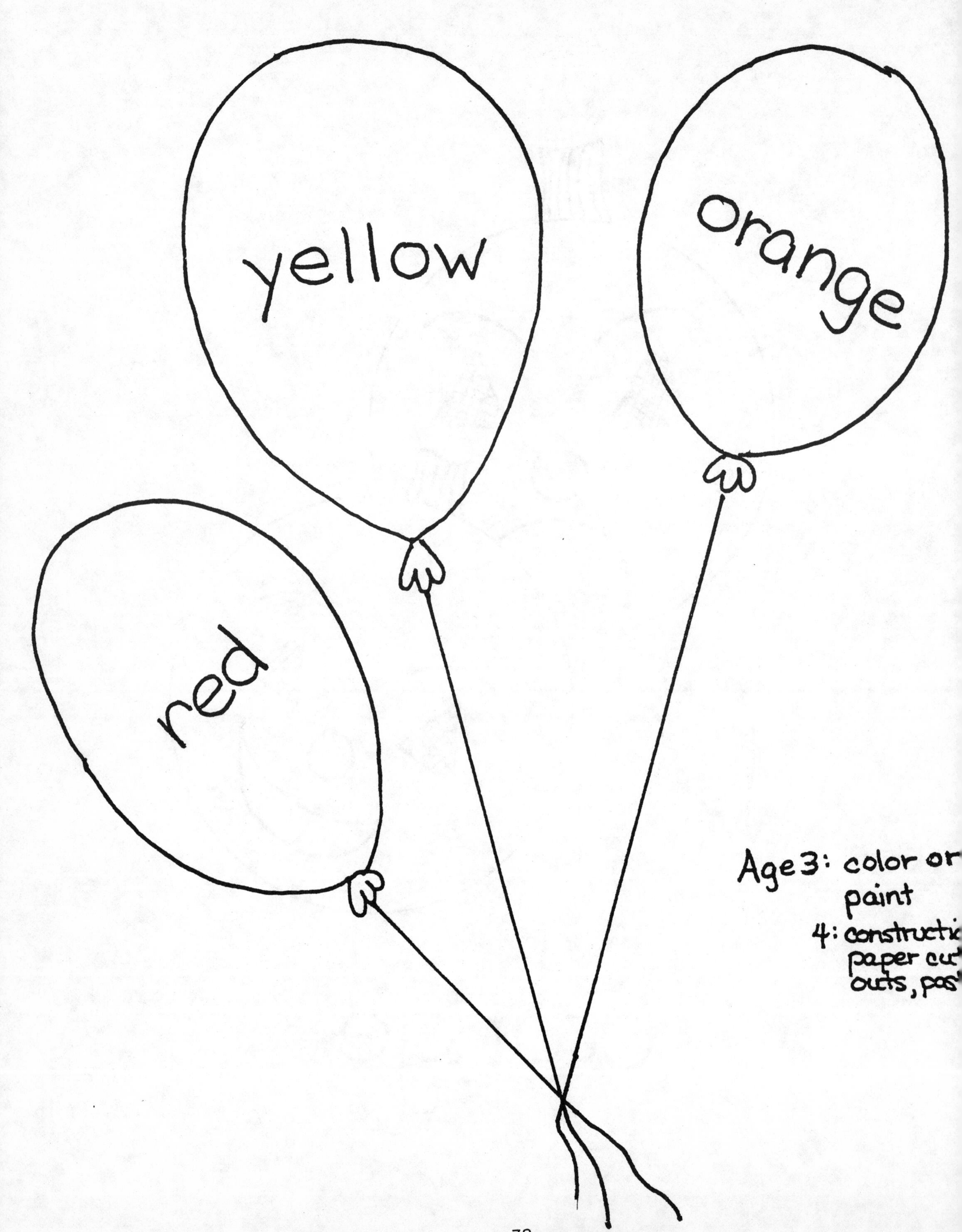

Age 3: color or
paint
4: constructi
paper cut
outs, pos

HUMPTY-DUMPTY

Humpty-Dumpty

Teacher: Give each child a hard boiled egg with a face marked on it. Egg to be eaten at home.

BLUE

blue

3-4 (9)

Age 3: color or paint
4: color-cut out, paste

Sing a song of sixpence

Four and Twenty Blackbirds

black

black boots

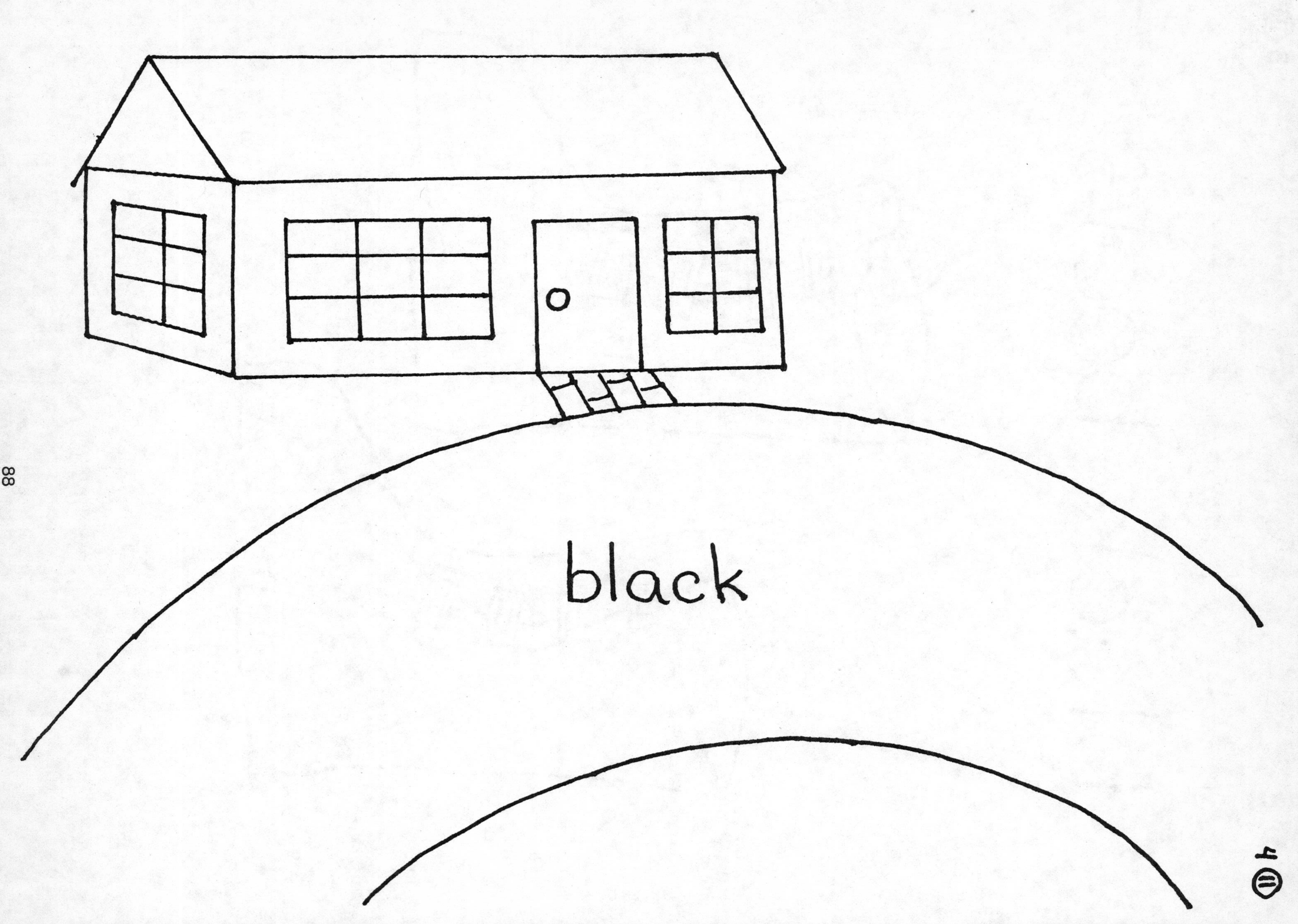
black
4 (11)

Little Jack Horner

4 12

Little Jack Horner

green

green

green

Age 3: paint
4: paste
on pieces
of green
egg carton

3-4 (15)

3 

4 (16)

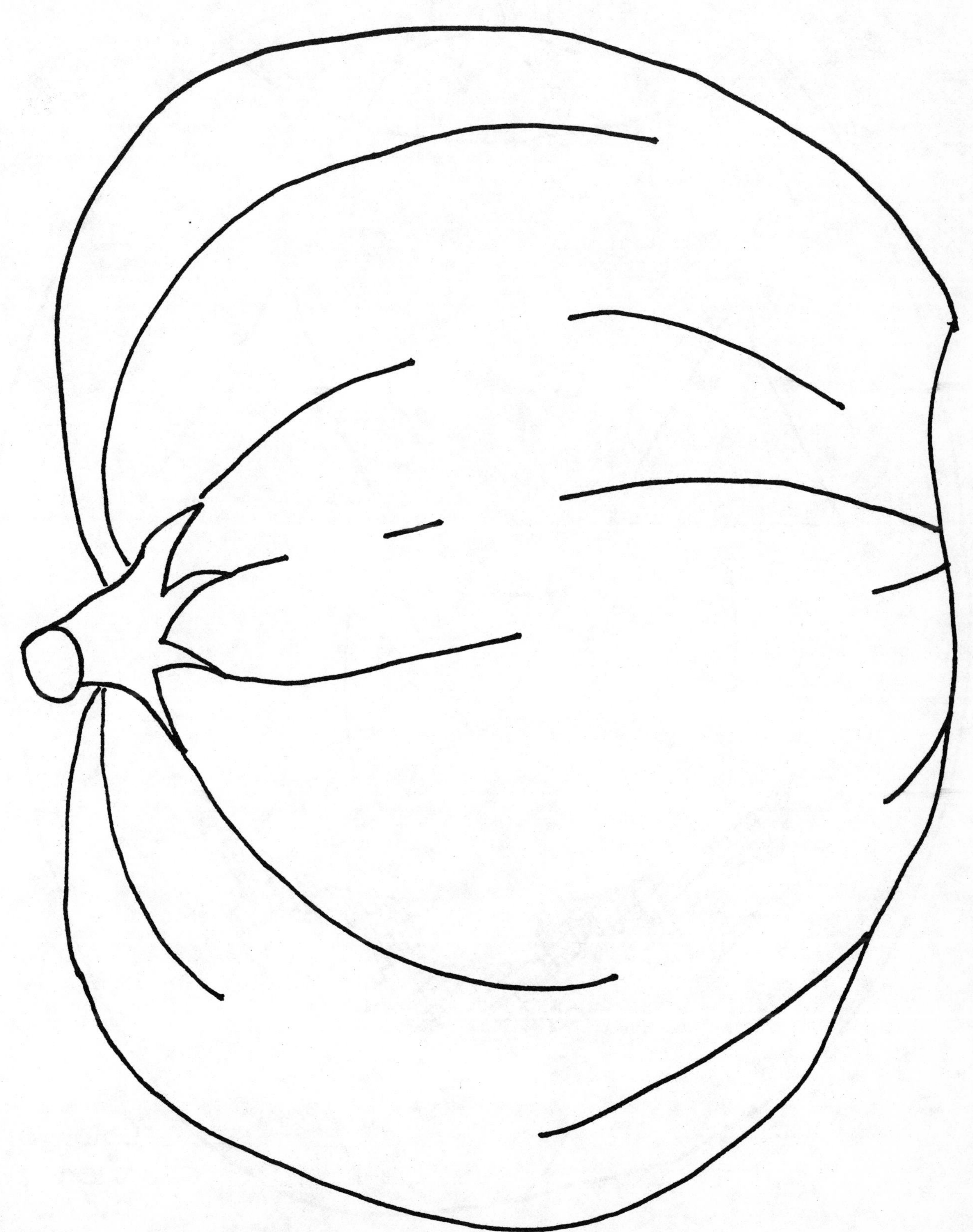

4 (17)

Age 3: color
black, paste
green circles
to eyes
Age 4: paint black,
cut out;
cut eyes,
attach
string
for mask.
3-4
19

NOVEMBER UNITS:

I. Indians
   A. This unit is designed for ages 2-4 years.
   B. The time period involved is two weeks and the presentation will correlate with the unit on Pilgrims and Thanksgiving.
   C. Key ideas
      1. The Indians were already living here when Columbus discovered America.
      2. The Indians did not understand the Pilgrims, but tried to be helpful and kind.
      3. Indians today have a proud heritage and prefer to be called NATIVE AMERICANS.

II. Shapes
   A. This is one of the basic units of the entire program and will be reviewed throughout the entire school year. This month is an introduction to the basic shapes that we encounter in daily living.
   B. Specific shapes to be covered
      1. Circle
      2. Square
      3. Triangle
      4. Rectangle
   C. Other shapes that can be included
      1. Star
      2. Diamond
      3. Bell
      4. Tear drop

III. Numbers
   A. This is another basic unit that will be reviewed throughout the year, and will be introduced this month.
   B. Specific numbers introduced are 1-5.

IV. Colors (continued)
   A. Review
      1. Red
      2. Yellow
      3. Orange
      4. Blue
      5. Black
      6. Green
   B. Introduce
      1. Brown
      2. Purple
   C. Color book (see Appendix I) is optional. This may be presented on days that the teacher needs to fill the program. They should be collected from the class and returned in booklet form to take home at the end of the month.

V. Holiday — THANKSGIVING

A. This can be correlated to the Indian unit, and should be presented the week of Thanksgiving.

B. Explain how the Indians and the Pilgrims helped each other and were thankful for each other.

C. Explain that this is a holiday that is celebrated only in America.

Special project: Cornucopia

Take a piece of brown construction paper and form a cone shape. Staple together. Provide nuts for the children to paste to the open end of the cone. Explain how this is a symbol of plenty and the end of a good harvest.

PROBLEM/CONCEPT	**SUGGESTED ACTIVITIES**
INDIANS: The Indians have a proud heritage.	Explain how resourceful the Indians have been; how they survived here long before the white man came, and how they lived off the land without destroying it. Show examples of Indian art, sign language and sand painting. Explain that different tribes formed together to make a nation. Some Indians were nomads, some were agrarian. Show the different types of houses the Indians made, using the materials you have available. 1. Cliff dwellings 2. Lean-to's 3. Teepees 4. Mud huts

Indians prefer to be called Native Americans.	Many different Indian tribes lived in what became the United States. They were a noble people with interesting and different customs.
SHAPES:	
Everything in the world has a shape.	Point to various objects and tell about their shape or the shapes that they are made up of.
Some objects are made of only one shape.	An orange is round, an ice cube is rectangular and an arrow point is triangular. Try to identify different shapes in the classroom. Have the children sit in a circle, march in a square, make a triangle with their arms. Show blocks of the various shapes, in different colors.
NUMBERS:	
Numbers are a part of our everyday world.	Calendars count the days of the month. Television stations have numbers to identify their position on the dial. We count plates, silverware, etc. when setting the table. Papers in class are counted to make sure everyone has one. We count money to know what we can buy.
Each number has its own symbol.	Show the numbers 1-10. Have a card with each number on it. Have the children line up and say the name of the number and point to the child. Then give the child the card with the number to show the symbol for the name. Introduce each number separately on different days. Group objects on the table in the number of the day. 1. Buttons 2. Pencils

Counting songs	Little Indians. 1-2-3-4-5-6-7-8-9-10 little Indian boys, etc. Use records available at the library.
THANKSGIVING:	Tell the story of the first Thanksgiving. Remember the hard time the Pilgrims had their first year in the new land. Explain their relationship to the Indians. Coordinate with the special holiday sheet.

November

(1) Calendar Begin: BROWN (squirrel)	(2) Begin: CIRCLE (circle)	(3) Continue CIRCLE Begin review BROWN (teddy bear)	(4) Begin: PURPLE Review: CIRCLE (grapes)	(5) Review: PURPLE Begin NUMBERS (1)
(6) Begin: SQUARE	(7) Review day BROWN PURPLE CIRCLE #1	(8) Introduce: TWO Review: SQUARE	(9) Continue: TWO	(10) Begin: TRIANGLE Review: TWO
(11) Begin: INDIANS THREE (teepee)	(12) INDIANS	(13) Continue: THREE Indian headband	(14) Review: THREE TWO ONE	(15) Review: SHAPES
(16) Introduce: FOUR Begin: PILGRIMS	(17) Continue Pilgrims Review: FOUR	(18) THANKSGIVING STORY Make project	(19) Review: FOUR	(20) Begin: FIVE RECTANGLE
(21) Review day SHAPES COLORS	(22) Review: FIVE			

NOVEMBER

SUN.	MON.	TUES.	WED.	THURS.	FRI.	SAT.

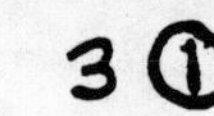

brown

4 ①

3 ②

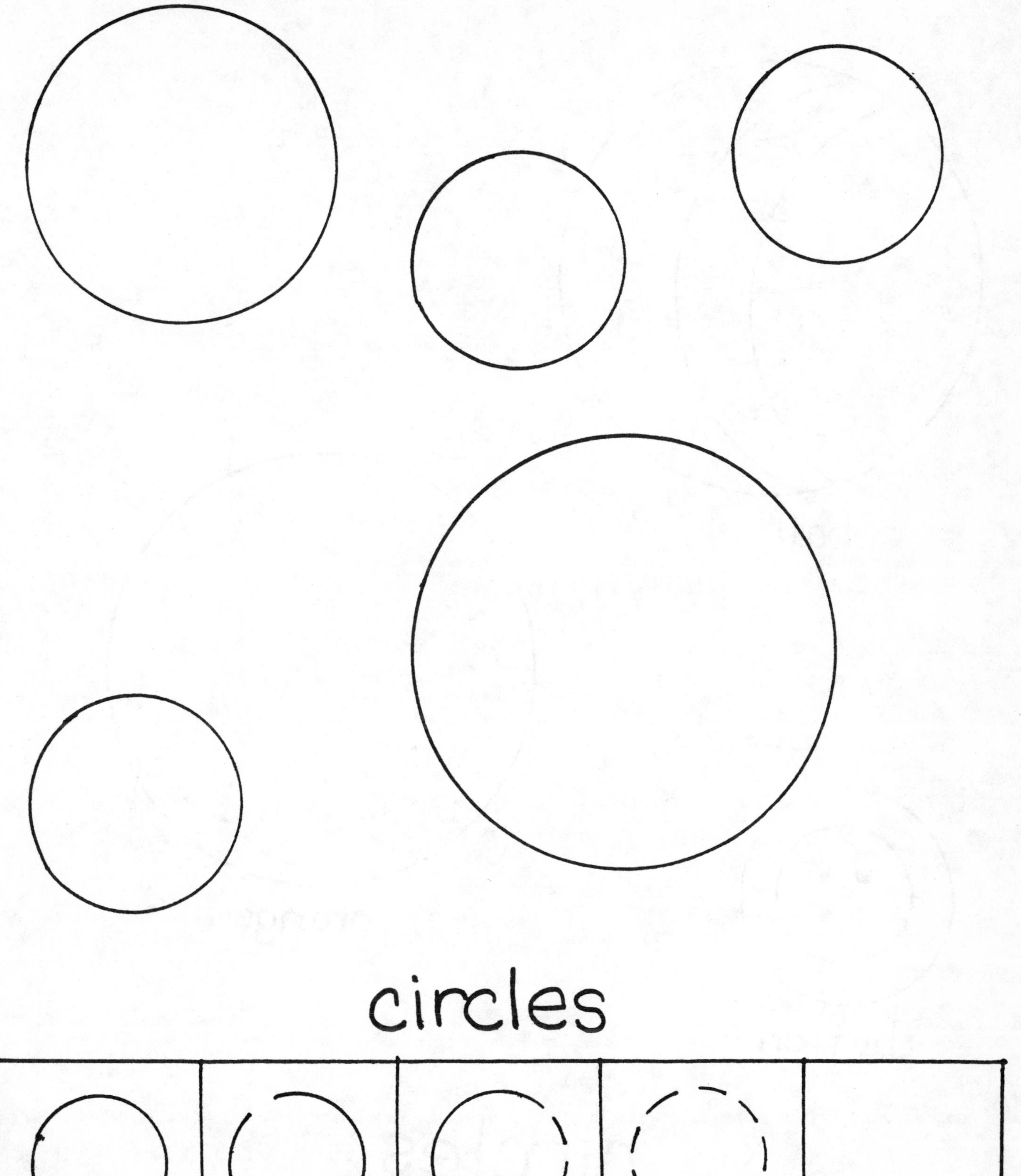

circles

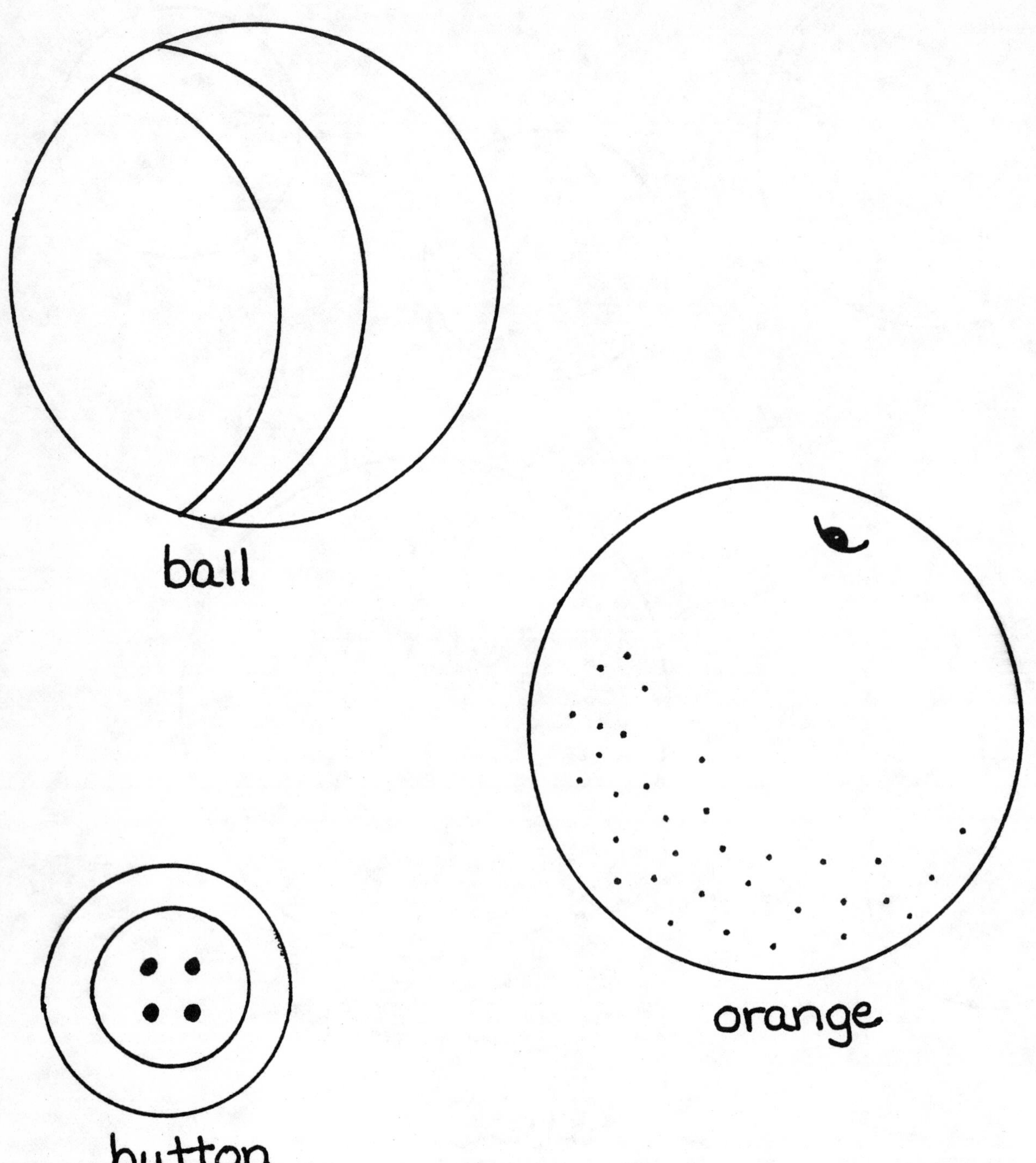

circles

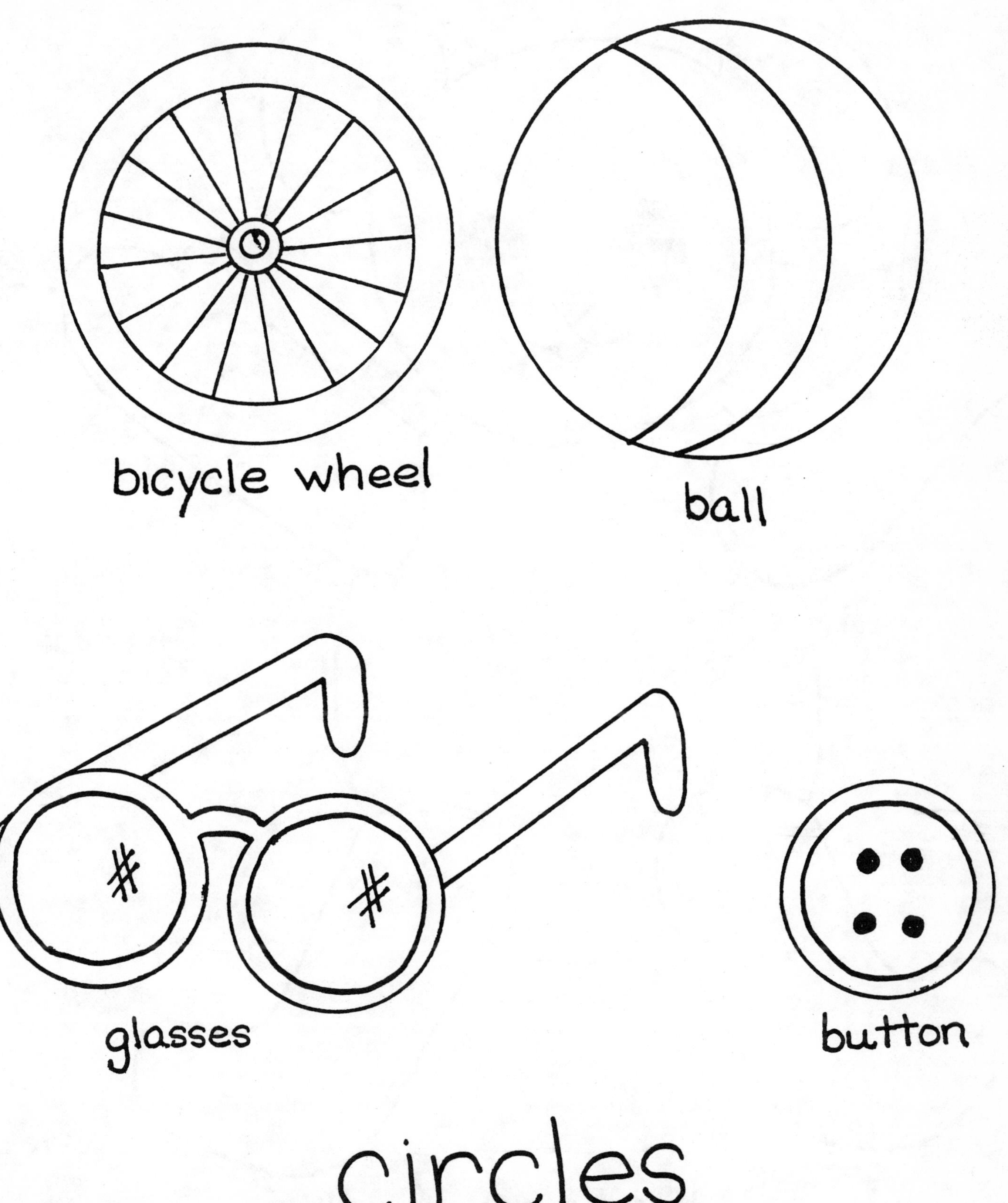

circles

brown

4 ③

brown

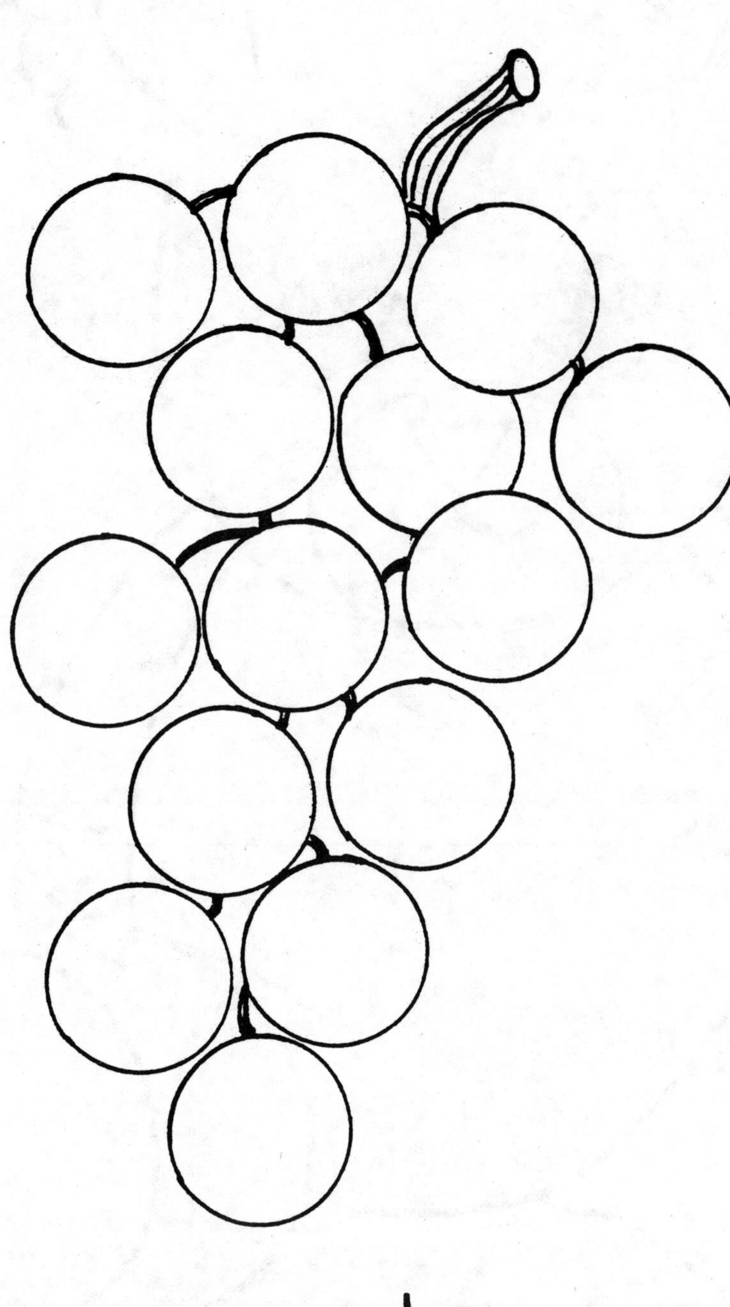

Age 3: color
4: paint

purple

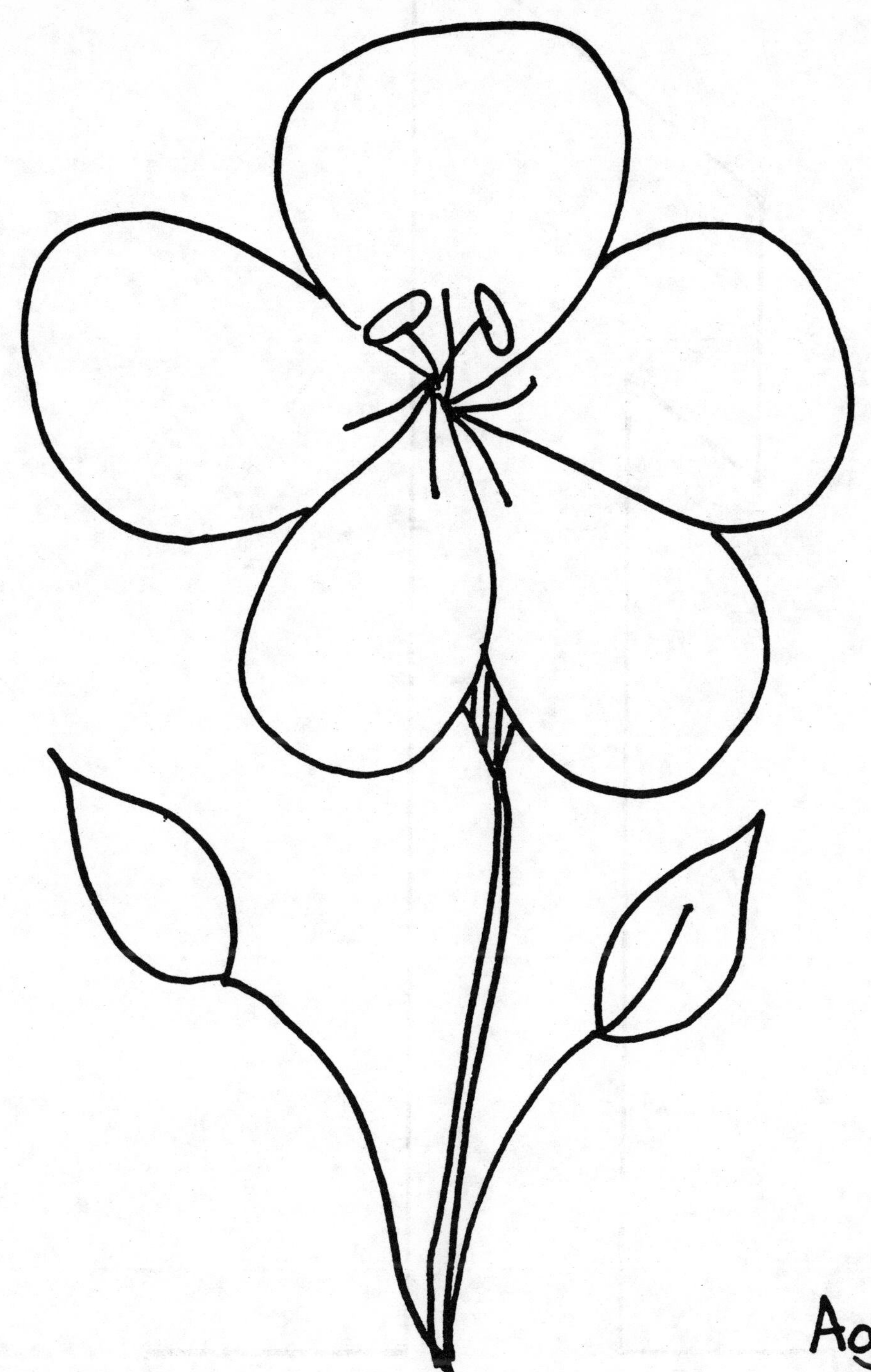

Age 3: paint
4: color

purple

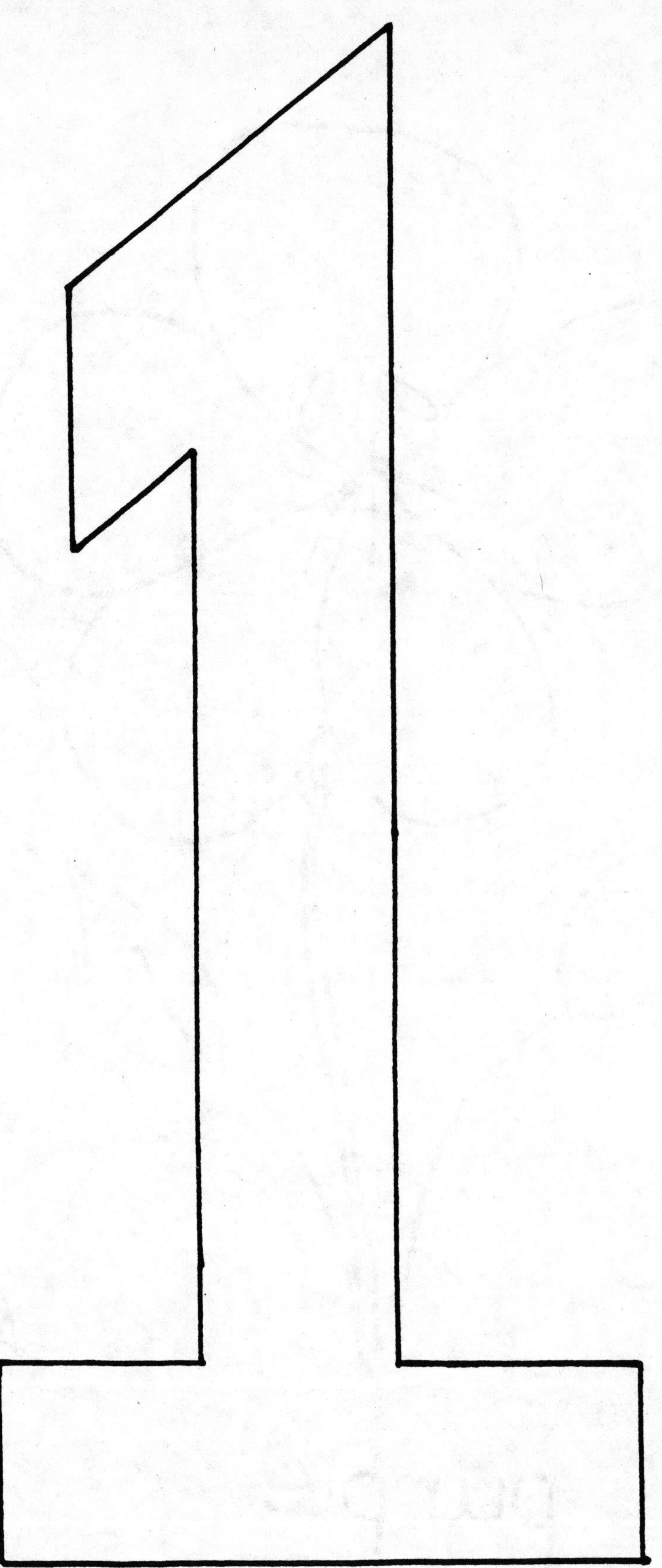

4⑤

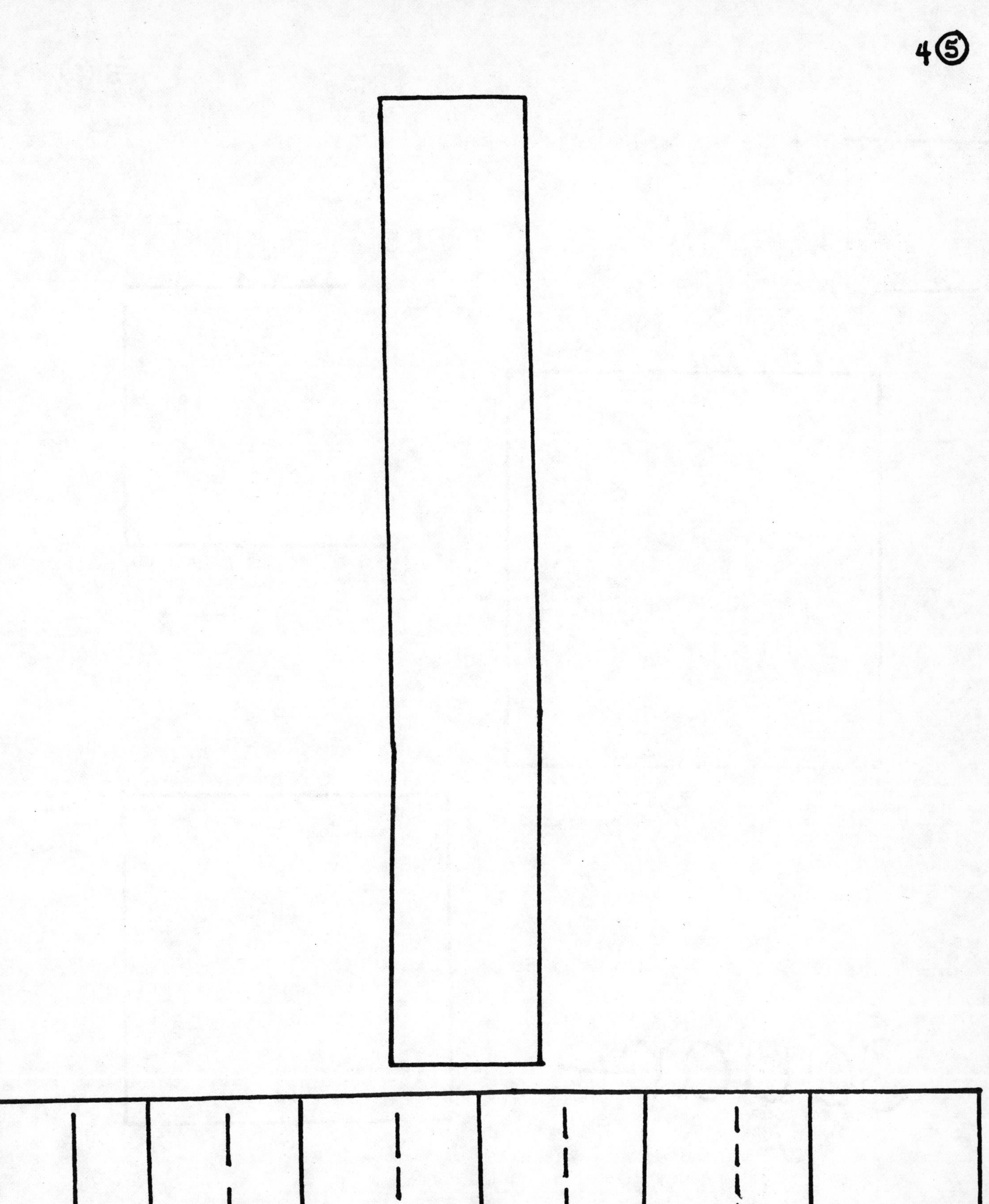

3 ⑥

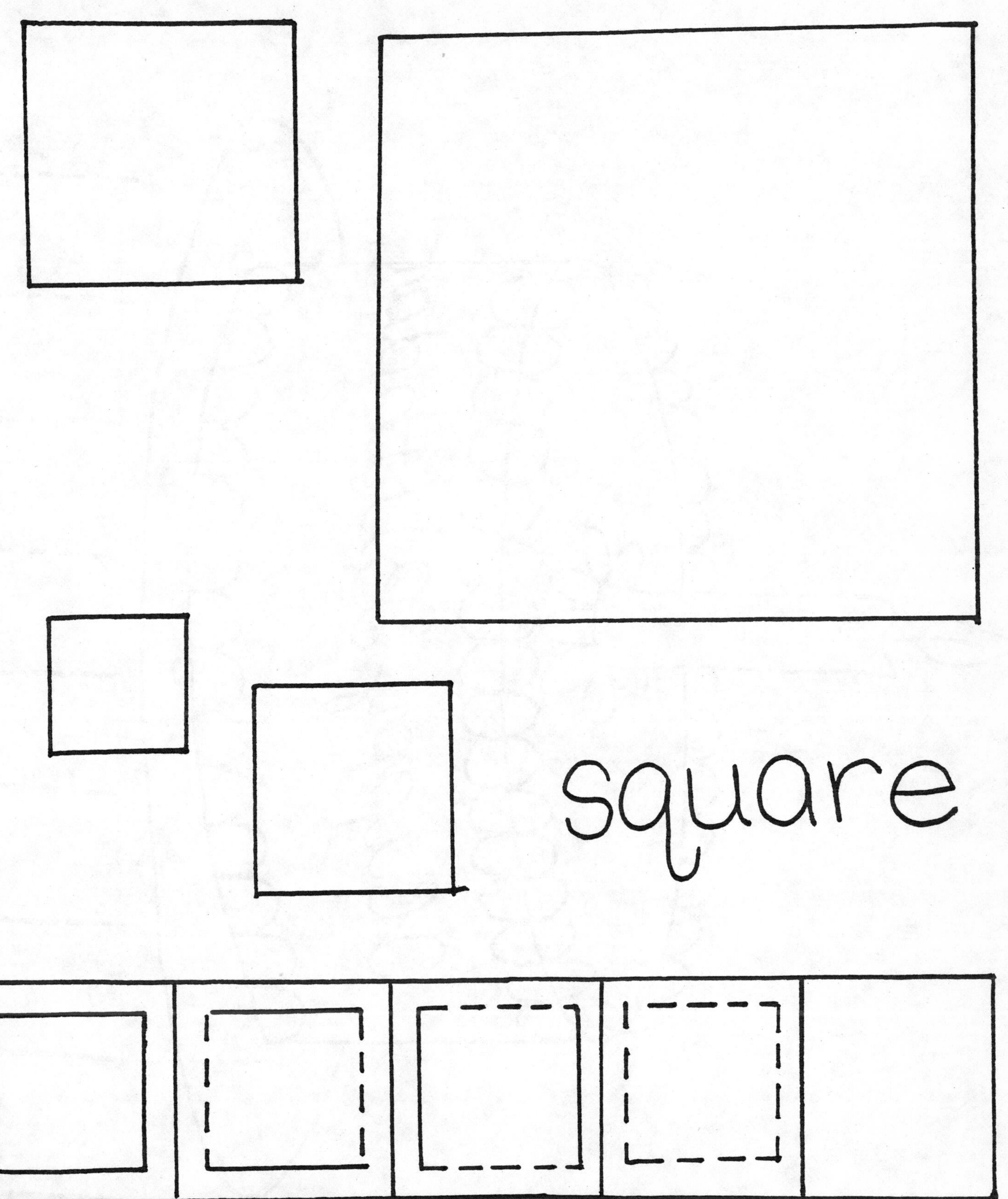
square

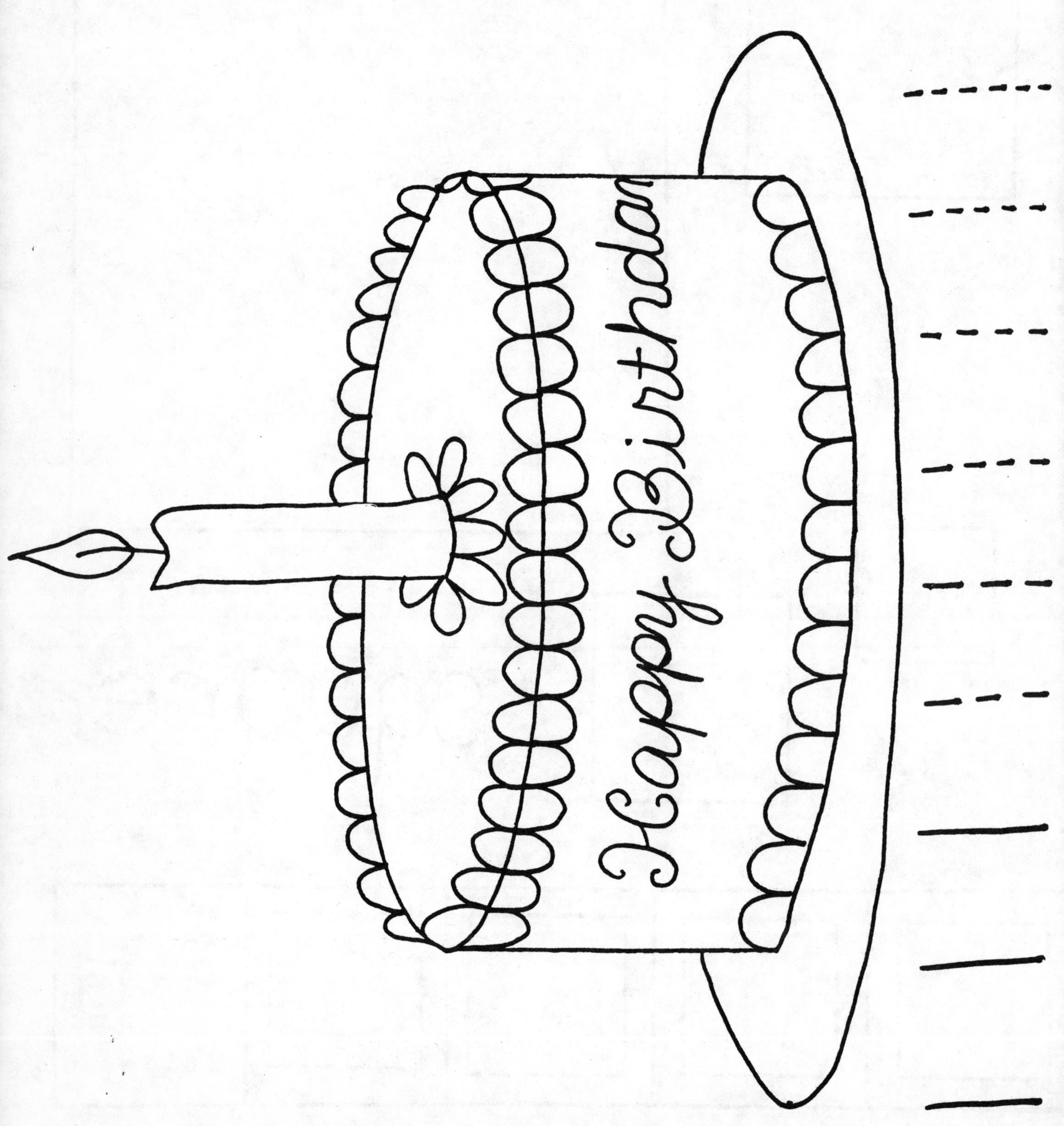
Happy Birthda

COLOR REVIEW

2

2	2	2	2	2

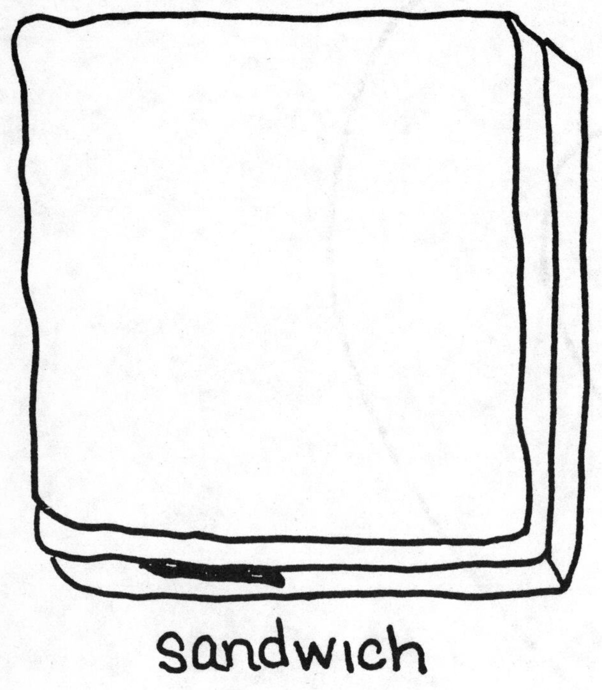

sandwich

napkin

block

square

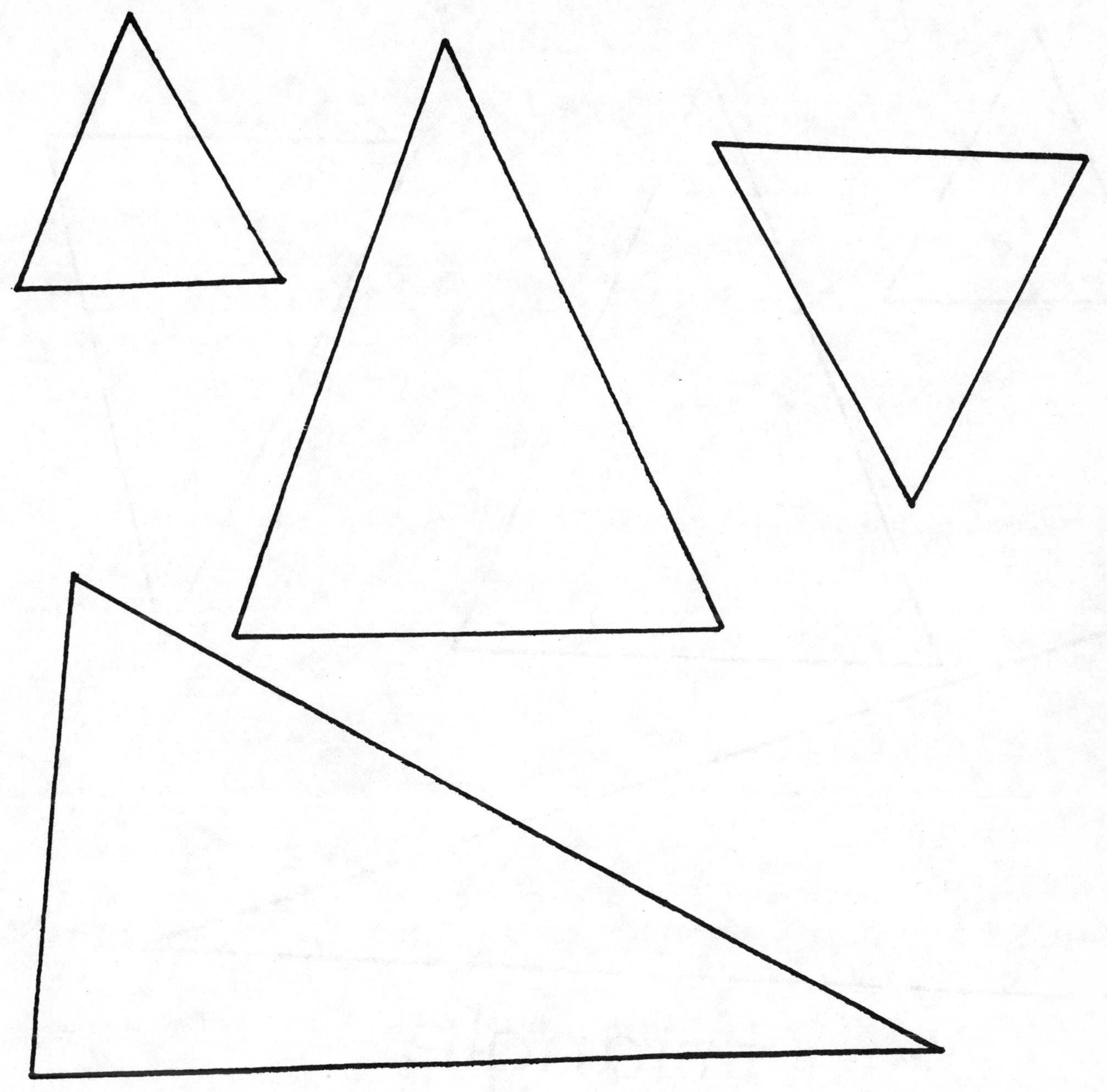

triangle

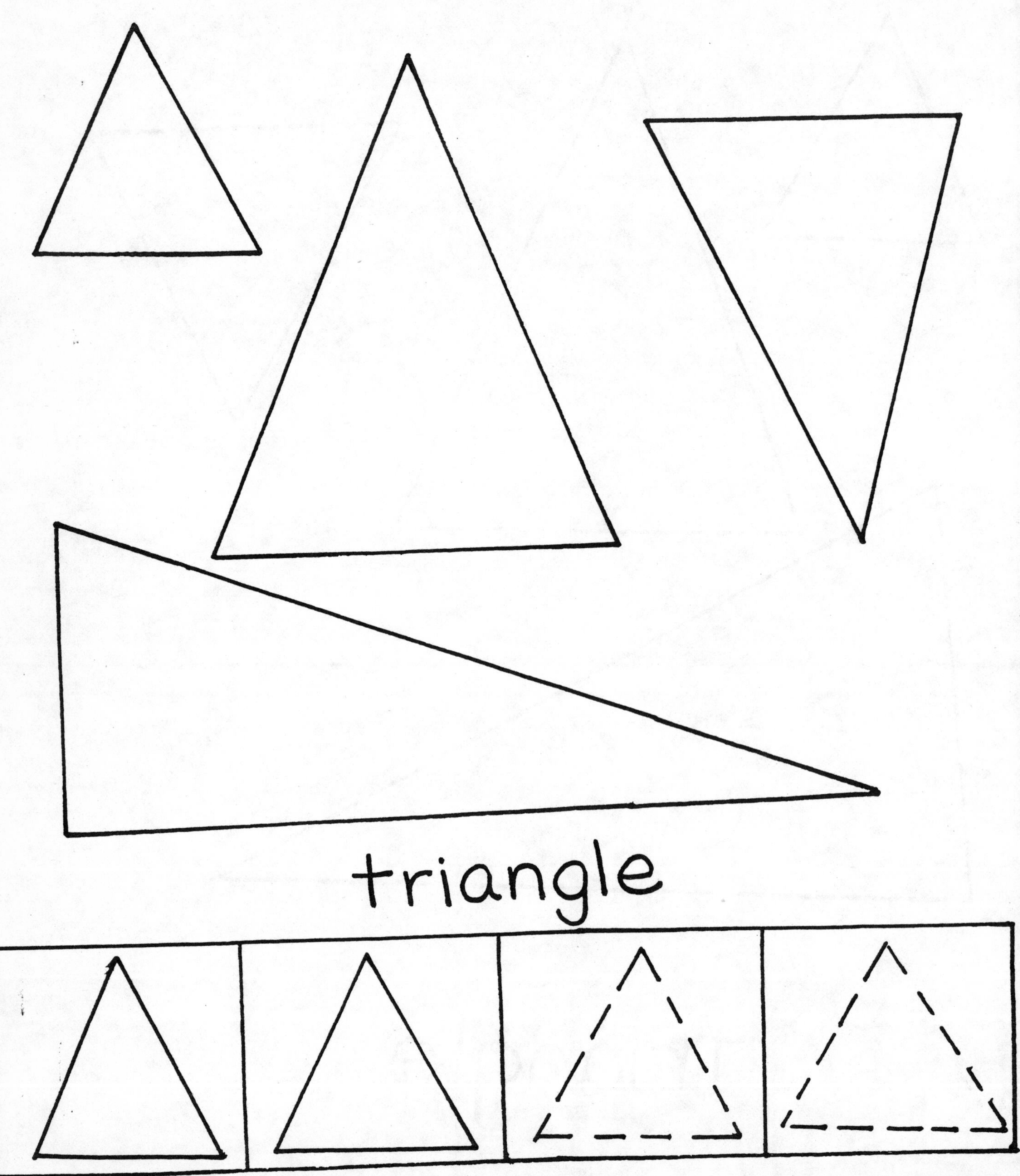
triangle

2

2

4 (11)

3 ⑪

3 (12)

4 (12)

1

2

3

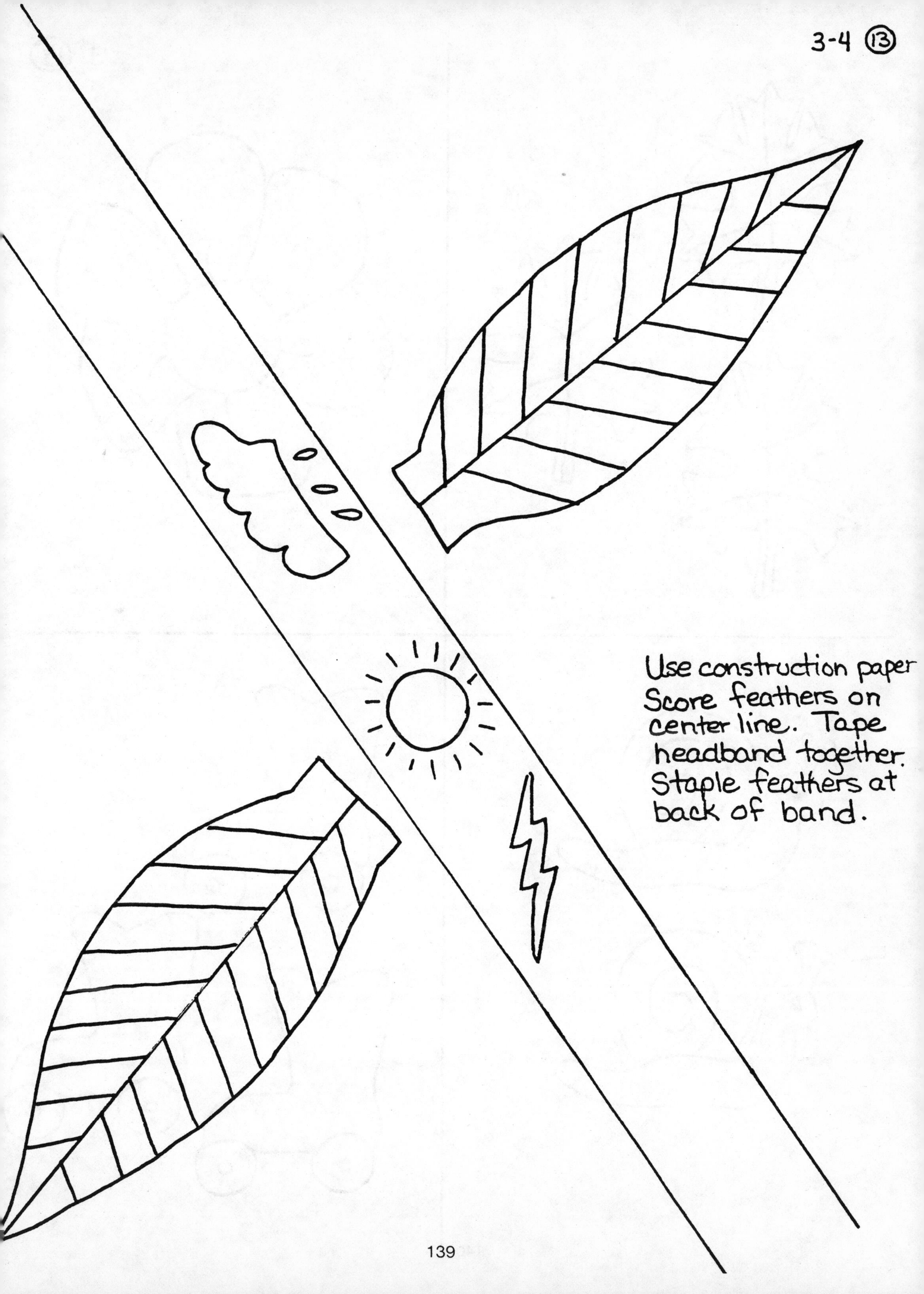

Use construction paper
Score feathers on
center line. Tape
headband together.
Staple feathers at
back of band.

3 14

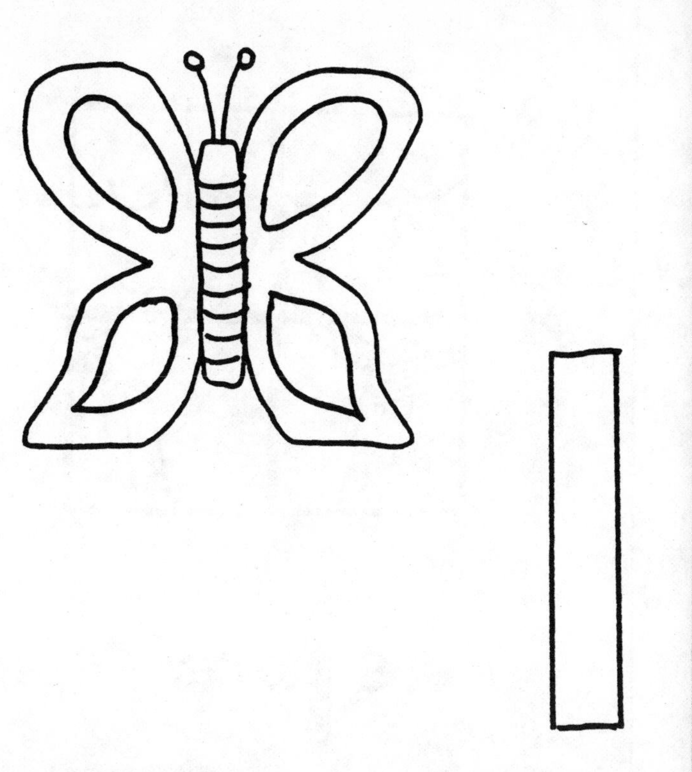

circle

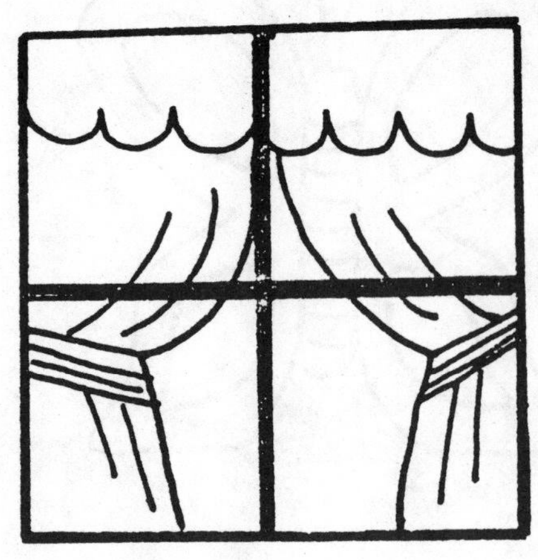

square

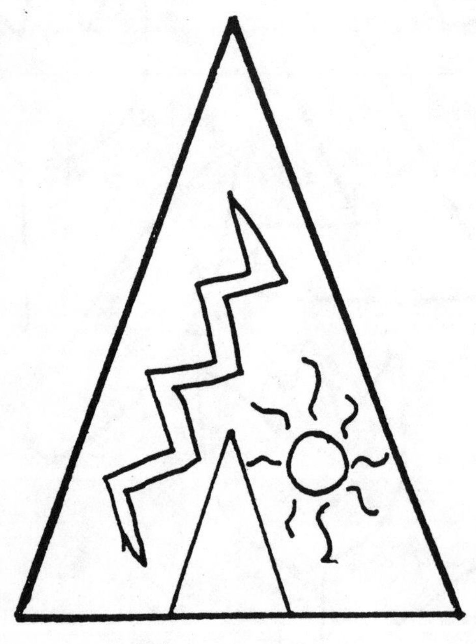

triangle

circle

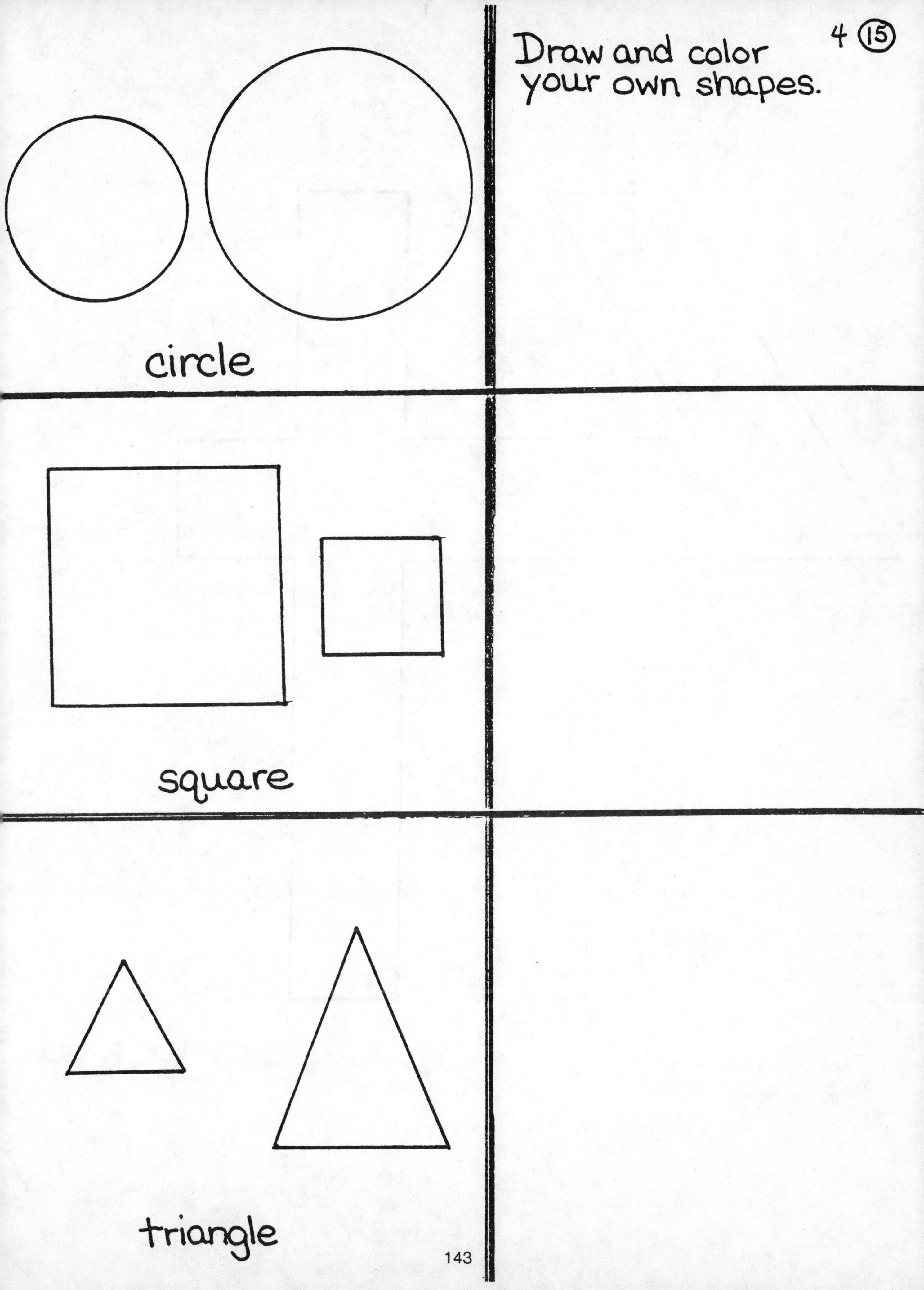
4 (15)
Draw and color
your own shapes.
circle
square
triangle

3-4 ⑱

4

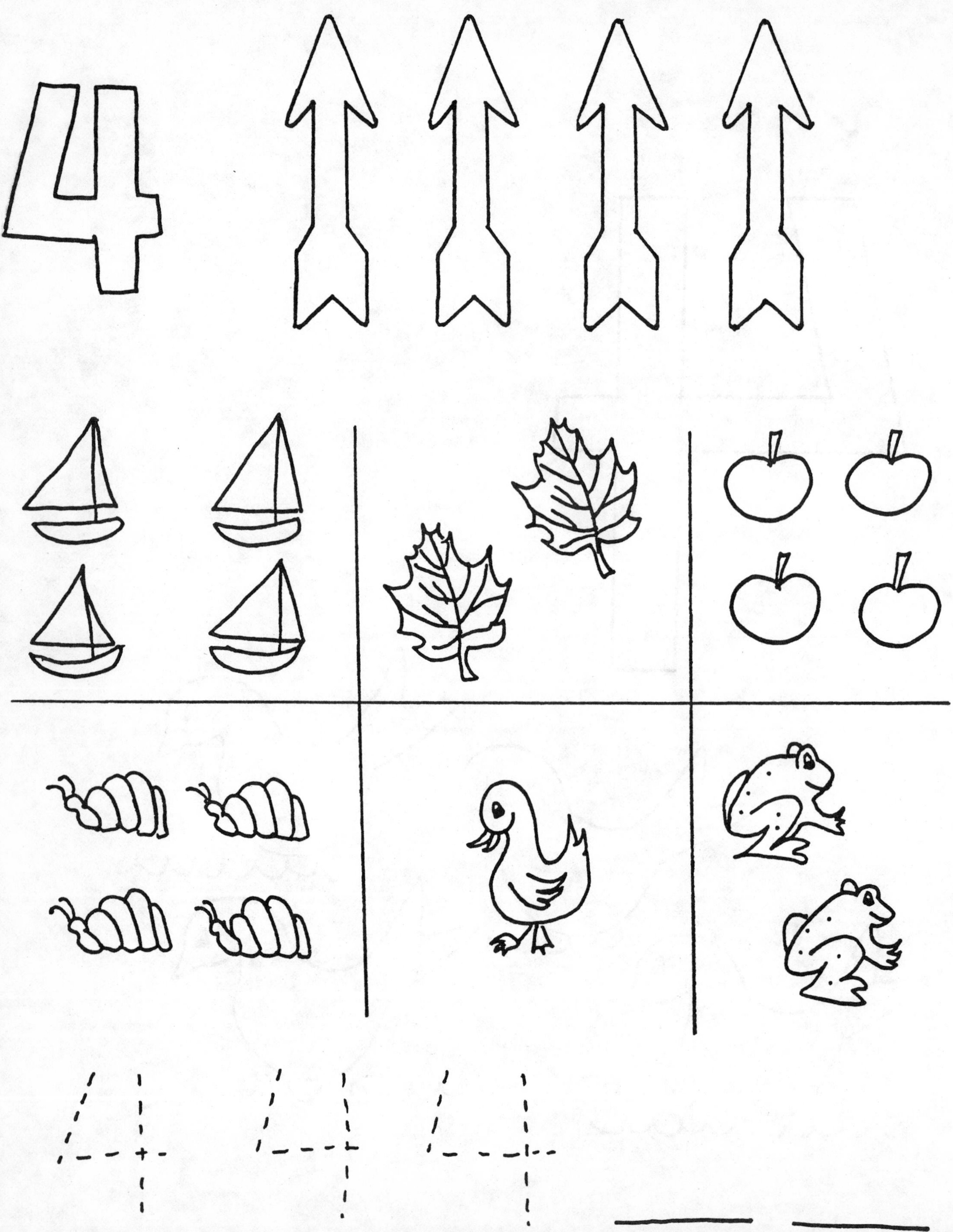

3 (20)

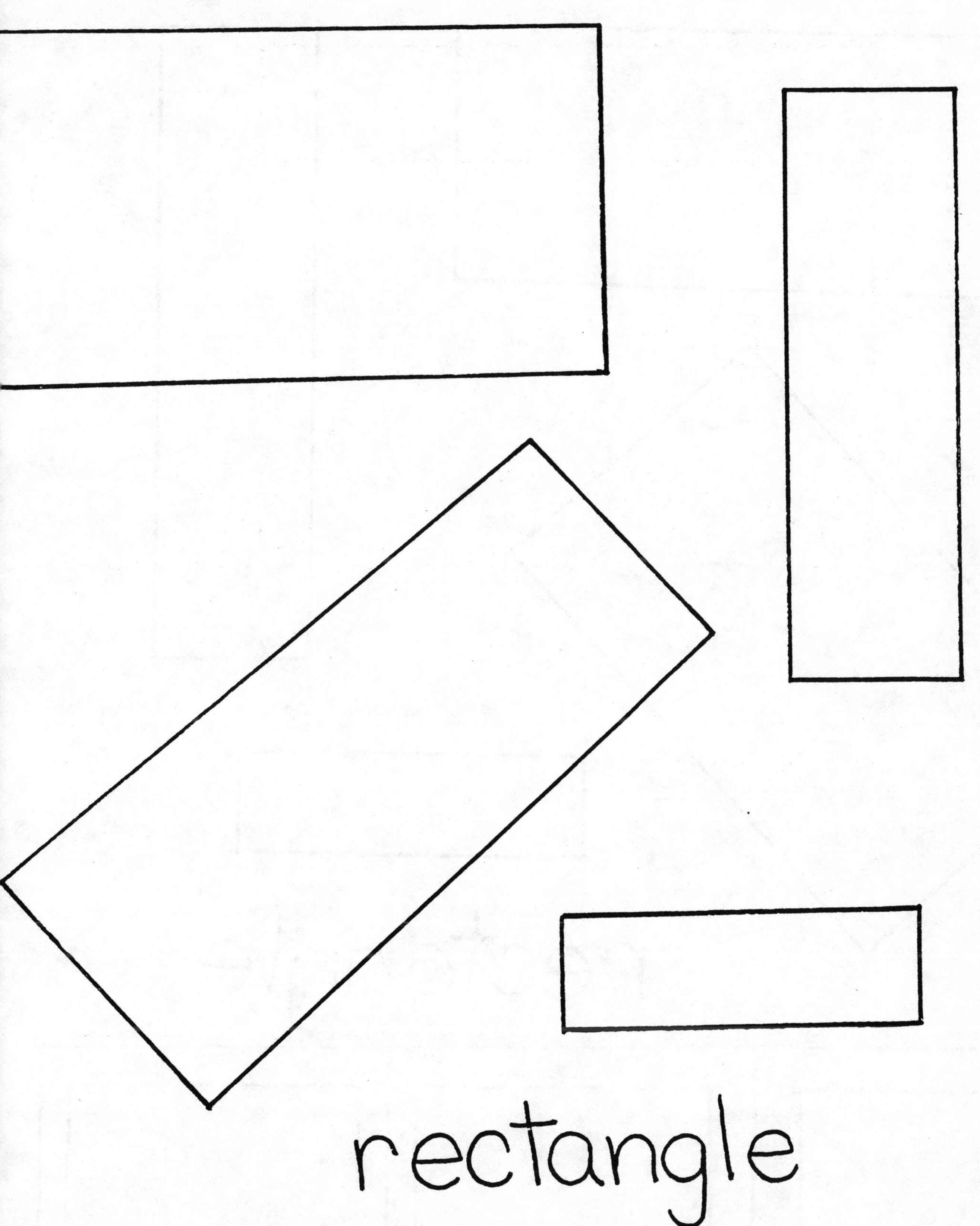

rectangle

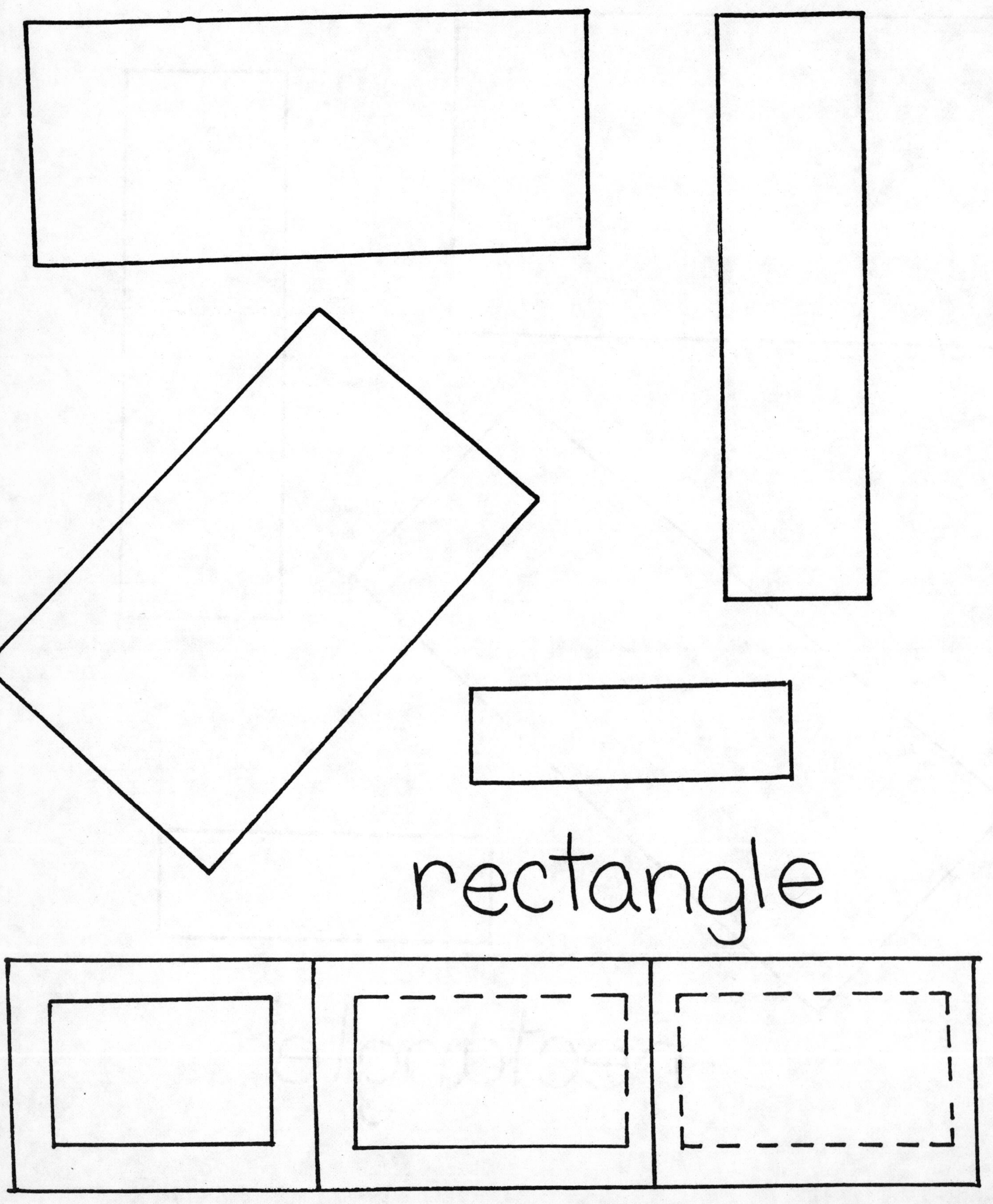
rectangle

SHAPE REVIEW

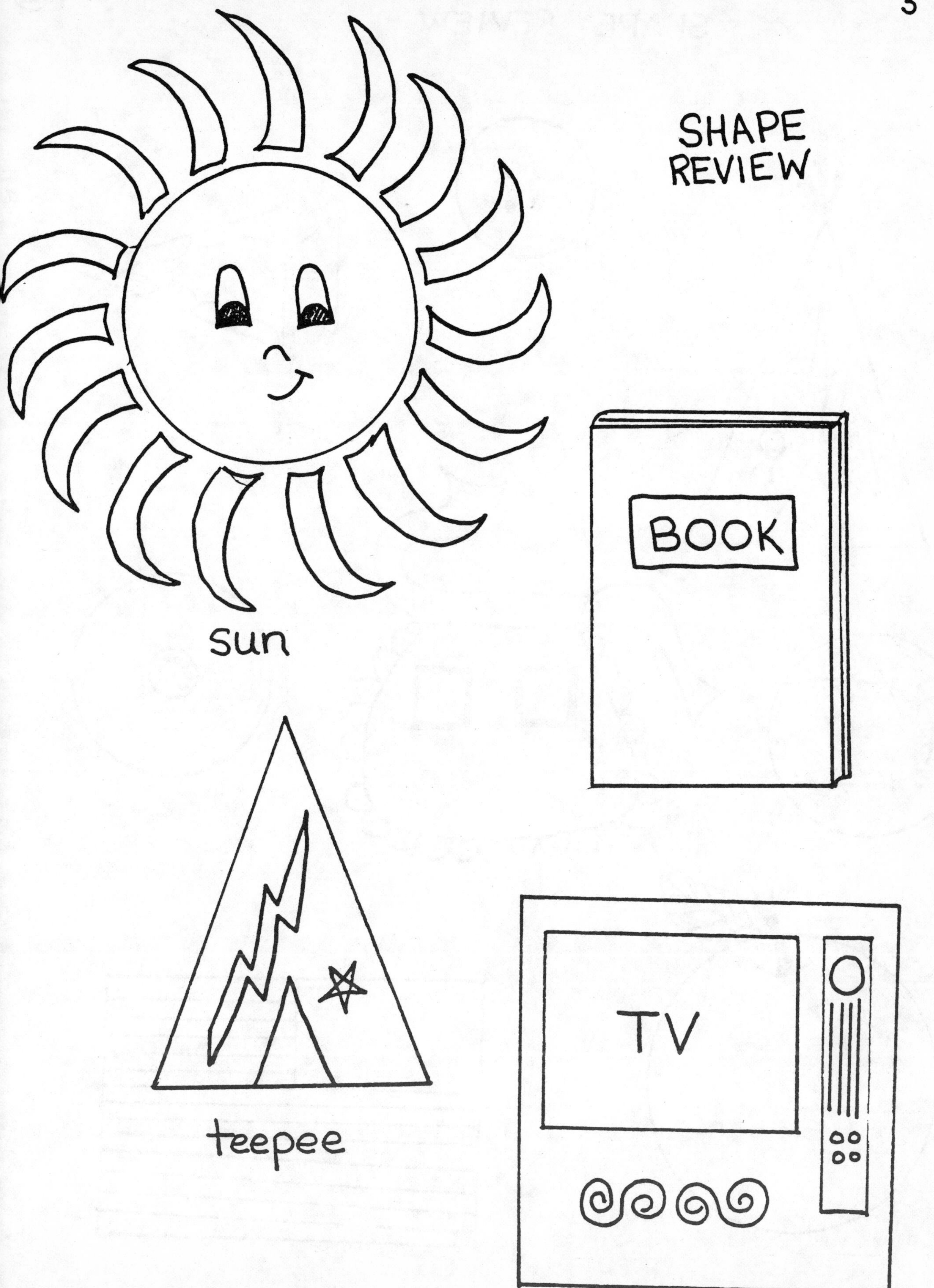

SHAPE REVIEW

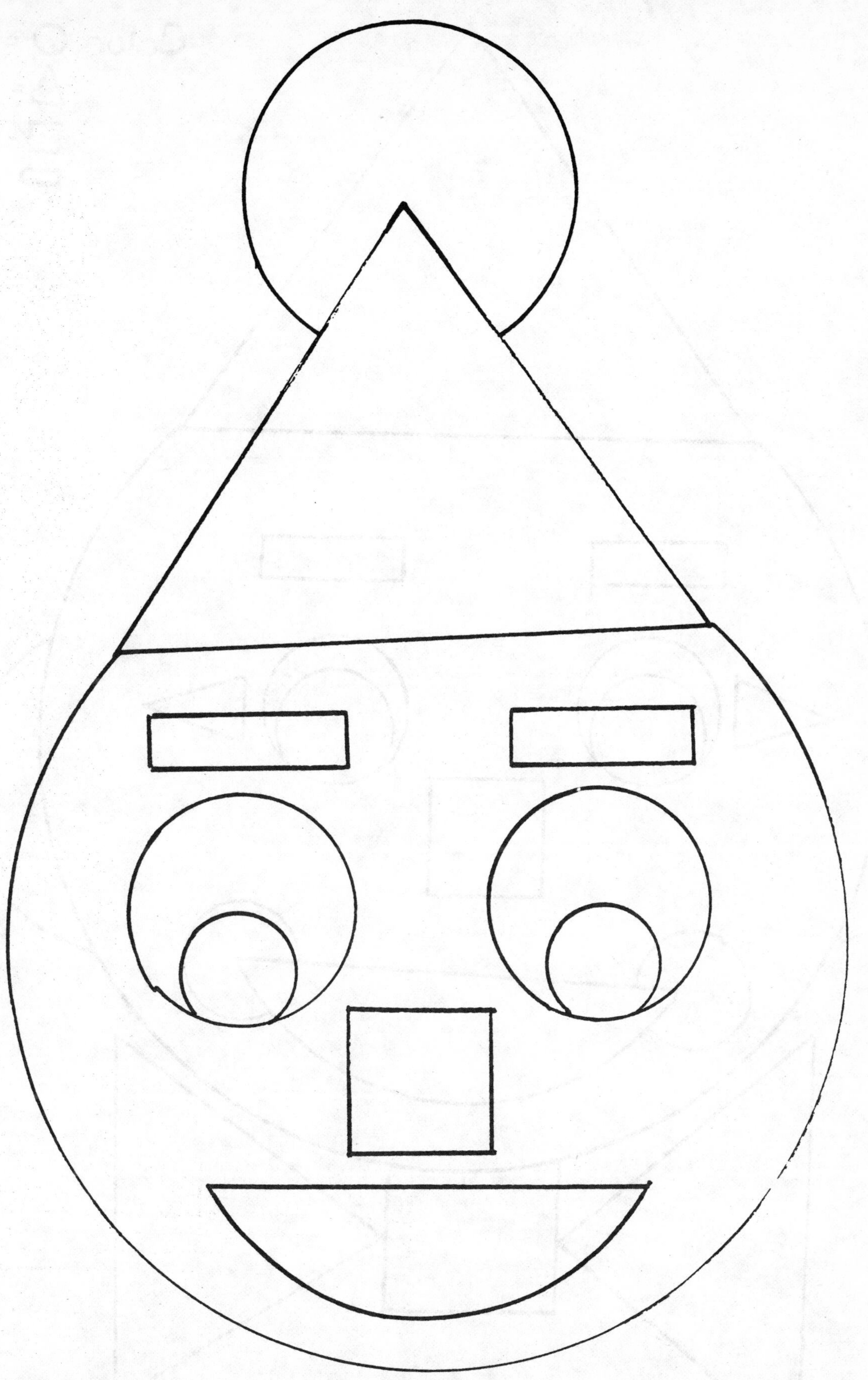

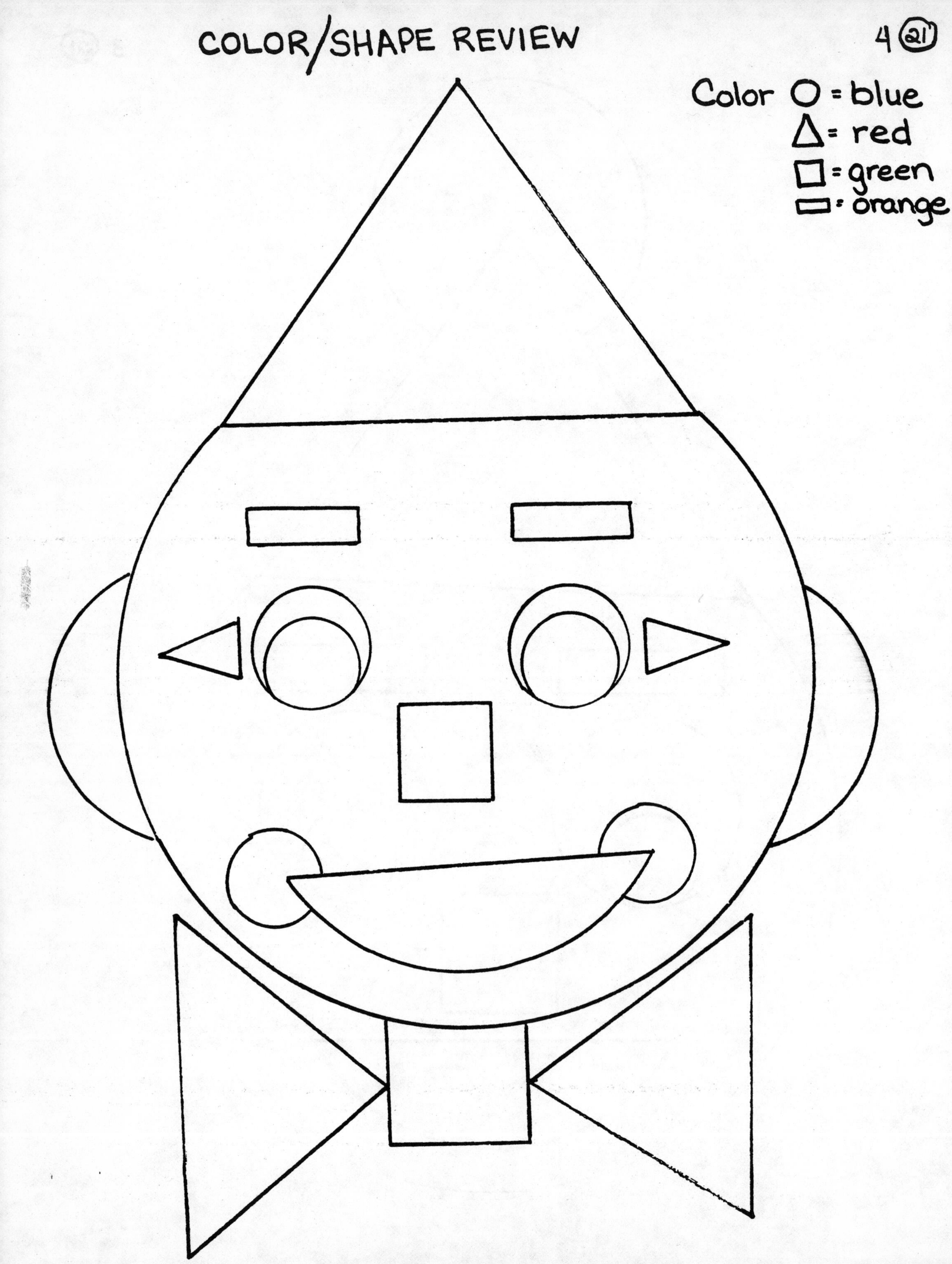
COLOR/SHAPE REVIEW
4 (21)
Color ○ = blue
△ = red
□ = green
▭ = orange

5

5

DECEMBER UNITS:

I. Numbers
   - **A.** A continuation of the basic unit begun last month.
   - **B.** Numbers introduced this month are 6-10.
   - **C.** The numbers introduced last month should be reviewed, as will this whole unit throughout the school year.

II. Nutrition
   - **A.** This unit is designed to help the children understand more about themselves, their bodies, and how they help to take care of themselves.
   - **B.** Basic food groups will be discussed.
   - **C.** Sample meals will be included in daily lesson color sheets. Age 3 will color or paint, age four will cut out pictures from magazines and paste them to the sheet.

III. This is a month of holidays and two are emphasized.
   - **A.** Chanukah (Hanukkah): The Jewish festival of lights celebrating the miracle of the lamp that stayed lit for eight days. (See Appendix III for detailed explanation).
   - **B.** Christmas: The Christian holiday celebrating the miracle of Jesus' birth. (See Appendix III for detailed explanation and drawings).
   - **C.** In a private school both religious holidays may be celebrated. Children should understand holidays from all cultures and neither holiday will be emphasized more than the other in this book.
   - **D.** SANTA is a concept associated with Christian religions and the use of this material is optional.

IV. Review
   - **A.** The last week of the month is usually a school holiday. If this program is used by a day care facility, it will be necessary to provide activities for this week however.
   - **B.** Basic units are reviewed at this time so as not to introduce material that will be missed by other children.
   - **C.** Review material
     1. Numbers 6-10
     2. Shapes
     3. Colors

PROBLEM/CONCEPT	SUGGESTED ACTIVITIES
NUTRITION: Our selves are important and we must learn to help take care of our own bodies.	Ask the children how a building is built. Relate the story of the three little pigs. 1. A house built of straw will not stand for long. 2. Good materials, well placed, make a strong house. 3. Correlate junk food to a well-balanced diet.
Emphasize the individual and his or her responsibility for good eating habits and manners.	Babies are fed by their parents. Growing girls and boys feed themselves, although the parents provide the food. Try role playing: Let the children be the parents and the teacher be the child.
Try to recognize the basic food groups that we should eat from each day.	Use the coloring sheets provided with this program. Cut pictures out of magazines to make a large class collage for each food group.
CHRISTMAS:	Tell the story of the miracle of the Nativity. See special holiday sheet in Appendix III. Review gift giving and the idea of presents. Make presents for parents. Color the tree (See Appendix III).
CHANUKAH (HANUKKAH):	Tell the story of the miracle of the lamp in the Temple. See special holiday sheet in Appendix III. Review gift giving and the idea of presents. Color the Menorah (See Appendix III).
NUMBERS: Songs:	Refer to November syllabus. Little Indians Twelve Days of Christmas (cut to ten for number purposes)

Holiday Gifts for Parents:

Age 3:

Supplies:

pom-pom braid
self adhesive strip magnets
small animal "craft eyes"
glue

Method:

1. Cut braid – two balls for each child
2. Attach magnet strips to bottom.
3. Glue eyes to head.

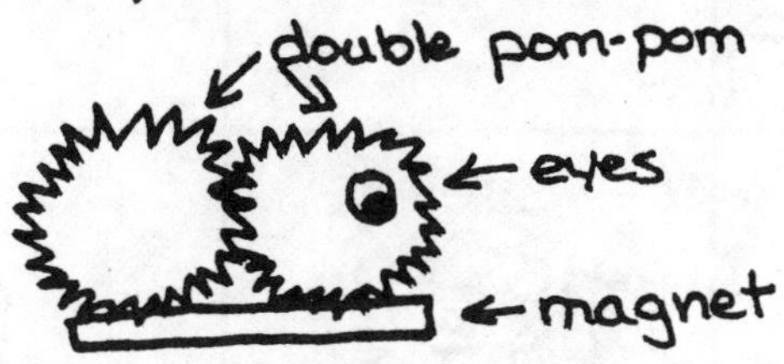

4. Use on refrigerator to hold notes.

Age 4:

Supplies:

pot pie pans
"Pam" no stick spray
plaster of Paris
poster paint

Method:

1. spray pans with "Pam"
2. mix plaster, pour 1" into pan
3. Have child make hand print
4. When dry, unmold and have child decorate with poster paint.

December

MONTH: DECEMBER

① Calendar	② Begin: SIX	③ Begin: NUTRITION	④ Concept of body and "me"	⑤ Review: SIX Breakfast
⑥ Begin: SEVEN	⑦ Review: SIX SEVEN	⑧ Begin: EIGHT	⑨ Review: EIGHT Lunch	⑩ Review: NUTRITION
⑪ Begin: Christmas (Santa) NINE	⑫ Make ornaments for room Dinner	⑬ Review: NINE Make presents for parents	⑭ Begin: TEN Discuss: winter (snowman)	⑮ Review: TEN Decorations
⑯ REVIEW: SIX — EIGHT	⑰ Review: SHAPES	⑱ Review: NINE - TEN	⑲ Review: Colors	⑳ New Year Picture
㉑ Channukah Menorah (See Appendix III)	㉒ Christmas Tree (See Appendix III)		Craft items: magazines cotton balls pom pom braid strip magnets, self adhesive "eyes" glue pie pans, plaster, poster paint	

DECEMBER

SUN.	MON.	TUES.	WED.	THURS.	FRI.	SAT.

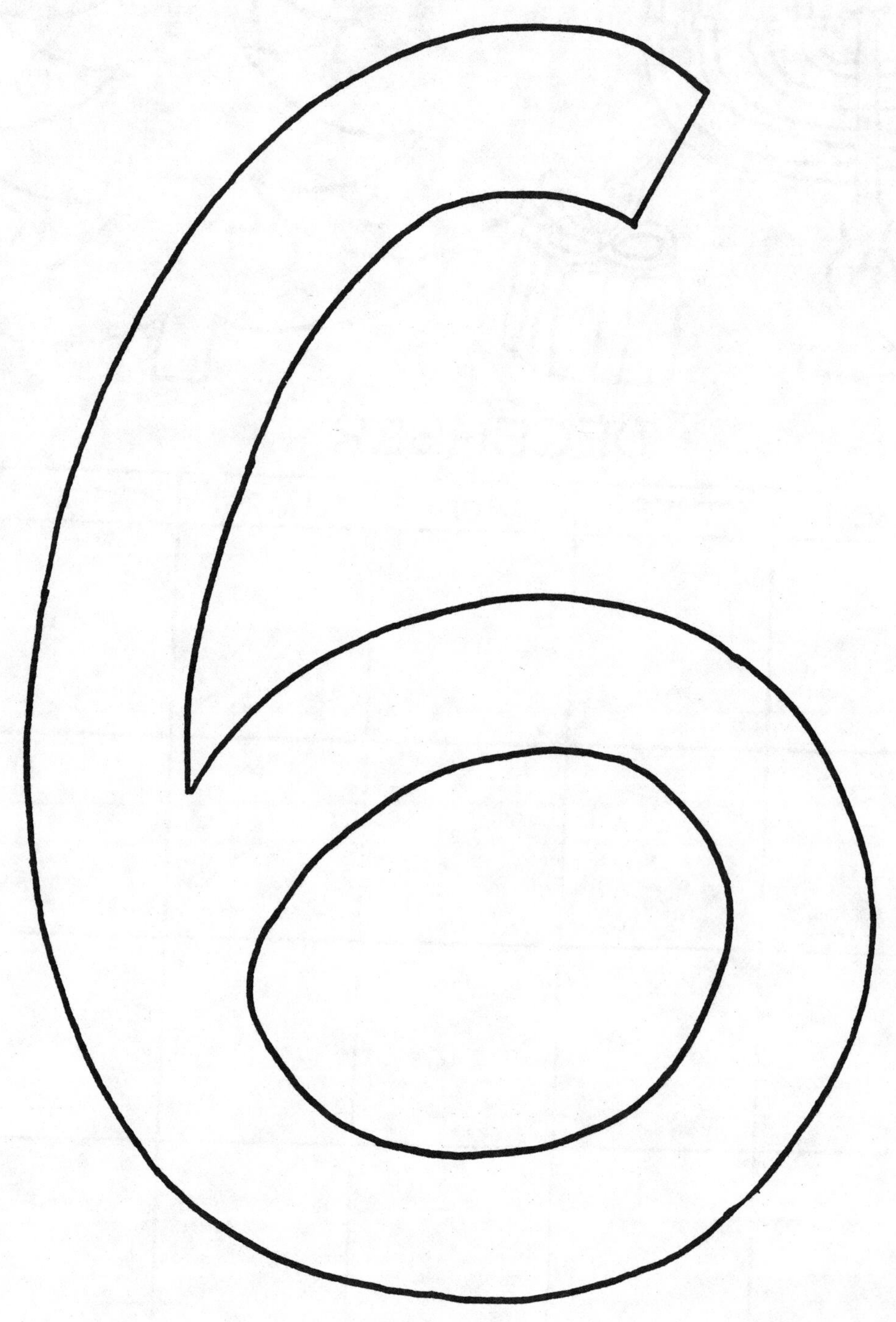

We need all kinds of food to help us grow. 3 ③

MILK

bread

dairy

fruit

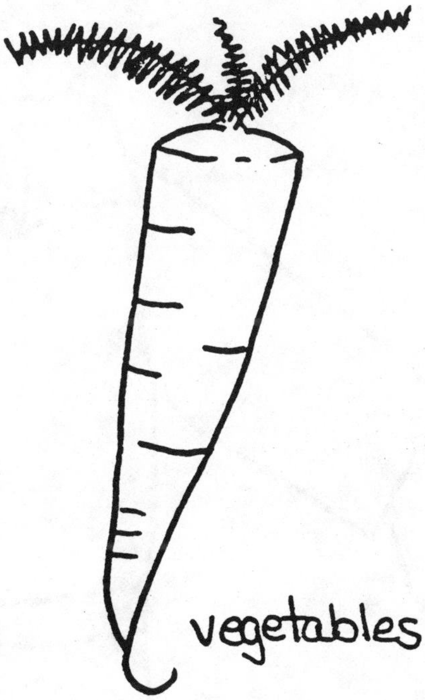

vegetables

DIFFERENT FOODS HELP US GROW

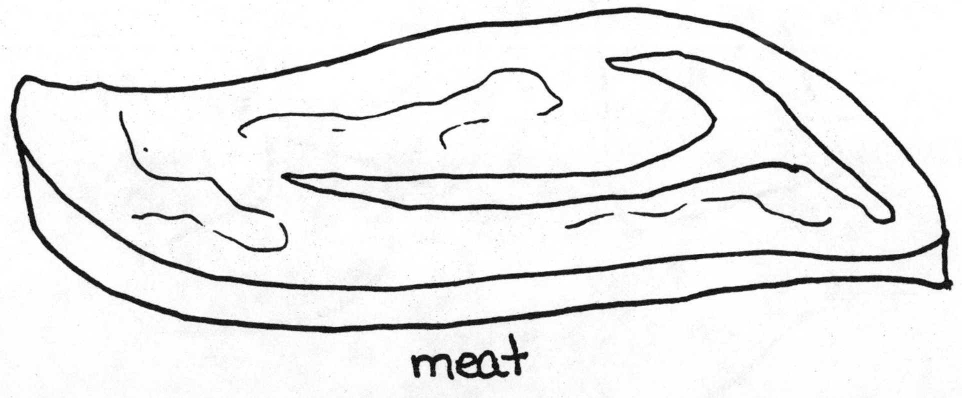

My name is ______________________________

My name is ______________________

3 ④

My name is ____________________

My name is ____________________

4 ⑤

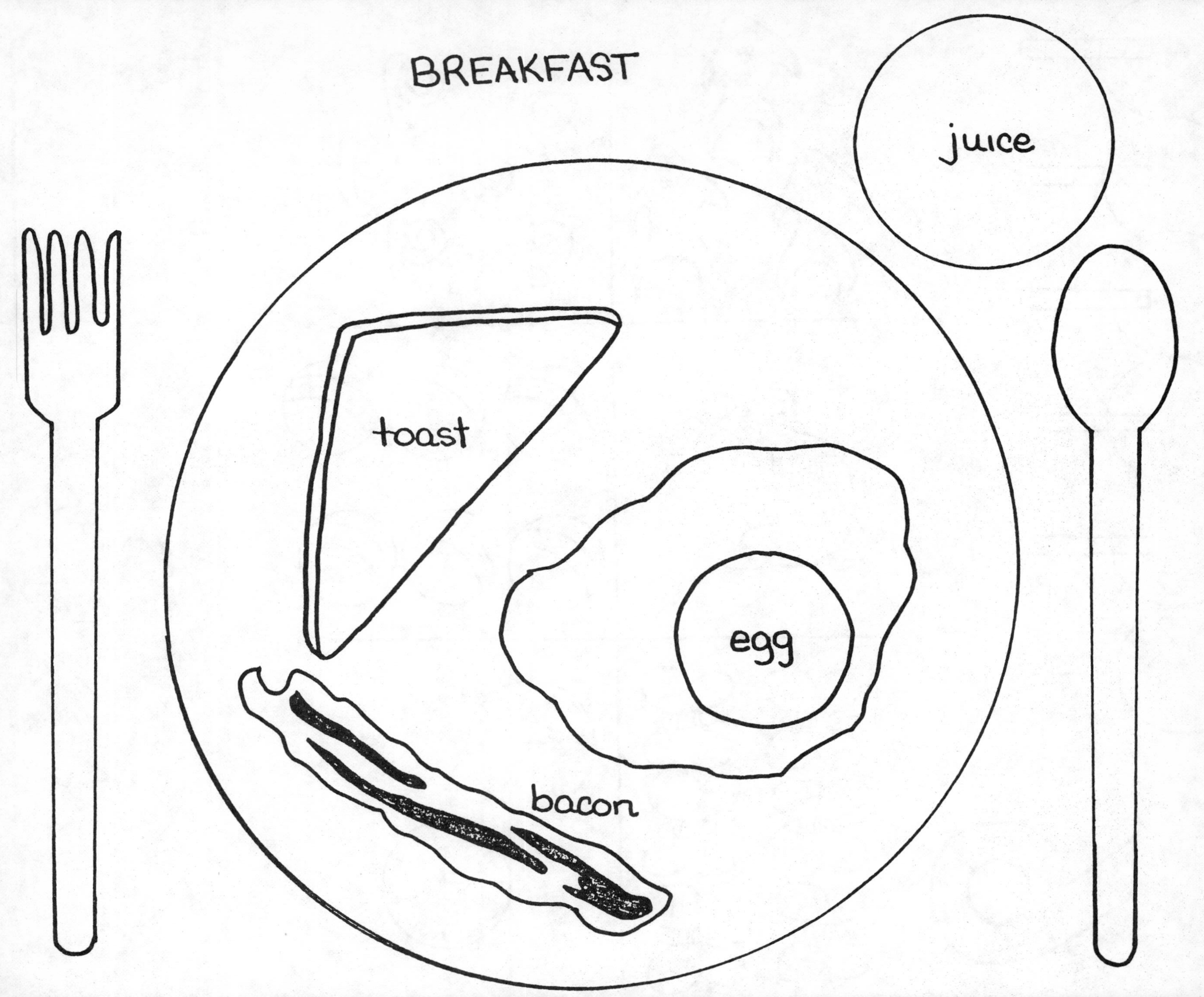
BREAKFAST
juice
toast
egg
bacon

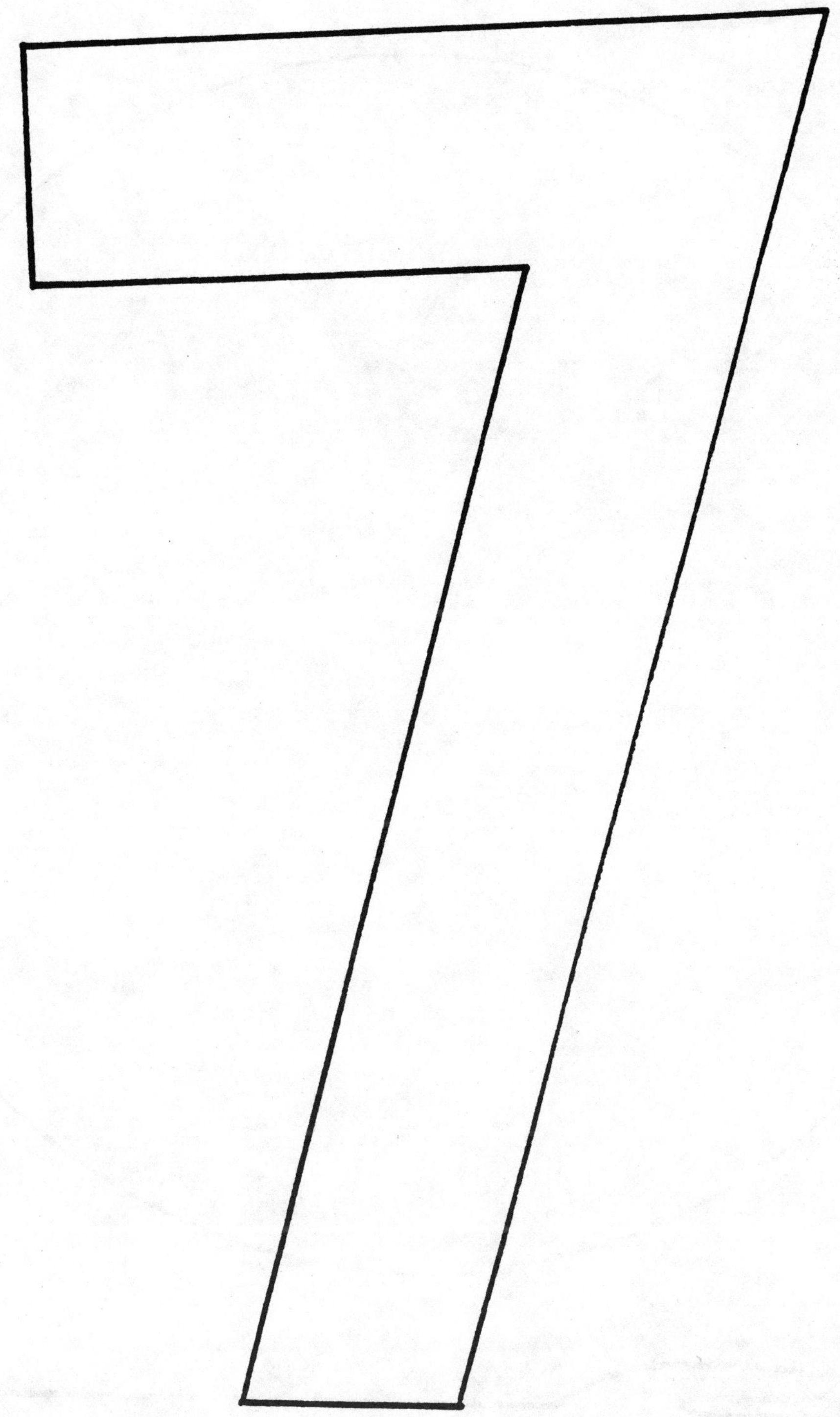

BREAKFAST

Cut out pictures from a magazine to show what

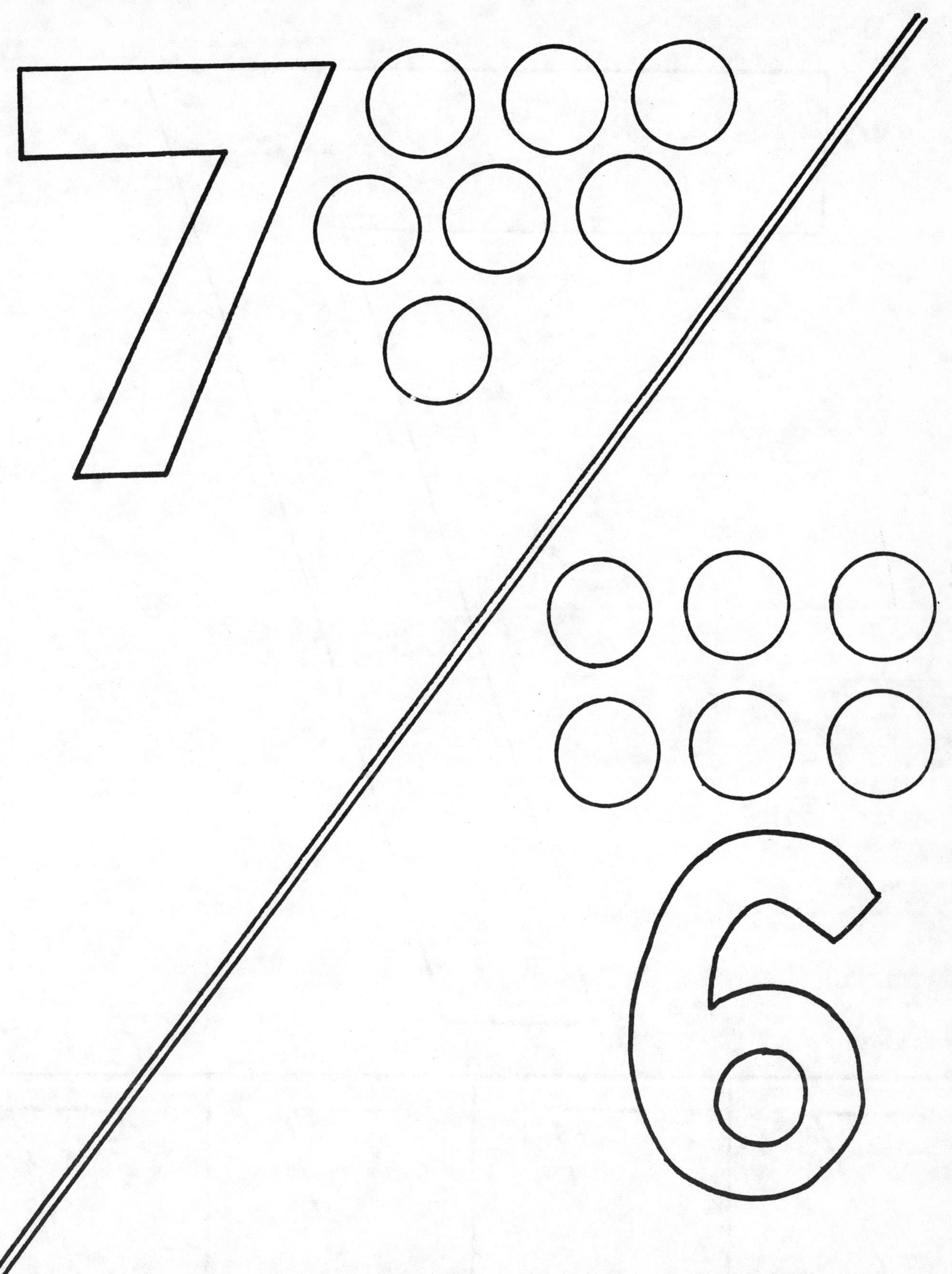

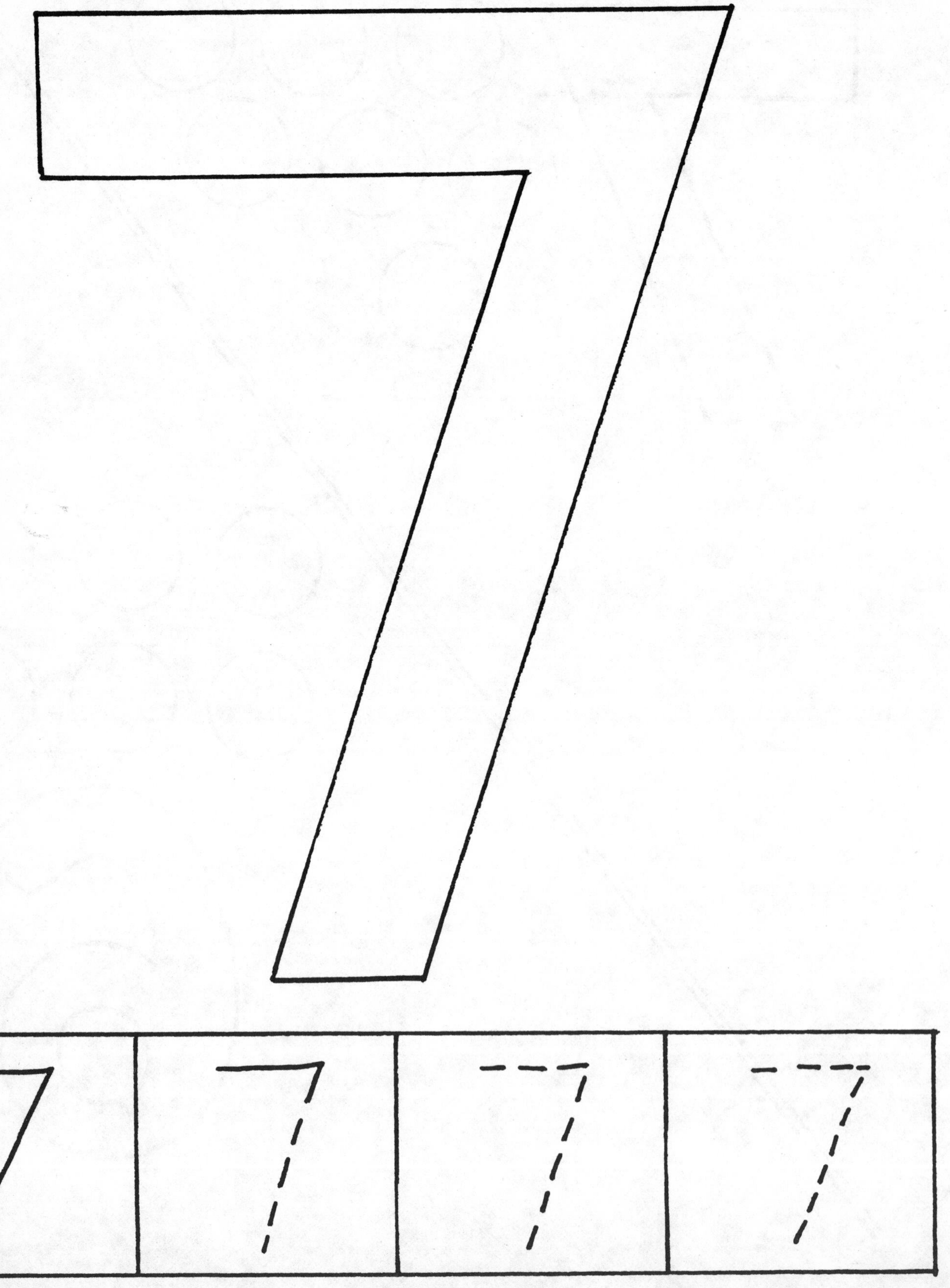

4 (7)

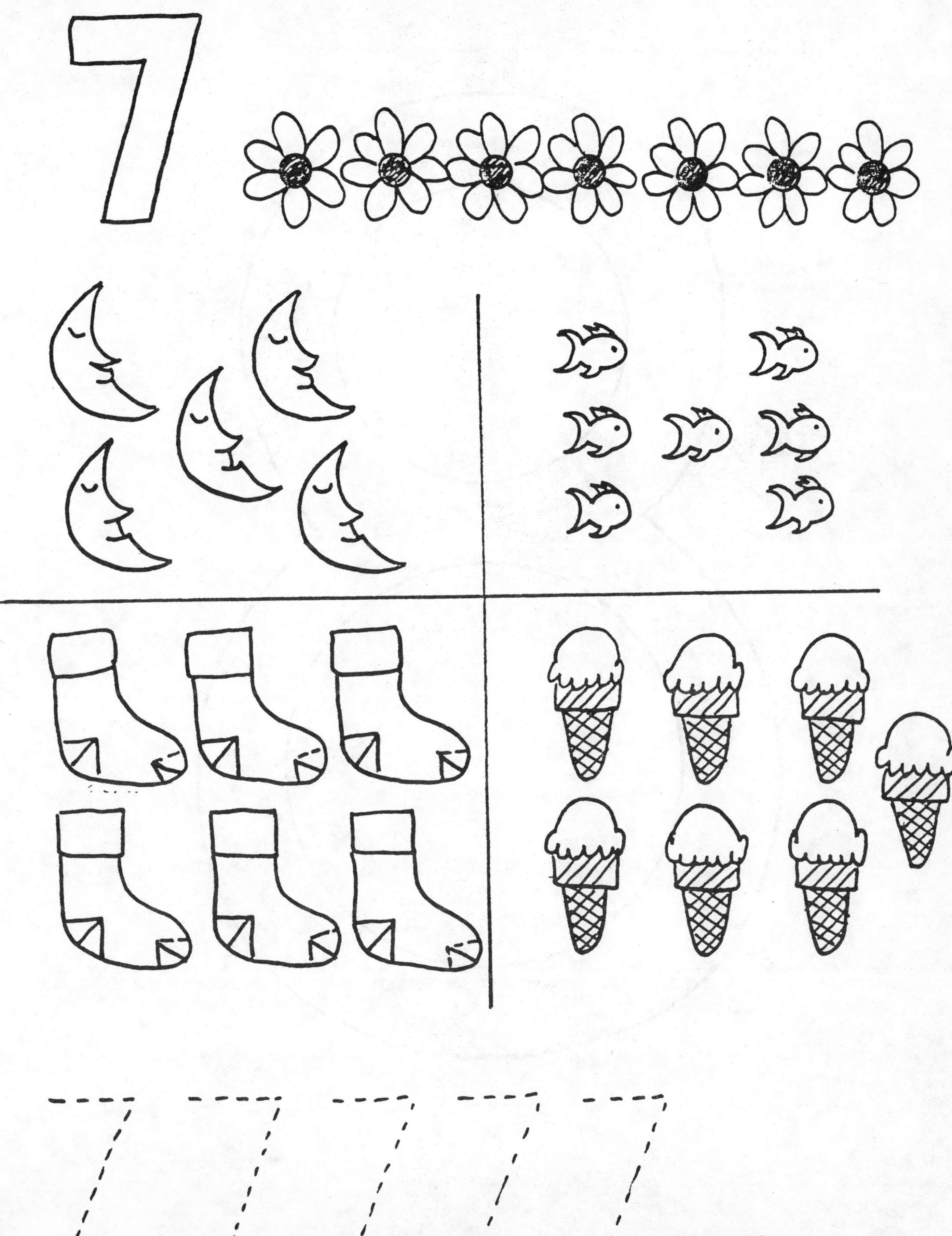

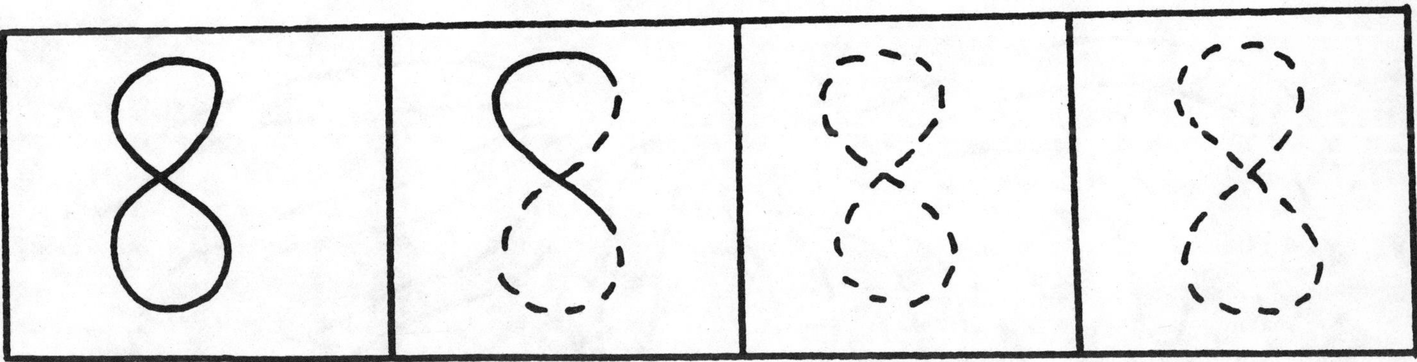

1
2
3
4
5
6
7
8

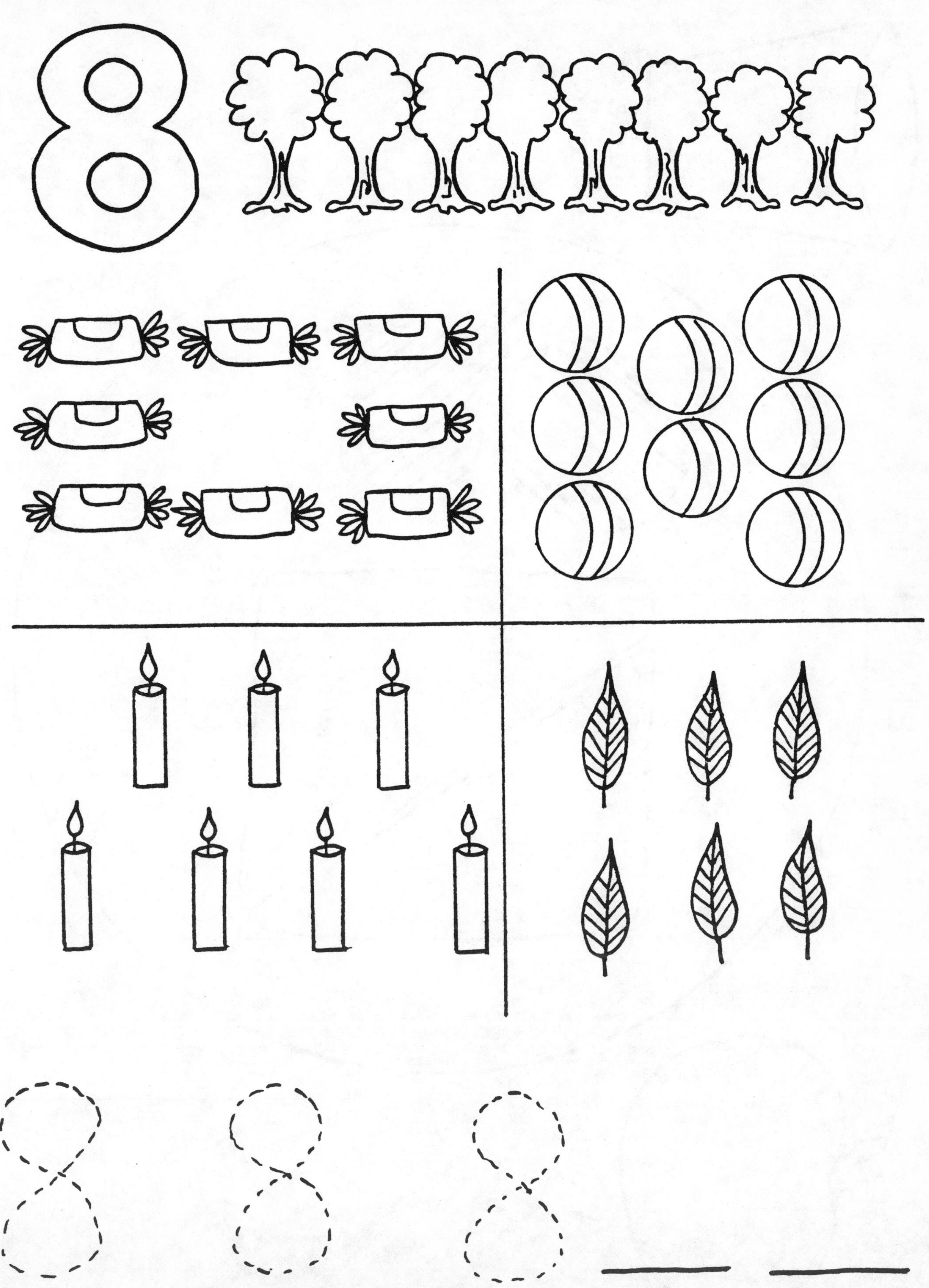

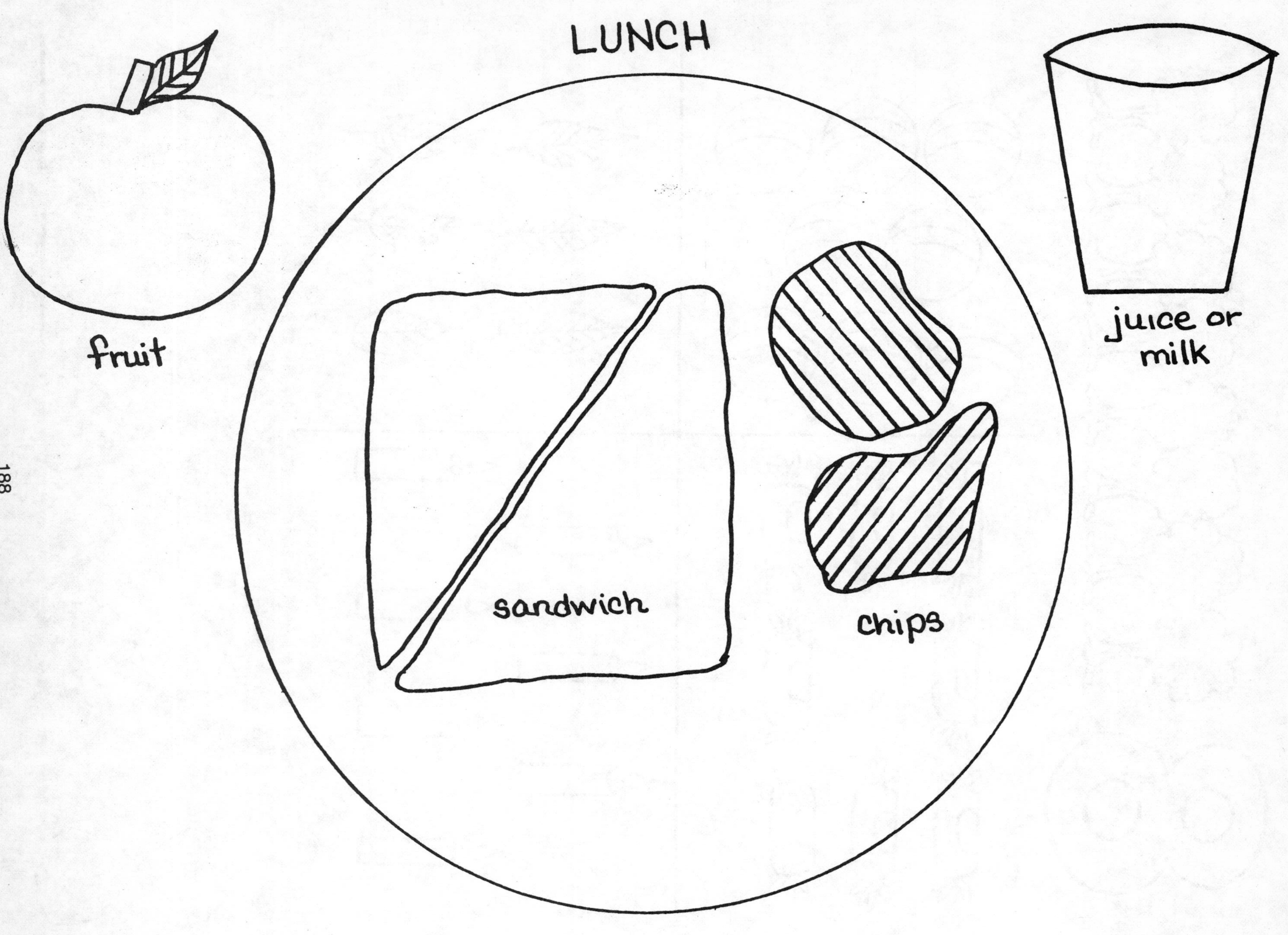
LUNCH
fruit
sandwich
chips
juice or
milk
3 9

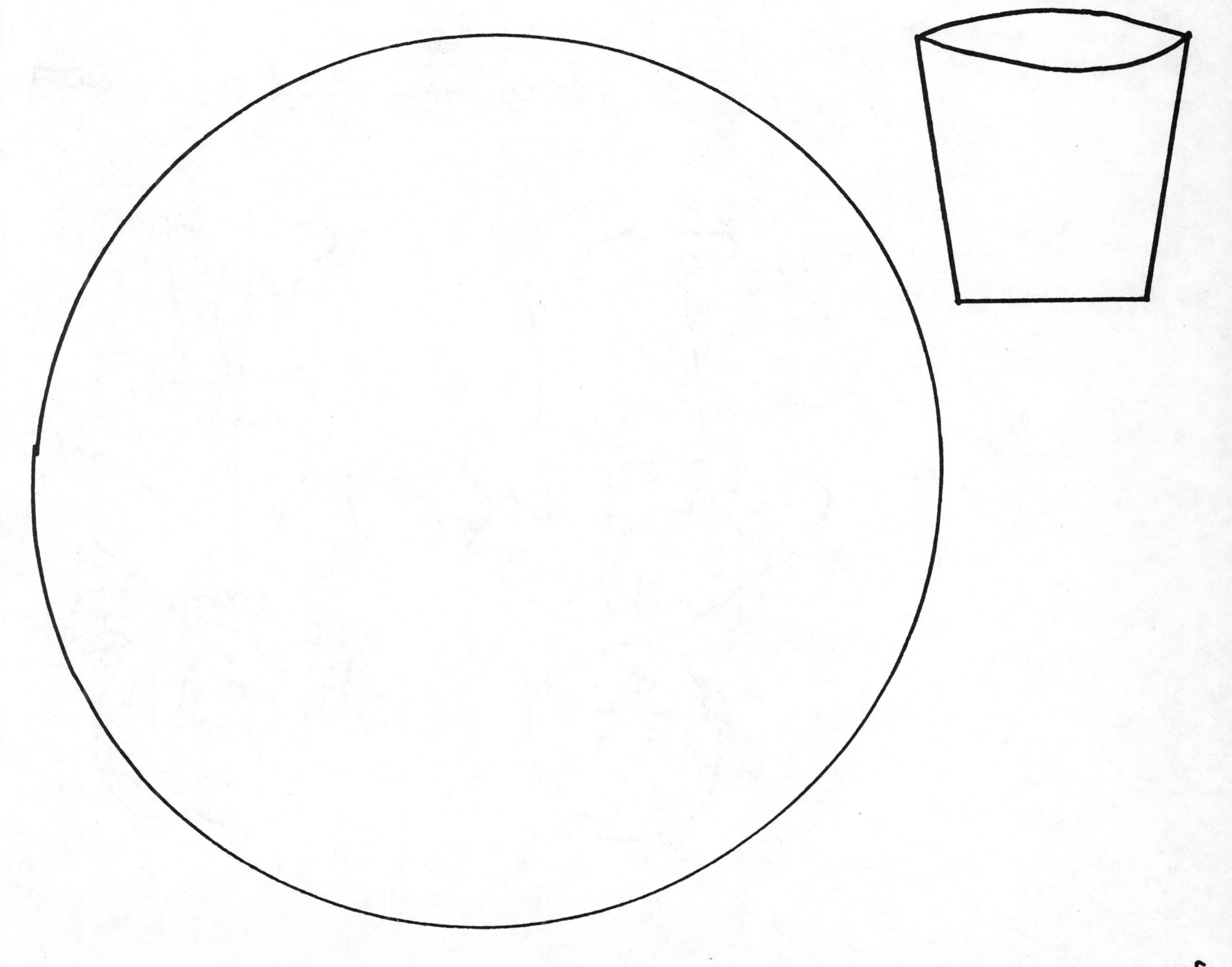

Cut out pictures from a magazine to show what you like to eat for lunch. Paste them on the plate.

4 ⑨

Eat Good Food Everyday!

dairy
bread, cereal
fruit
vegetables
meat, fish
Eating Good Food Helps Us Grow
4 10

Age 3: color
4: color, paste cotton balls on hat.

Cut out, decorate with yarn, glitter, cotton balls, etc.

DINNER

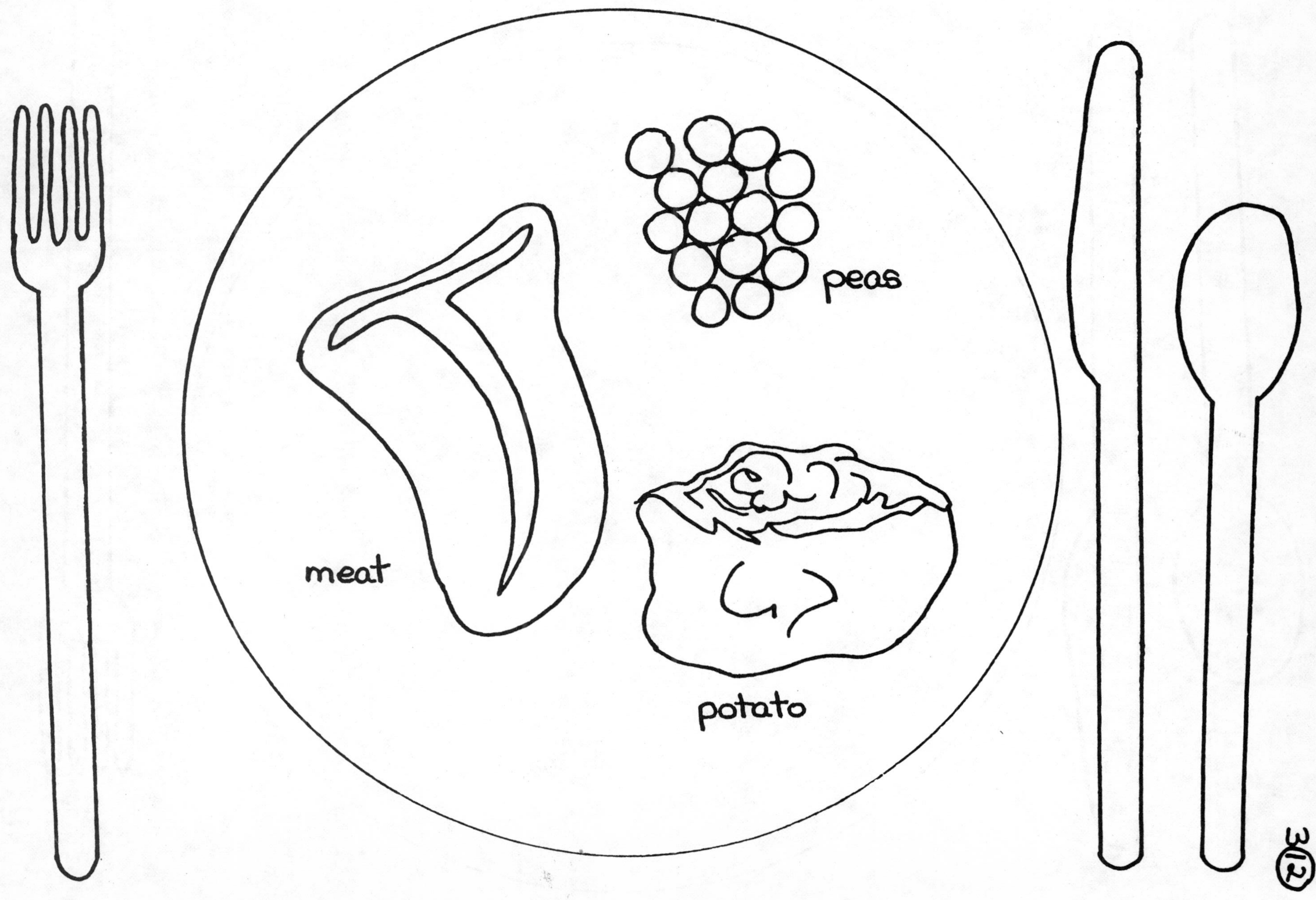

DINNER

Cut out pictures from a magazine to show what you like to eat for dinner. Paste them on the plate.

4 (12)

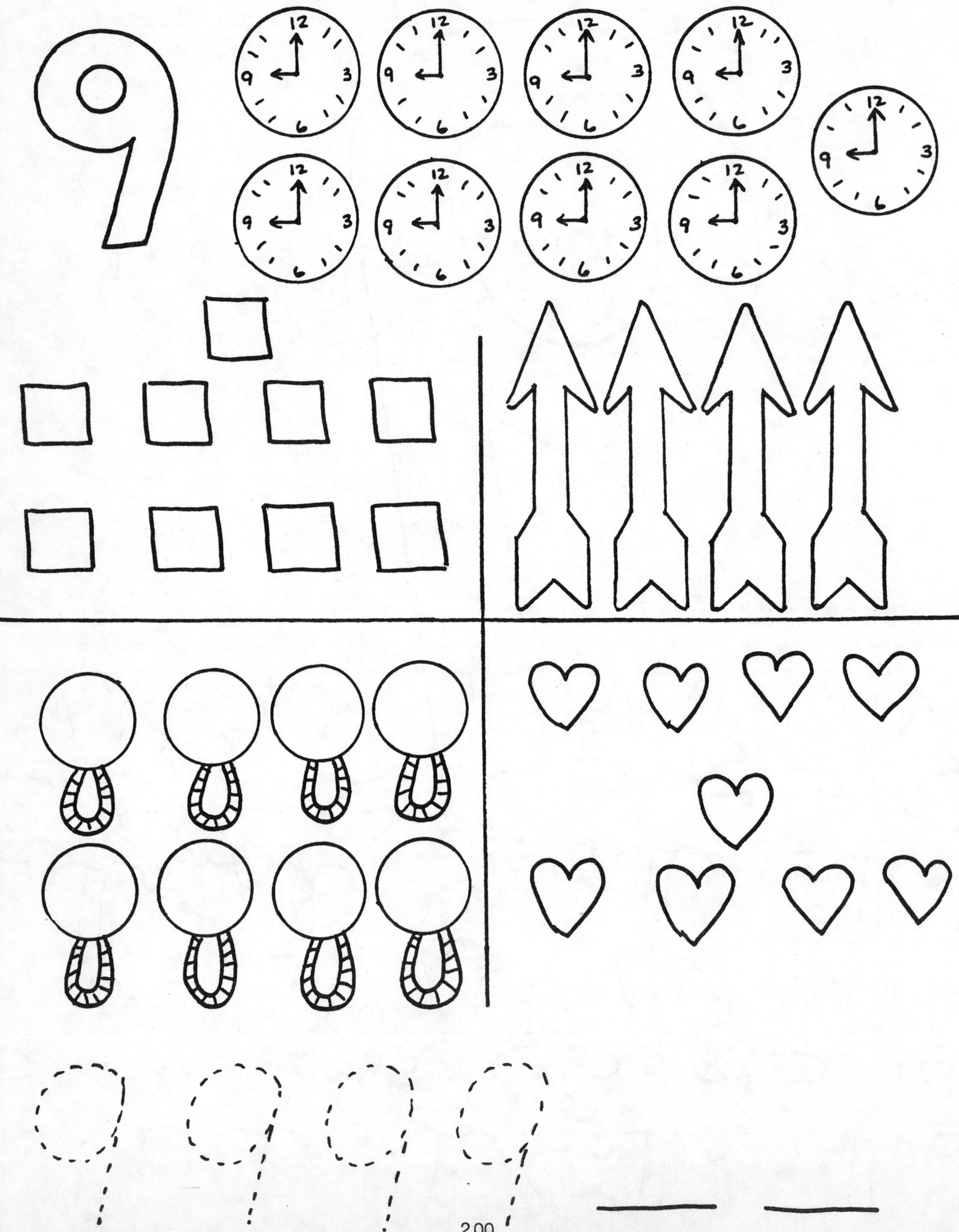
9

This is the season for giving gifts. What would you put in this present, and who would you give it to?

3 (14)

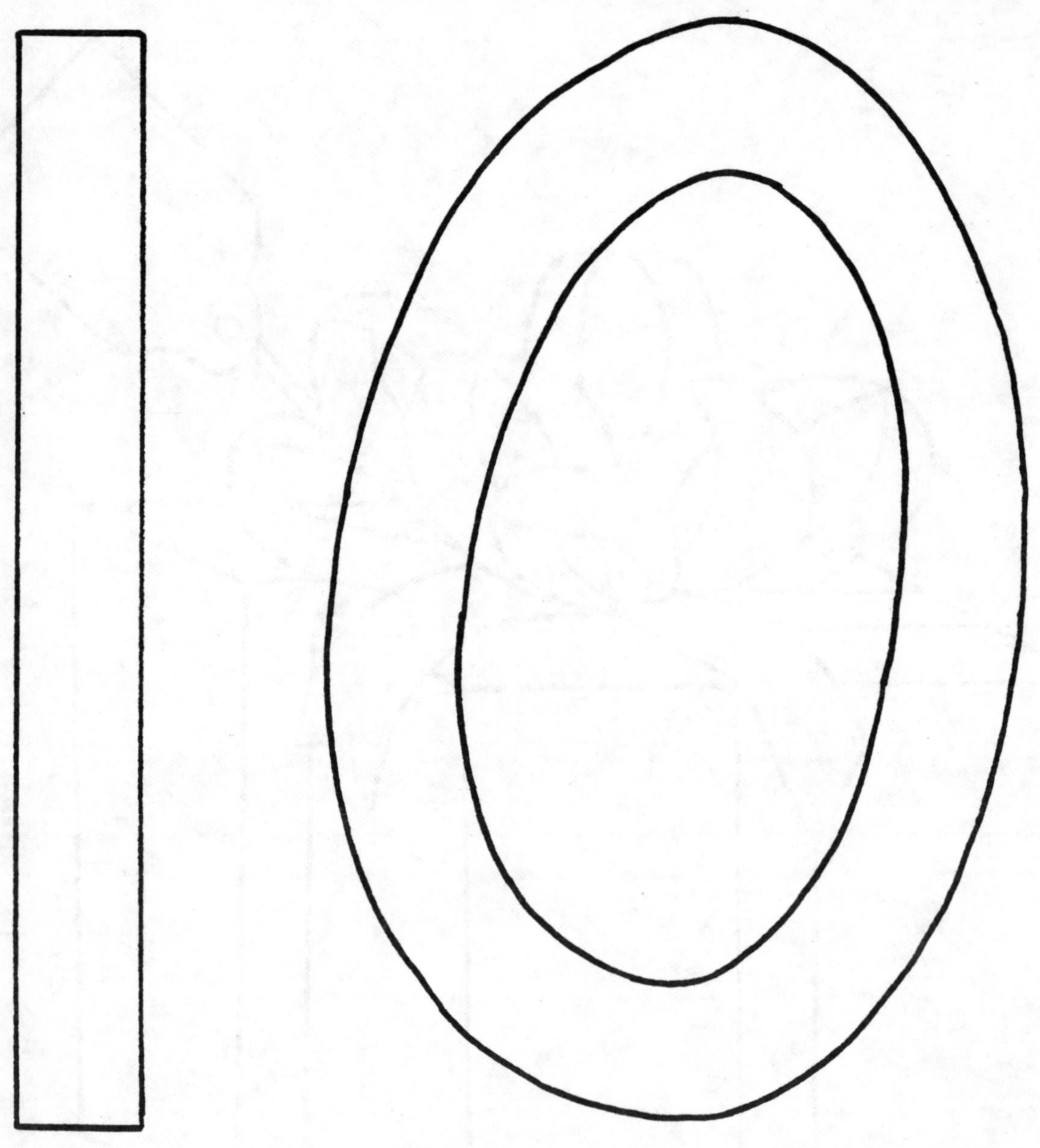

3-4 (14)

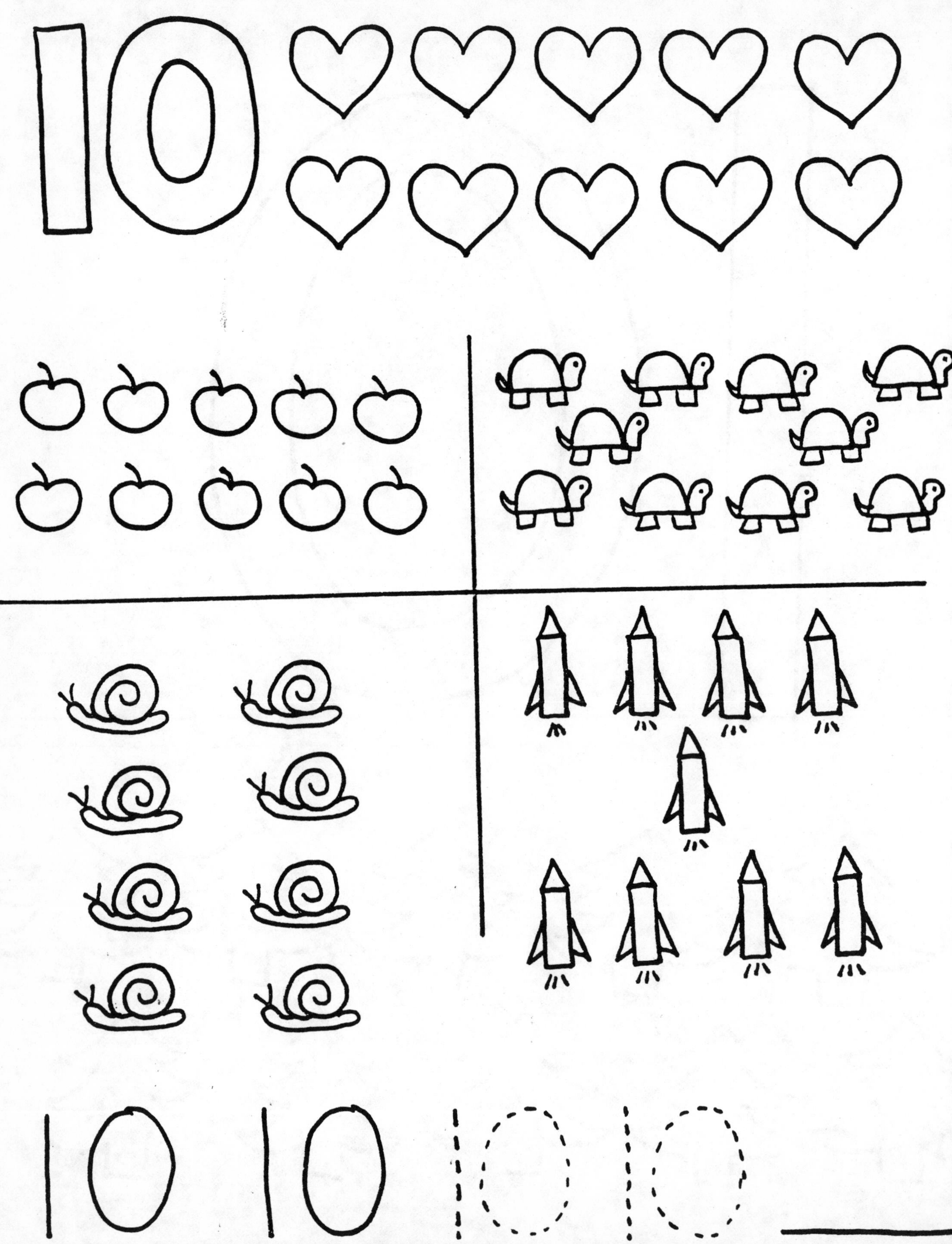
10
10 10 10 10

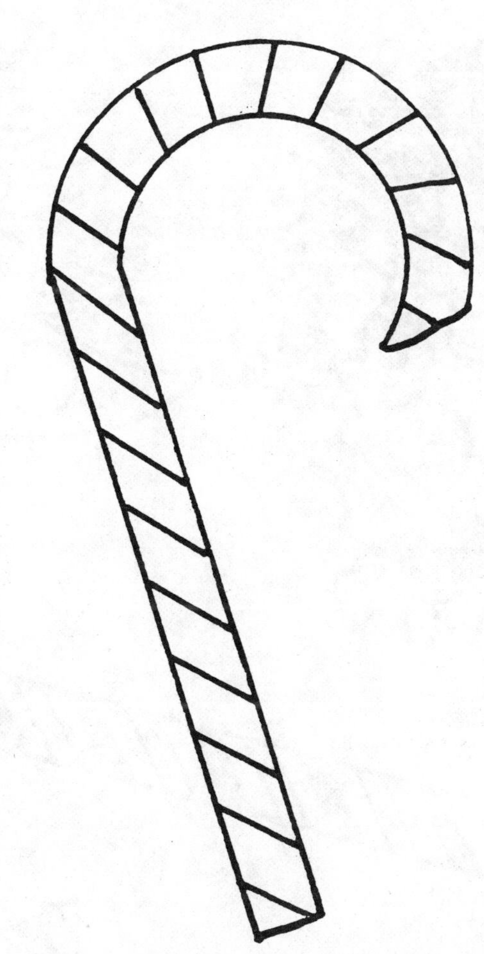

NUMBER REVIEW

Draw a line to the right group:

6

7

8

SHAPE REVIEW

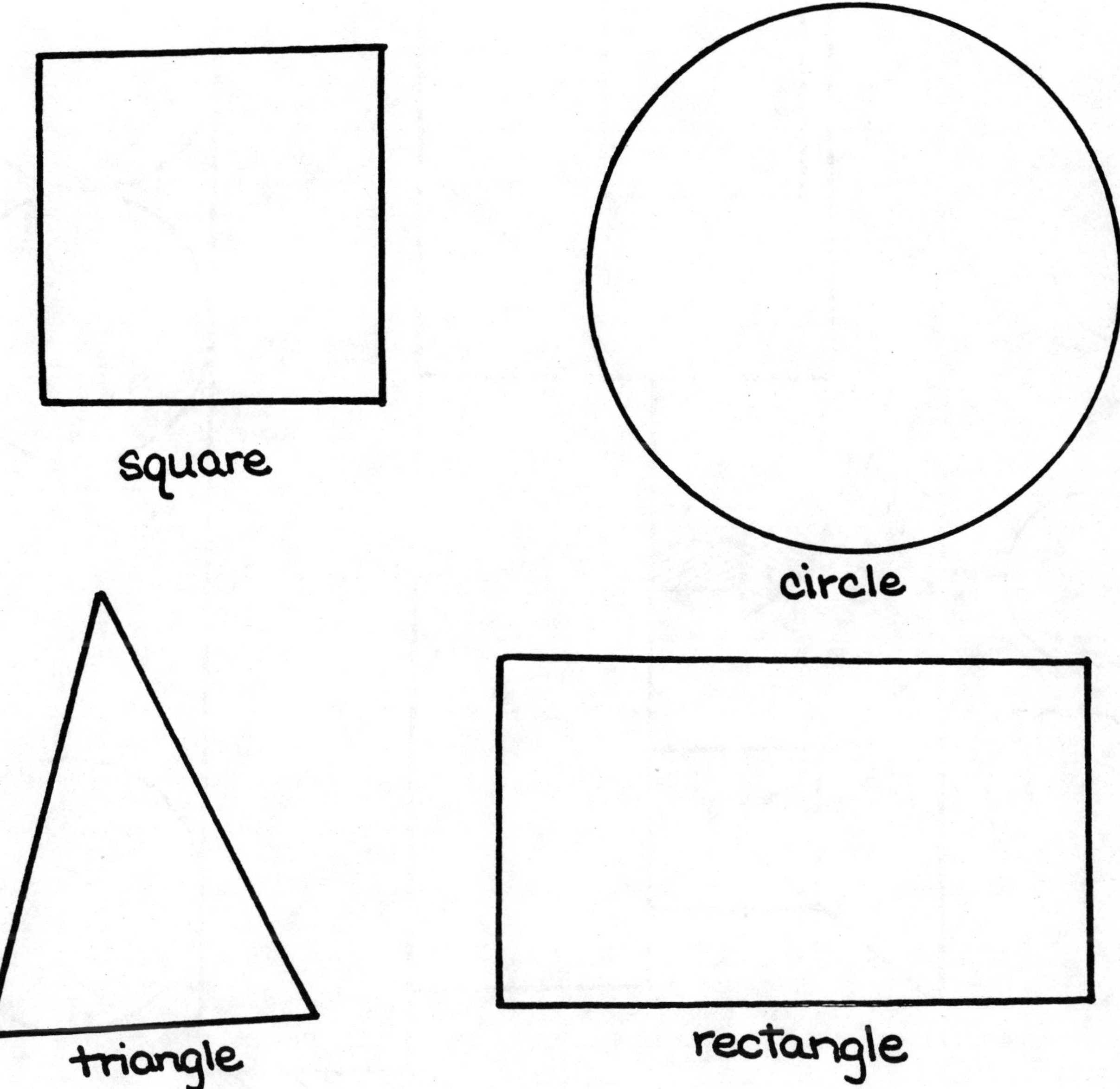

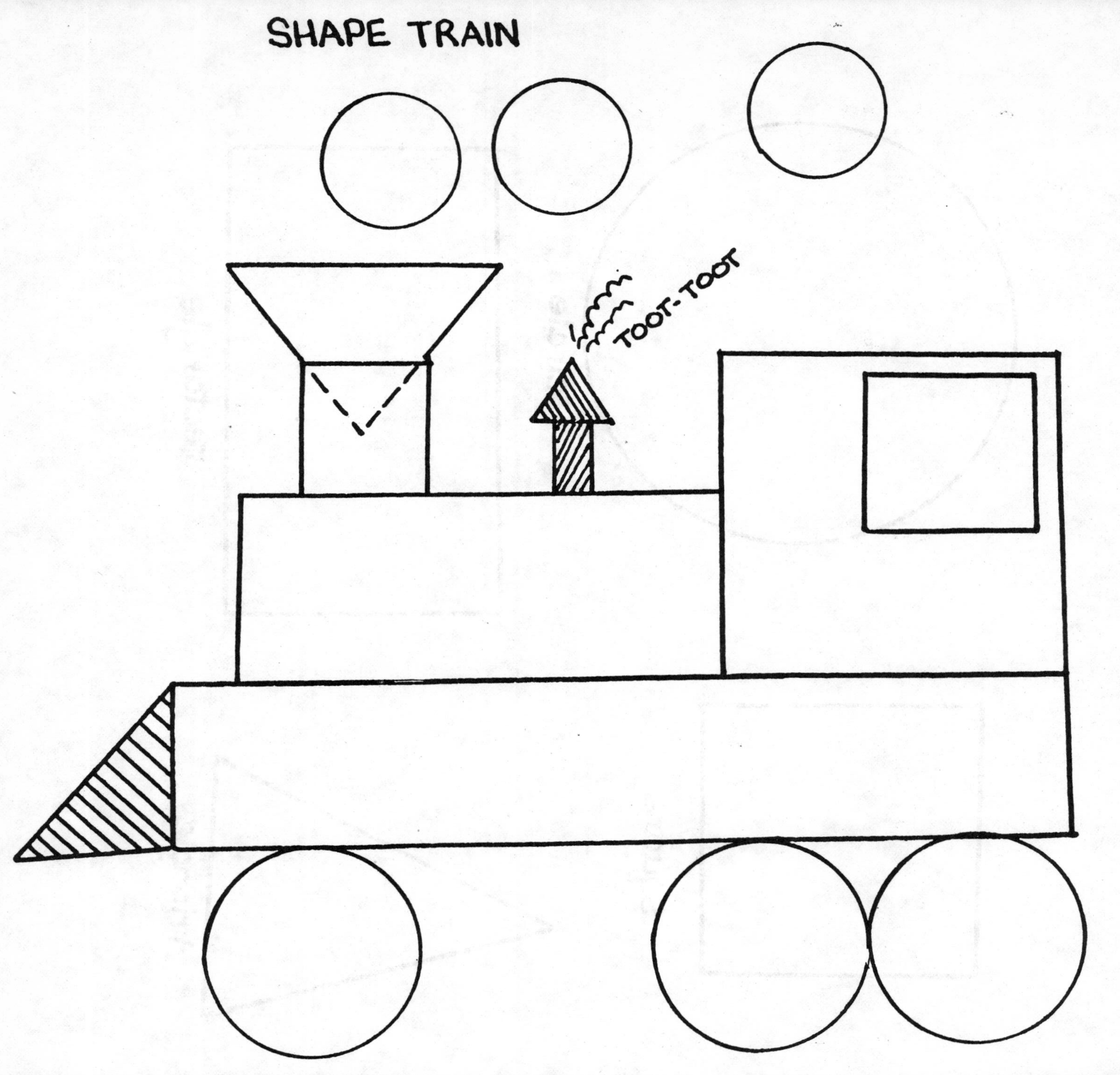
SHAPE TRAIN
TOOT-TOOT

9
10

Draw a line from the number to the right group.

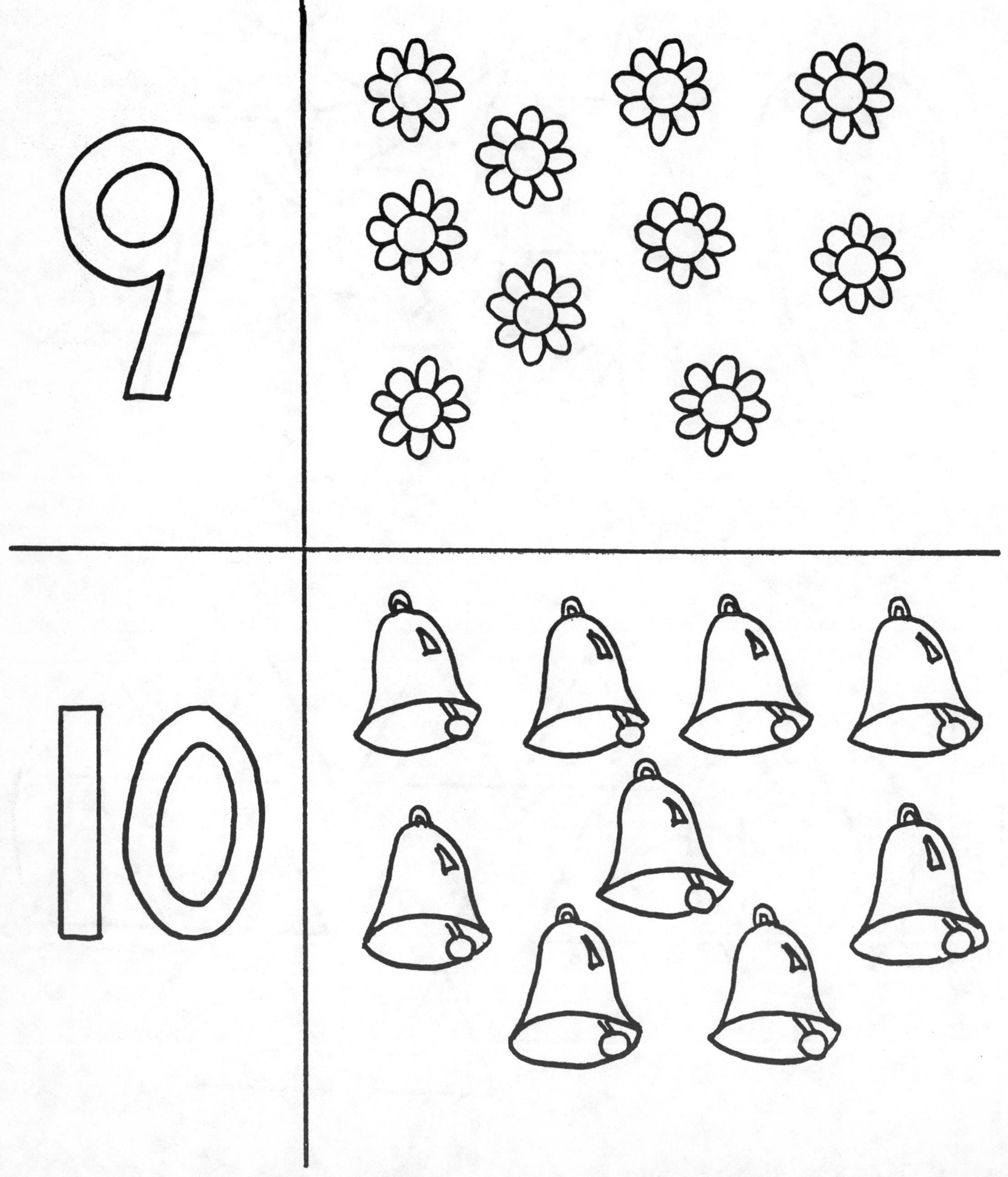

COLOR REVIEW

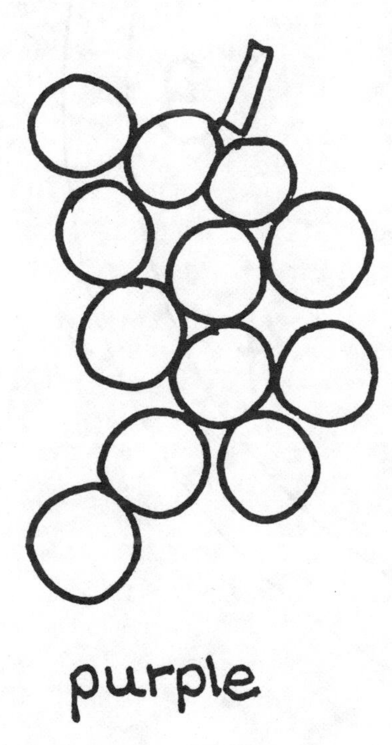

3-4

JANUARY UNITS:

I. Alphabet
   - **A.** Introduction of letters
   - **B.** Uppercase stressed for younger ages, uppercase and lowercase taught to age 4 group.
   - **C.** Word recognition
     1. Child's own name
     2. Basic classroom words (door, window, cupboard, sink, etc.)
   - **D.** Only part of the alphabet will be introduced (A-H). This is a unit that will continue throughout the spring months and should be reviewed for the rest of the school year.

II. Seasons of the year
   - **A.** This unit begins in January because it is the beginning of the calendar year.
   - **B.** Winter, Spring, Summer and Fall, which is somewhat of a review.
   - **C.** One week is spent on each season.
   - **D.** Stress should be made on the climate. In the south seasonal changes are slight while in the north they are greatly different.

III. Family pets
   - **A.** Young children should be taught that animals are alive and need care. They are not **things.**
   - **B.** Stress responsibility.
   - **C.** Christmas pets can suffer if a child loses interest.
   - **D.** Pets covered
     1. Dog
     2. Cat
     3. Bird
     4. Fish
     5. Turtle
   - **E.** If the teacher agrees, children may bring in pets for a "show and tell" time. Try to schedule dogs and cats on different days.

IV. FOUR YEAR OLDS ONLY: ALPHABET BOOK
   - **A.** Used as a review for the children.
   - **B.** Kept in the classroom to be brought home at the completion of the unit as a whole book. This will allow the parents to see the completed work.

PROBLEM/CONCEPT	SUGGESTED ACTIVITIES
ALPHABET: Try to have the children recognize letters as symbols.	Cut letters out of felt to let the children feel the contours of each one. Have a child turn around and trace a letter on his or her back. See if he or she can recognize which letter it is.

	Paste the words for sink, door, etc. on the appropriate site and show that the letters are only the name for that thing, not the thing itself.
The alphabet has an order.	Explain that we will learn the alphabet in a certain order, but that when the letters are mixed up differently, they form words. Sing the alphabet song, but make sure the children sing each letter individually; hold up a sign, or point to each letter on a poster as the song is sung.
Each letter has a sound.	As each new letter is introduced, walk around the room and say the name of the object that begins with that sound. Ex. B: Bathroom Ball Bulletin Board Try to illicit responses from the children of words that begin with the letter of the day.
FAMILY PETS:	
Responsibilities	Who feeds the pet? Who makes sure water is available? Who walks (cleans up after) the pet? Who takes the pet to the vet when it gets sick?
Handling	Can you touch this pet? Does he like it? Should you wake him if he is asleep? Do you play with him as if he were a toy? Are you rough or gentle? If parents agree, have a child bring a pet to school for a day to let the other children see the live animal. (Make sure it is returned in the same condition.)
Love	Can a pet be forgotten once the first thrill is over? Is this an ongoing friendship?

SEASONS:	
Climate	In the south the changes are minimal. In the north they are more dramatic. Pictures colored for this unit use dramatic differences for emphasis. Winter — cold, snow Spring — warmer, rain Summer — hot, sun Fall — cool, cloudy
Vegetation, animals	The cycle of the year is told in the seasons. Regeneration in the spring, death in the fall, sleep in the winter and fulfillment in the summer. Winter — a time of waiting Spring — new life Summer — growing time Fall — harvest

January

(1) Introduce Alphabet: Begin A Calendar	(2) Begin seasons of the year (winter) Age 4: cut out snowflakes	(3) Continue winter (snowman) Age 4: A page for booklet	(4) Begin: B	(5) Begin: spring (renewal) Growing flowers Age 4: B page for booklet
(6) Begin: Pets care handling feeding (dog)	(7) Continue pets Begin: C (cat)	(8) Continue spring Age 3: duck 4: spring scene Review: A - B	(9) Continue pets Age 3: fish 4: Aquarium Age 4: C page for booklet	(10) Begin: summer long days fun activities Begin: D
(11) Continue: pets (bird) Age 4: D page for booklet	(12) Continue: summer (sailboat) Review: C - D	(13) Continue: pets (turtle) Begin: E	(14) Finish summer Age 4: E page for booklet	(15) Begin: fall harvest Begin: F
(16) Continue: fall colored leaves Age 4: F page for booklet	(17) Fall animal stories (squirrel) Review: E - F	(18) Fall festivals Halloween Thanksgiving Begin: G	(19) Review family pets: dog cat bird fish	(20) Review seasons Age 4: G page for booklet
(21) Begin: H Review			CRAFT ITEMS: Brown paper bags Green egg cartons	

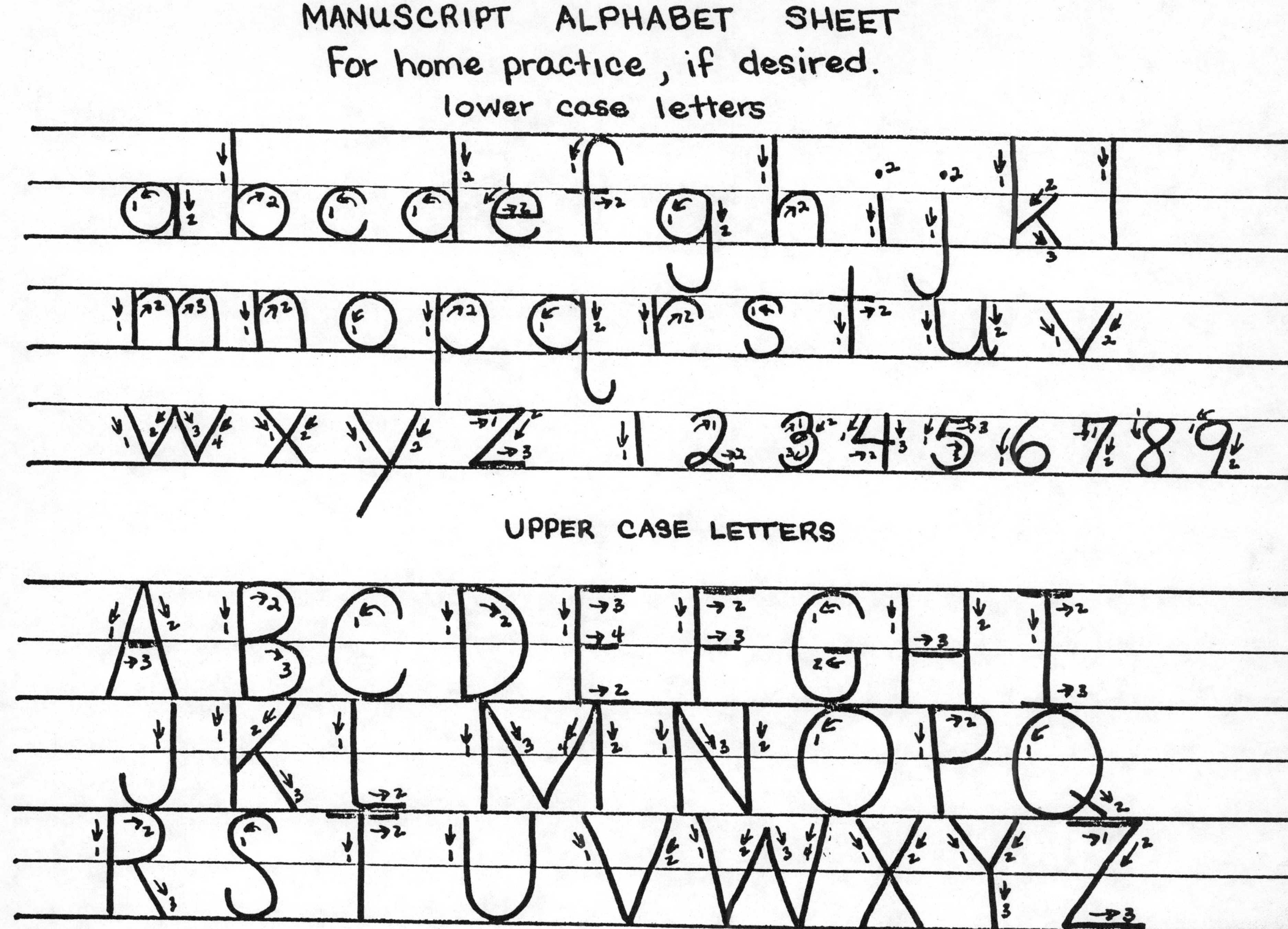
MANUSCRIPT ALPHABET SHEET
For home practice, if desired.
lower case letters
UPPER CASE LETTERS

3-4 ①

JANUARY

SUN.	MON.	TUES.	WED.	THURS.	FRI.	SAT.

A
a
apple

WINTER
3-4 ②

3 ③

3 ④

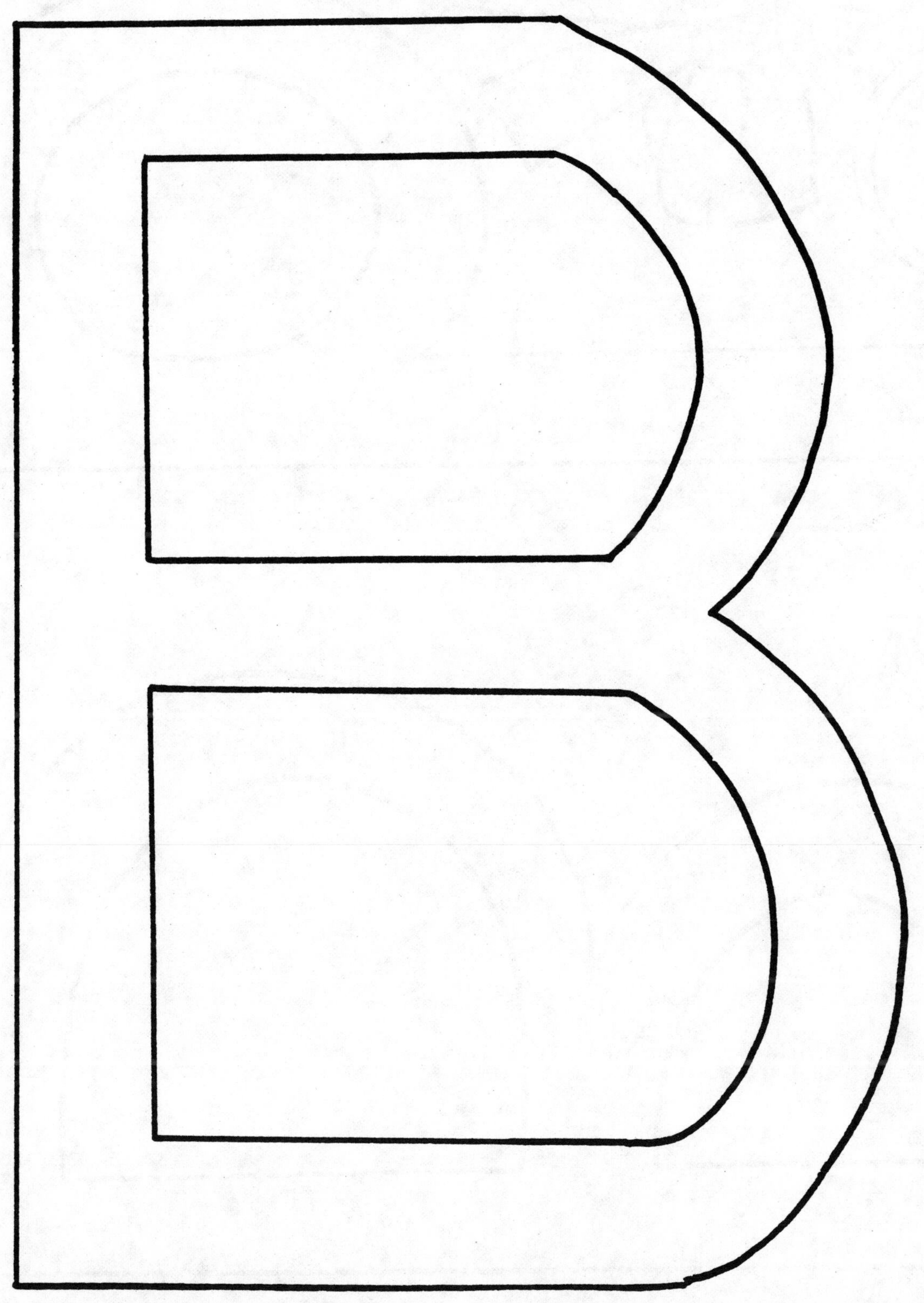

buttons
bow

SPRING

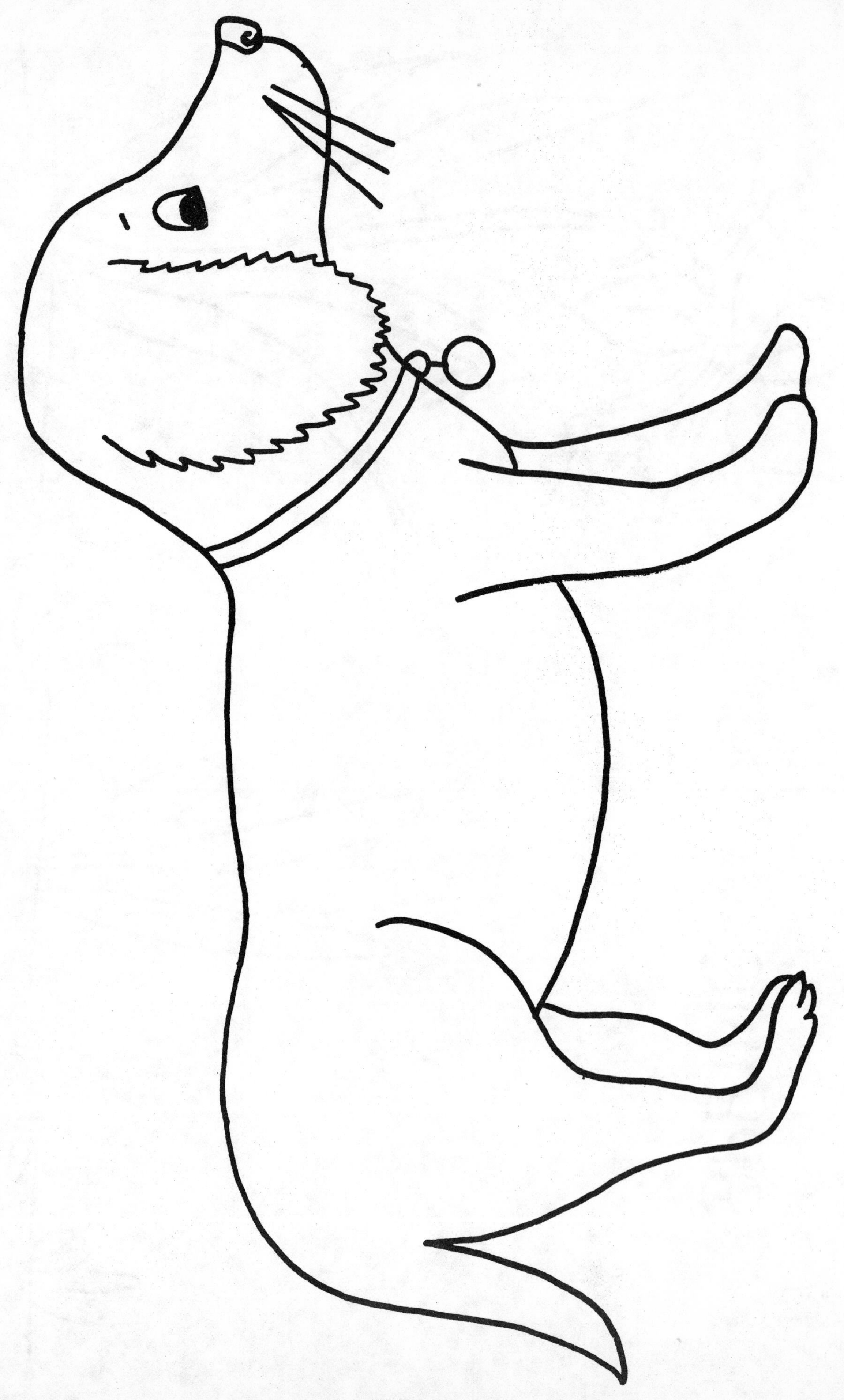

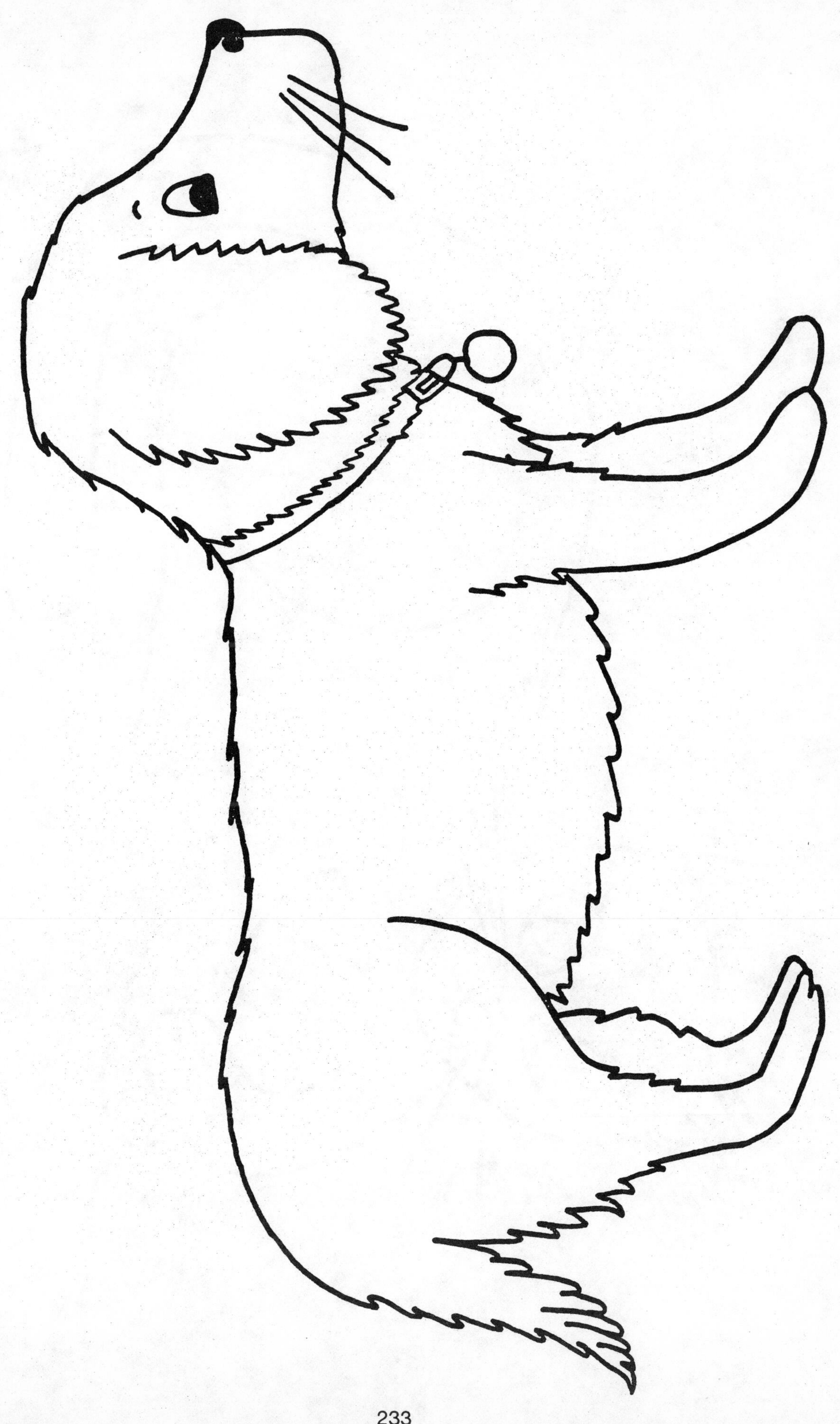

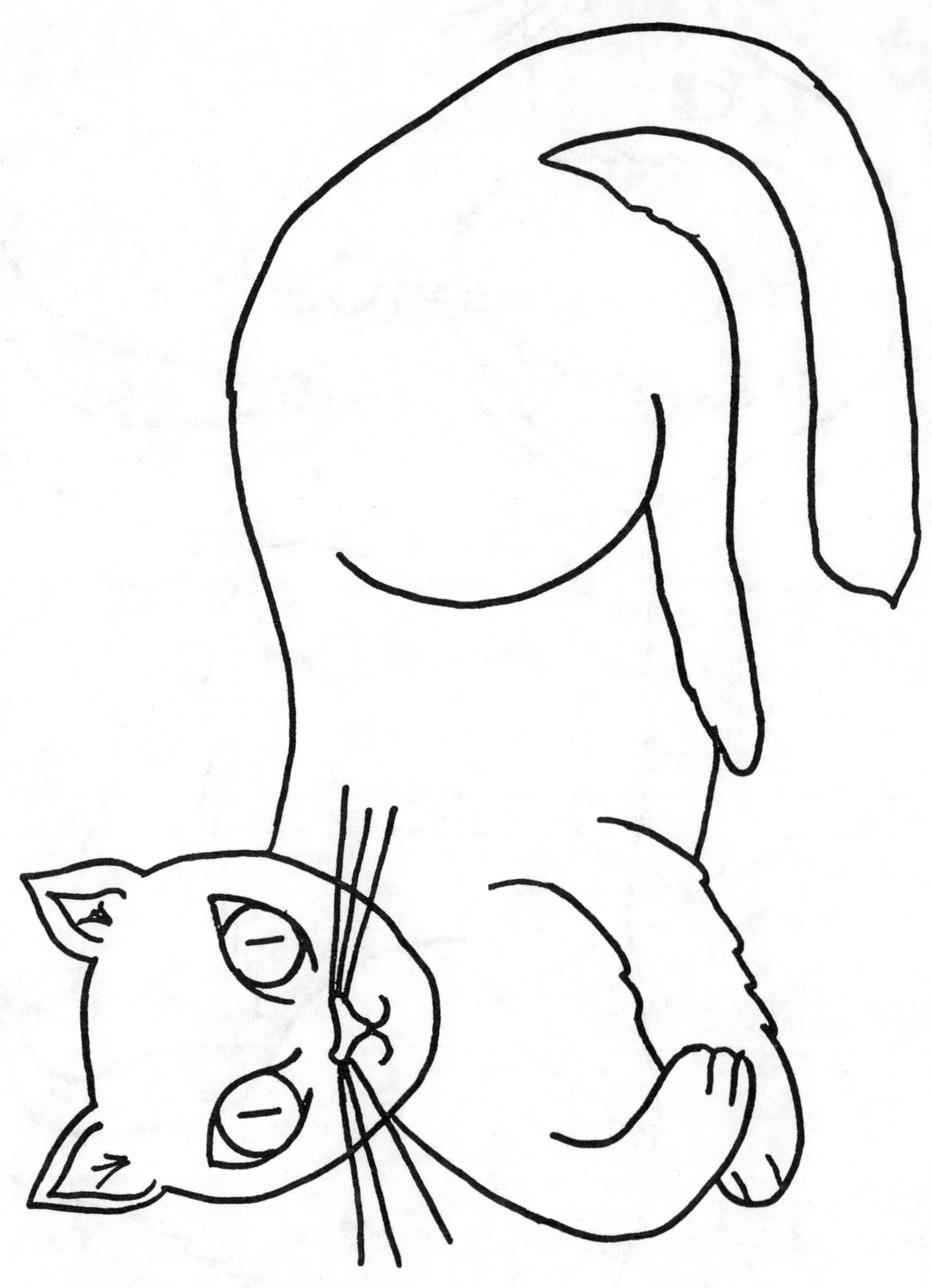

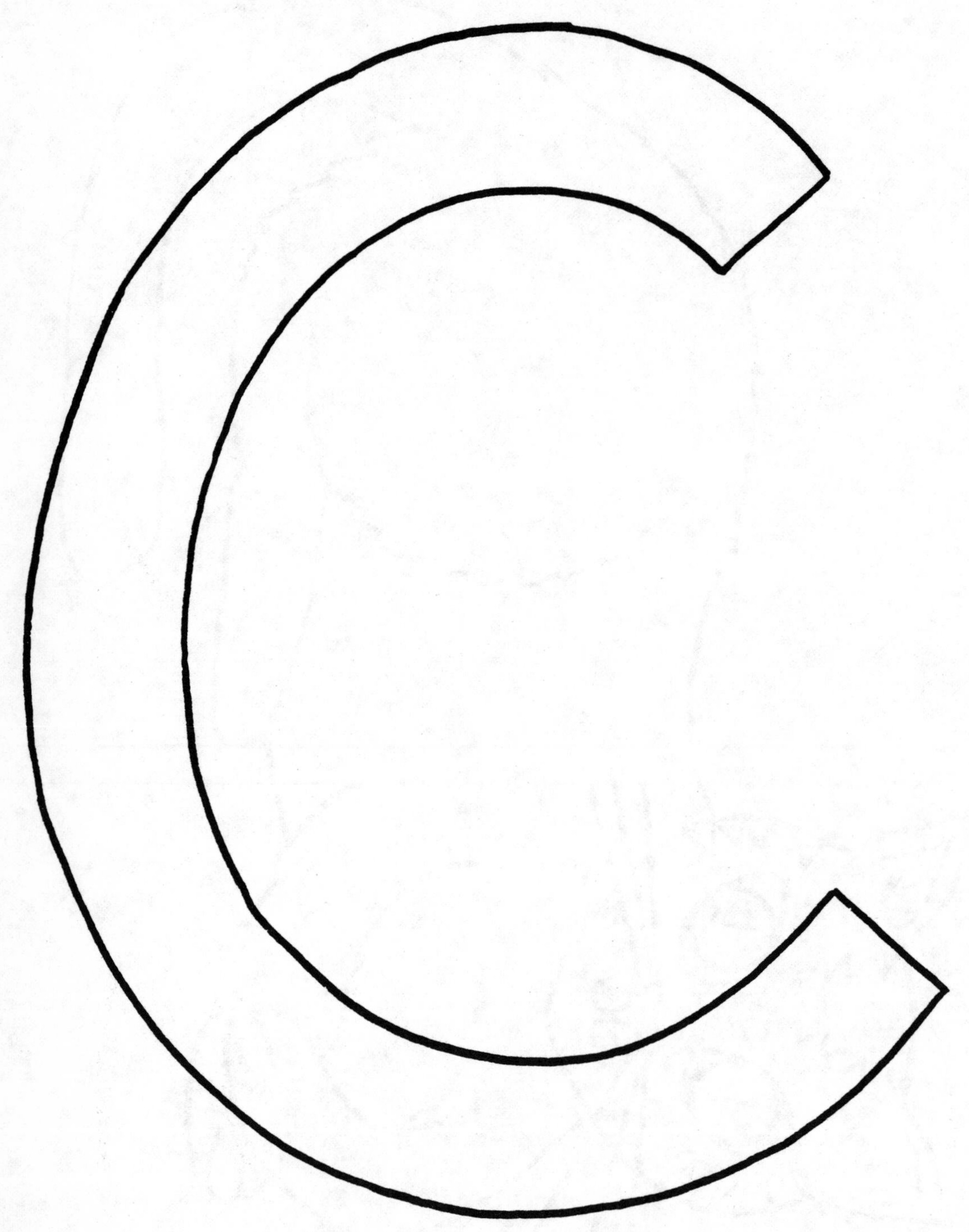

4 ⑦

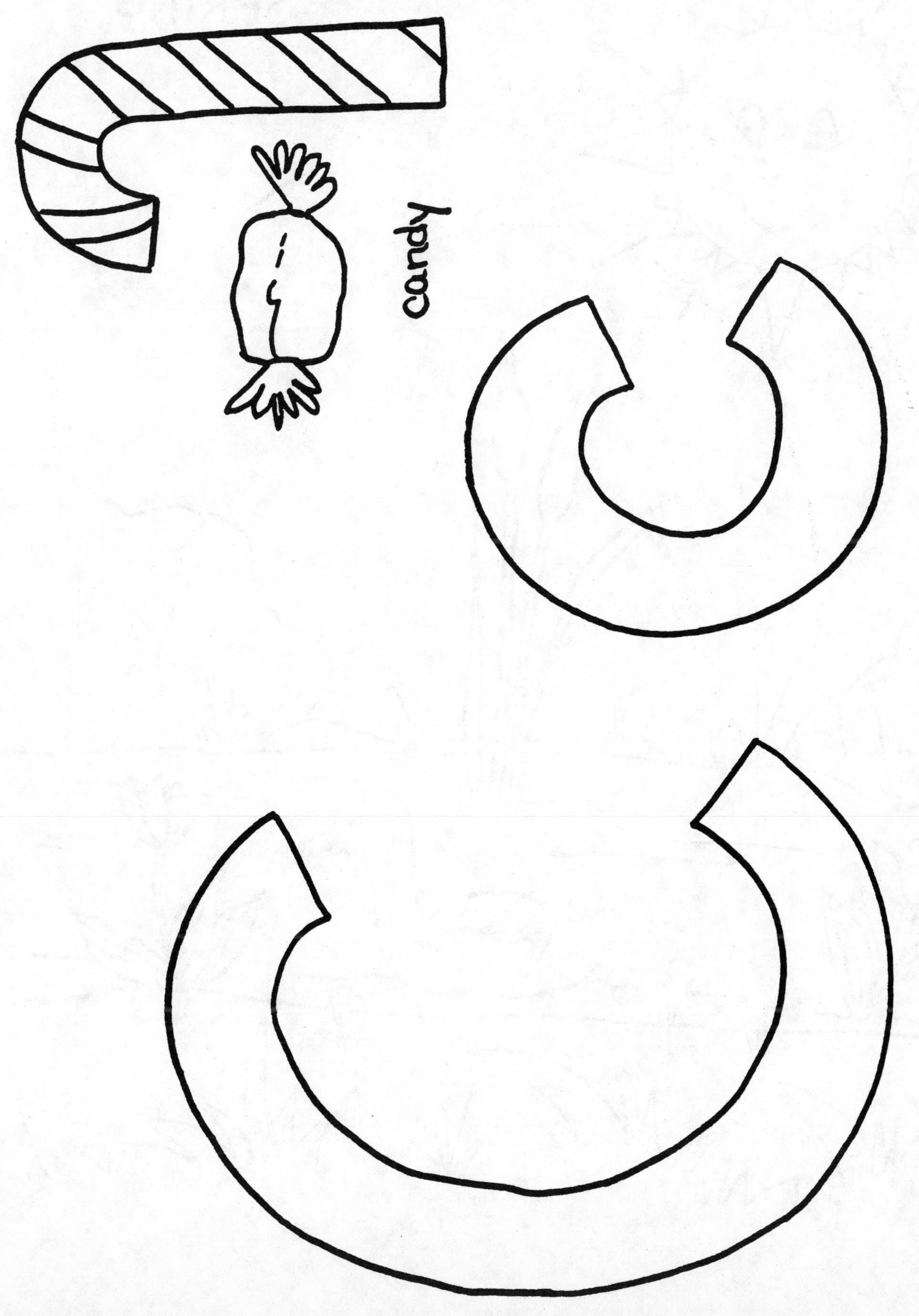

4 (8)

REVIEW

3 ⑧

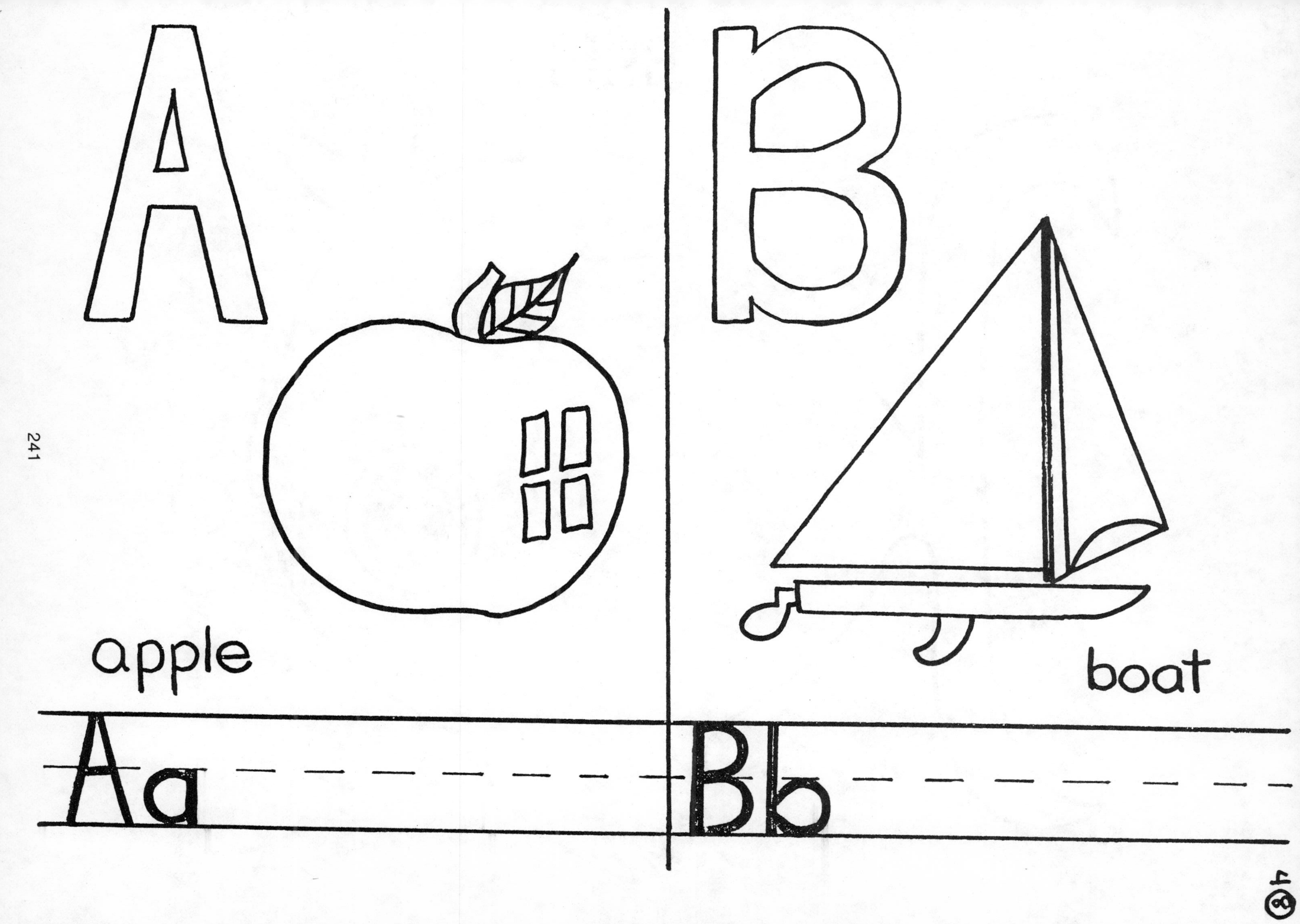
A
apple
Aa
B
boat
Bb
4⑧

3 (9)

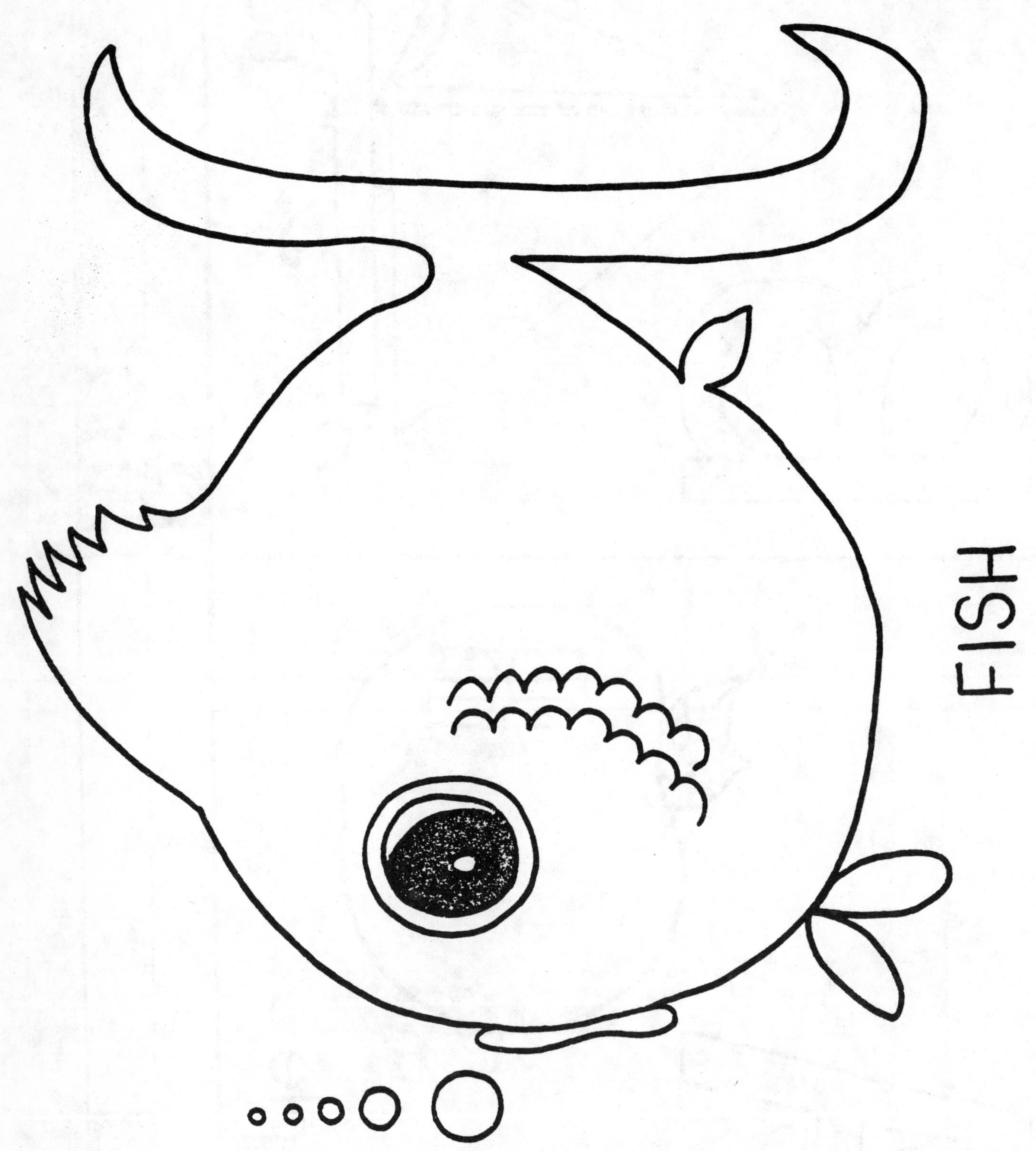

FISH

4 (9)

SUMMER FUN

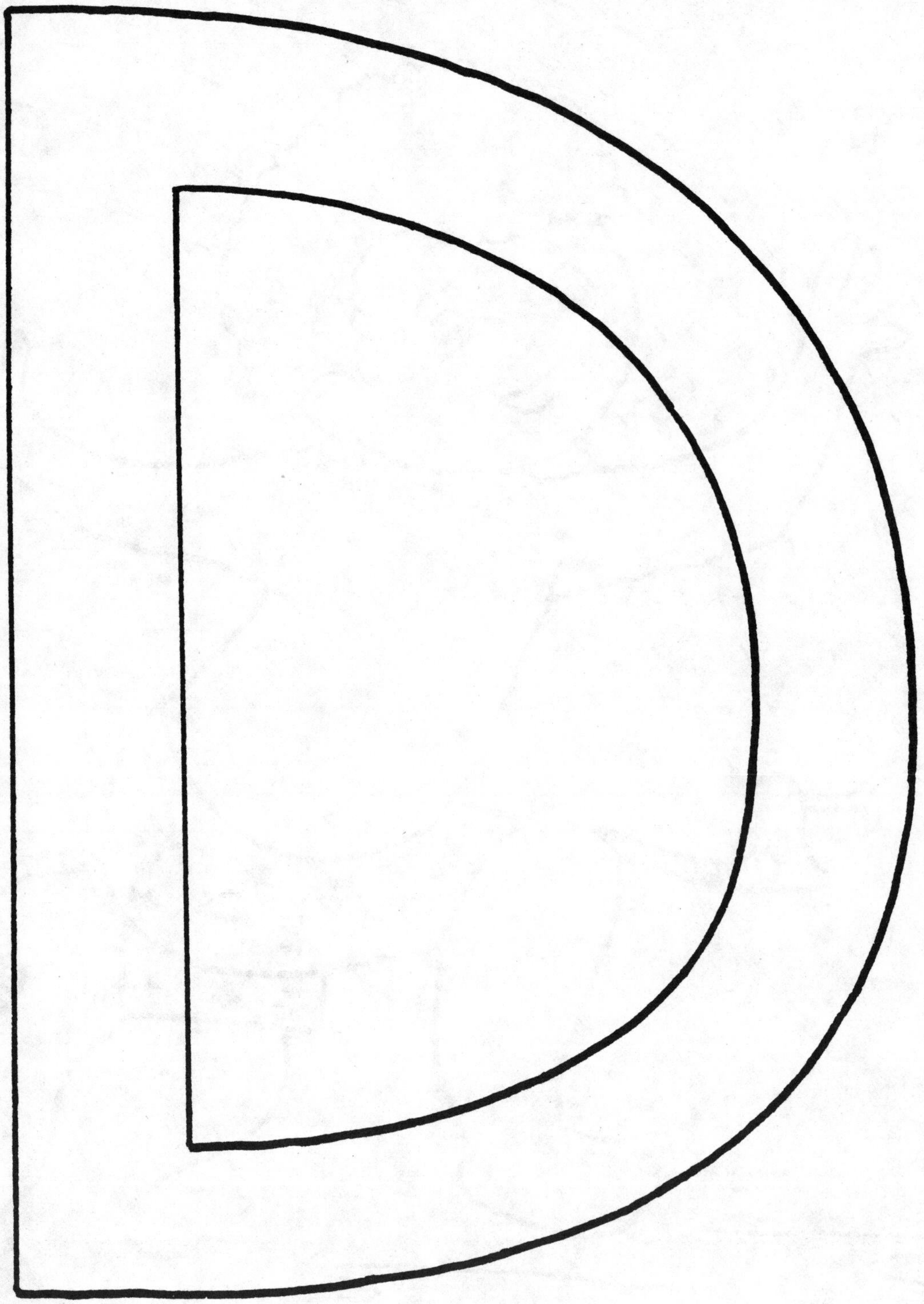

Dd
dog

BIRD

BIRD

7080

REVIEW

3 (12)

C
D
candy
dog
Cc
Dd
4 (12)

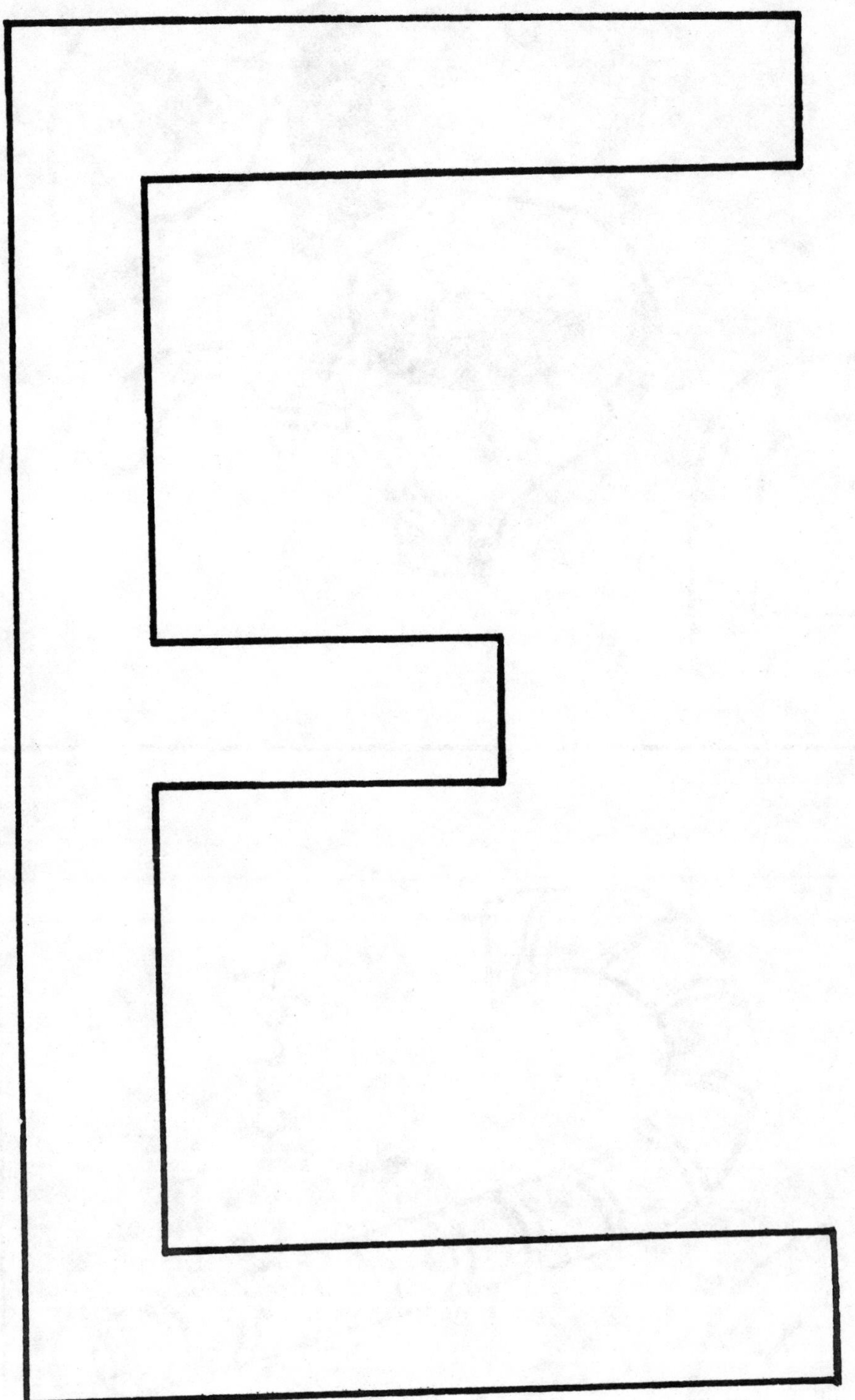

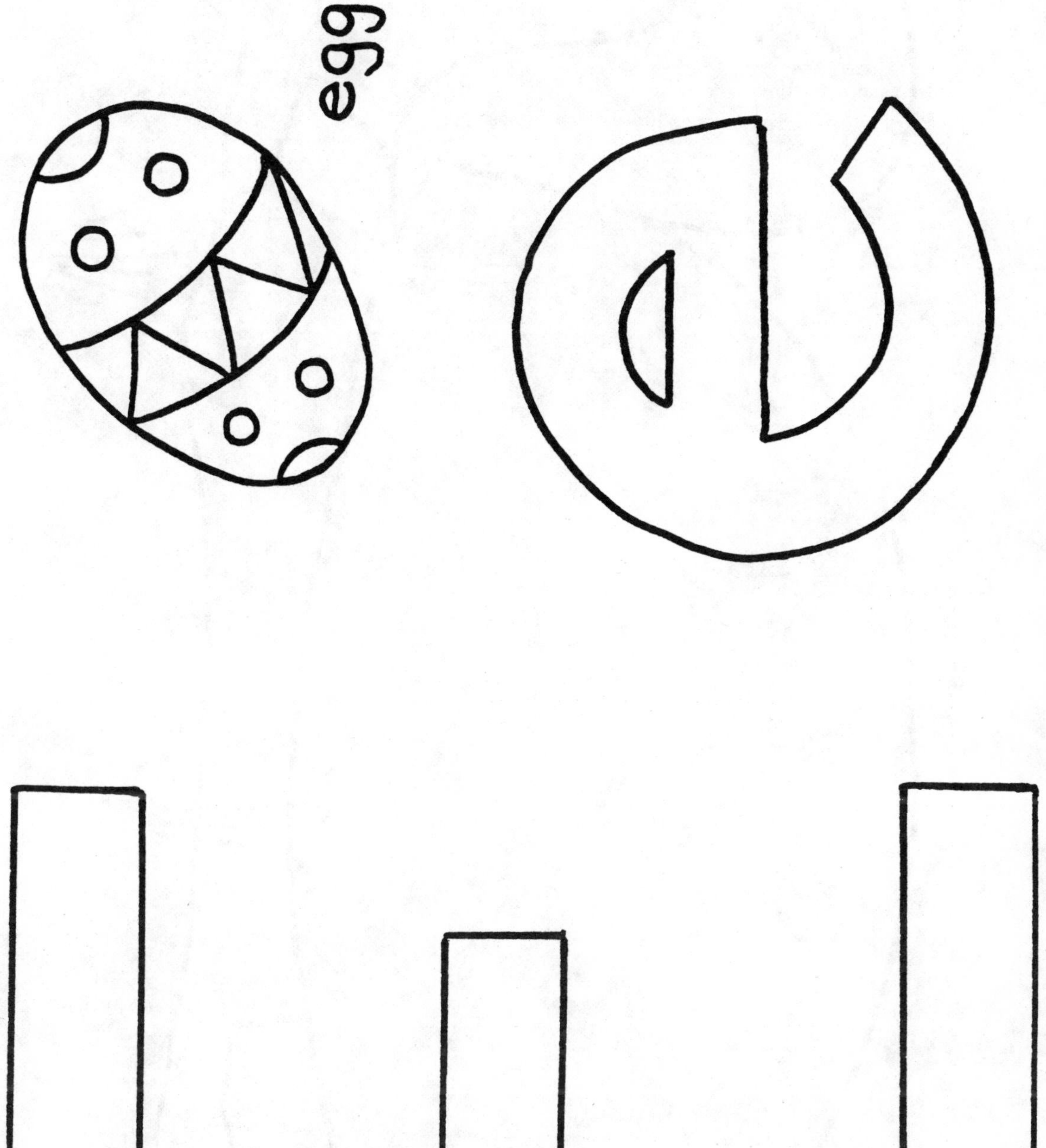

egg

Paste bits of green egg cartons to shell.

TURTLE

3 (13)

TURTLE

3-4 14

FALL

F

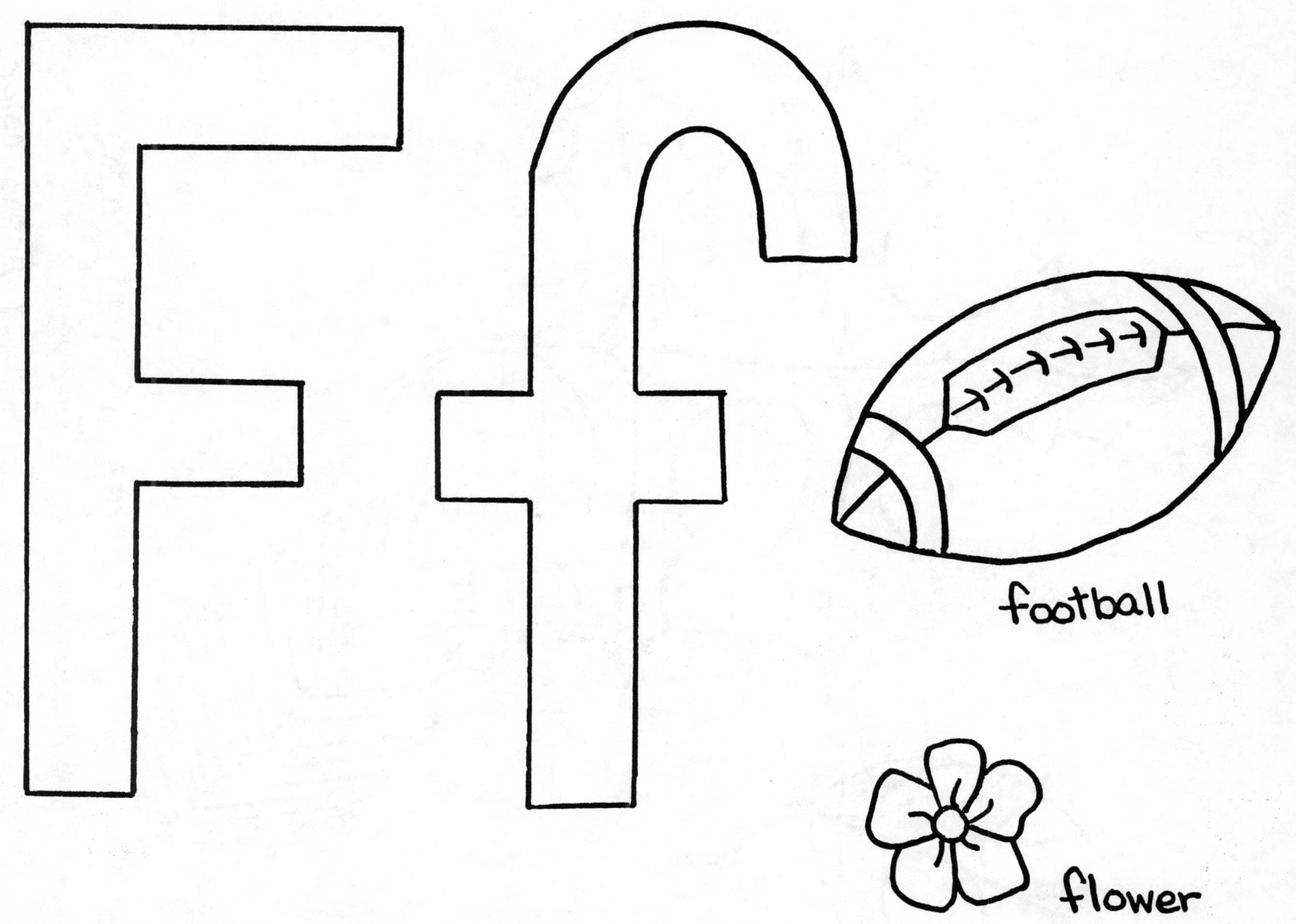

4 15

FALL LEAVES

Age 3: color
4: paint

Try teanng small pieces of brown paper bags and paste them to the tail.

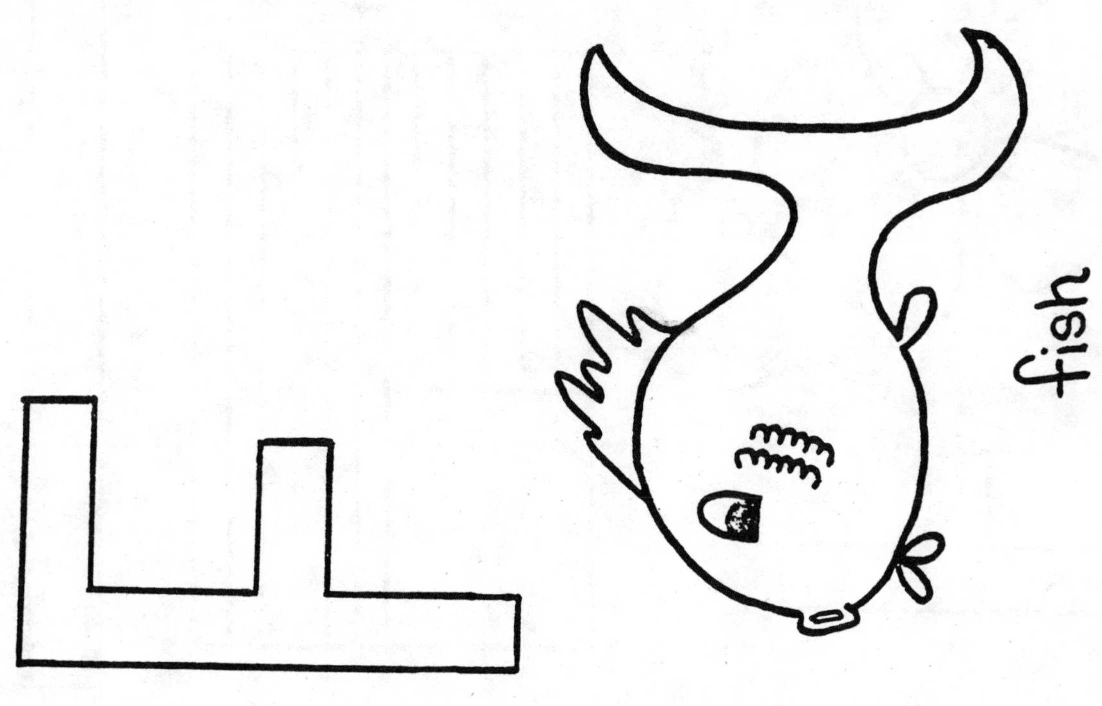
F
fish

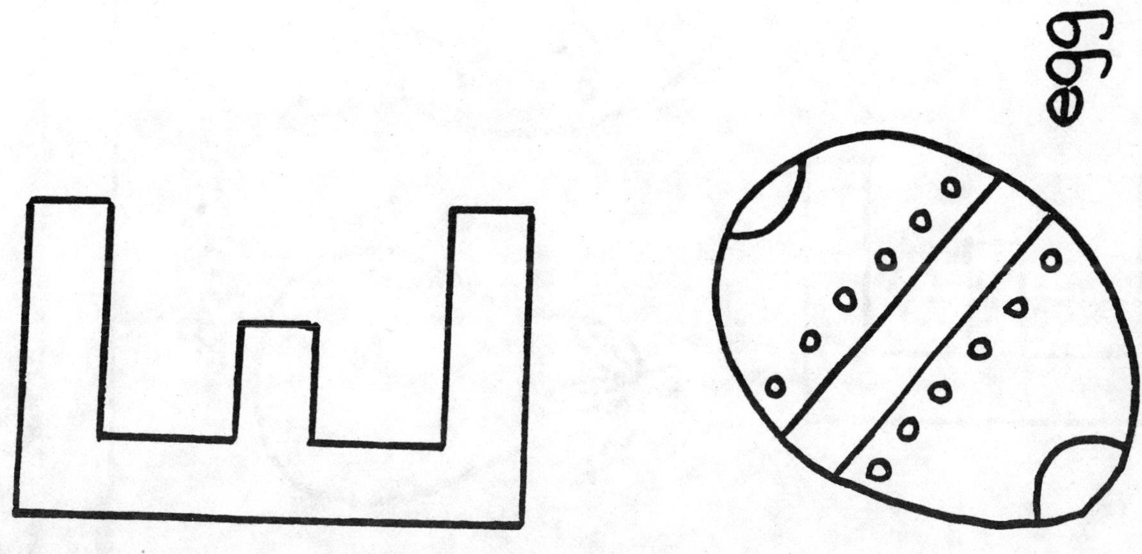
E
egg

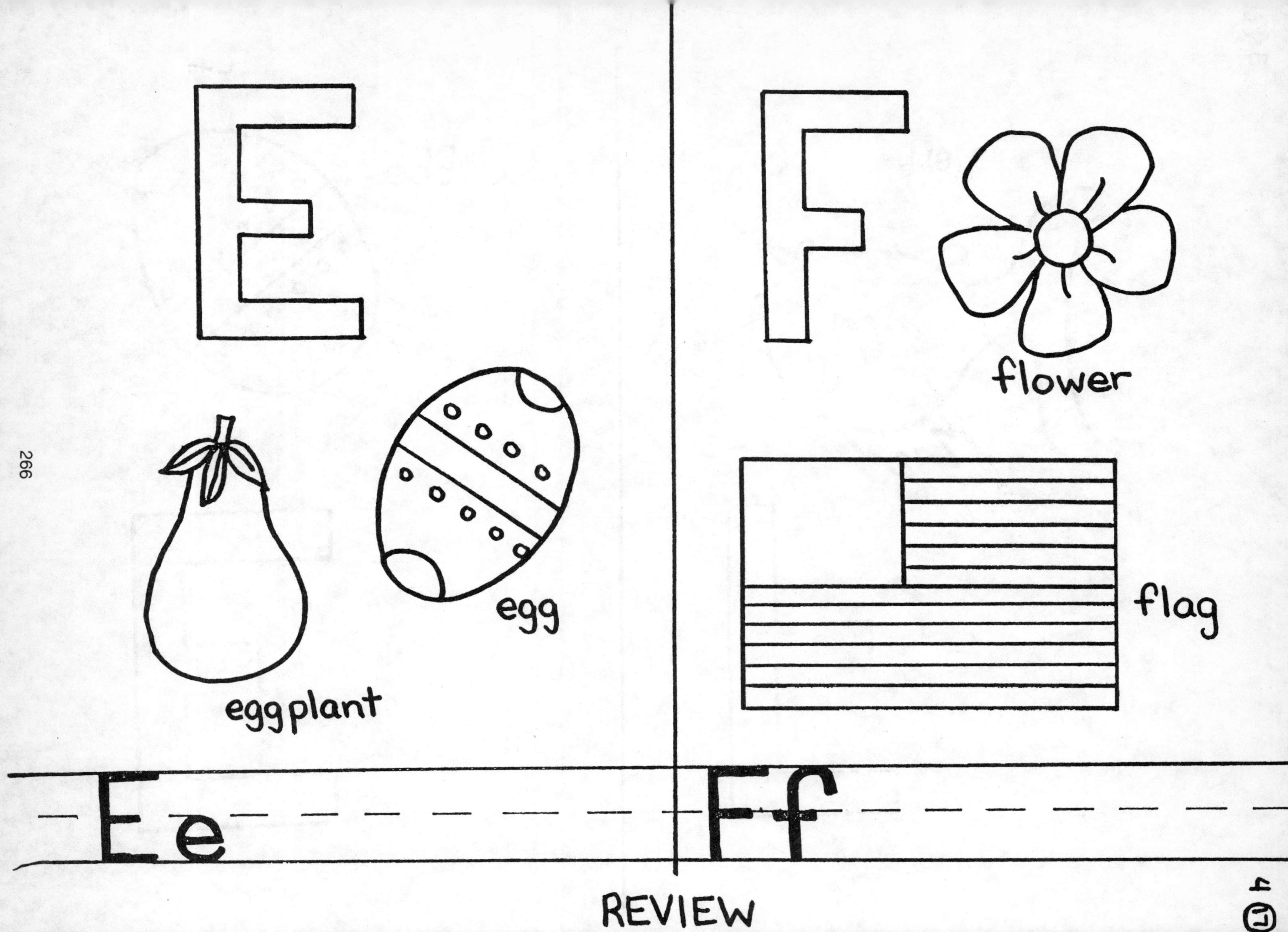
E
F
flower
eggplant
egg
flag
Ee
Ff
REVIEW
4 (17)

FALL FESTIVALS

Halloween

Thanksgiving

Age 3: Color
4: paint

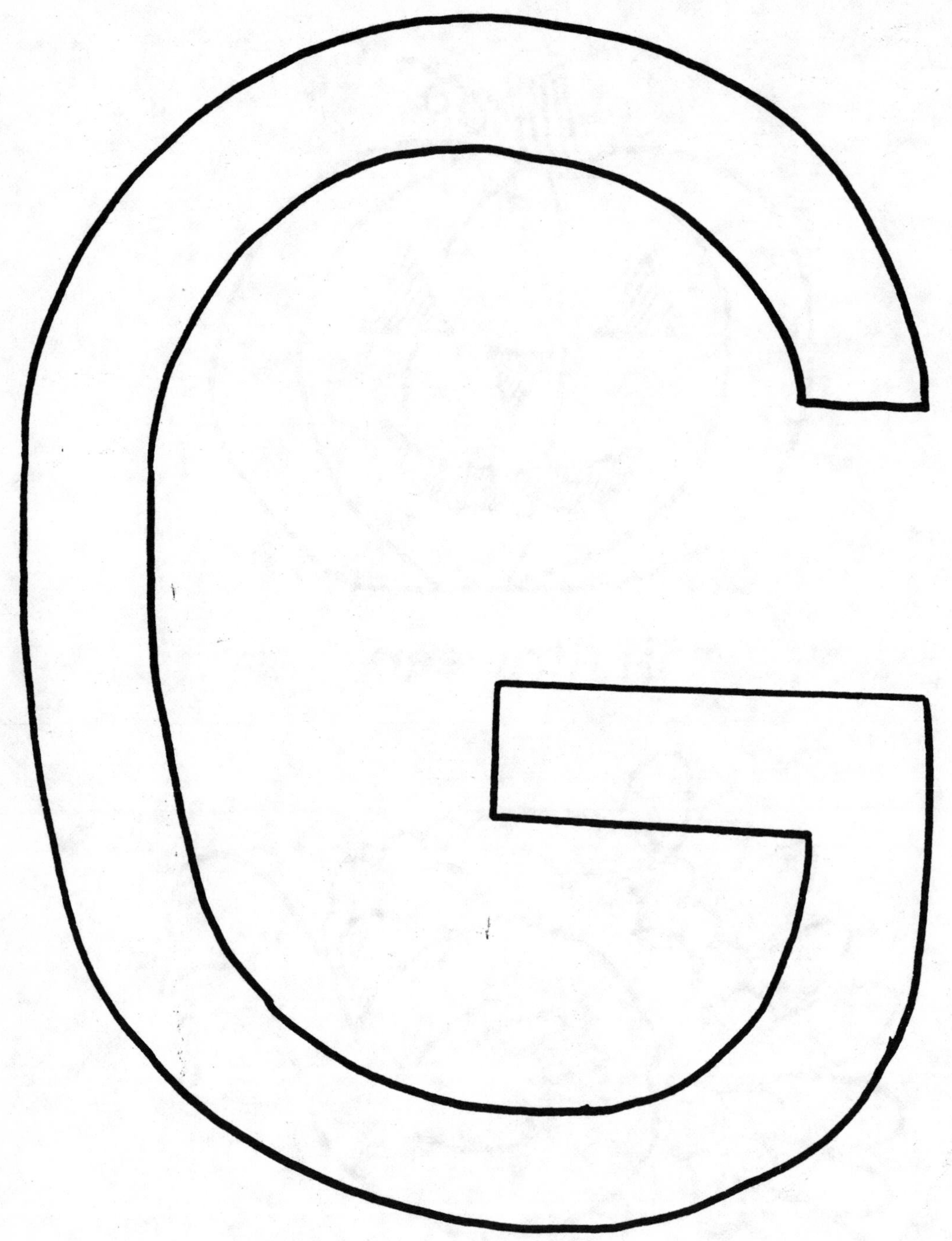

G g
glass
goat

Review: Family Pets

Cat

Dog

Fish

Bird

Review: Seasons

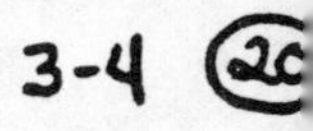

Winter

Spring

Summer

Fall

3 (21)

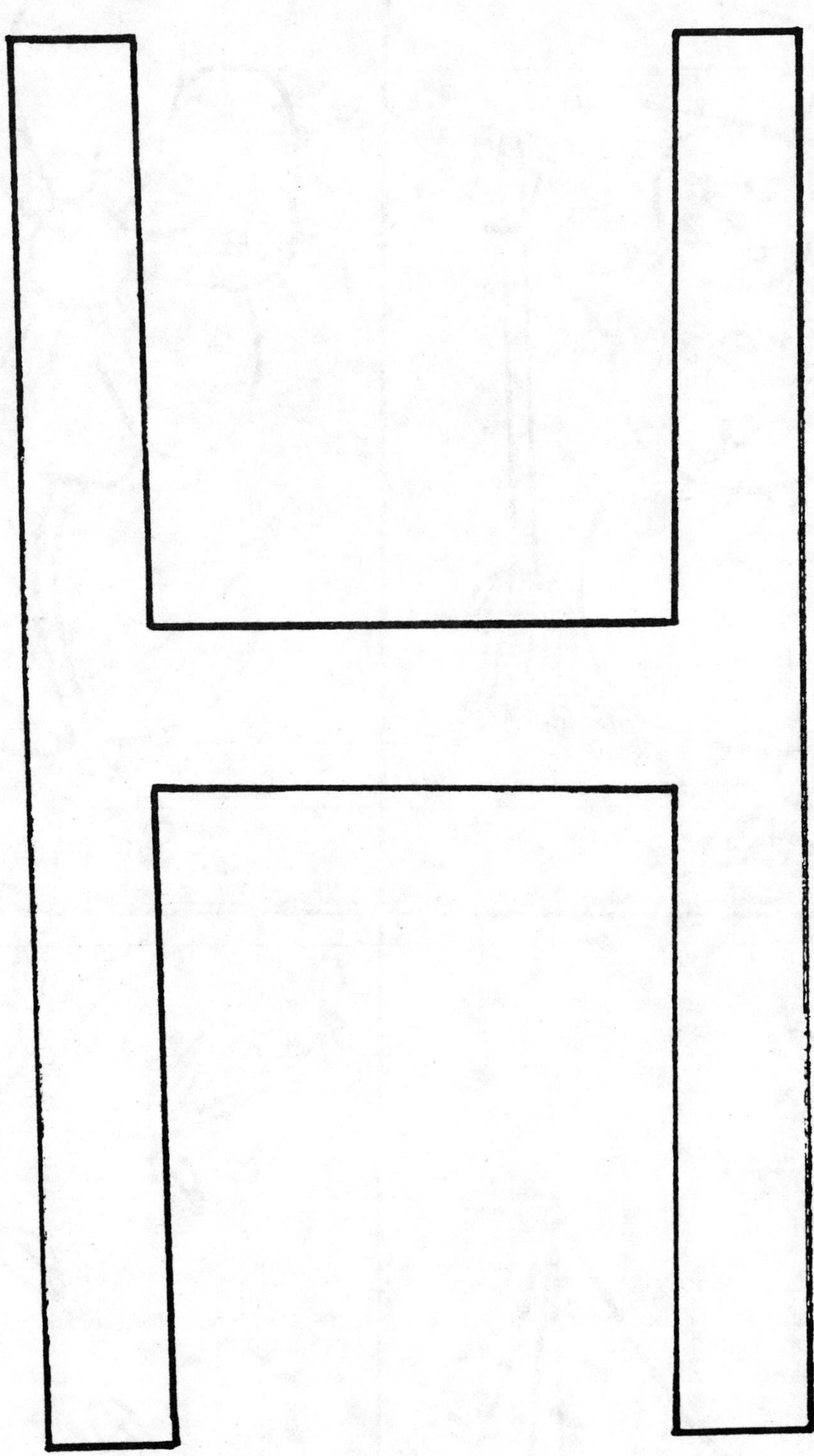

hat
heart

FEBRUARY UNITS:

I. Alphabet

A. Introduction of letters I-L

B. Uppercase is stressed for younger ages, uppercase and lowercase for age 4 group.

C. Word recognition

1. Continue working on child's own name.
2. Re-emphasize classroom words.

D. Continuation of the unit begun last month. A review of all the letters covered during both months appears at the end of this month.

II. Review

A. Shapes

B. Colors

C. Numbers

D. Alphabet A-L

III. Valentine's Day

A. The true children's holiday for this month will be celebrated for an entire week prior to the day itself.

B. Love and friendship for everyone should be stressed.

C. Several projects are included in the basic unit for the month, but please expand if your children would like to do more.

D. If Valentine's Day falls on a school day, see Appendix III for holiday sheet and explanation of why we celebrate.

IV. President's Day

A. The third Monday of February is President's Day.

B. It celebrates both Lincoln's and Washington's birthdays.

C. A simple explanation of our government and the election process is in order. Elect the helper of the day.

D. The myths about both men are fun to hear, and the children should be exposed to them.

1. Washington and the cherry tree.
2. Lincoln and the long walk to return the library book.

V. FOUR YEAR OLDS ONLY

A. Continue alphabet book.

B. Keep the book in the classroom to be taken home at the end of the unit.

PROBLEM/CONCEPT	SUGGESTED ACTIVITIES
SHAPES REVIEW:	Point out the shapes of objects in the classroom. Cut the shapes out of construction paper and play a match-up game.
COLOR REVIEW:	Make sure the children are coloring the pictures presented in their true colors. Purple does not an apple make.
ALPHABET: Introduce new letters of the alphabet.	Refer to January syllabus. Have the children make the letters like a marching band.
VALENTINE'S DAY:	Make a Valentine mail box for the room, or have the children bring in shoe boxes to decorate and fill individually. See Appendix III for explanation of this holiday.
PRESIDENT'S DAY:	See Appendix III for explanation of this holiday. Role playing: Have the children pretend to be Lincoln splitting rails for fences in Illinois. Be sure to mention that he was born in Kentucky, lived awhile in Indiana and finally settled in Illinois. Tell some of the myths that surround Washington's history. 1. Cherry tree. 2. Throwing the coin across the Delaware River. Mention the Revolution and the harsh winter suffered at Valley Forge before Washington became the first President. Show the pictures of Lincoln and Washington on the $5.00 and $1.00 American currency.

February

MONTH: FEBRUARY

1 Calendar Shape review: square Age 4: H page for booklet	2 Letter review: G, H. Shape review: circle	3 Begin letter I Shape review: triangle	4 Shape review rectangle Age 4: I page for booklet	5 Begin decorating for Valentine's Day Color valentine
6 Begin: letter J Shape review (bird)	7 Story of LINCOLN (cabin) Valentine picture.	8 Review: I, J Make valentine Age 4: J page for booklet	9 Begin: letter K Valentine birds and mouse.	10 Review no.'s 1, 2, 3 Age 4: letter K for booklet
11 Begin: letter L Review: no's 4, 5, 6	12 GEO. WASHINGTON myths Review: no.'s 7, 8, 9	13 Review: letters K, L Age 4: L page for booklet	14 Alphabet review: A, B, C	15 Alphabet review: D, E, F
16 Alphabet review: G, H, I	17 Alphabet review: J, K, L	18 Alphabet fun pages	19 Valentine's Day – see Appendix III	20 Presidents' Day – see Appendix III
			Craft items: construction paper: RED GREY PINK YELLOW	BLUE GREEN PURPLE

3-4①

FEBRUARY

SUN.	MON.	TUES.	WED.	THURS.	FRI.	SAT.

REVIEW: SHAPES - SQUARE

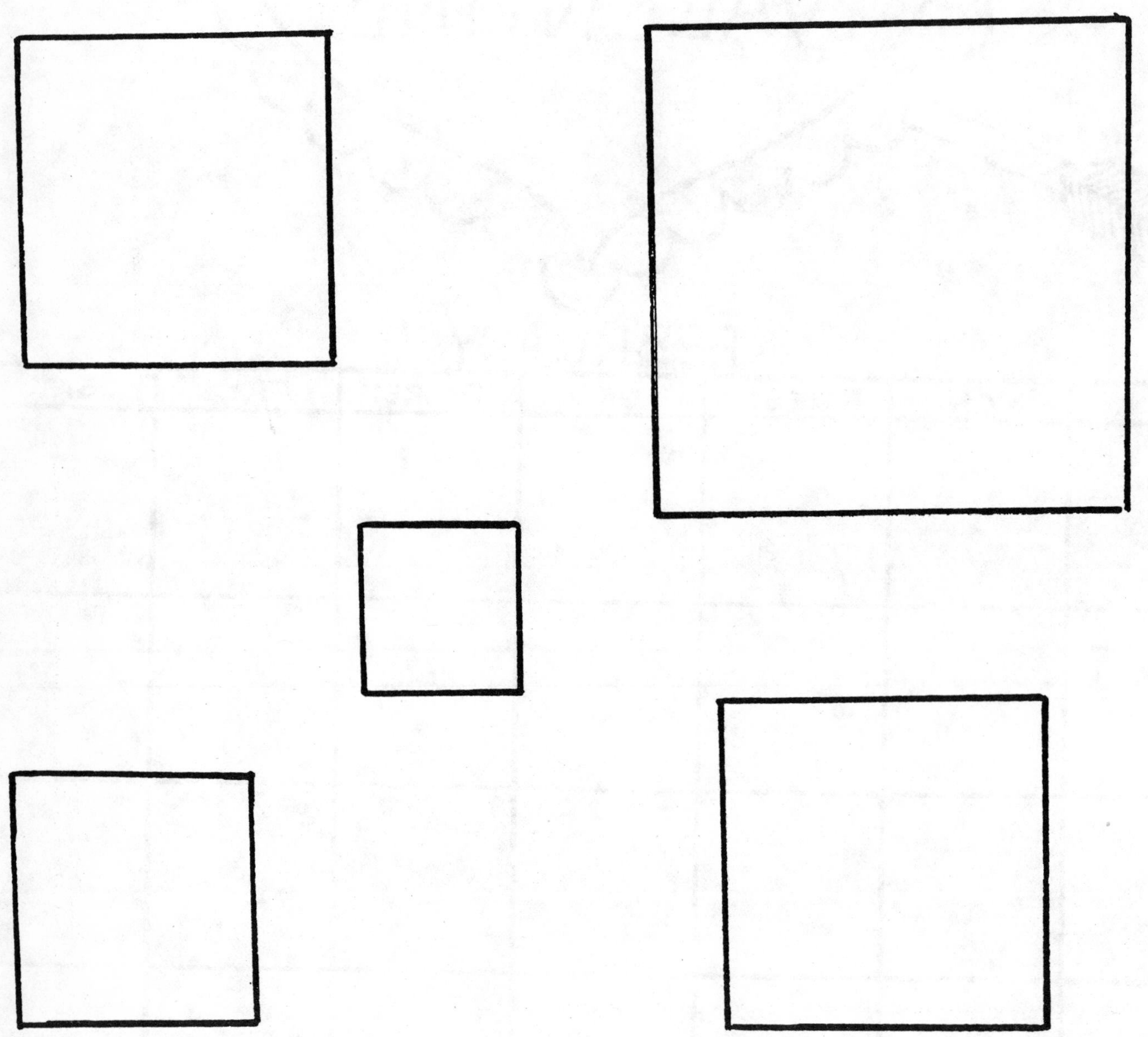

Color each square a different color.

REVIEW: SHAPES - SQUARE

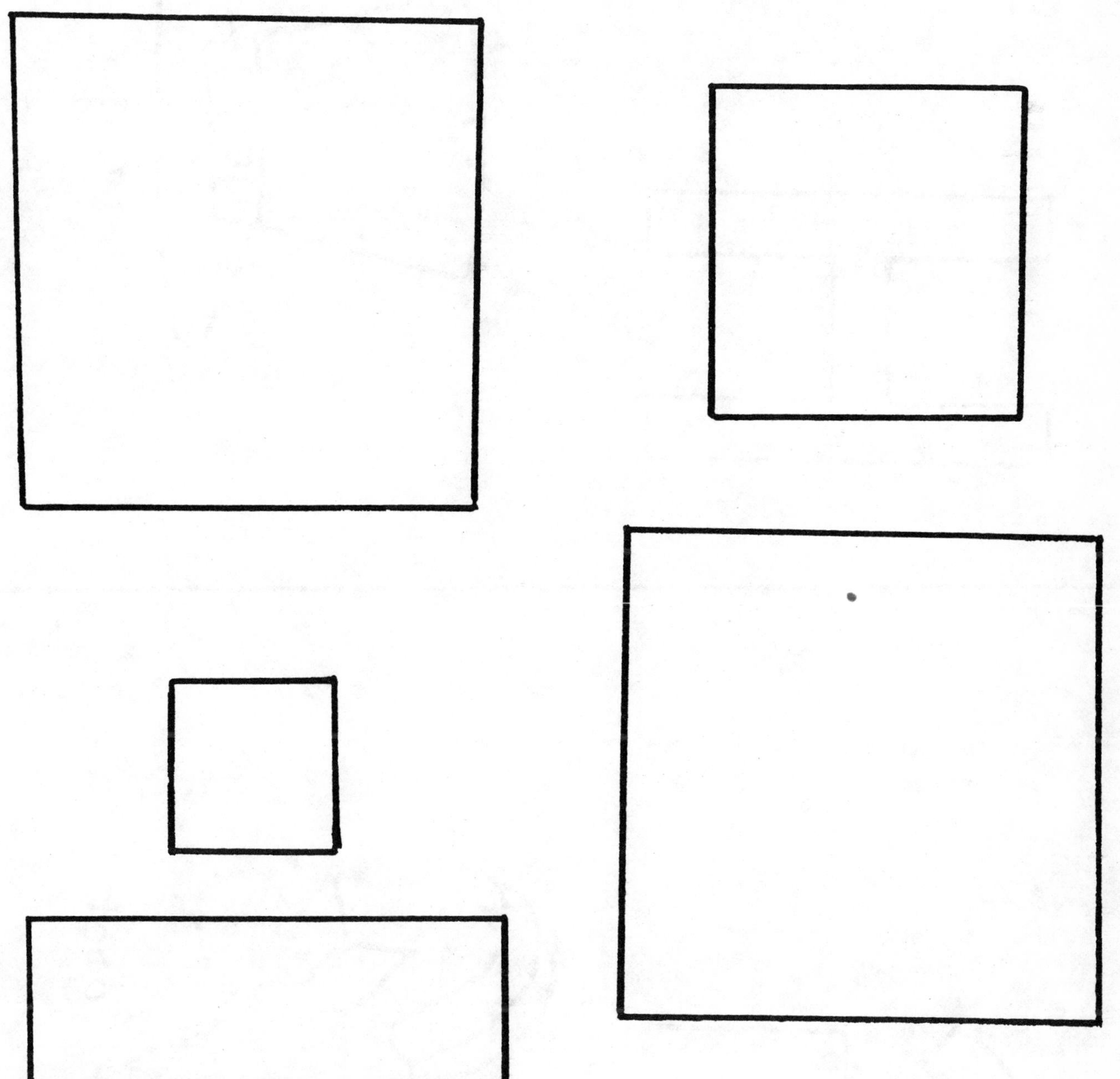

1. Mark an "X" on the shape that is not a square.
2. Paste pre-cut matching squares on these shapes.

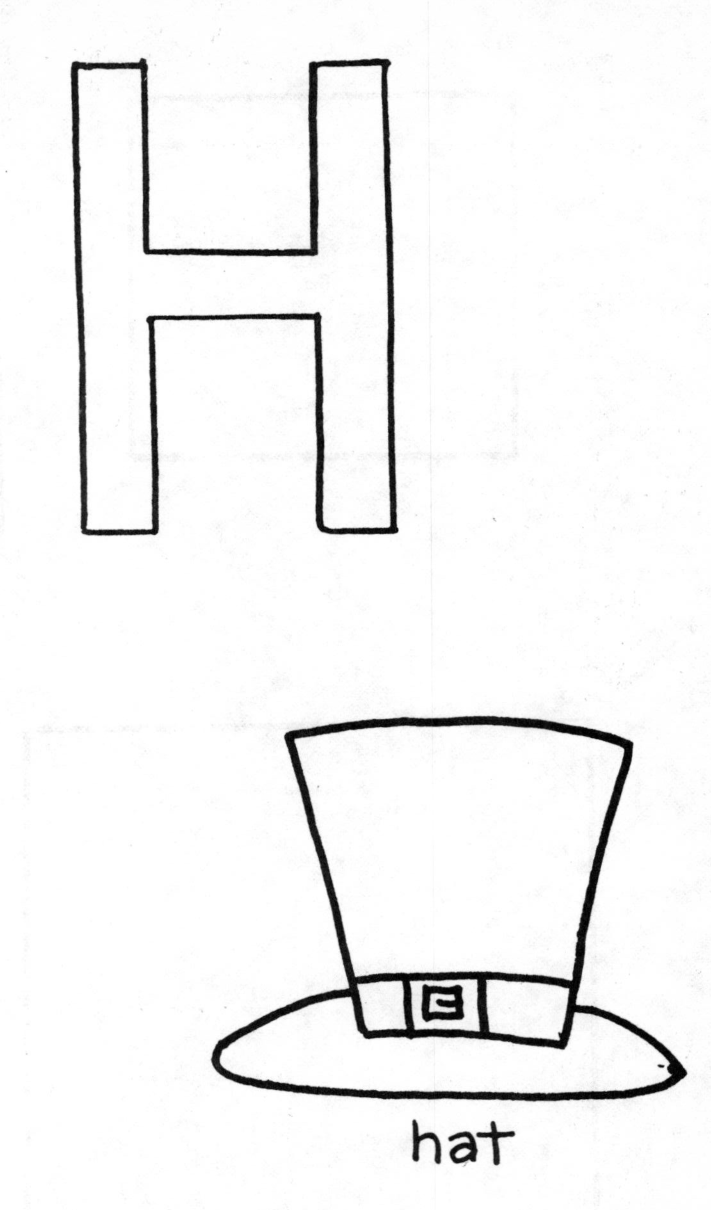

REVIEW

3 ②

G
glass
grass
H
hand
heart
house
Gg
Hh

REVIEW : SHAPES - CIRCLE

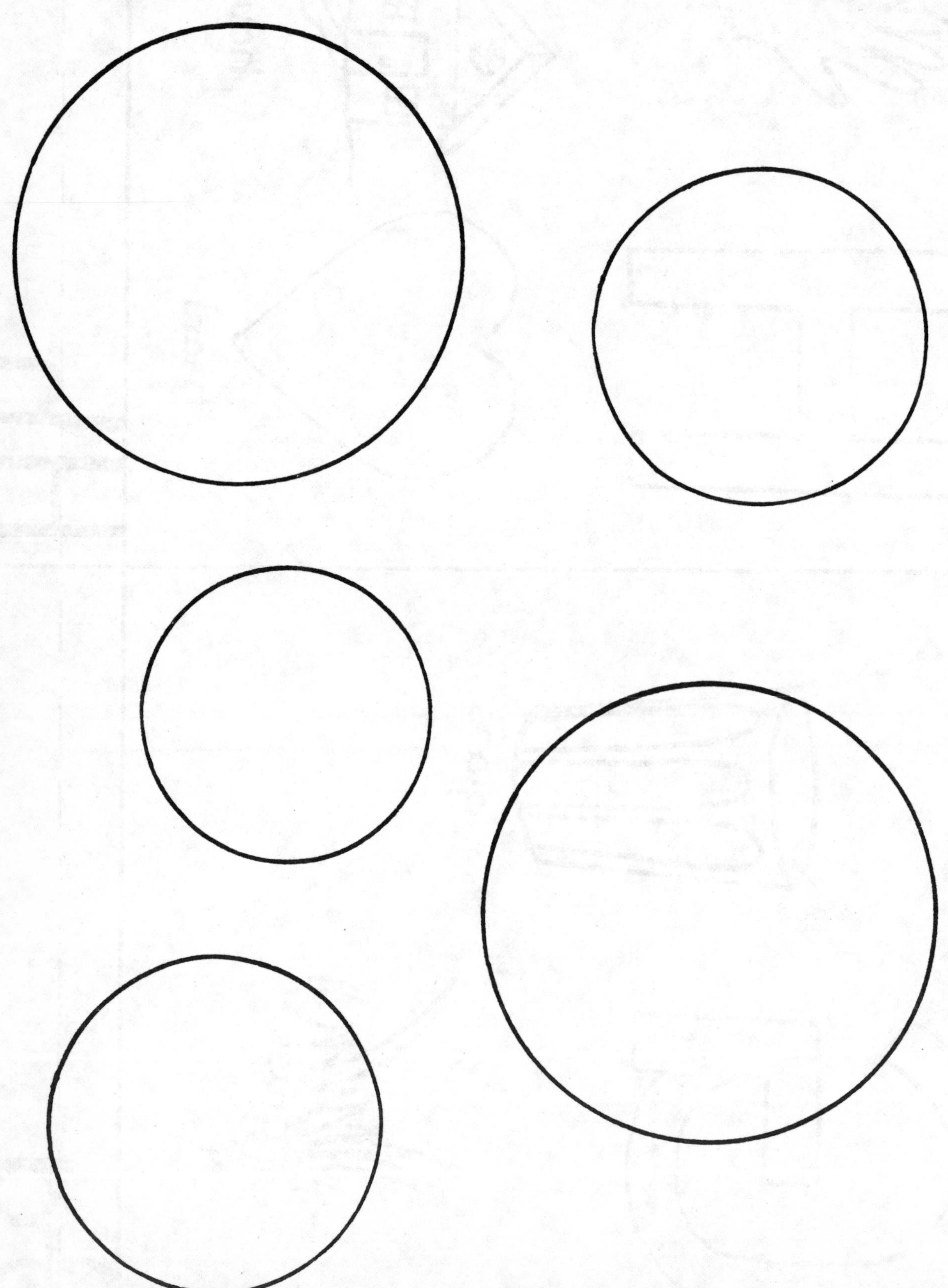

REVIEW: SHAPES – CIRCLE

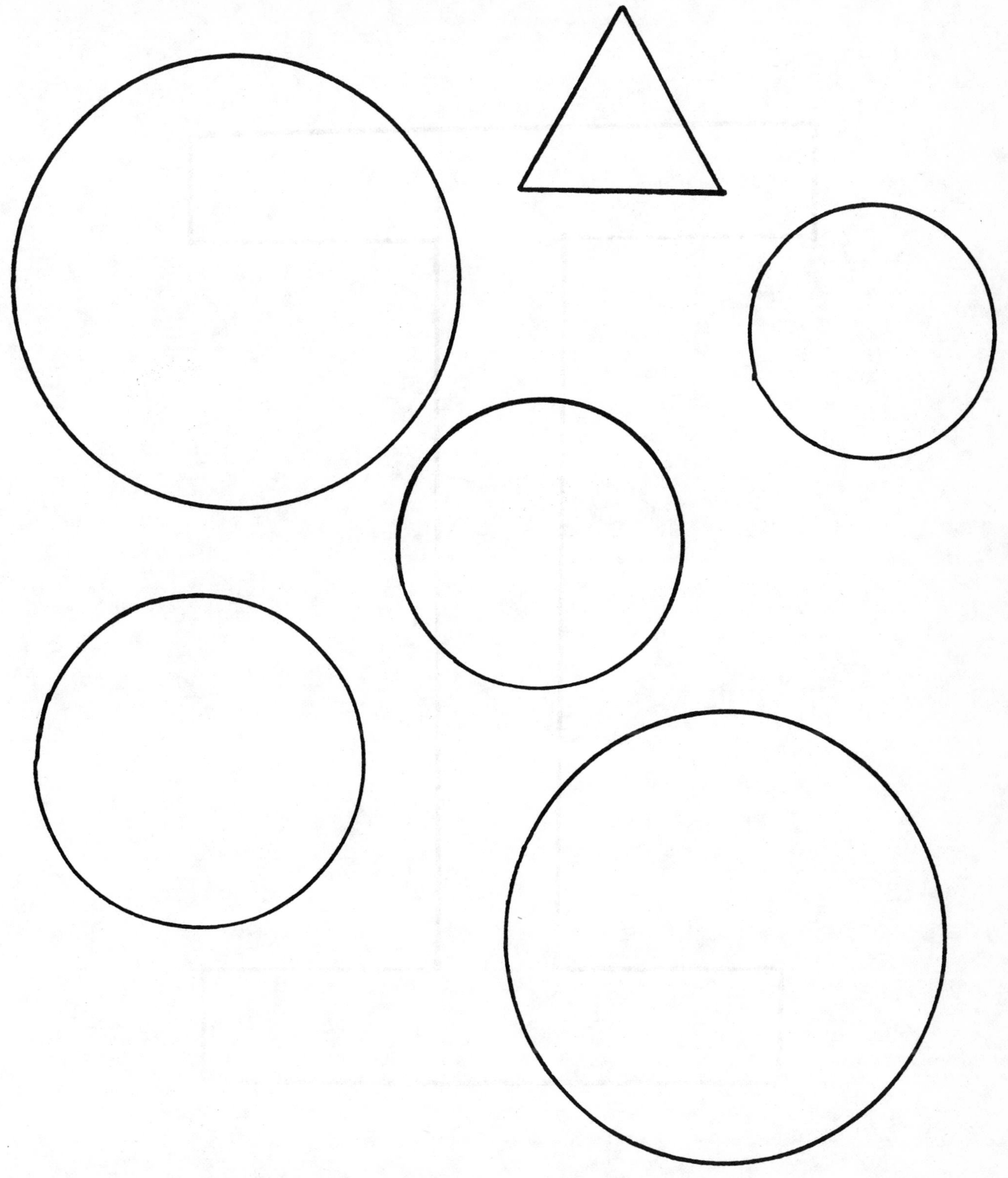

1. Mark an "X" on the shape that is not a circle
2. Paste pre-cut circles to matching shapes.

3 ③

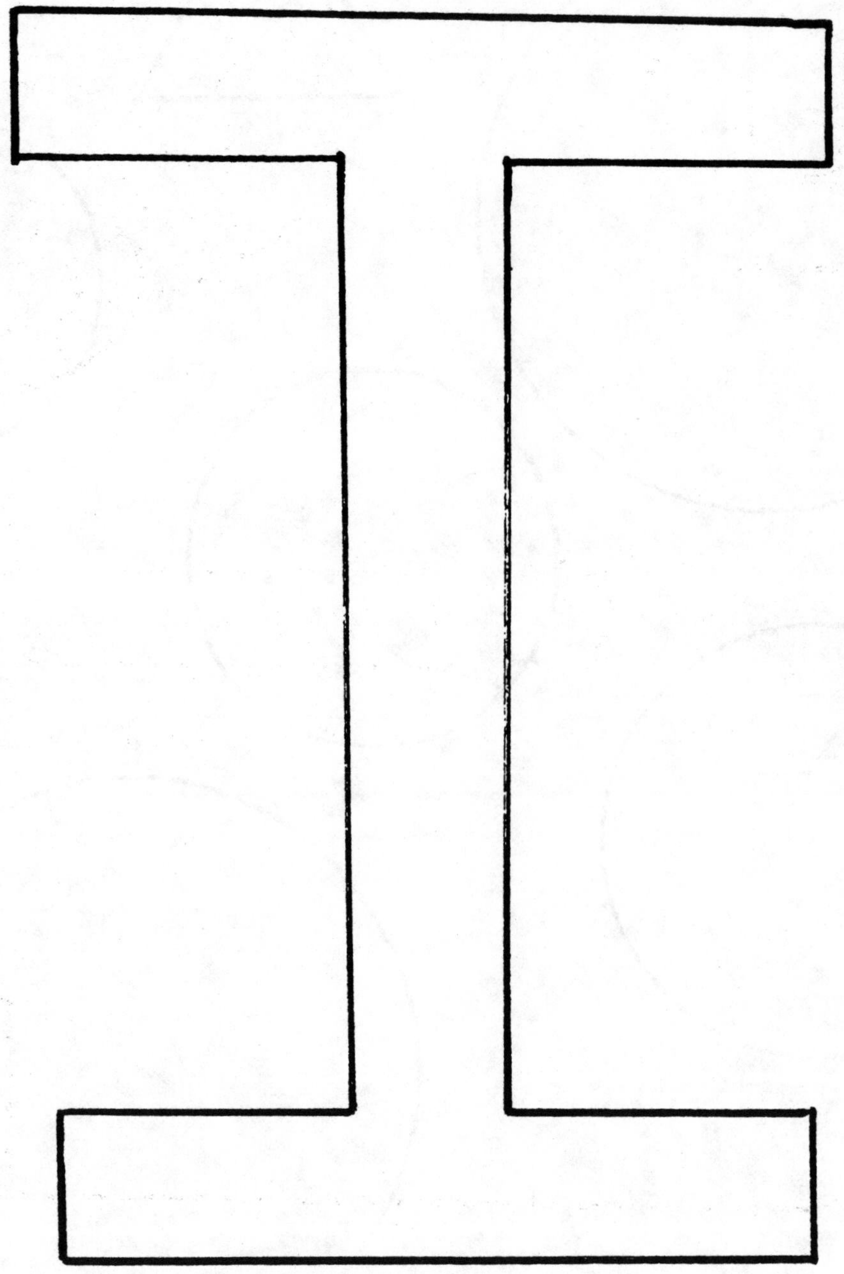

icicles
igloo

REVIEW: SHAPES - TRIANGLE

REVIEW: SHAPES – TRIANGLE

1. Mark an "X" on the shape that is not a triangle
2. Paste pre-cut triangles to matching shapes.

REVIEW: SHAPES – RECTANGLE

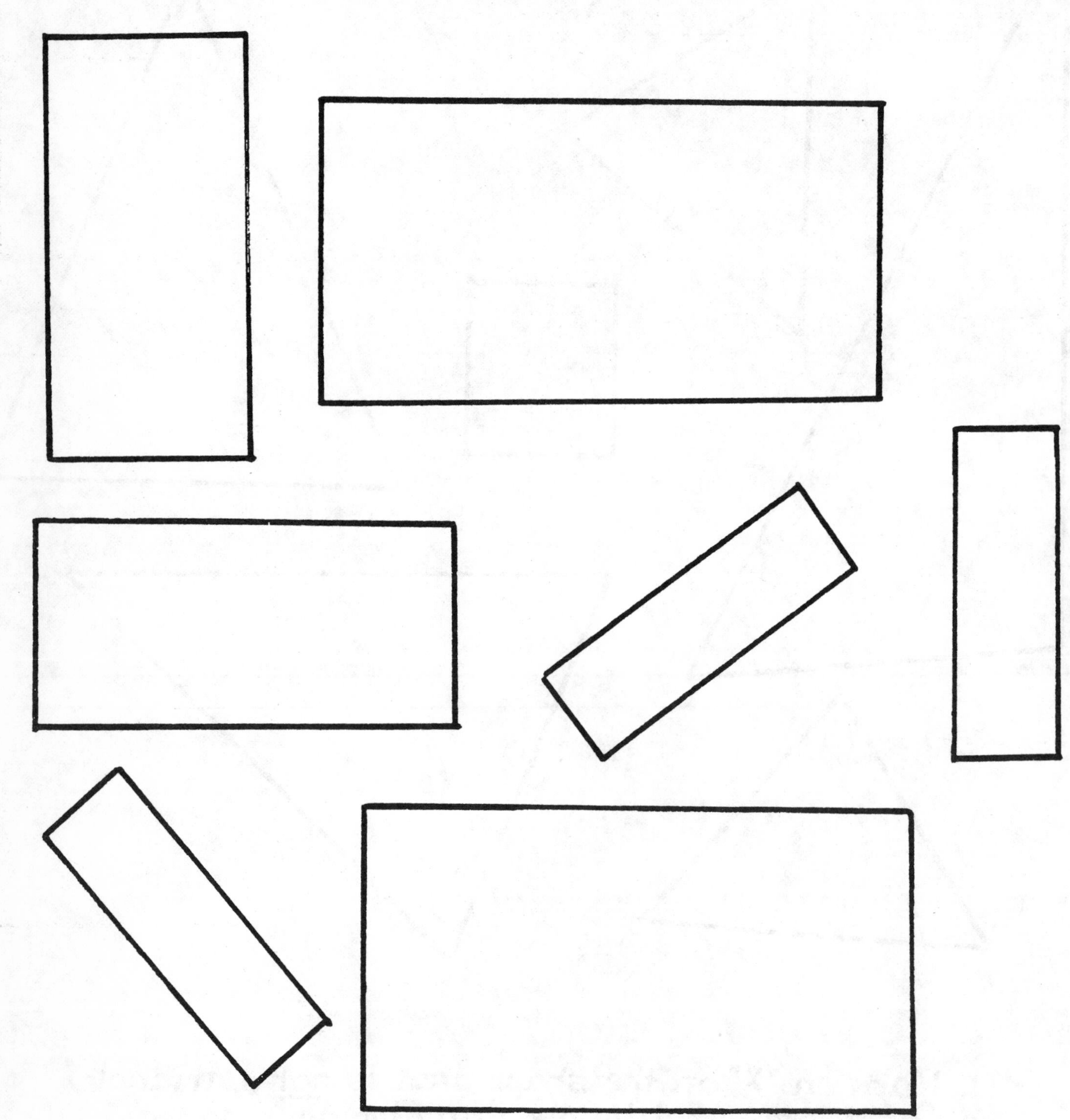

REVIEW: SHAPES - RECTANGLE

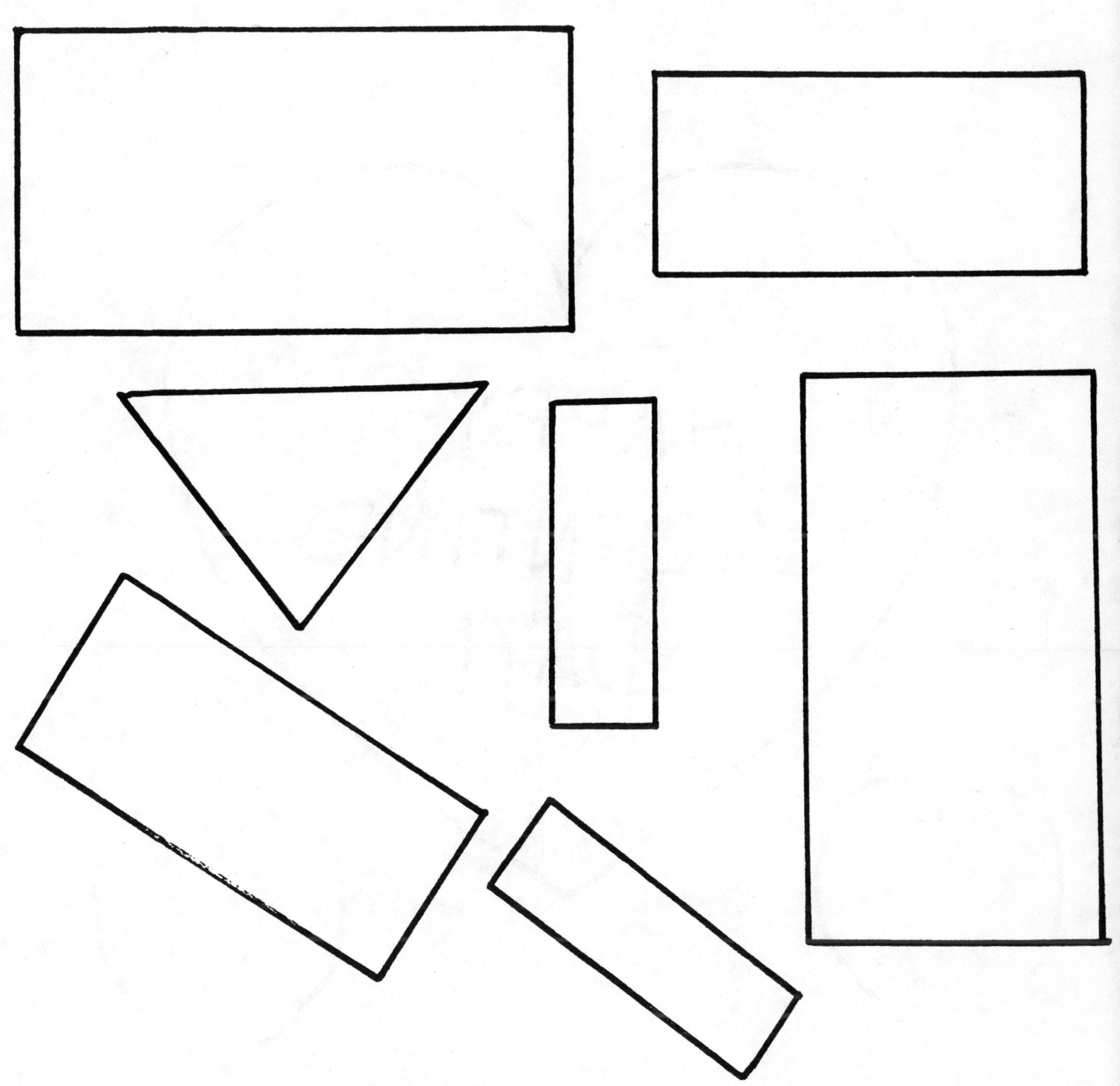

1. Mark an "X" on the shape that is <u>not</u> a rectangle.
2. Paste pre-cut rectangles to matching shapes.

3⑤

Happy
Valentine's
Day!

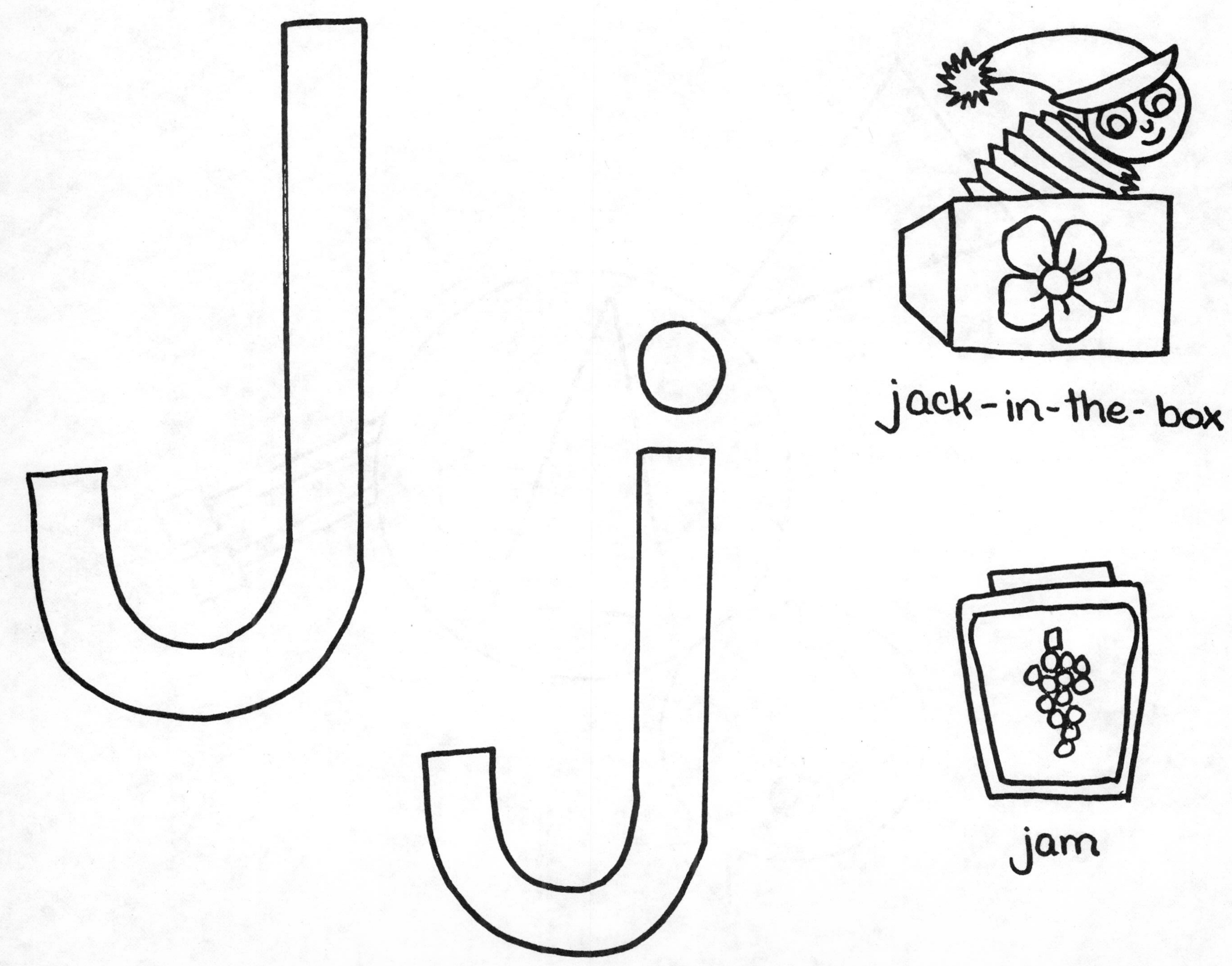
jack-in-the-box
jam

SHAPE REVIEW

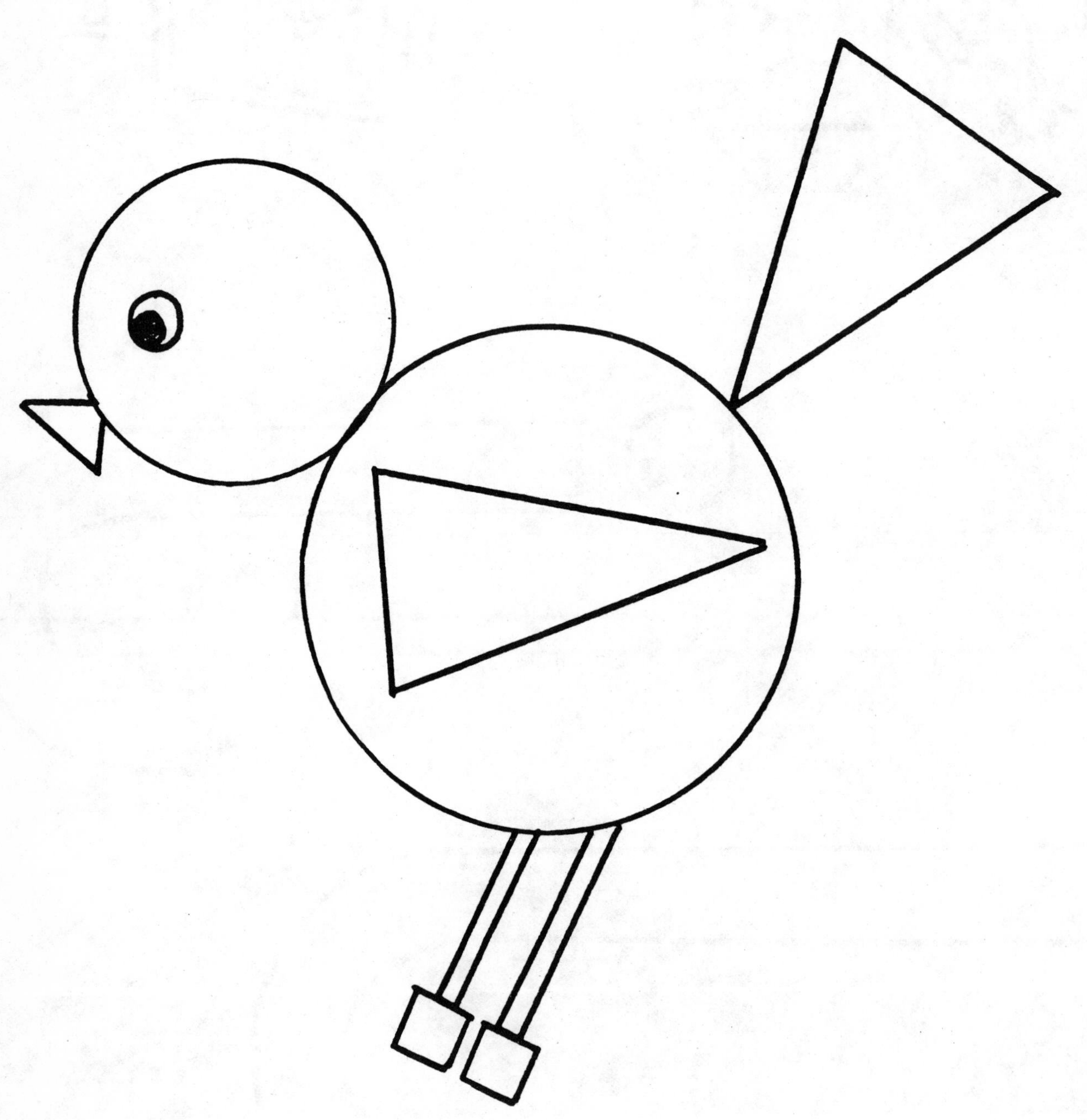

4 ⑥

SHAPE REVIEW

LINCOLN'S FIRST HOME - A LOG CABIN

Valentine
Mail Box

BE
MINE

Color valentine red

Age 3: cut out, paste arrow to heart
Age 4: cut out, paste arrow to heart
make snowflake doily, pasté valentine on top.

3 (8)

REVIEW

I
icicles
igloo
ice cream cone
J
jelly
jack-in-the-box
I i
J j
REVIEW . J

Color the Valentine Bird

3⑨

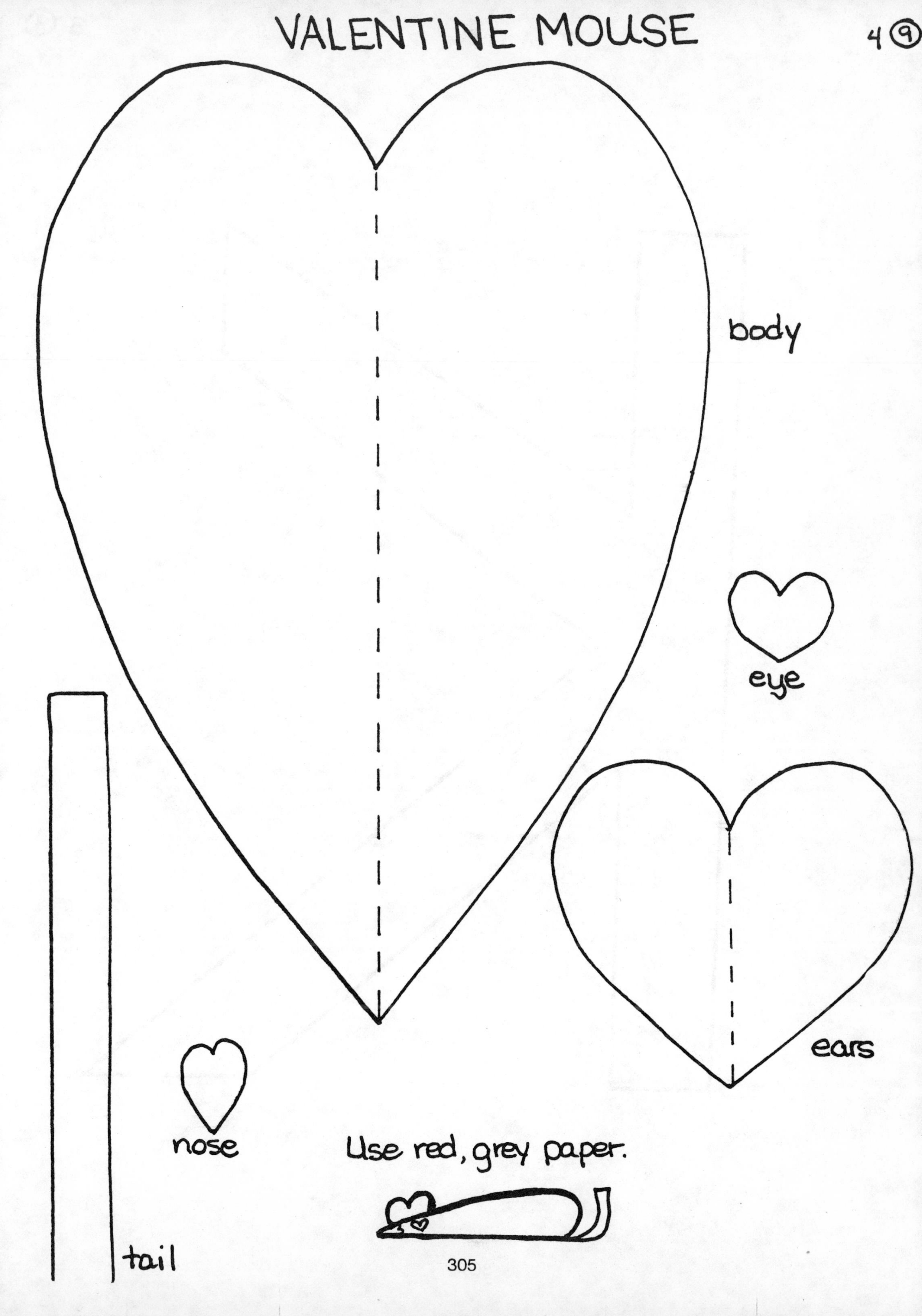
VALENTINE MOUSE
4 9
body
eye
ears
nose
Use red, grey paper.
tail

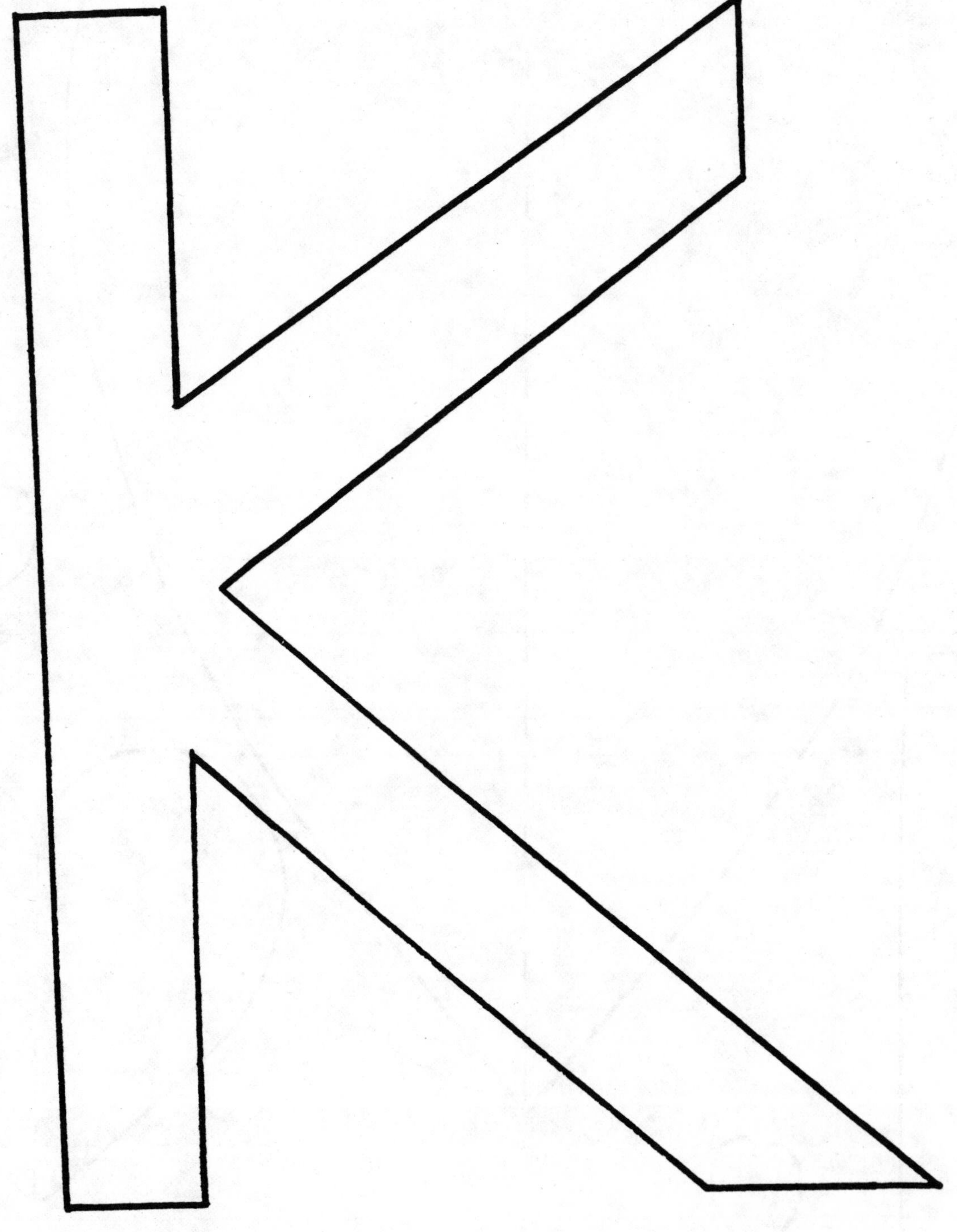

kite
kangaroo

Draw a line from the number to the correct group.

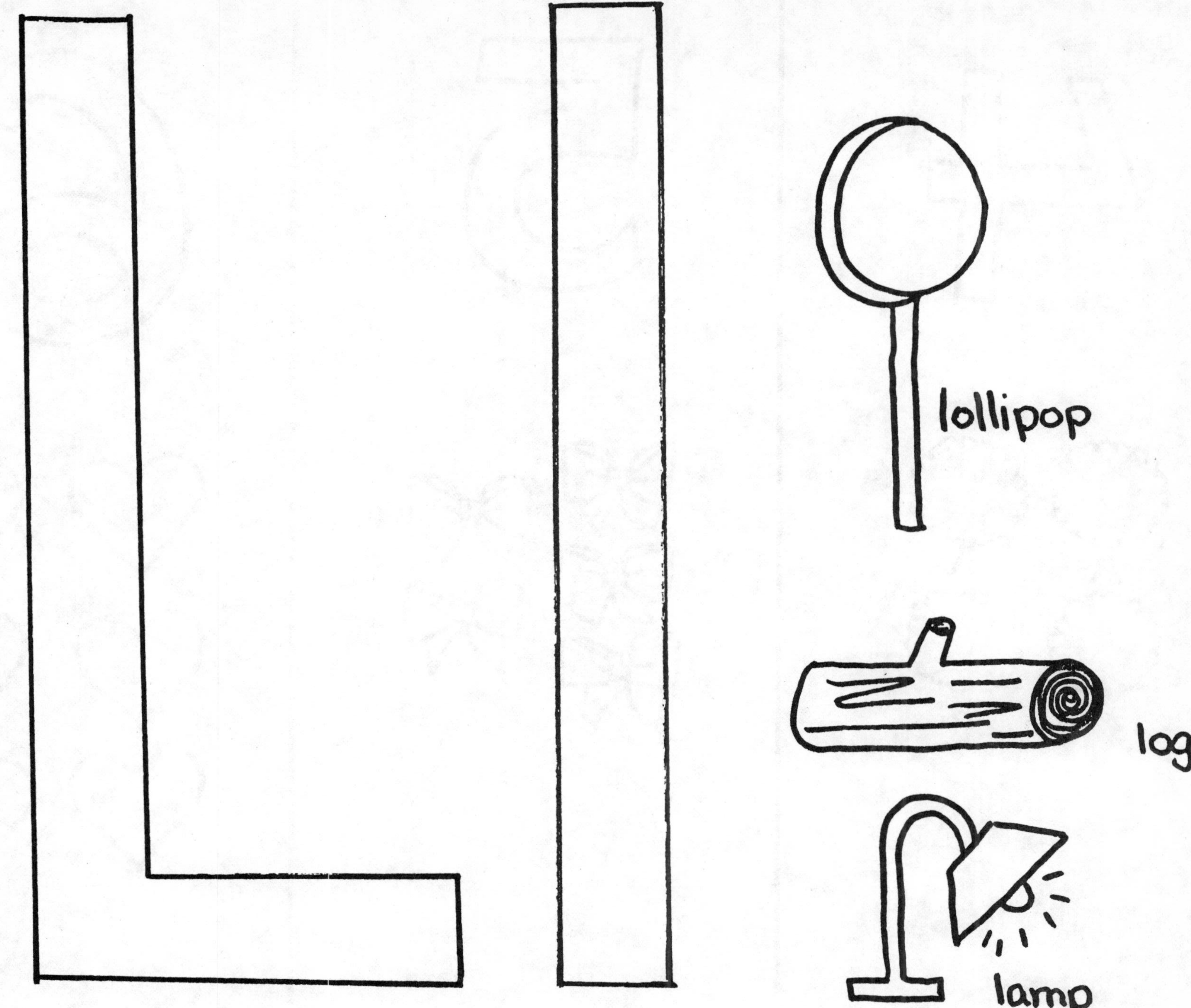
lollipop
log
lamp

3⑪

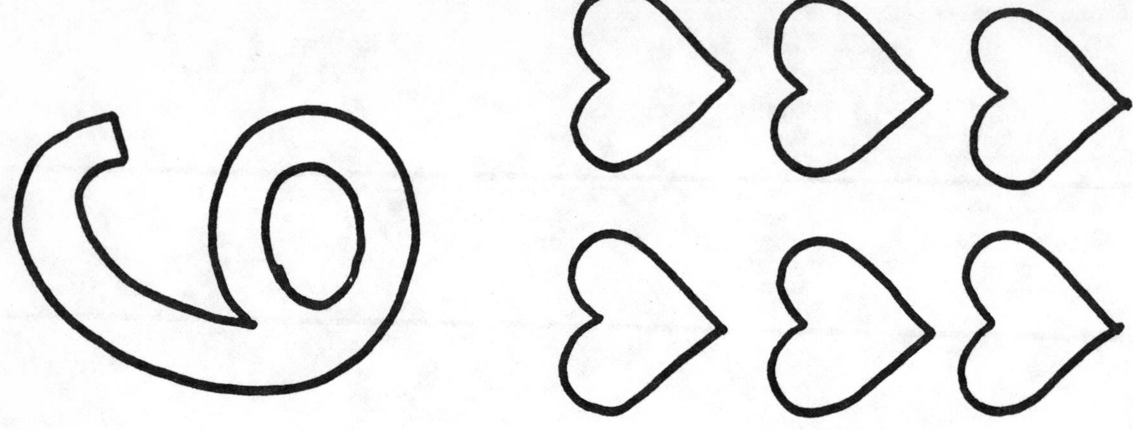

Draw a line from the number to the correct group.

5

6

4

Did George Washington really chop down his father's cherry tree?
3-4 12

9

8

7

Draw a line from the number to the correct group.

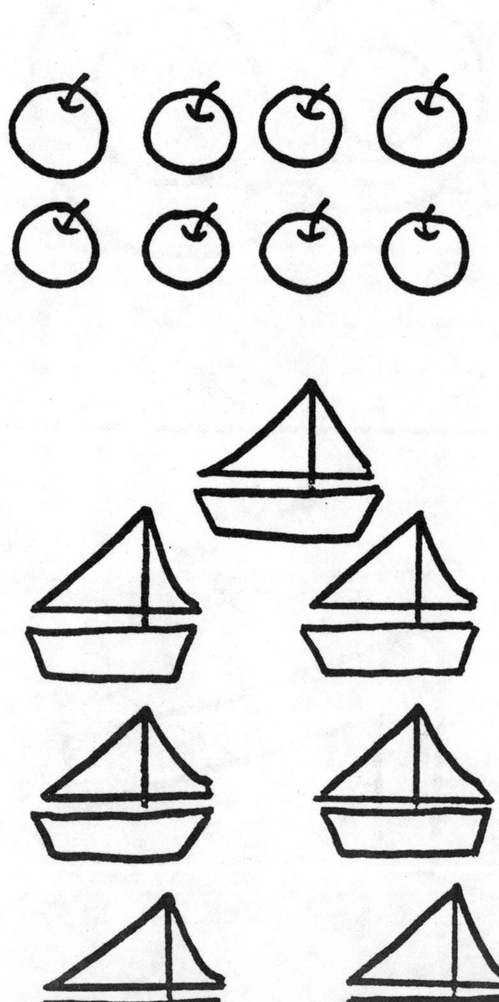

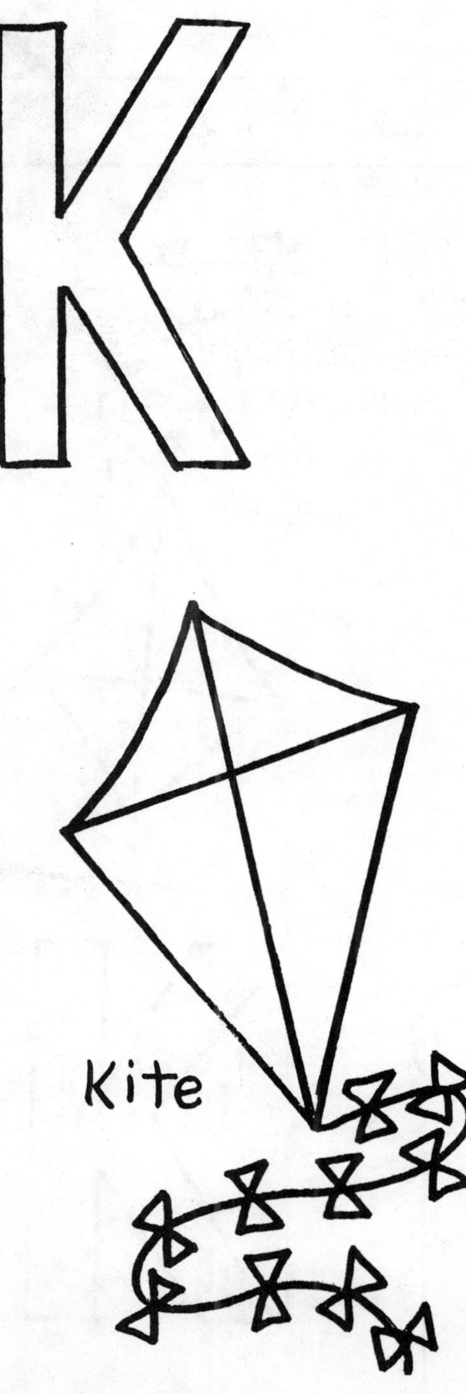

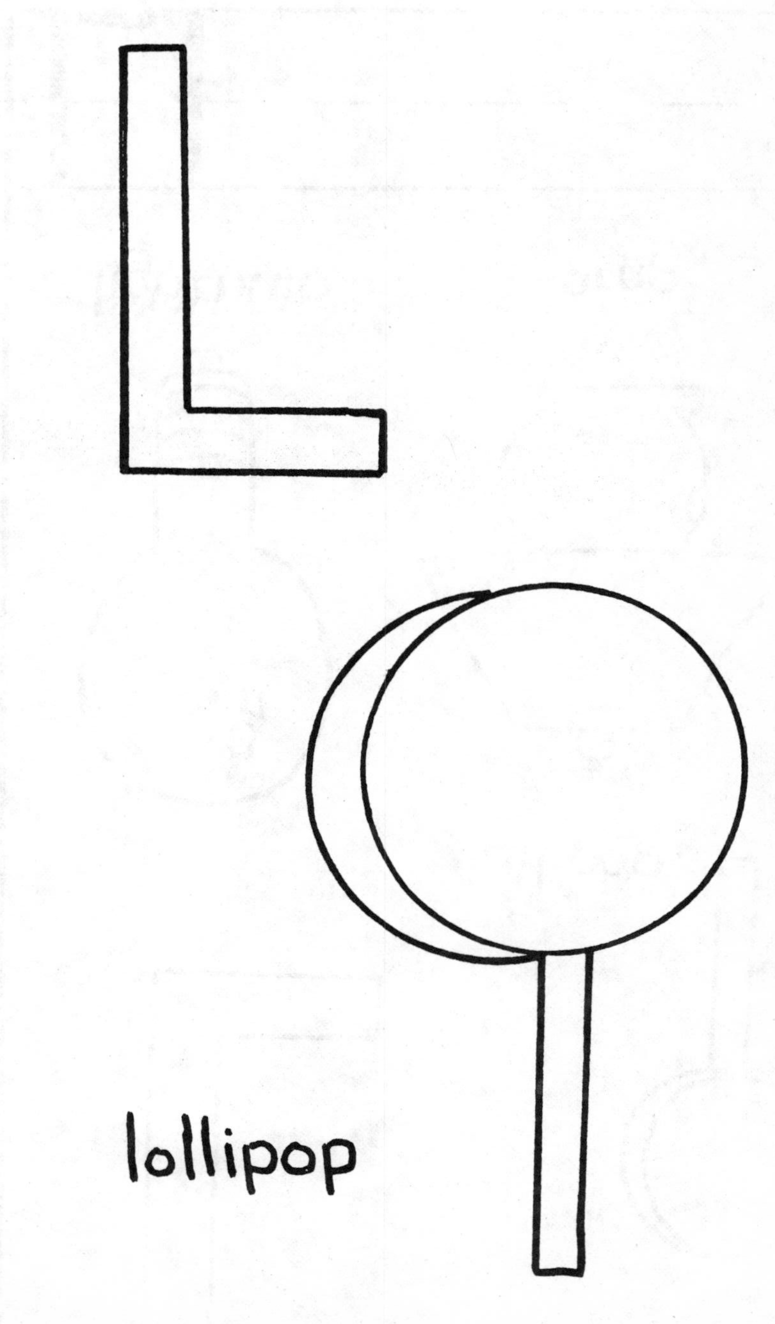

REVIEW

K
kettle
kite
kangaroo
L
lollipop
lightbulb
lamp
Kk
Ll
4 13

ALPHABET REVIEW

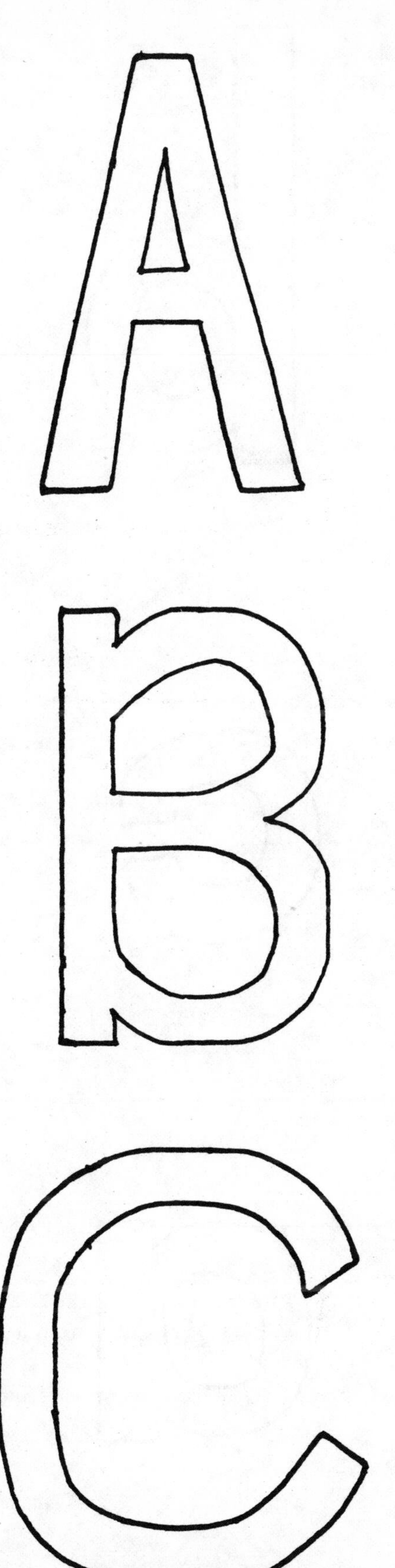

apple

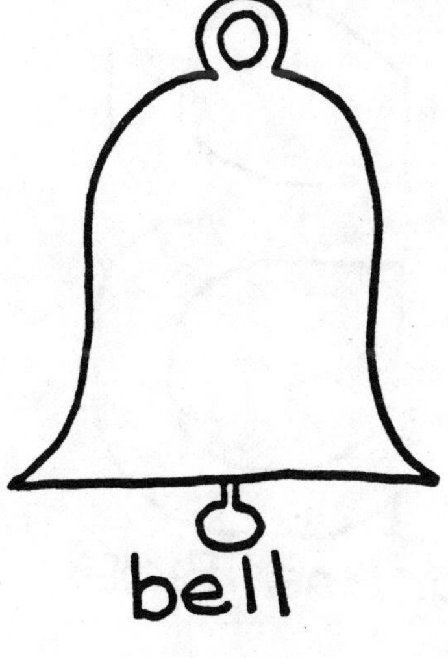

bell

cap

Match the CAPITAL LETTERS to the lower case letters.

ALPHABET REVIEW

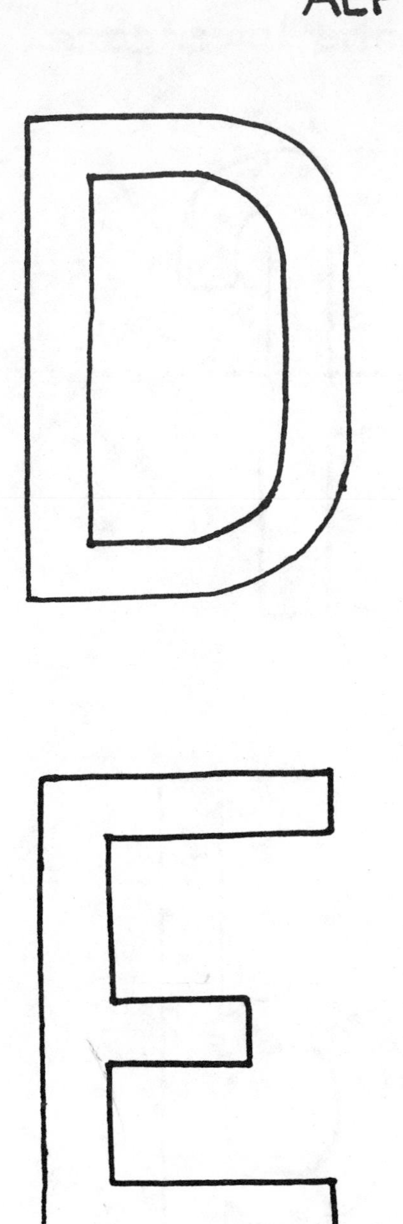

dog

egg

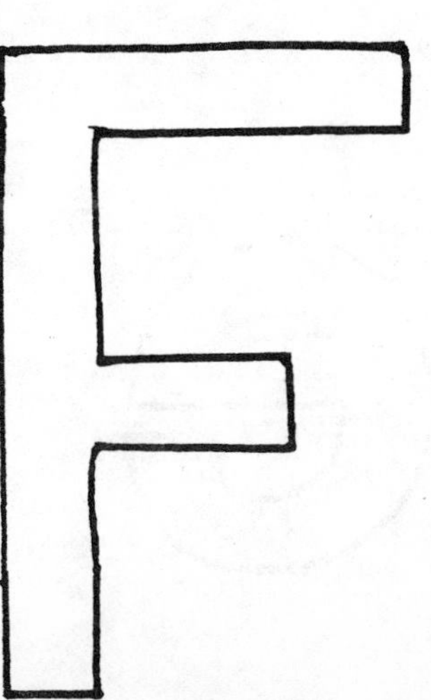

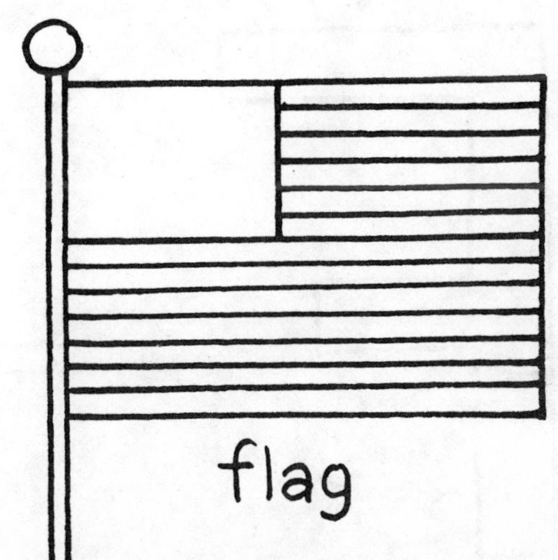

flag

ALPHABET REVIEW

Match the CAPITAL LETTERS to the lower case letters.

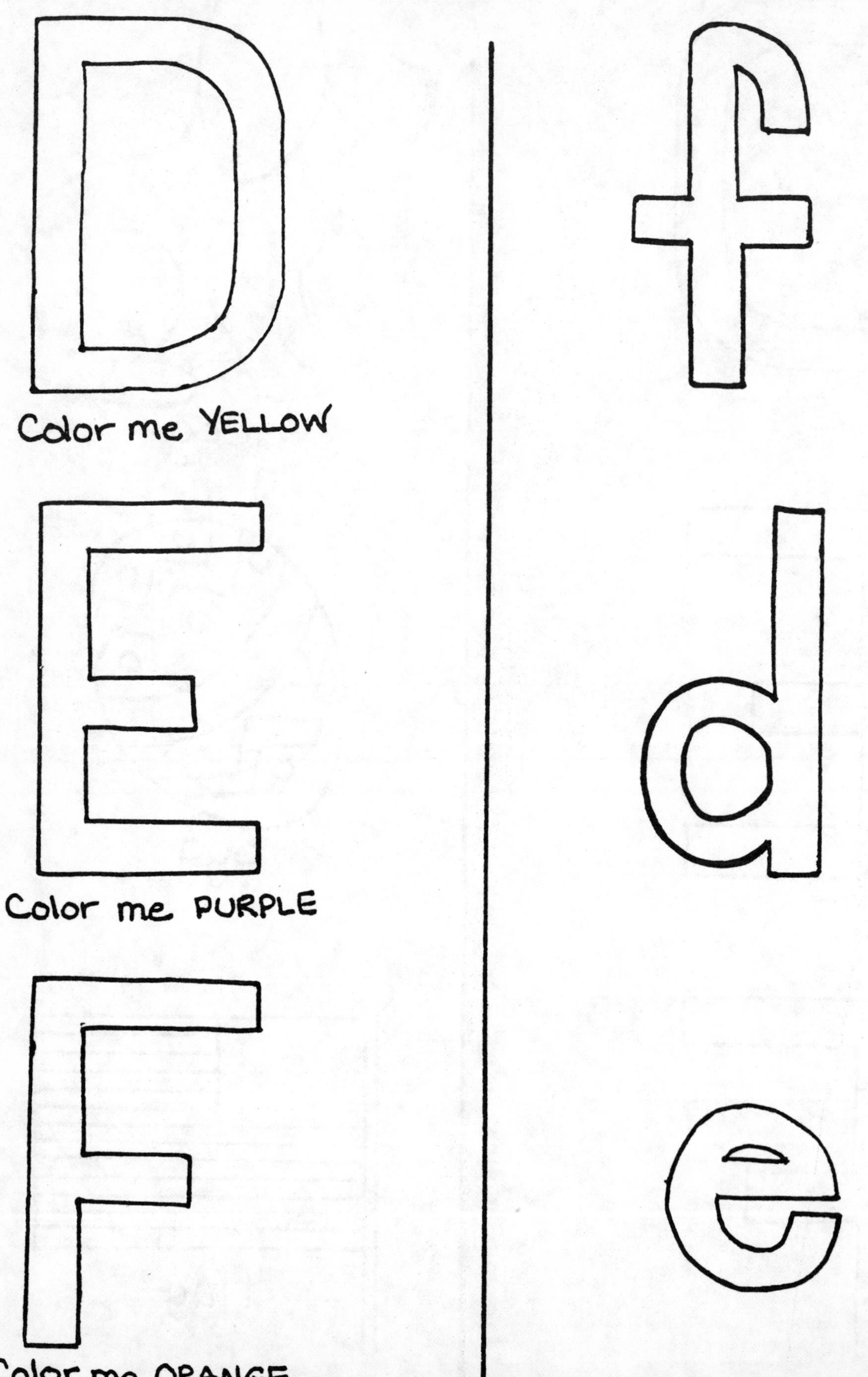

ALPHABET REVIEW

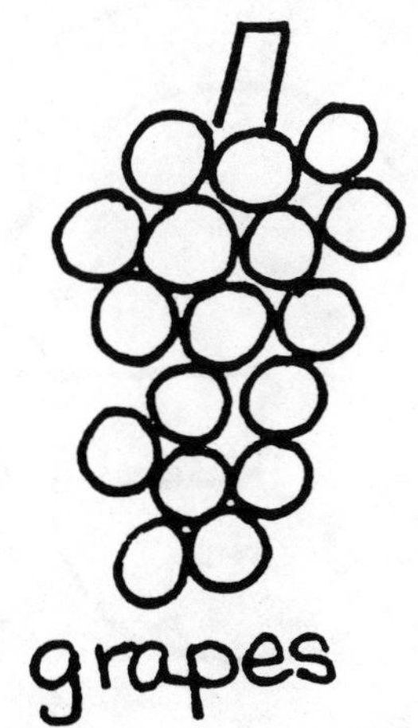

grapes

house

ice cream cone

ALPHABET REVIEW

Match the CAPITAL LETTERS to the lower case letters.

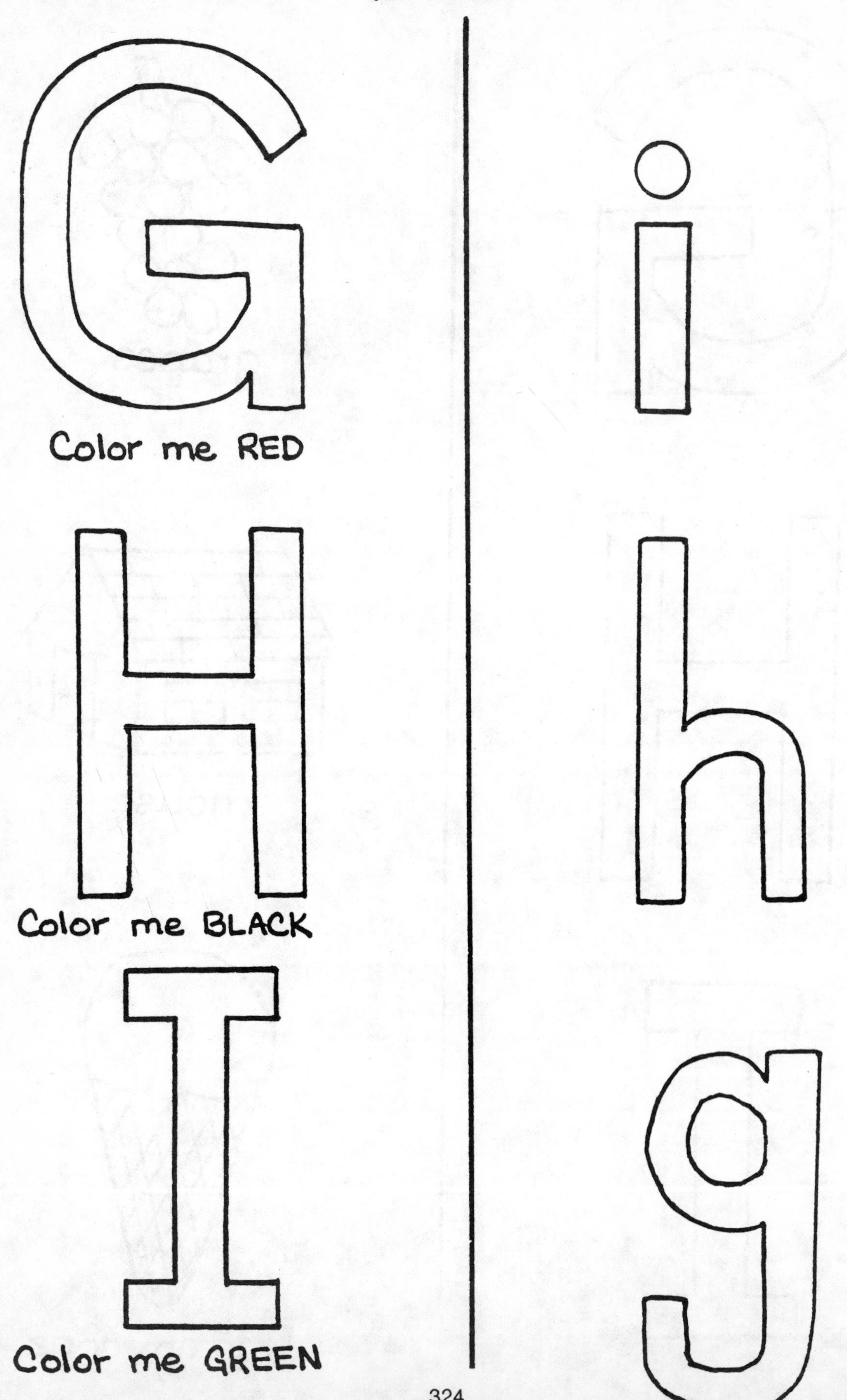

ALPHABET REVIEW

ALPHABET REVIEW

Match the CAPITAL LETTERS to the lower case letters.

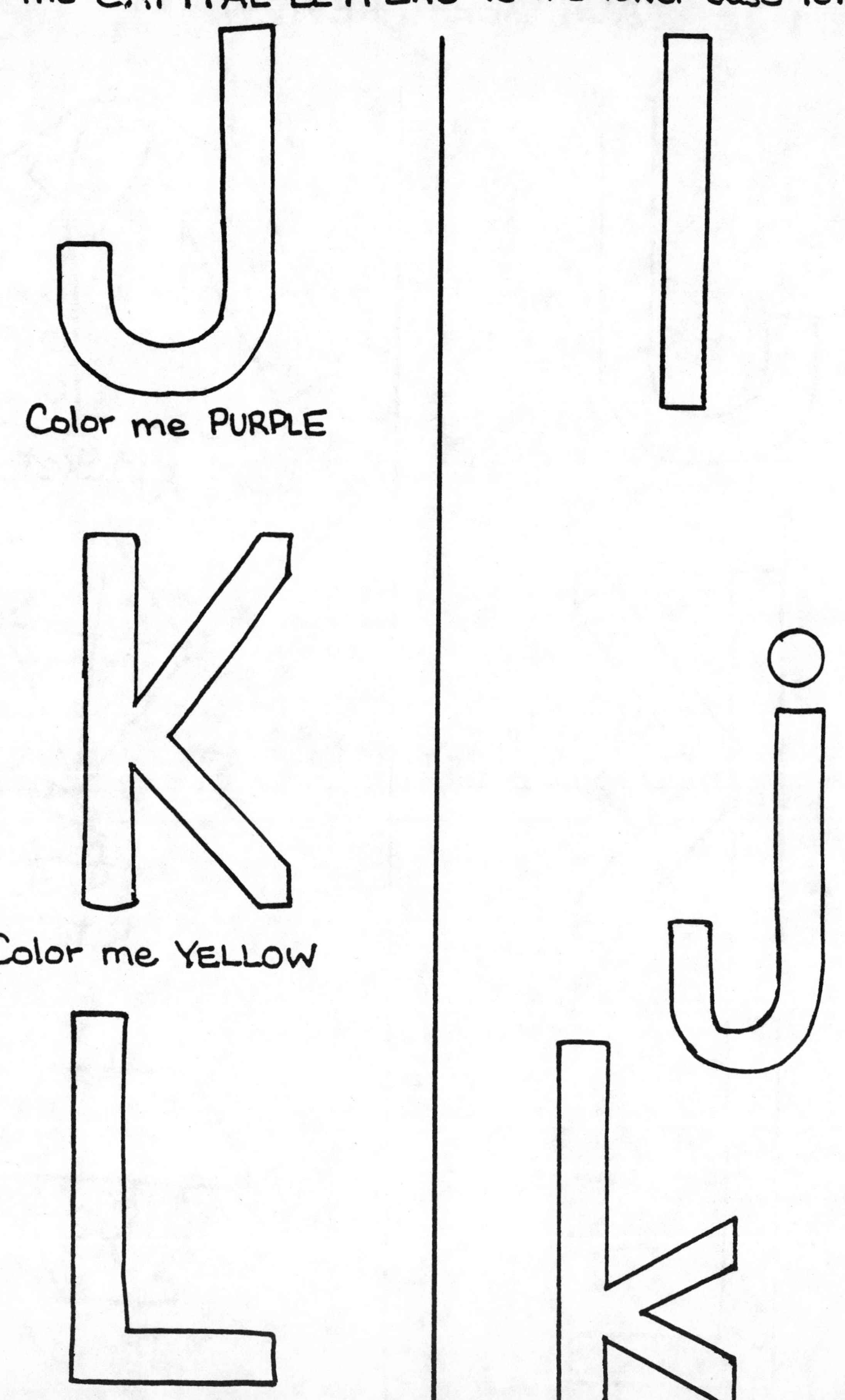

ALPHABET FUN PAGE

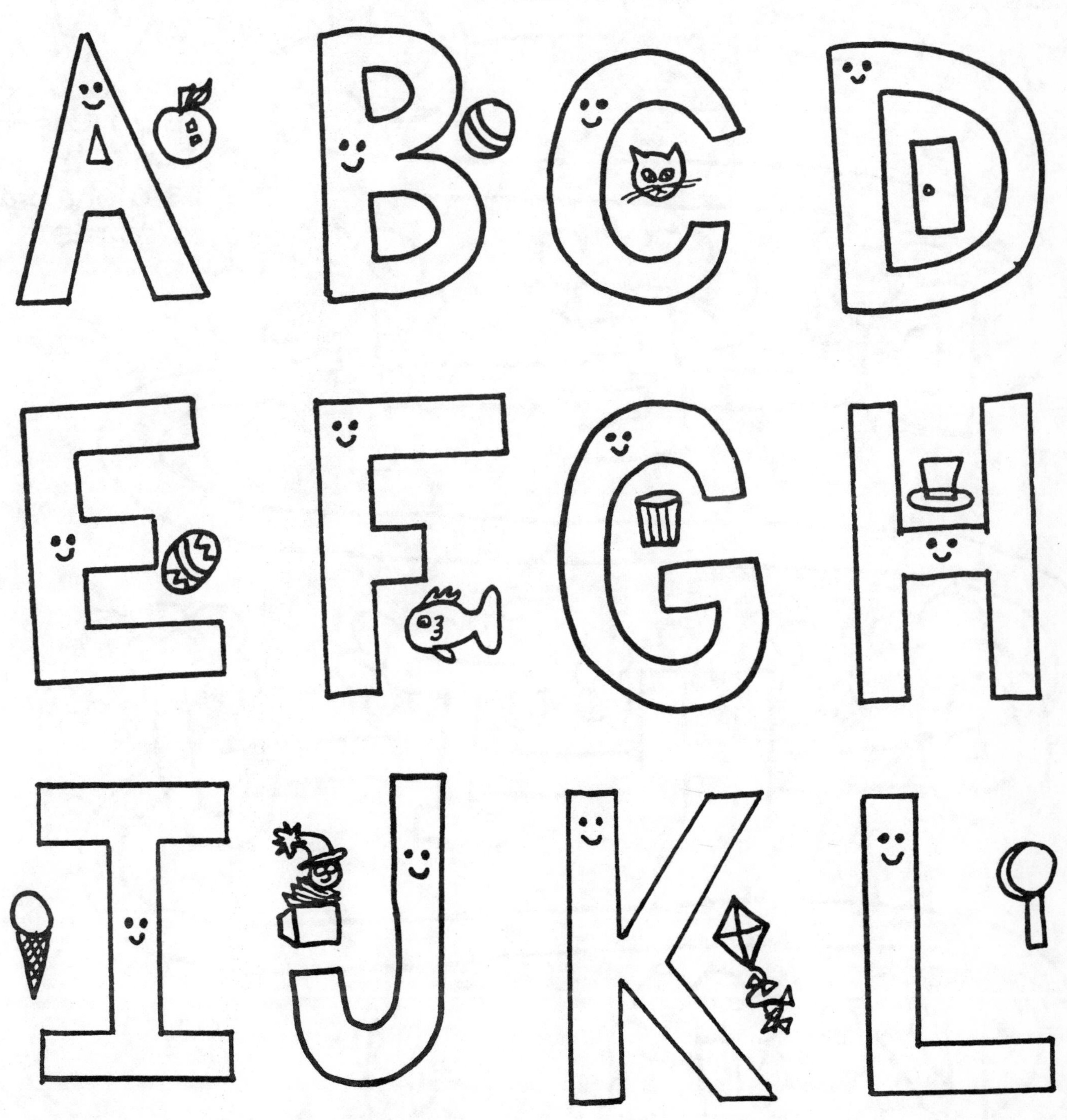

Fly Frederick home through the alphabet forest.
A
B
C
D
E
F
G
H
I
J
K
L

MARCH UNITS:

I. Alphabet
  A. Introduction of letters M-S.
  B. Uppercase stressed for younger ages, uppercase and lowercase for age four group.
  C. Word recognition
    1. Continue working on child's own name
    2. Re-emphasize classroom words
  D. This is a continuation of the unit begun in January. A review of all the letters covered so far appears at the end of the month. It is an intensive review, and this is all that is covered on these three days.

II. Weather
  A. A concentration on the basic types of weather changes
    1. Precipitation
    2. Temperature
  B. Breakdown for classes
    1. Age 3: very basic — rain, snow, warm, cold, clothing to wear on rainy and sunny days.
    2. Age 4: Specific — lightning, rain, snow, how the weather helps plants grow, wind.

III. Spatial Concepts
  A. This unit introduces the child to relationships between objects and space.
  B. Antonymn approach — opposites teach
    1. Big, small
    2. Up, down
    3. In, out
    4. Over, under
    5. First, last
    6. Right, left
    7. Top, bottom

IV. St. Patrick's Day: See Appendix III.

V. Easter (If the holiday should fall this month, see Appendix III.)

VI. Review
  A. Alphabet group
  B. This unit is concentrated at the end of the month and covers the letters A-R.

PROBLEM/CONCEPT	SUGGESTED ACTIVITIES
ALPHABET:	Refer to January syllabus.
WEATHER: Temperature Changes	Keep a classroom chart of daily outdoor temperatures. Note if sunny or cloudy and comment about how this affects the temperature.

Precipitation	Rain, snow, hail, sleet — explain that they are all forms of water, and that the temperature of the air determines what form it will take.
Thunder	Have the children watch you drop a book from overhead. Explain that lightning is like looking at the book falling, and thunder is the noise it makes when this happens. (The book hits the floor.) If they see lightning, they will probably hear thunder since they always go together. Sing the "Who's Afraid of Thunder" song: Who's afraid of thunder? Thunder's just a lot of noise. Just like the loud racket When girls and boys play with toys. First the lightning goes flash, Then the thunder goes crash. Tell me who's afraid of thunder? Not these girls and boys!
Clothing	Discuss the proper clothes to be worn outdoors when it's cold, wet, warm, snowy. Make a felt cut-out of a child and other cut-outs of different kinds of clothing. Let one child dress the "doll" for the day's weather outdoors.
Song:	"Umbrellas". See last page of monthly suggestions.
SPATIAL CONCEPTS: Opposites in prepositions and adverbs	Let the children act out the words for the day. Ex. Let one child sit **on** the table and another get **under** it. Let someone be **first** and **last.**
ST. PATRICK'S DAY:	See Appendix III.
EASTER:	If the holiday falls this month, see Appendix III.
ALPHABET REVIEW:	Sing the alphabet song as you point to the letters. Do this two or three times a day. Ask the children with names beginning **A** to stand. Repeat for **B,** etc.

UMBRELLAS

Um-ber-ellas, um-ber-ellas
Toot-a-la-ma, Toot-a-la-ma, Toot-a-lay,
Any um-ber-ella, Any um-ber-ella
To fix, today?
He'll mend your um-ber-ellas
And go on his way.
Singing Toot-a-la-ma, toot-a-la-ma, toot-a-lay.
Toot-a-la-ma, Toot-a-la-ma, toot-a-lay!

If there's a lull
And things get dull,
He'll sharpen knives for everyone in the neighborhood.
He's very good.
He'll mend a clock
He'll fix a box
He'll do anything, but he'd rather sing:

Toot-a-la-ma, toot-a-la-ma,
Toot-a-la-ma, toot-a-la-ma,
Any um-ber-ellas to fix today?

March

(1) Calendar Begin: M	(2) Begin: weather Age 3: sun, rain Age 4: weather chart M page for book	(3) Wind: Bring hair dryer to class	(4) Begin: N	(5) Rain and Snow Age 4: N page for booklet
(6) Review: M, N	(7) Begin: O Clothes for rainy days	(8) Clothes for sunny days Age 4: O page for booklet	(9) Big and Small	(10) Begin P Tall and Short
(11) Up and down Age 4: P page for booklet	(12) Review: O, P In and Out	(13) Begin: Q	(14) Over and Under Age 4: Q page for booklet	(15) First and Last Review: In, Out, Over Under
(16) Top and Bottom Begin: R	(17) Right and left Age 4: page R for booklet	(18) Review: Q, R	(19) Begin: S Review: up, down, above, below, on, beside	(20) Review: A – F Age 4: S page for booklet
(21) Review: G – L	(22) Review: M – R	CRAFT ITEMS: Brads Cotton balls Construction paper: yellow magazines	(23) St. Patrick's Day (See Appendix III)	(24) Easter (See Appendix III)

MARCH

SUN.	MON.	TUES.	WED.	THURS.	FRI.	SAT.

M

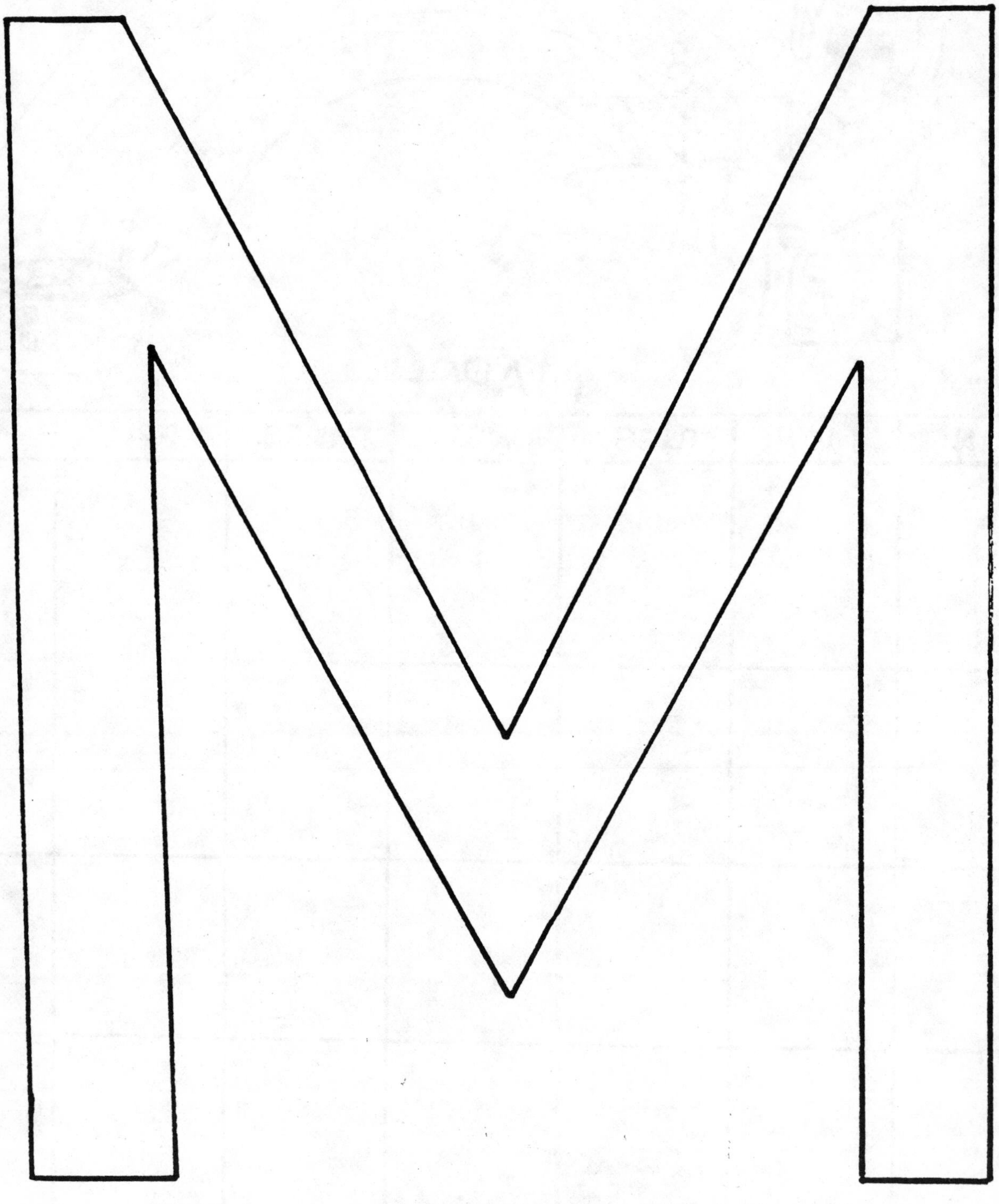

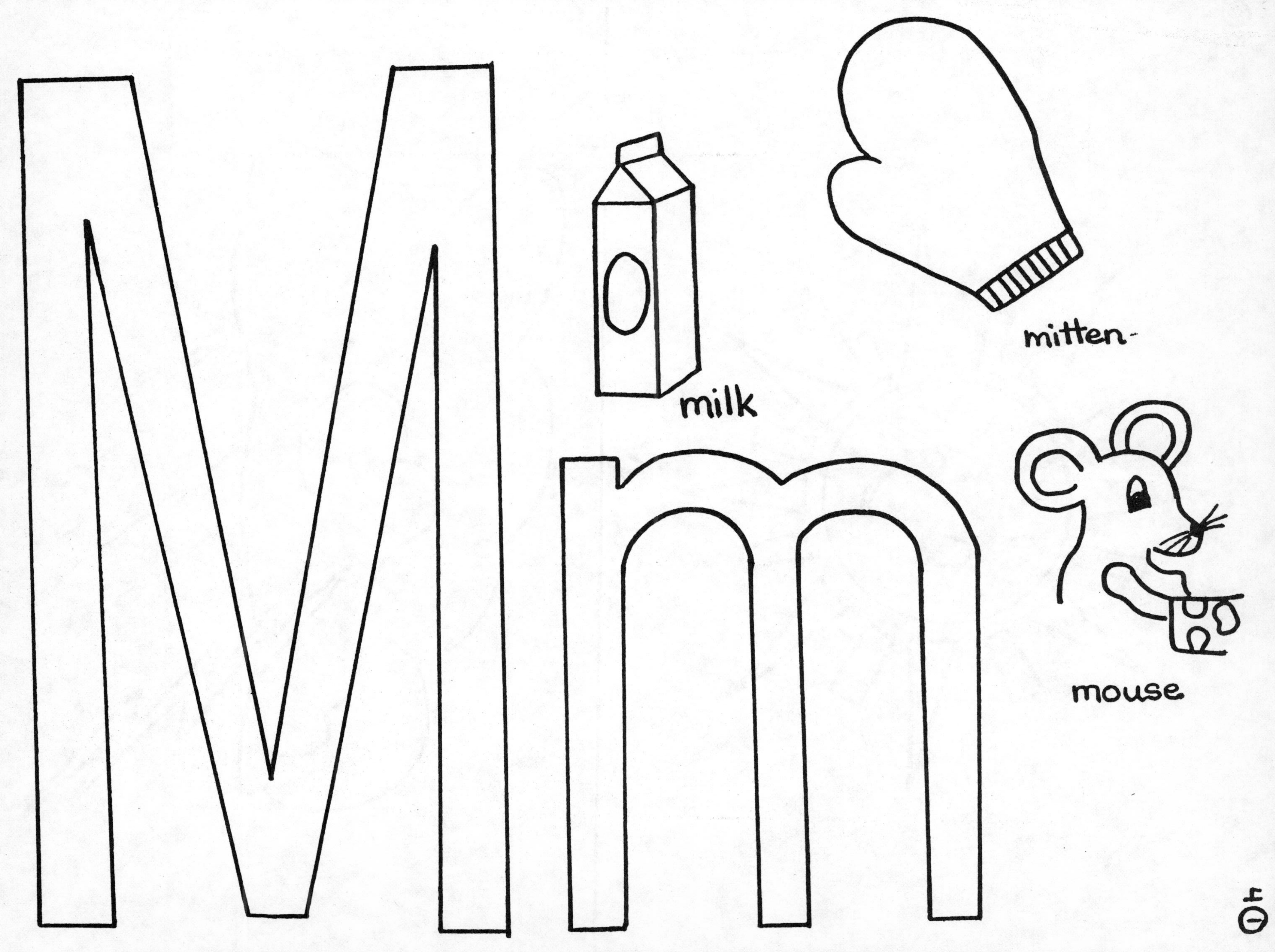

milk
mitten
mouse
4①

SUNNY

RAINY

WEATHER CHART

SUNSHINE

RAIN

cutting line ↑

Attach arrow to o with brad

Color arrow before cutting

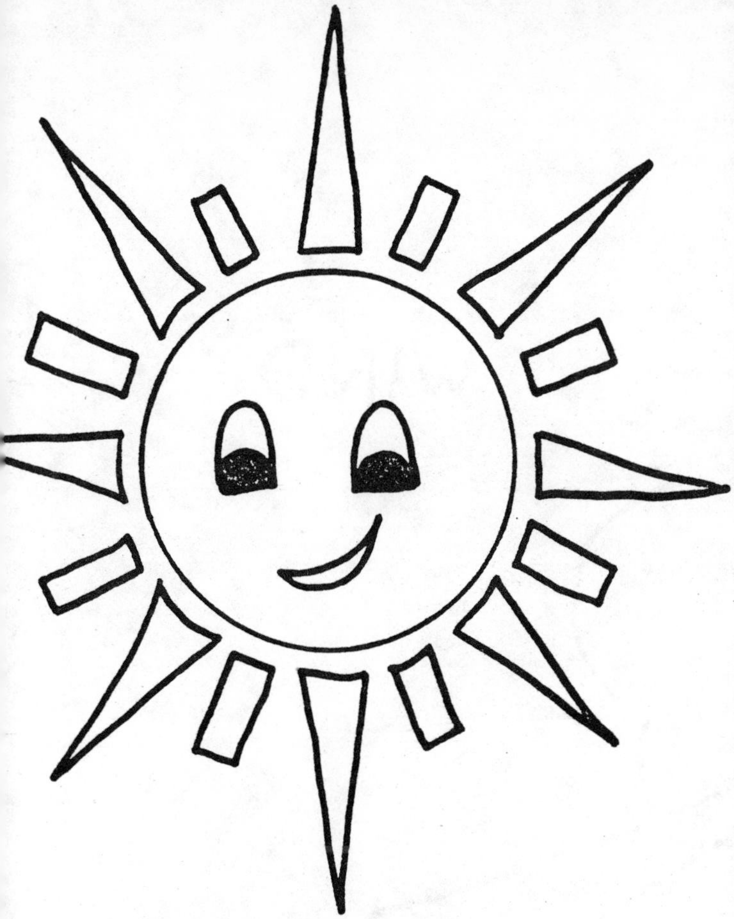

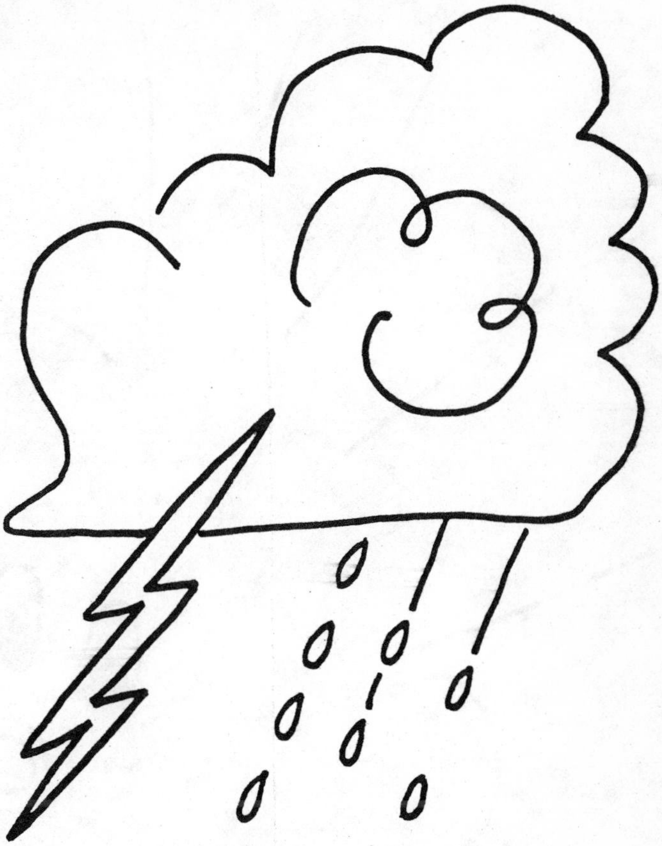

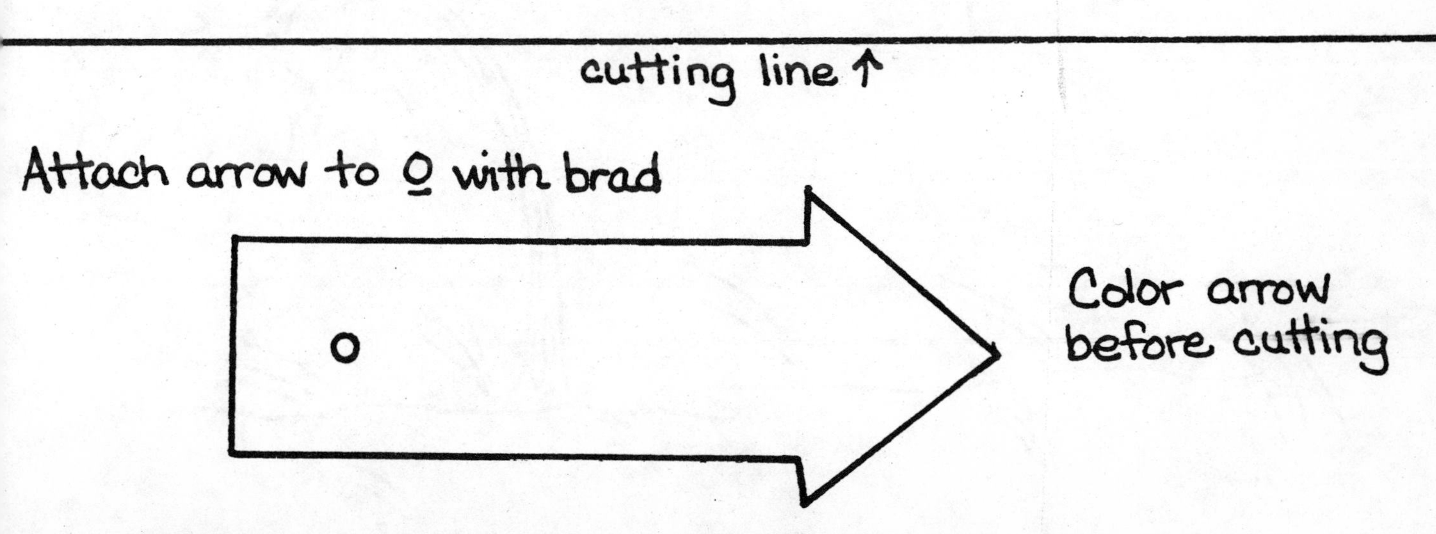

WIND

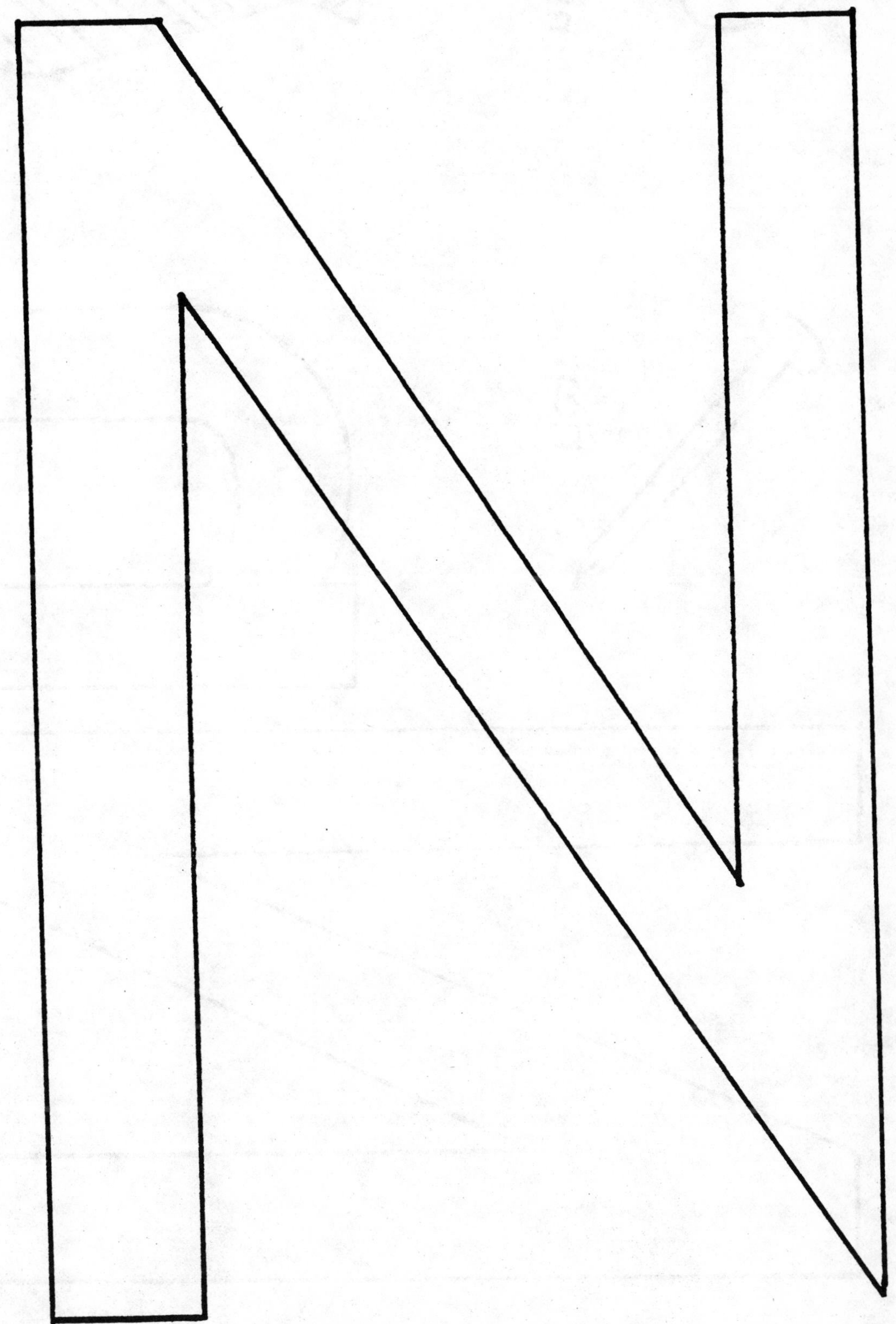

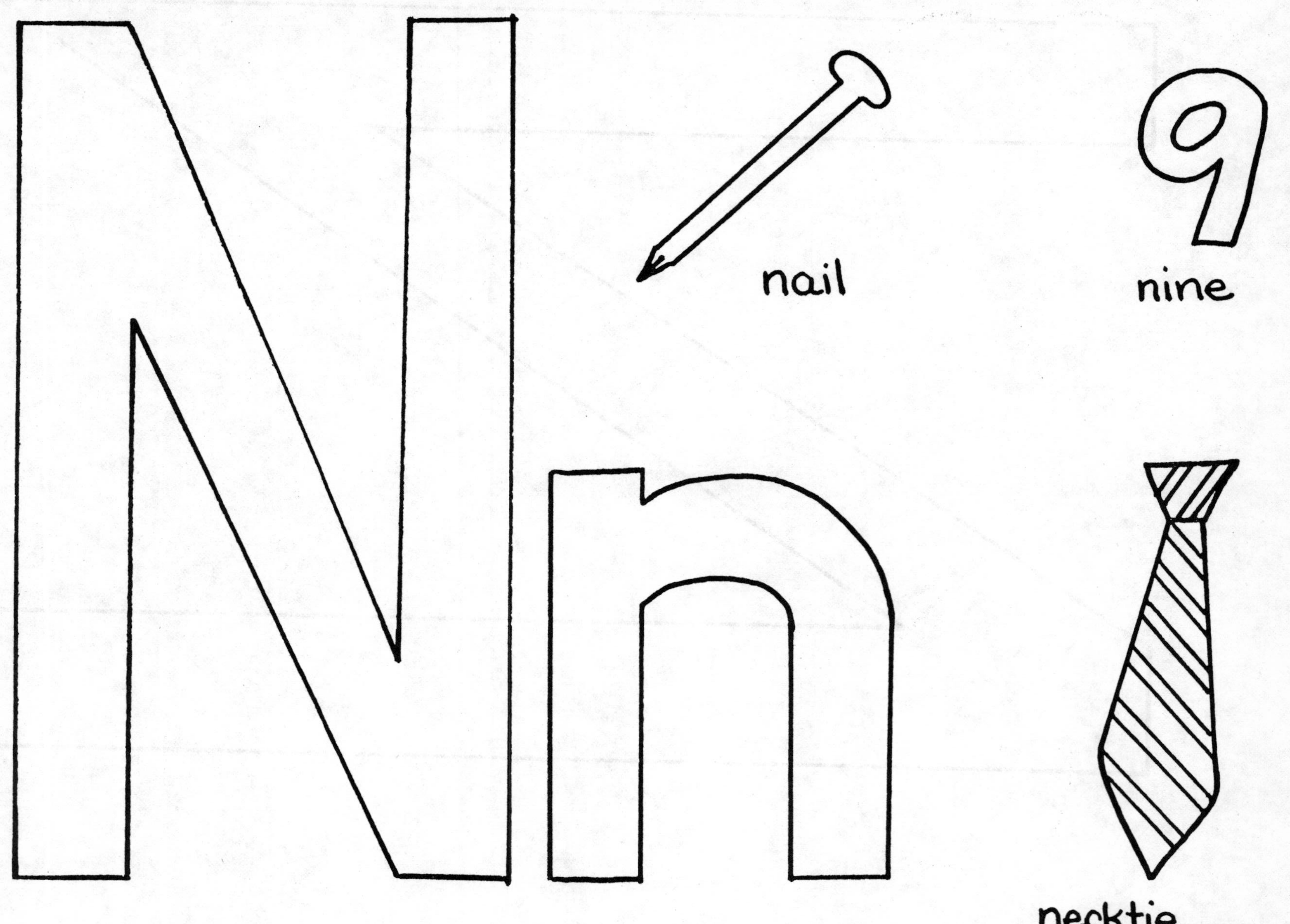

4 ④

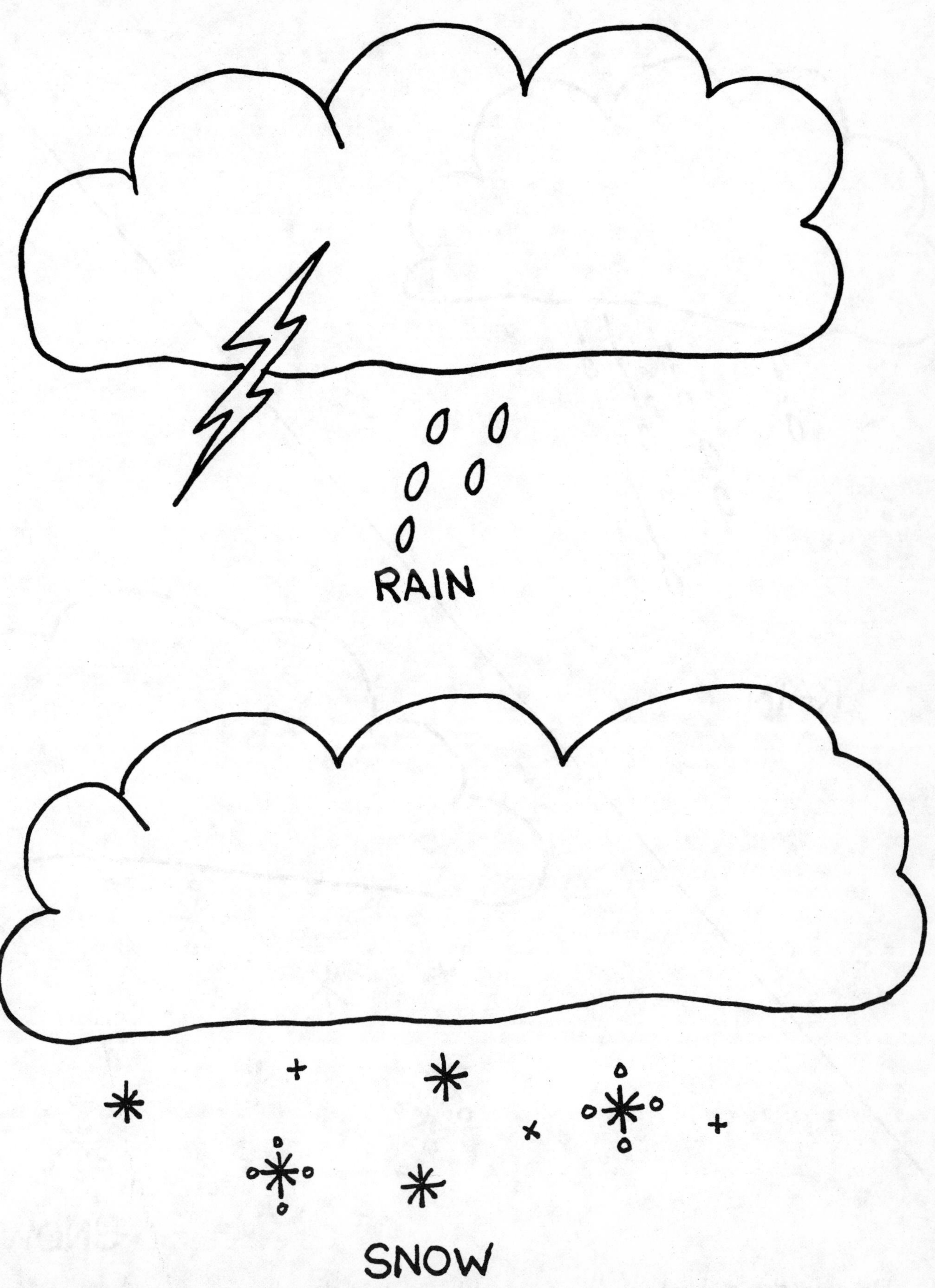
RAIN
SNOW

Teacher: pre-cut lightning bolts for each child. 4 ⑤

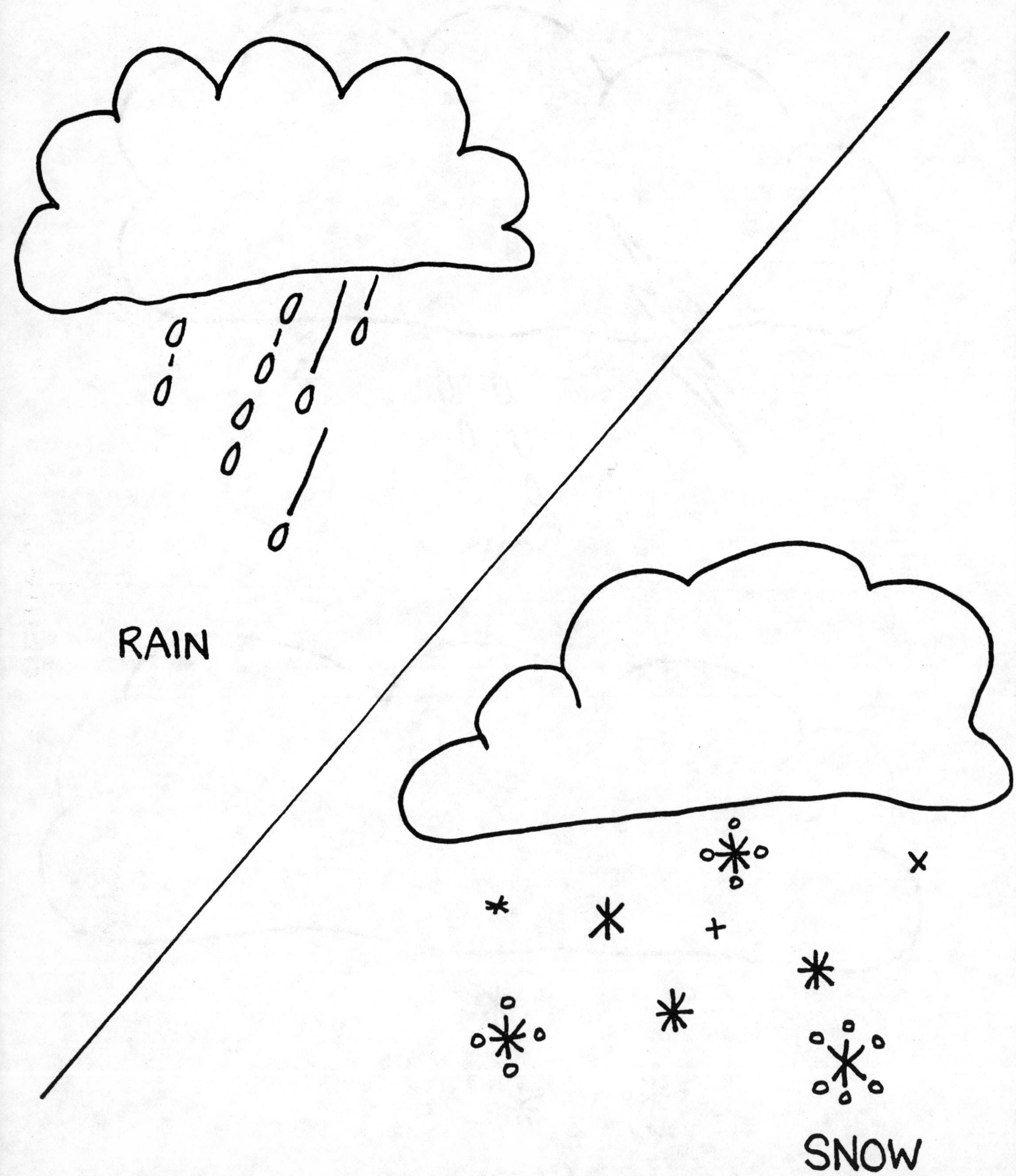

Paste the lightning on the right cloud

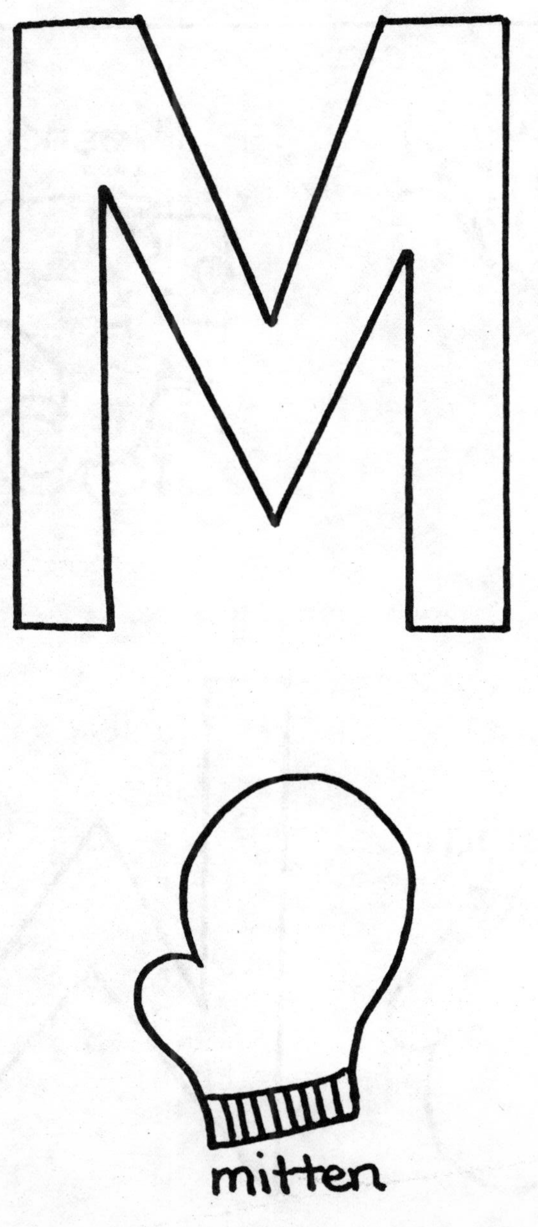

REVIEW

36

M
mitten
N
necktie
mouse
mop
nail
nine
Mm
Nn

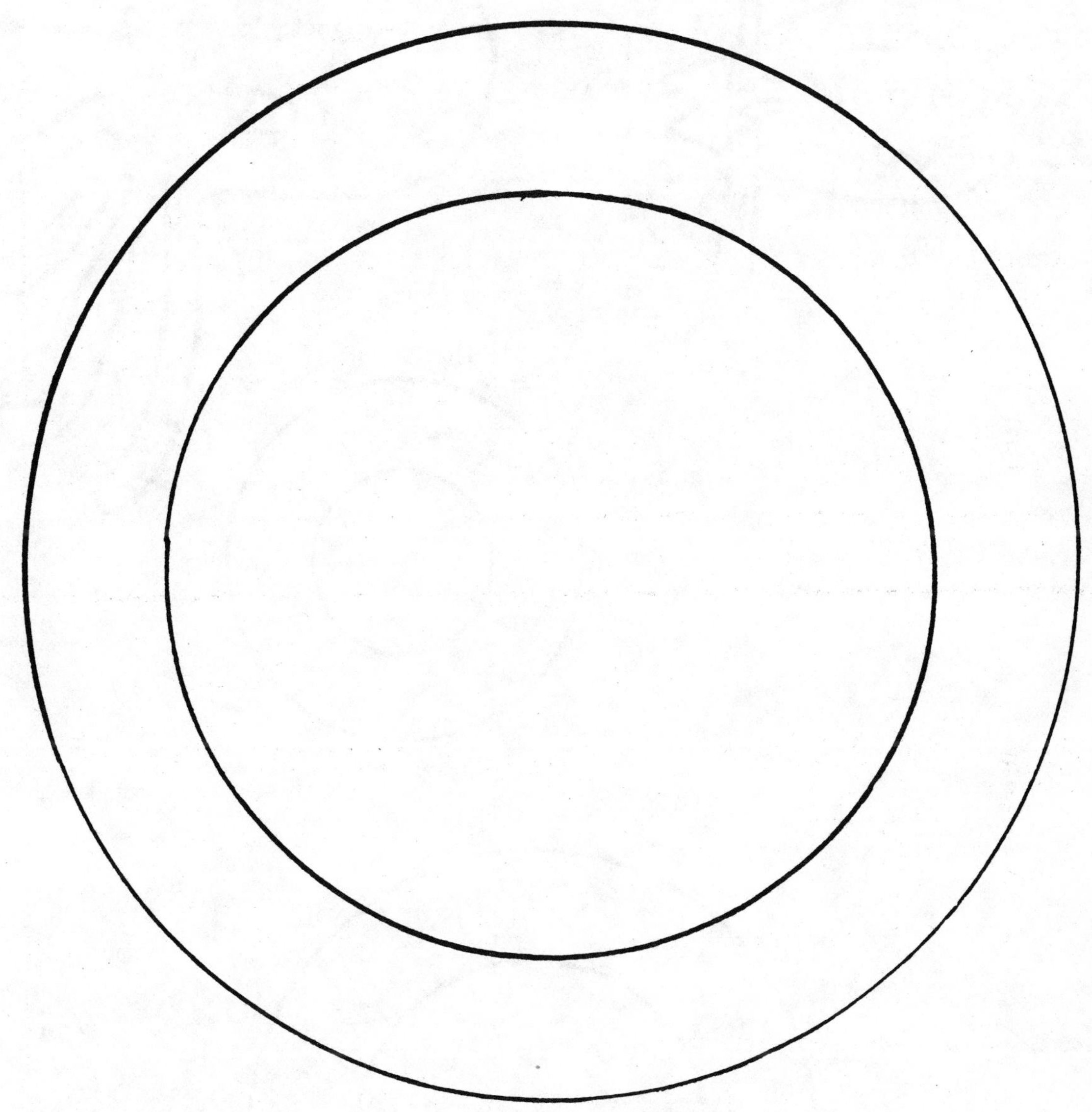

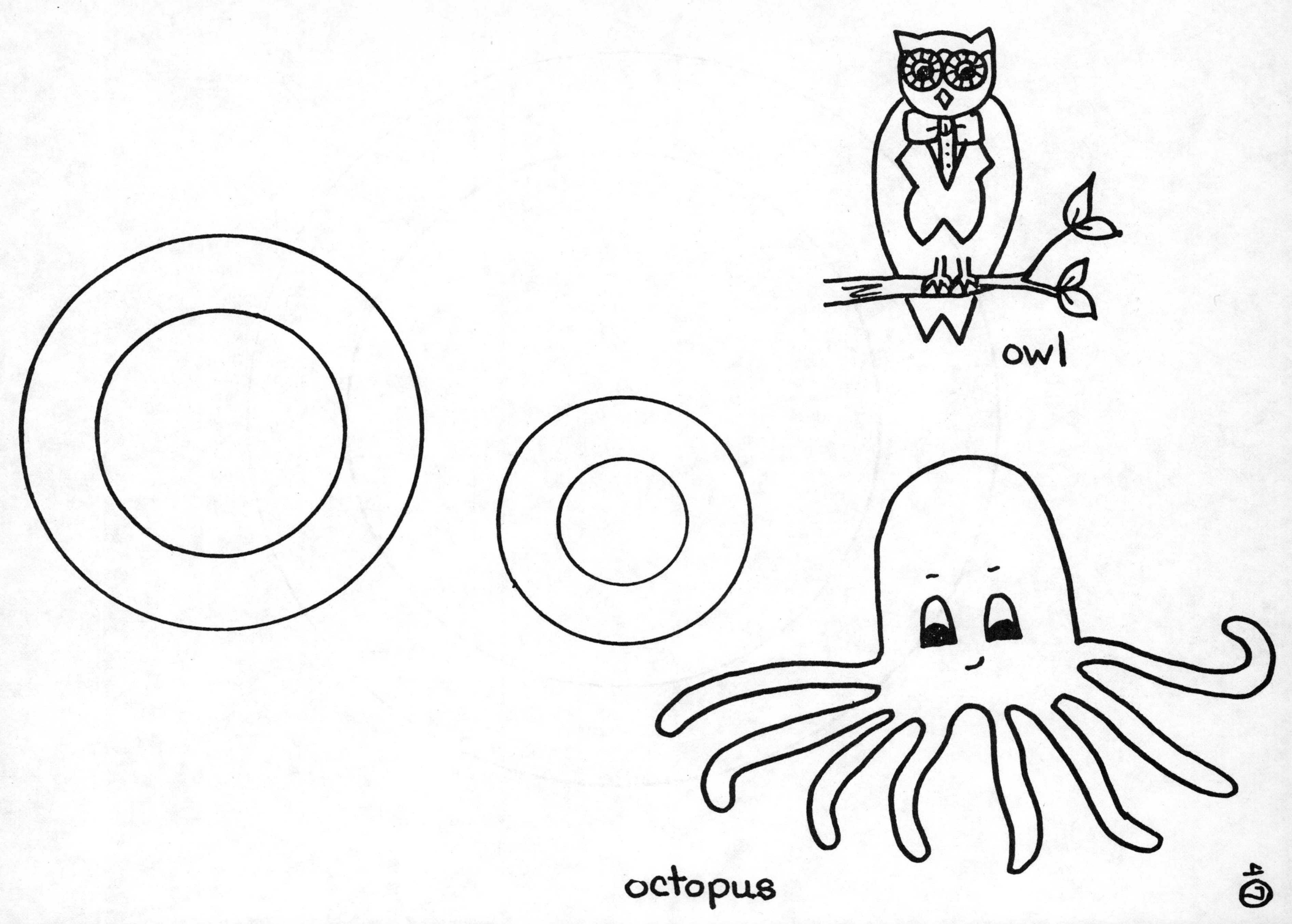
owl
octopus

We dress this way on a rainy day.

What would you wear on a rainy day?

Circle the answers.

We dress like this on hot, sunny days.

How would you dress for a warm, sunny day?

Circle the answers.

BIG

small

3 (9)

BIG AND SMALL

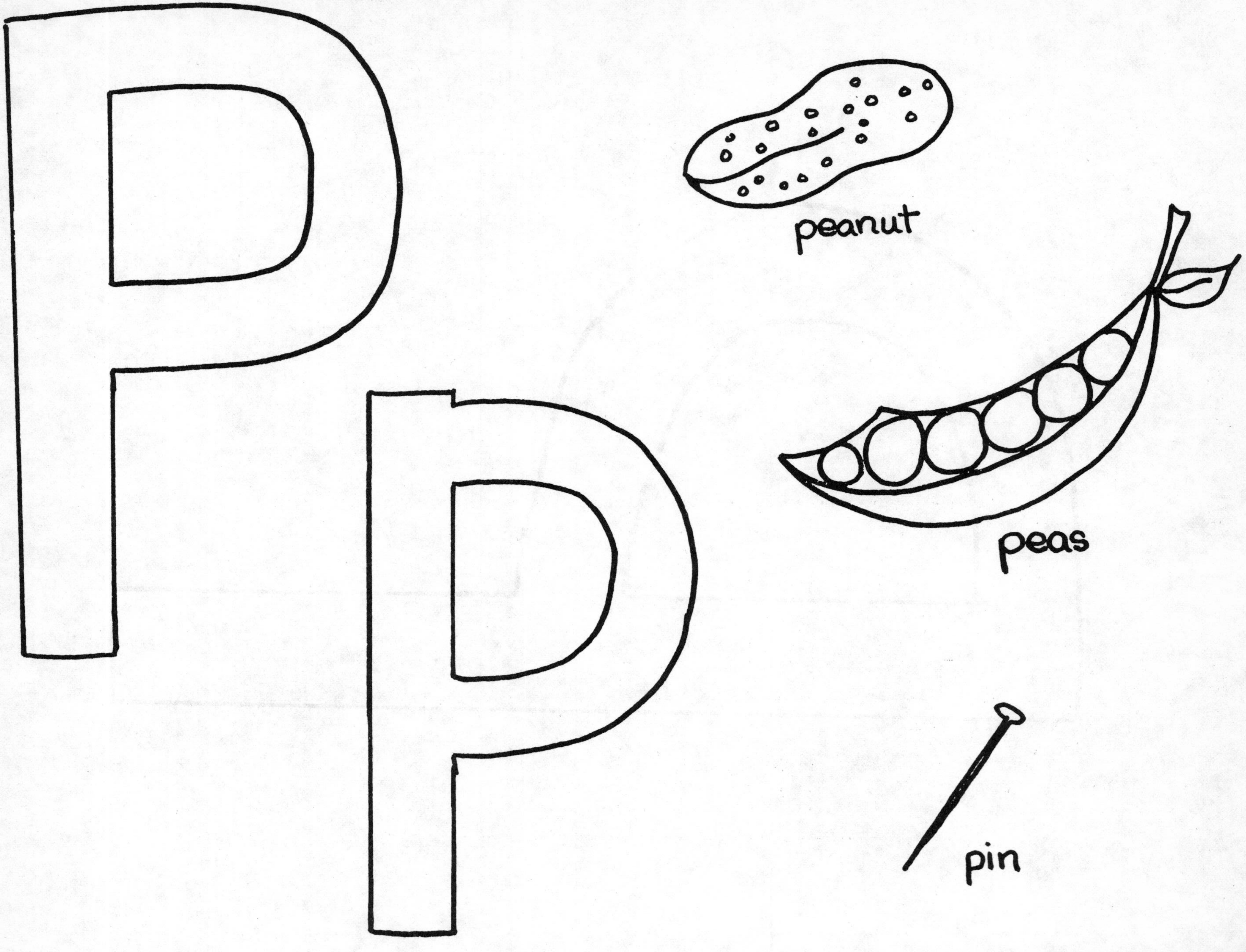

peas

pin

peanut

3 (10)

TALL AND SHORT

TALL AND SHORT

UP
DOWN

Halfway down the stairs
Is a stair
Where I sit.
There isn't any
Other stair
Quite like
It.
I'm not at the bottom
I'm not at the top
So this is the stair
Where
I always
Stop.

UP

DOWN

Halfway up the stairs
Isn't up,
And isn't down.
It isn't in the nursery,
It isn't in the town.
And all sorts of funny thoughts
Run round my head:
"It isn't really
Anywhere!
It's somewhere else
Instead.

A.A. Milne

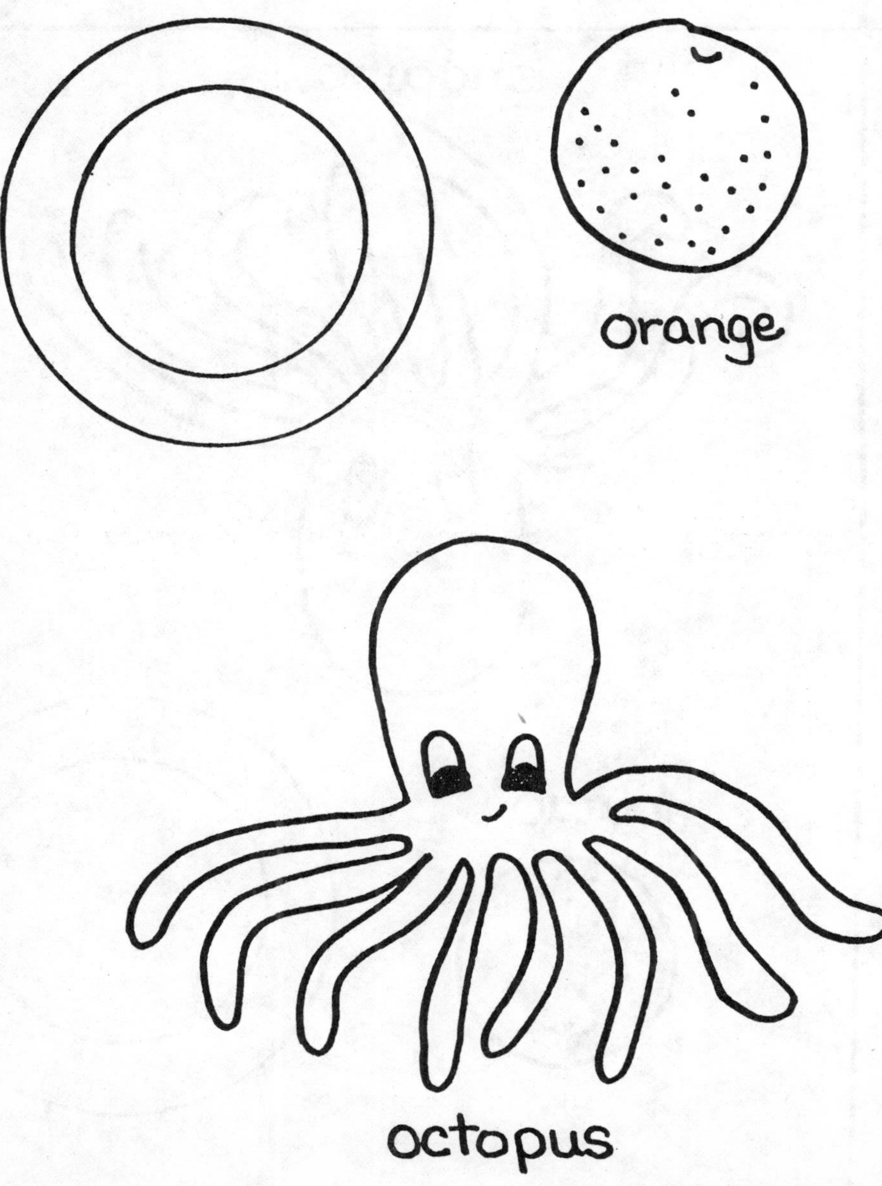

REVIEW

3 (12)

O
orange
octopus
P
pin
plant
peanut
Oo
Pp

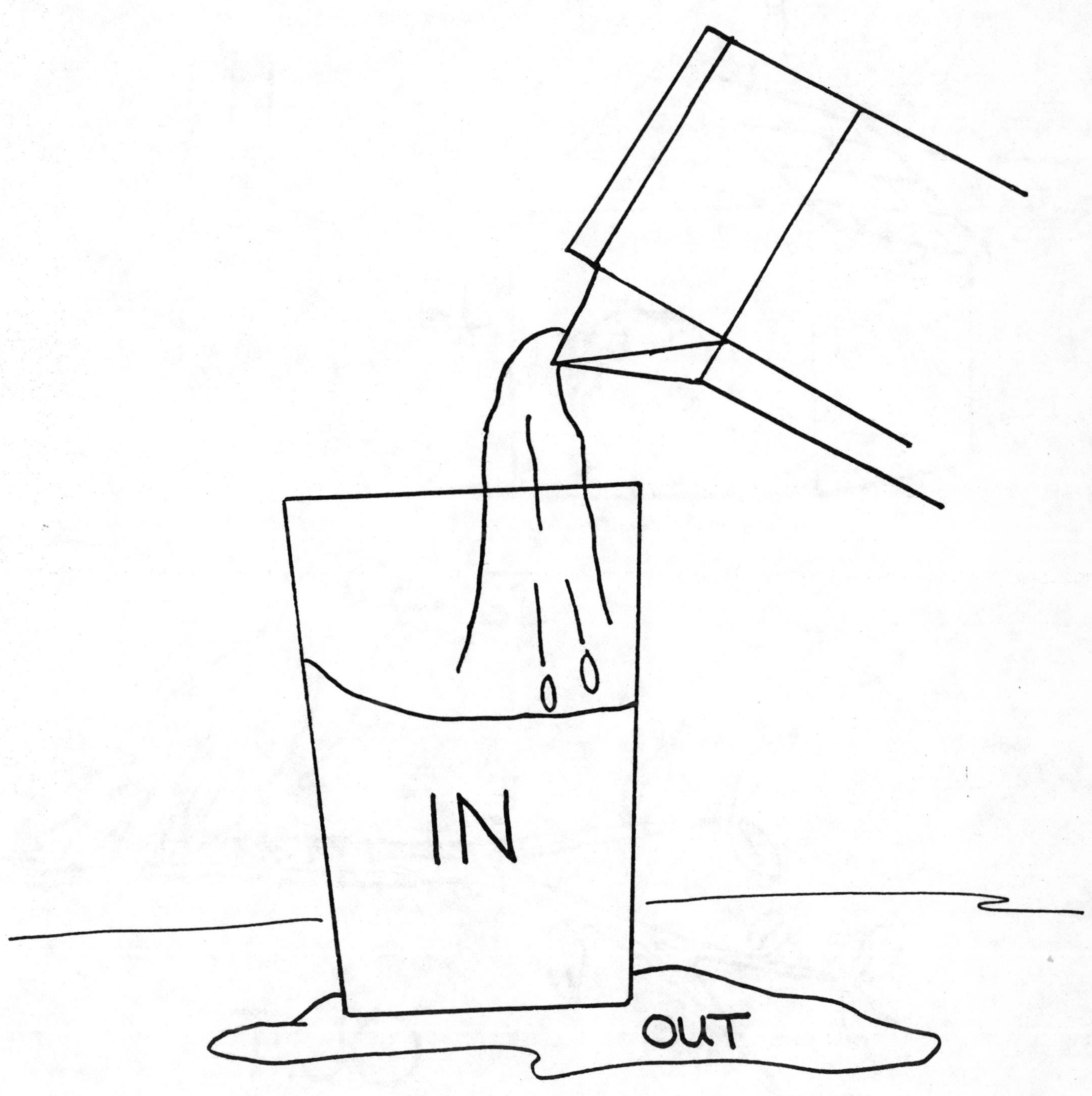
IN
OUT

IN
OUT

25¢
quarter
queen

OVER
UNDER

OVER
UNDER

Which is first?

Which is last?

Age 3: color
Age 4: paint

IN

OUT

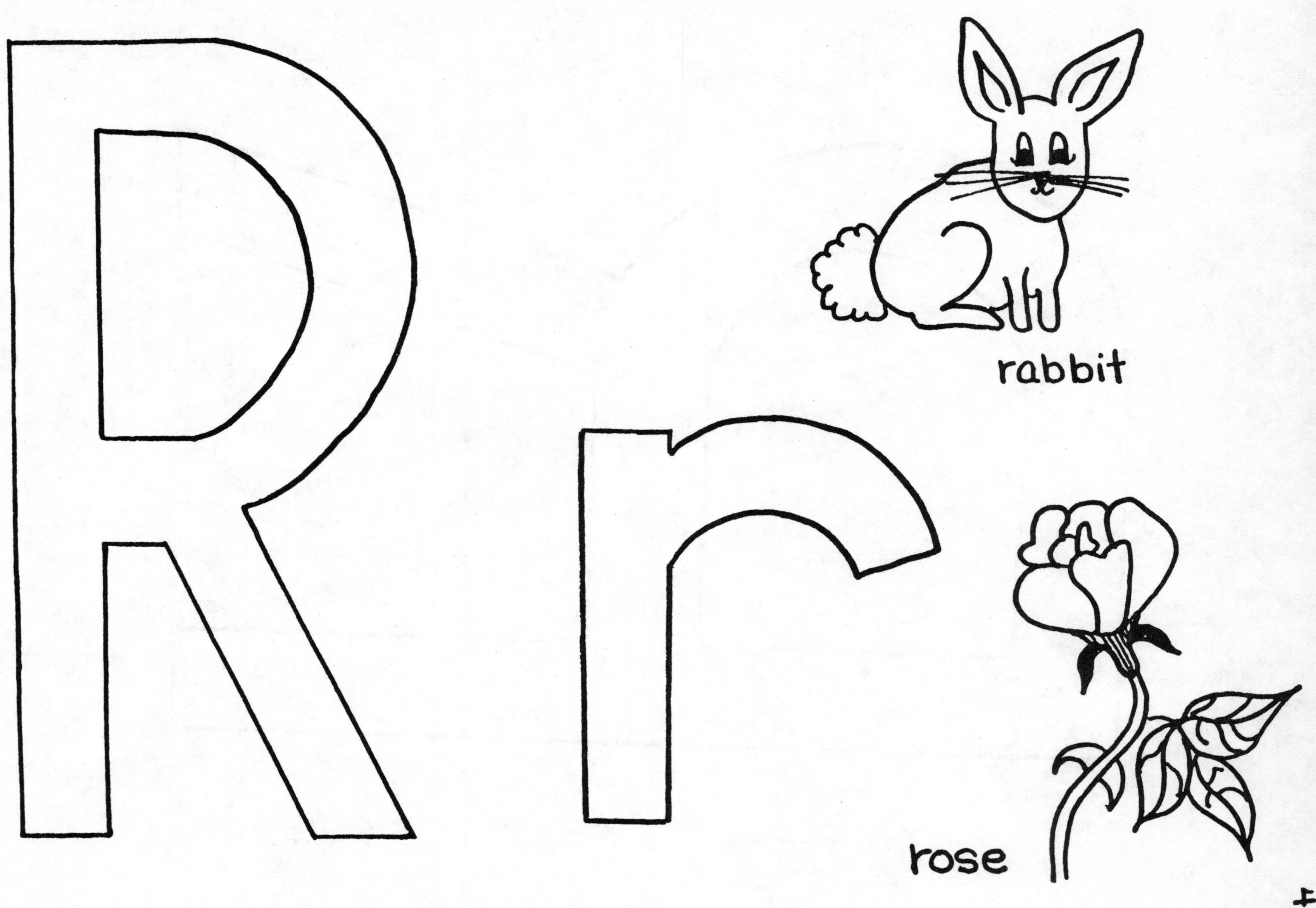
R r
rabbit
rose

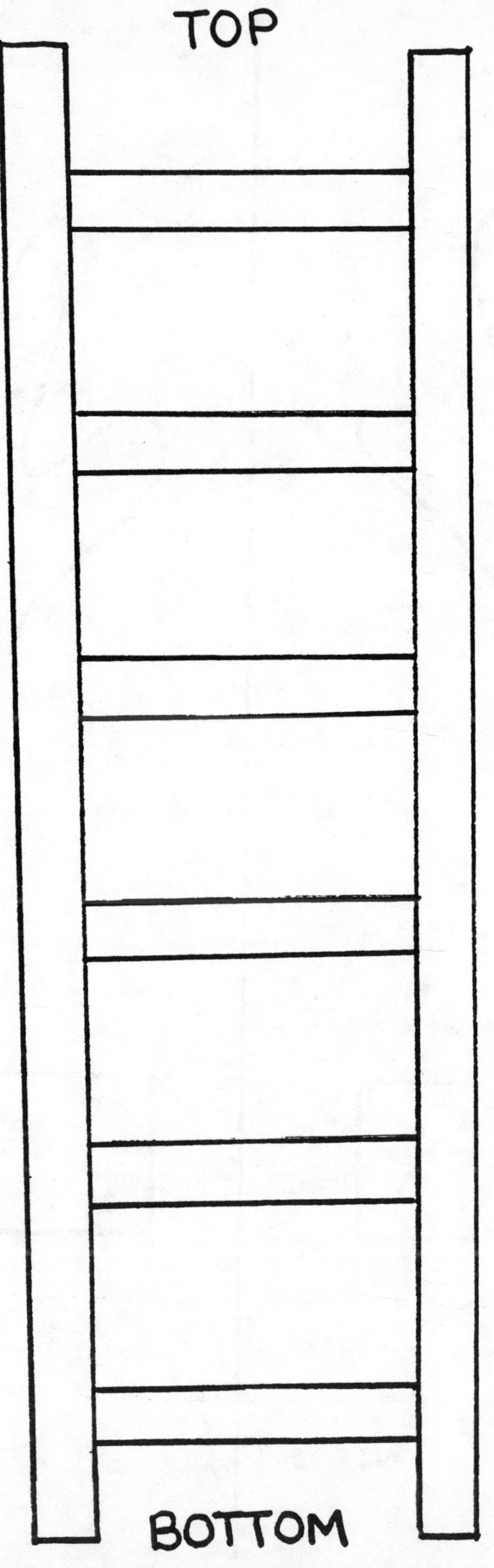

Age 3: paste a magazine picture of a person at the bottom.

Age 4: paste craft sticks over picture: make a ladder.

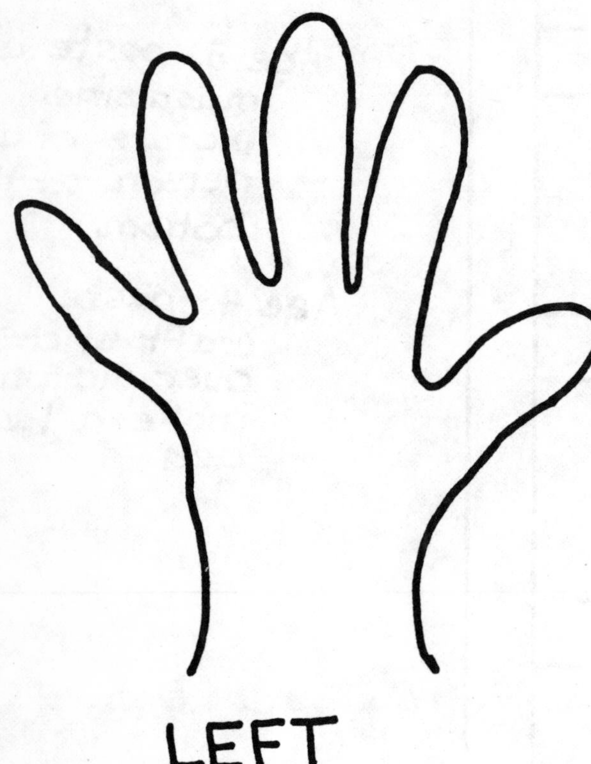

LEFT

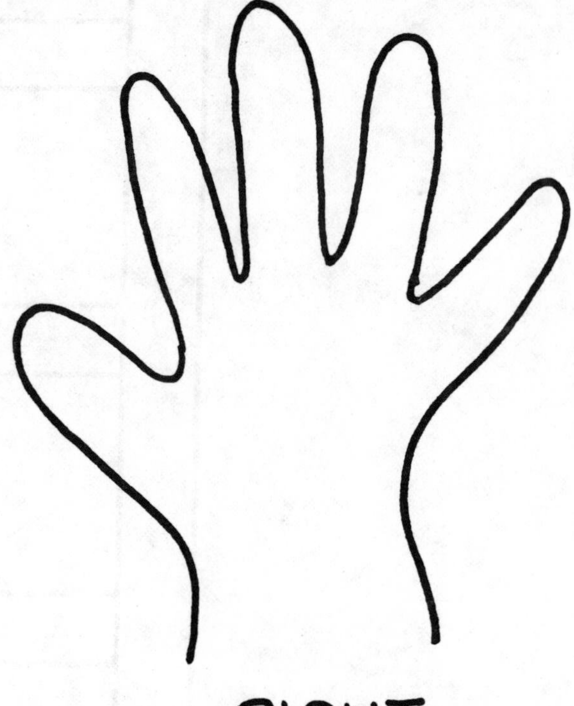

RIGHT

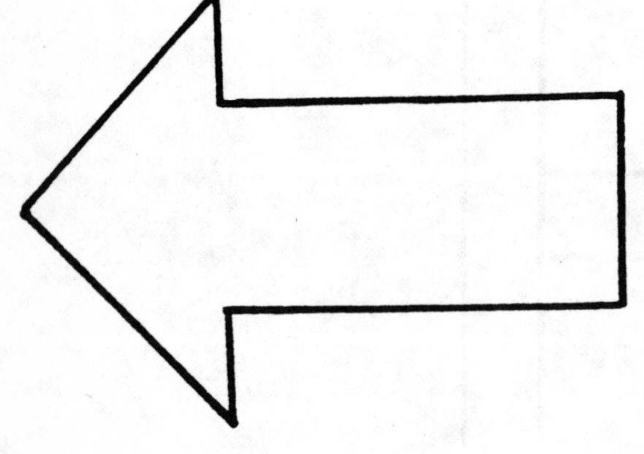

Draw around your LEFT hand.

Draw around your RIGHT hand.

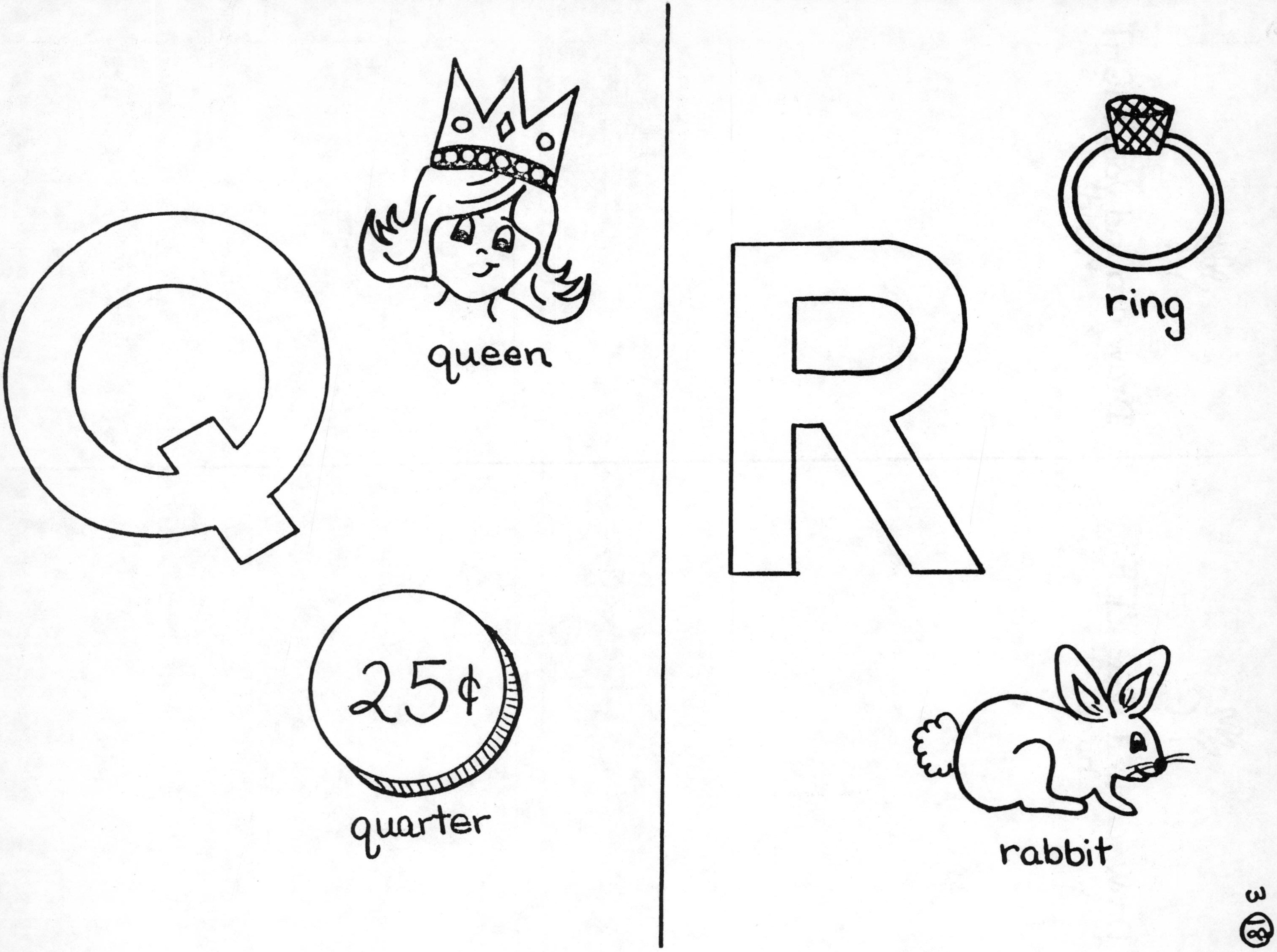

Q

queen

25¢

quarter

rabbit

Q
queen
25¢
quarter
R
rose
ring
rabbit
Qq
Rr
4 18

3 (19)

sun
snake
sock

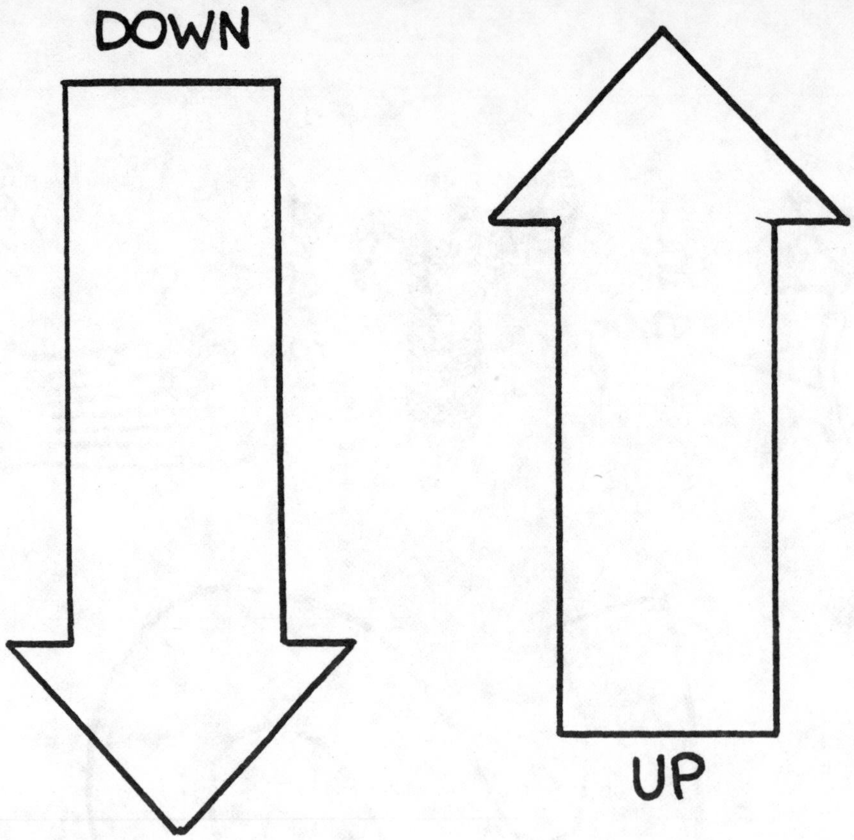

DOWN

UP

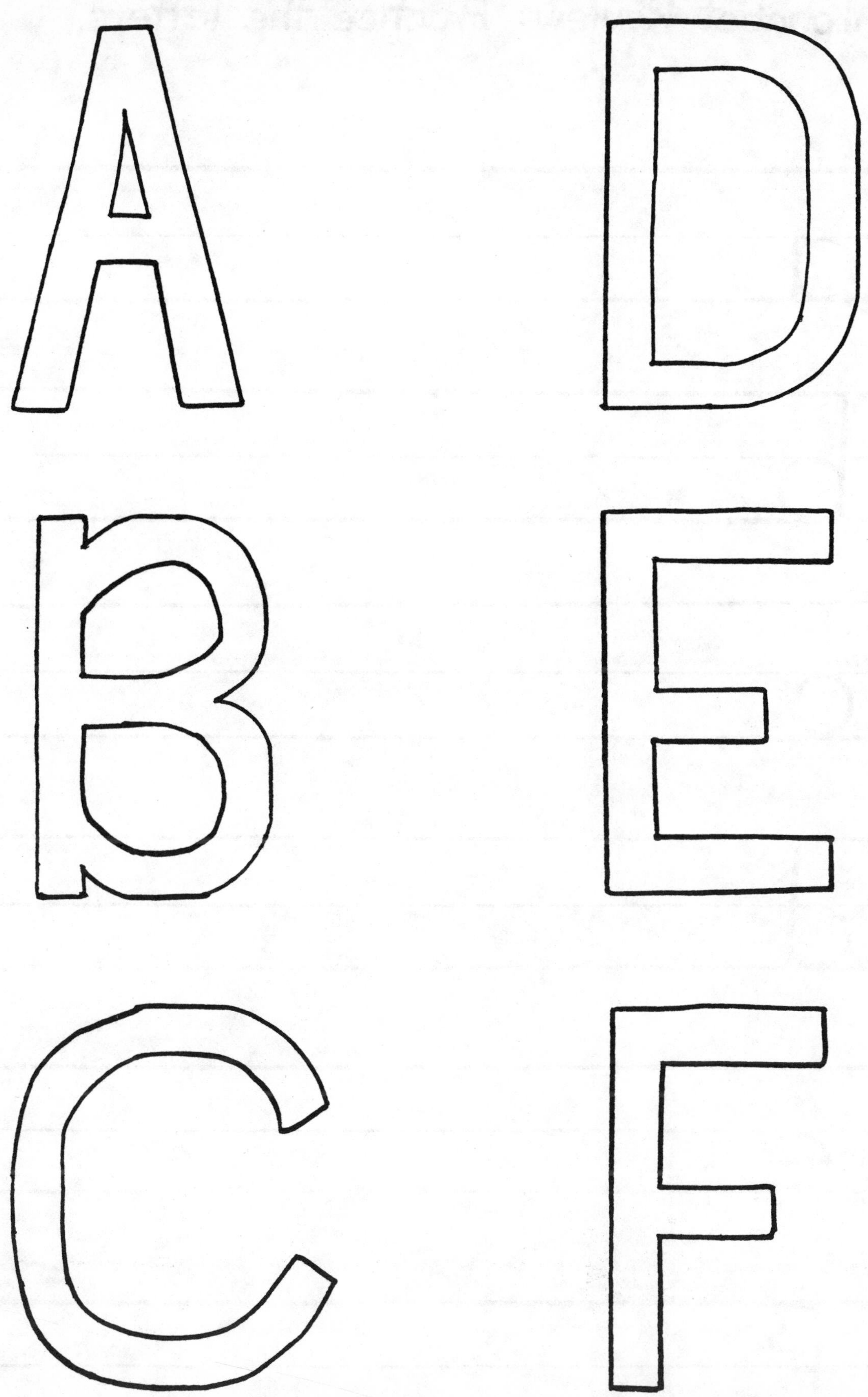

Make each letter a different color.

Alphabet Review: Practice the letters.

Aa

Bb

Cc

Dd

Ee

Ff

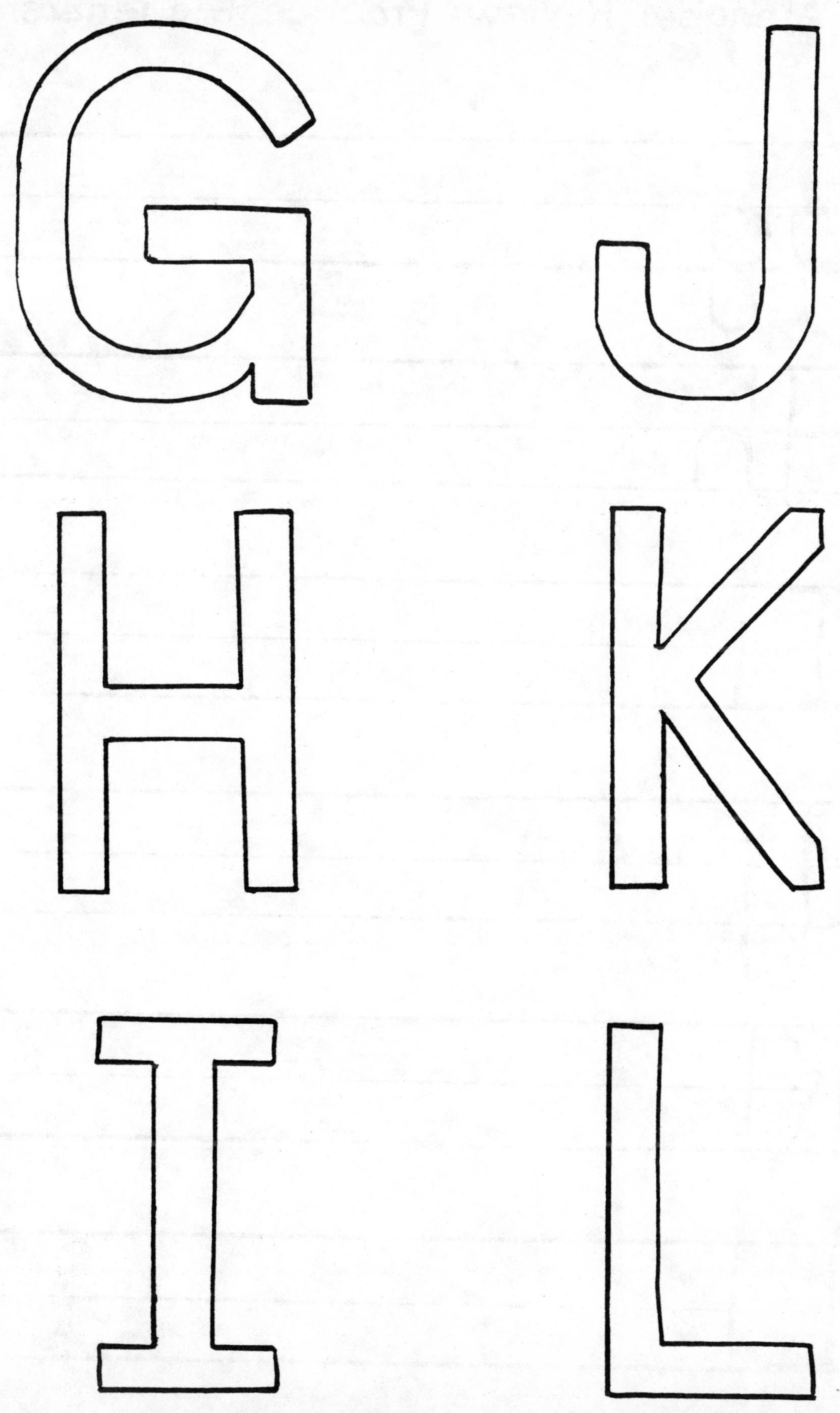

Make each letter a different color.

4

Alphabet Review: Practice the letters.

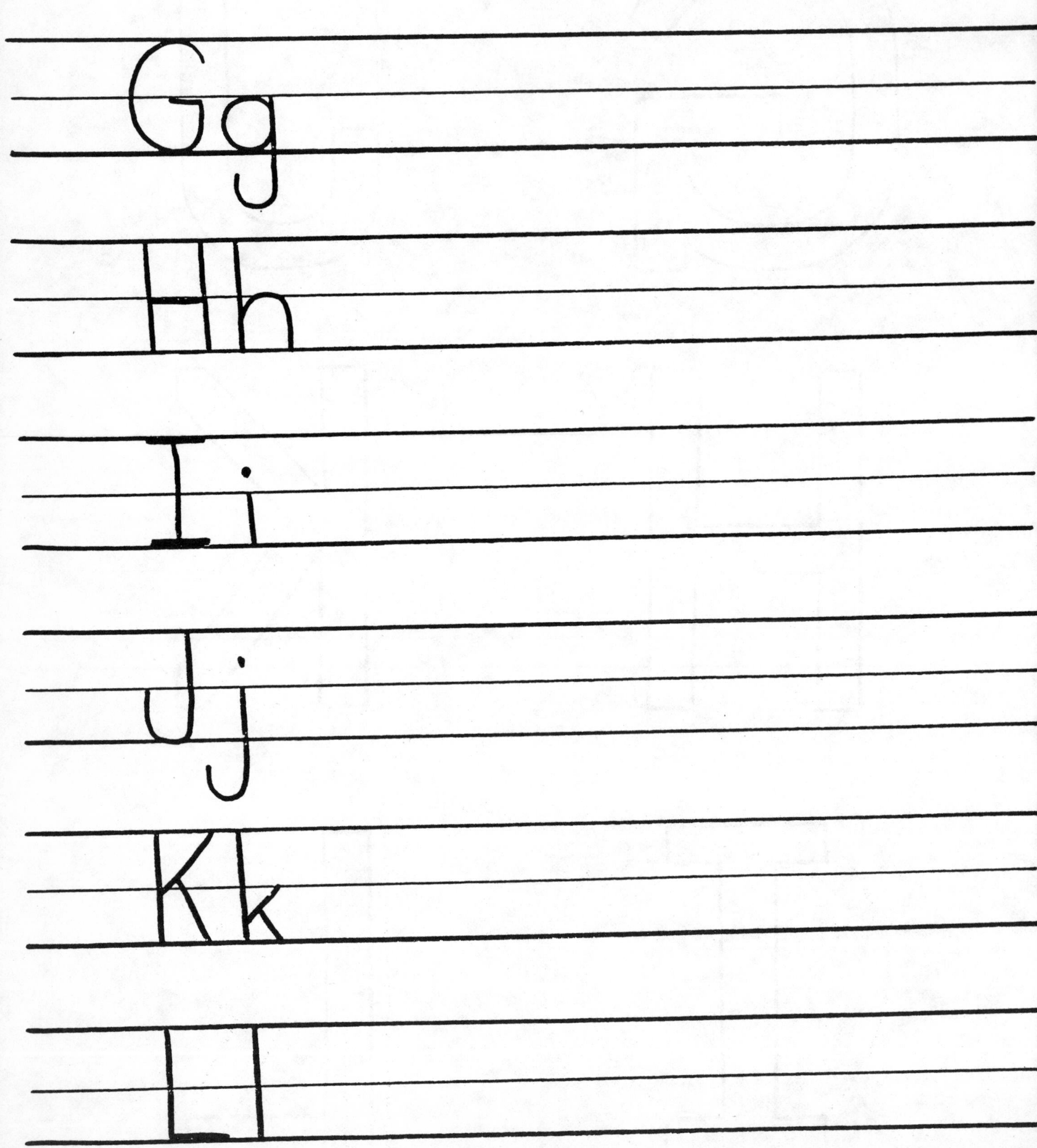

Make each letter a different color.

Alphabet Review: Practice the letters.

Mm

Nn

Oo

Pp

Qq

Rr

APRIL UNITS:

I. Alphabet
  A. Introduction of letters T-Z.
  B. Uppercase stressed for younger ages, uppercase and lowercase for age four group.
  C. Word recognition
    1. Continue working on child's own name.
    2. Re-emphasize classroom words.
  D. This is the final part of the unit begun in January. A review of all the letters covered so far appears next month, but continued review will be helpful.

II. Farm
  A. Animals and their care
    1. Cow
    2. Pig
    3. Chicken (project for age 4)
    4. Horse
    5. Goat
    6. Ducks
  B. Physical plant of the farm
    1. Buildings
    2. Machinery
  C. Chores
    1. Taking care of all of the animals
    2. Planting seeds
    3. Care of the crop
    4. Taking the crop to market — used as a transition to the next unit.

III. Transportation
  A. Discuss the various modes of transportation for people and things (goods).
  B. Specific vehicles:
    1. Truck
    2. Train
    3. Car
    4. Airplane
    5. Rocket
    6. Boat
  C. Teacher should emphasize other types (bus, helicopter, etc.) which are not presented as daily projects.

IV. Alphabet Booklet (Age 4 only)
  A. Complete this month
  B. Tie together with string or staple together and send home at the end of the month.

PROBLEM/CONCEPT	SUGGESTED ACTIVITIES
ALPHABET:	Refer to January syllabus.
FARM:	Introduce various common animals on the farm.
Farm Animals	Make a bulletin board with the animals shown. Cut a circle out of yellow paper and attach it around the animal of the day.
	Play "The Farmer in the Dell"
	Explain each animal's usefulness on the farm. The cow gives milk, as does the goat; the pig provides meat, the chicken lays eggs, and the horse pulls a wagon or provides transportation.
	Chicken project for age 4 group: Cut out chicken, wing and egg. Paste egg under wing area, attach wing with paper fasteners.
Farm buildings and machines	The barn provides shelter and storage.
	The tractor is a machine that helps the farmer plant more, and takes some of the work away from the horse.
Chores	Everyone on the farm must do their share of the work, just like members of the family have chores at home.
	Explain that farmers must take care of their animals.
Crops	Making the soil ready involves a lot of work.
	Age 4: Plant seeds in cups of soil and/or vermiculite.
	Discuss taking care of the crop and not watering too much.
TRANSPORTATION:	Discuss the different modes of transportation for goods and people.

A bulletin board with pictures of the various vehicles will provide a starting point each day.

This unit moves from the one on the farm through the use of the truck which takes the crops to market.

Sing the bus song:

The wheels on the bus go round and round,
round and round, round and round,
The wheels on the bus go round and round,
all through the town.

The horn on the bus . . .
The people on the bus . . .

Sing "Row, Row, Row Your Boat"

Tell the story of the **"Little Engine That Could".**

Be sure to emphasize that there are all kinds of transportation (feet), not just the kinds of pictures that they are coloring or painting in school.

ALPHABET BOOKLET:	Age 4 only — Complete this month and send home.

Optional Project for age 4 : Piggy Bank

Materials needed:

- 64 oz. (½ gal.) Clorox bottles - 1 for each child.
- 1" diameter corks, cut in half - 4 halves for each child.
- Brown construction paper
- Pink construction paper
- Pink pipe cleaners (1 for each child)
- Glue
- Magic markers

Method:

1. Clean bottles before class, remove labels
2. Cut quarter size slot in top (handle side)
3. Cut pink circle to cover top of screw cap for nose; glue in place.
4. Cut brown irregular shapes for spots on body; glue in place.
5. Use magic markers (teacher) to draw eyes under handle location.
6. Poke small hole in flat end for tail. Wrap pipe cleaner around pencil to form coil and insert at least 1" into hole.
7. Attach (glue) corks to bottom for feet.
8. Glue pink ears in place.

April

(1) Calendar Introduce: T	(2) Begin farm unit; animals (cow) Age 4: T page for booklet	(3) (pig) Review: S, T	(4) Begin: U (chicken)	(5) Age 3: Egg hatch Age 4: chicken with egg. U page for booklet
(6) (horse)	(7) Begin: V (goat)	(8) (tractor ducks) Age 4: V page for booklet	(9) Review: U, V Begin: crops, getting fields ready	(10) PLANT SEEDS Begin: W
(11) barn and silo Age 4: W page for booklet	(12) Backyard farmer and care of crop	(13) Farmer with animal. Must care for all	(14) Begin: X (gathering eggs – chores)	(15) Begin unit on transportation — TRUCK crops to market. Age 4: X page for booklet
(16) Review: W, X (train)	(17) Begin: Y (car)	(18) (airplane) Age 4: Y page for booklet	(19) Begin: Z (rocket)	(20) Review: Y, Z (boat) Age 4: Z page for booklet
(21) Easter (See Appendix III)		Craft items: Paper fasteners Cotton balls Lima beans Dixie cups Vermiculite		

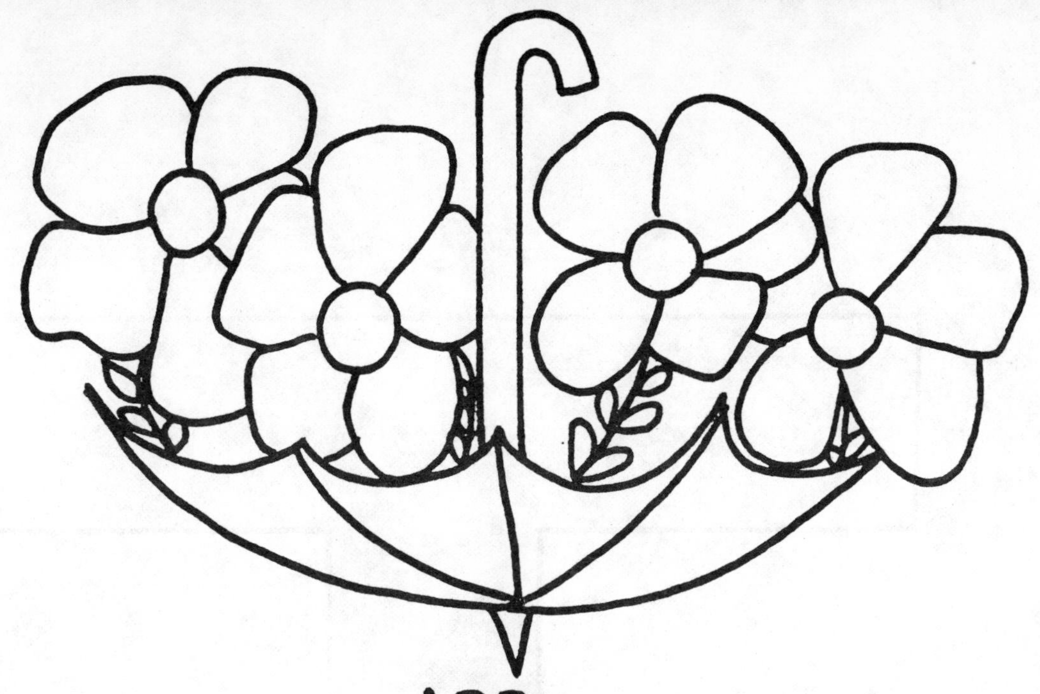

APRIL

SUN.	MON.	TUES.	WED.	THURS.	FRI.	SAT.

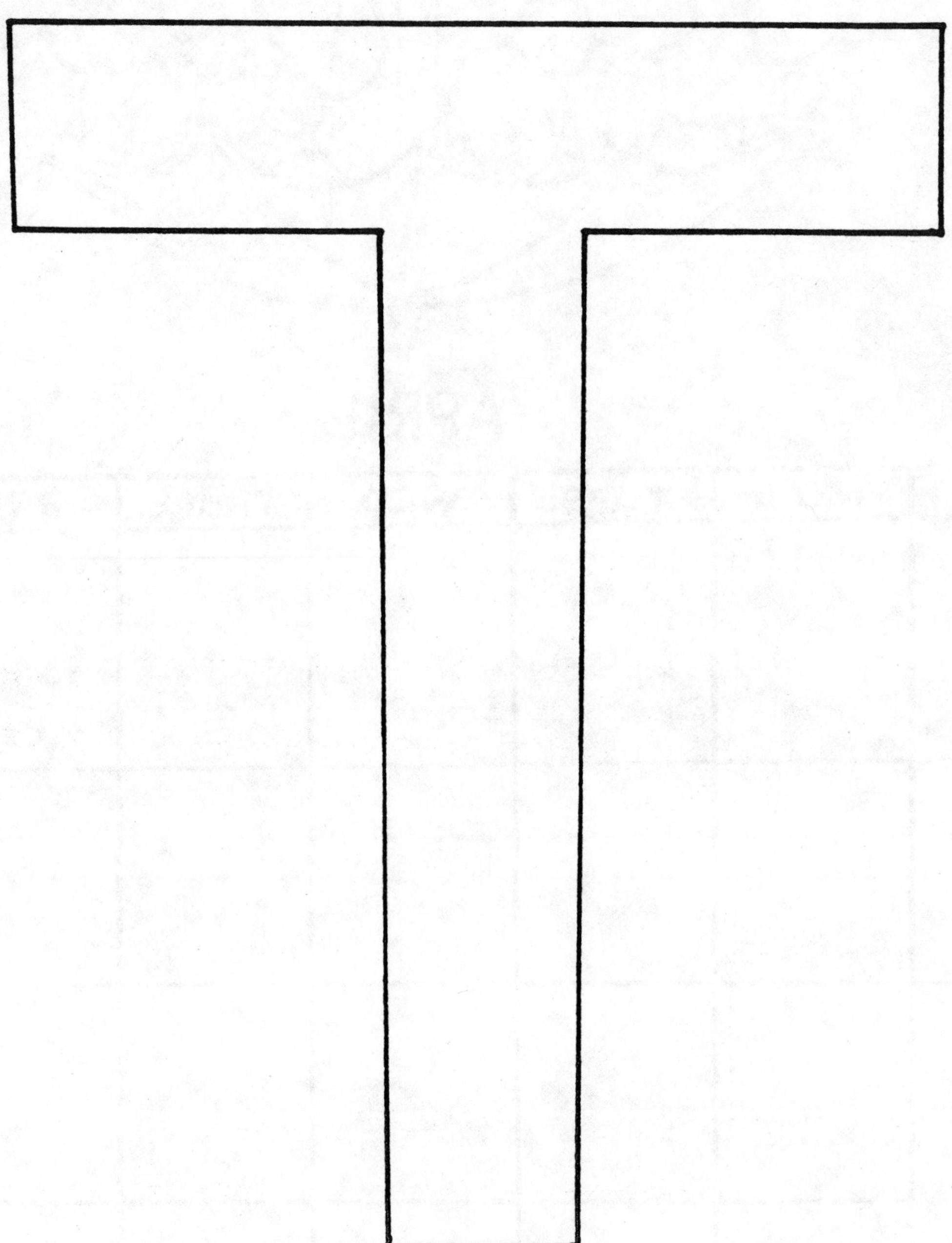

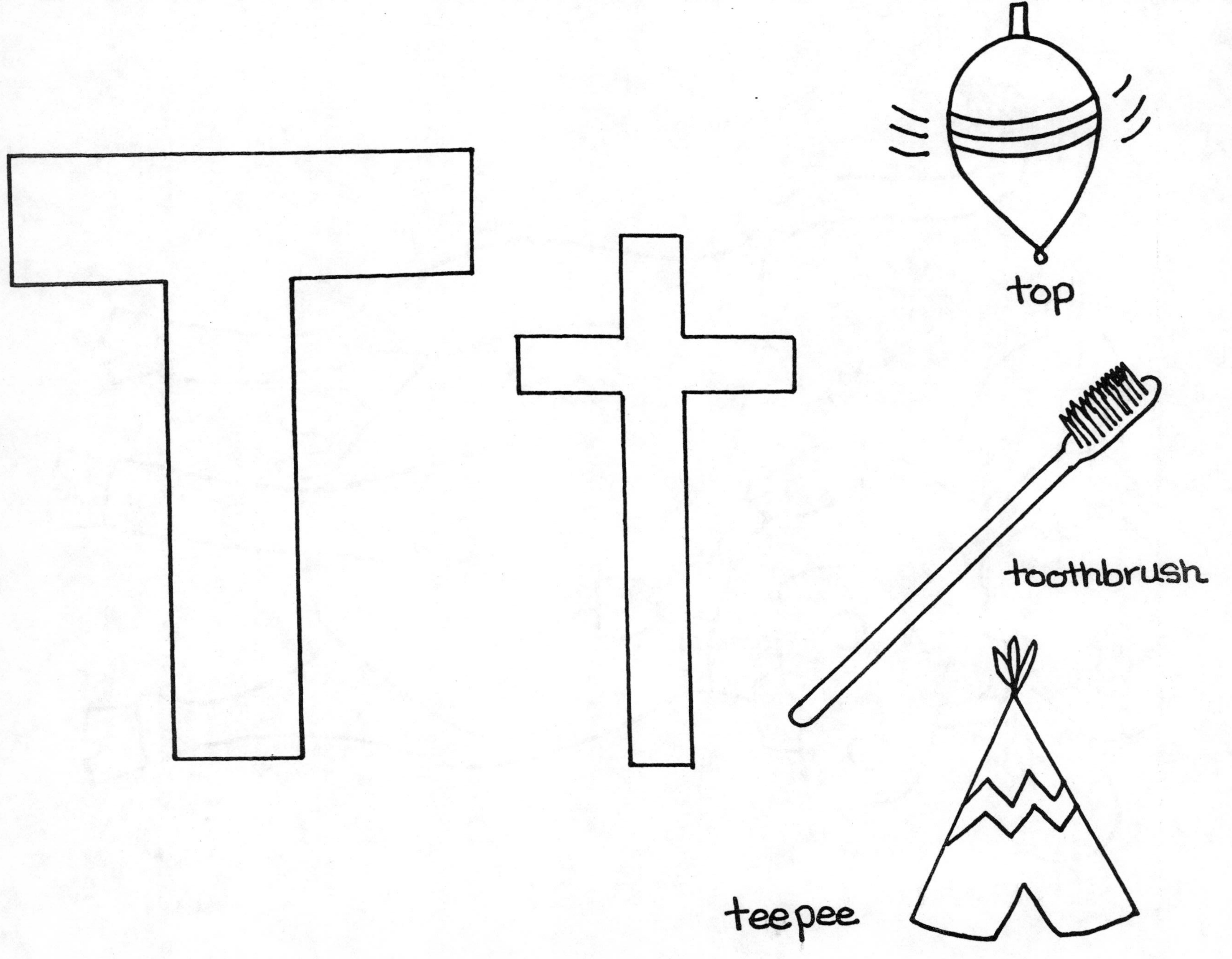

4①

COW

COW

PIGS

PIG

turtle

3③

S
sun
star
snake
T
tack
turtle
teepee
4③

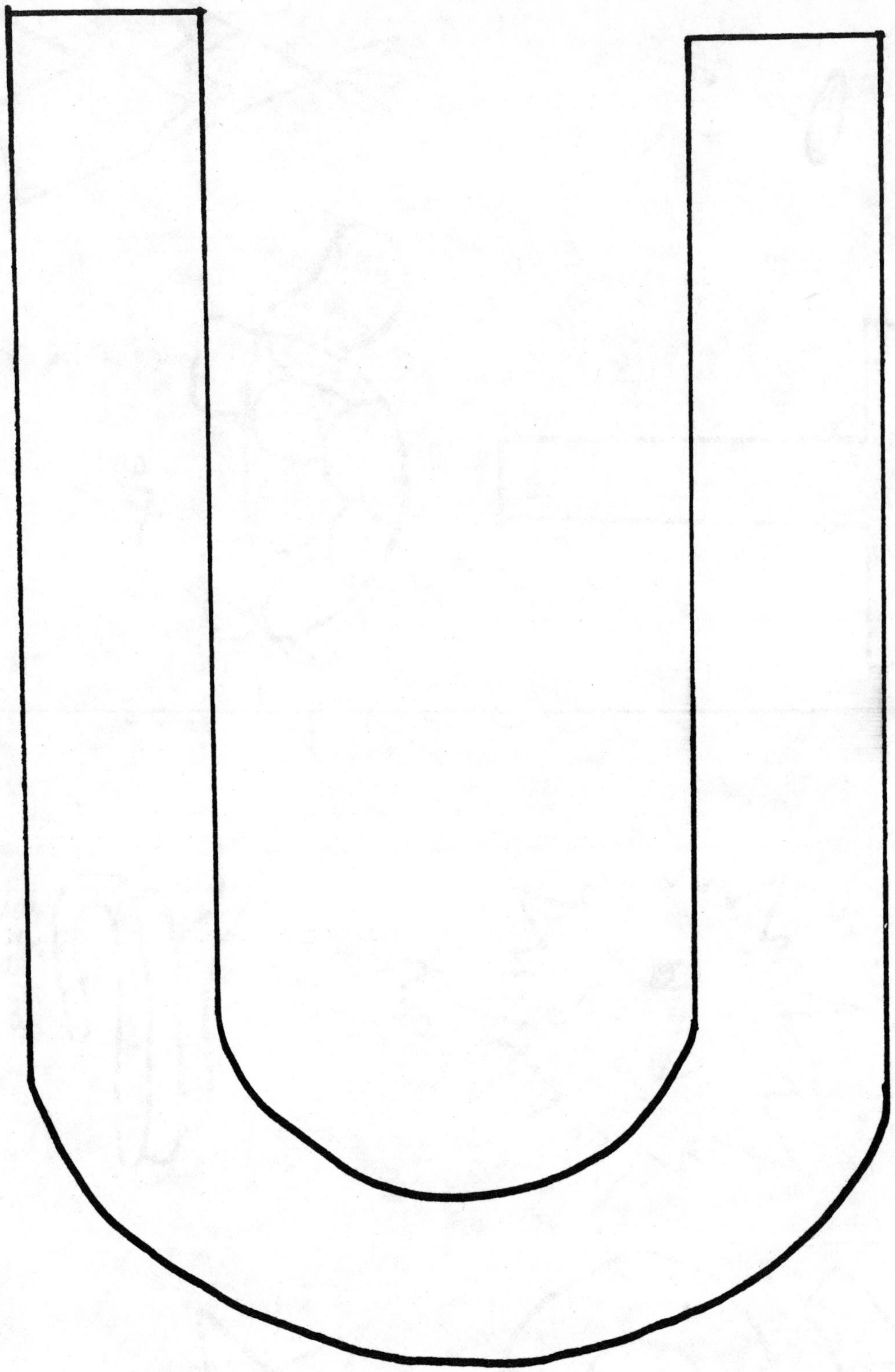

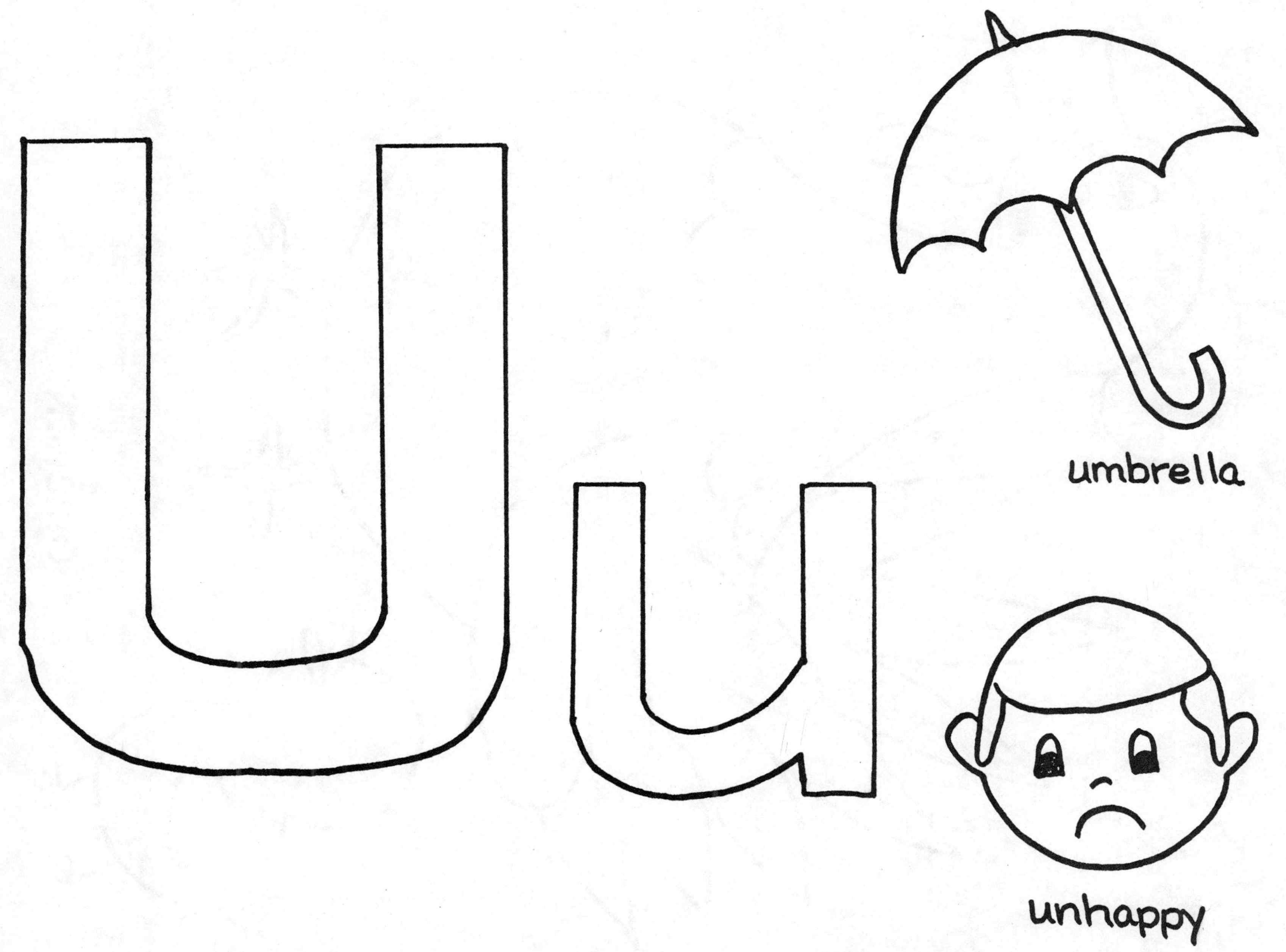
umbrella
unhappy

CHICKEN

CHICKEN

BABY CHICK

Cut out-paste
egg under wing;
attach wing with brad.
4 ⑤
See second
sheet for egg
cut-out

fold
fold

36

HORSE

HORSE

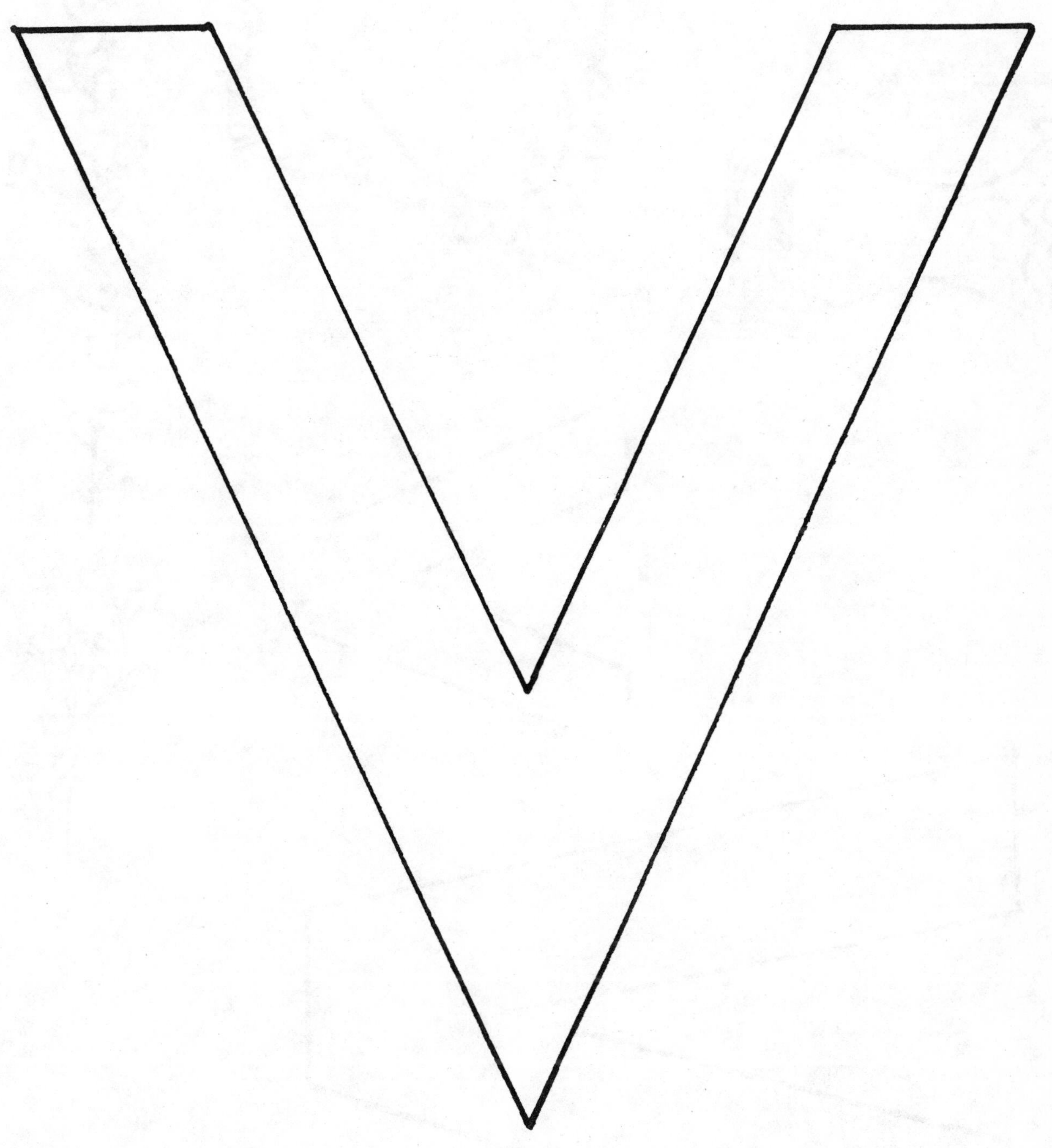

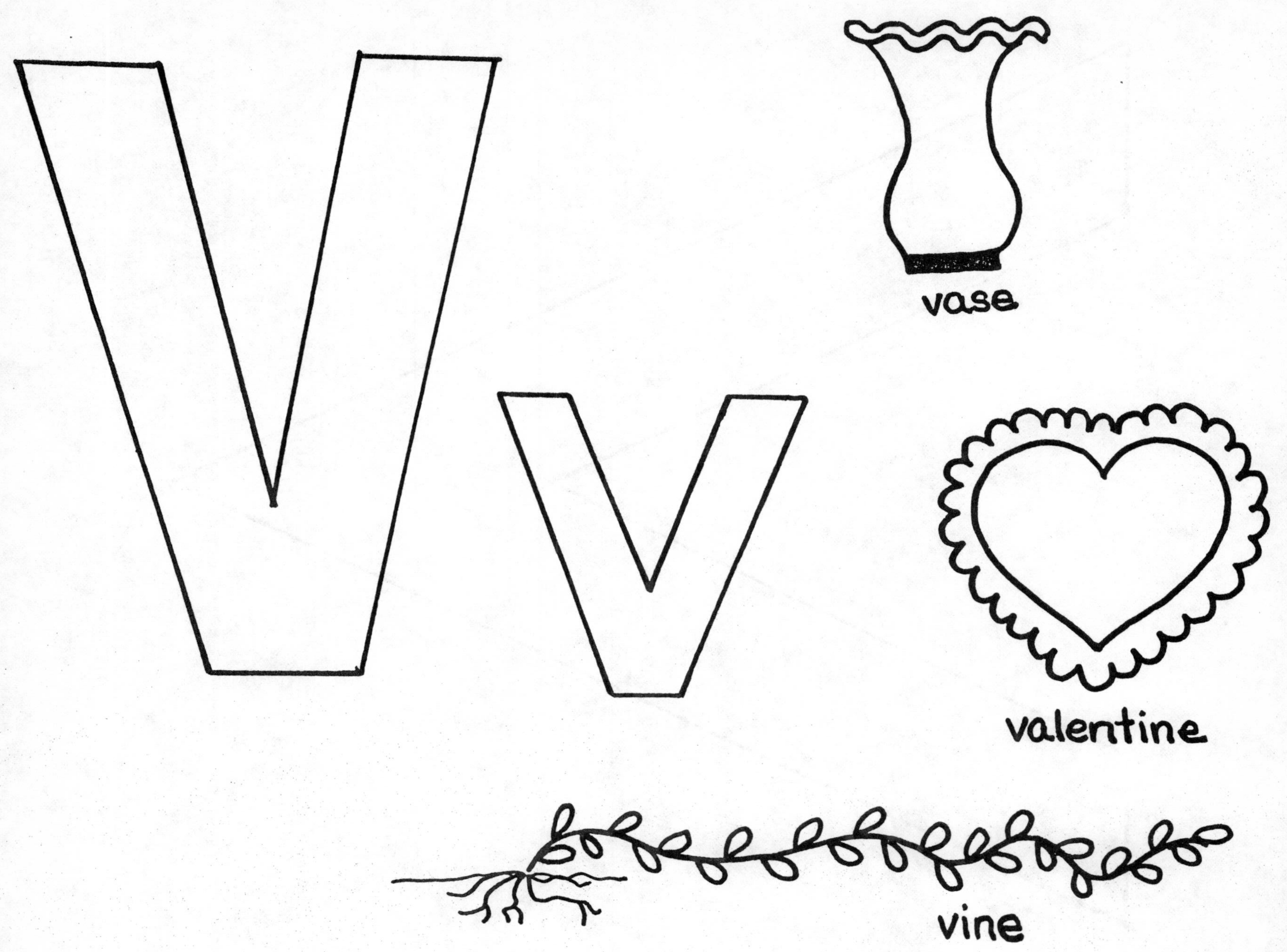
vase
valentine
vine

GOAT

GOAT

TRACTOR

4 8
TRACTOR

DUCK

DUCKS

4(8)

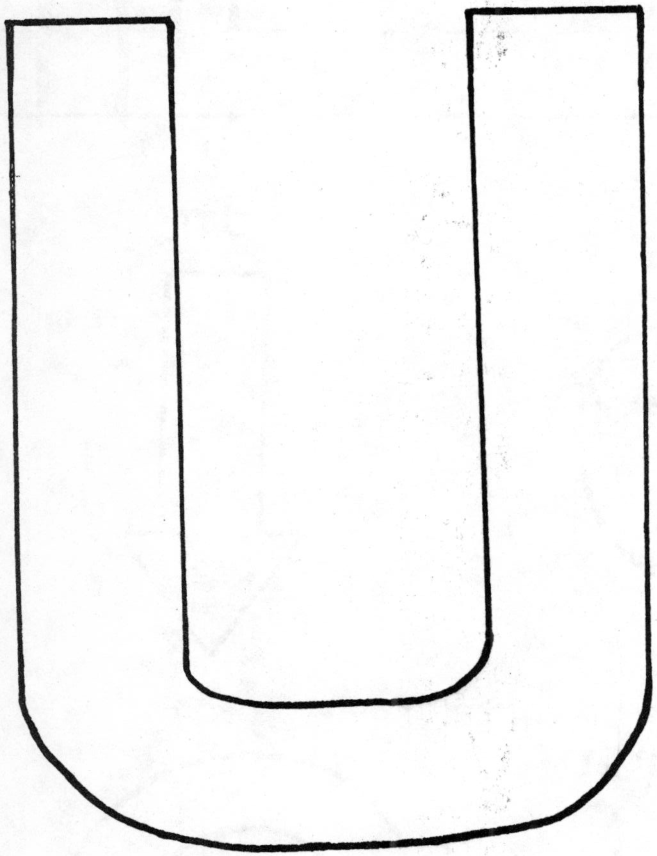

U

V

umbrella

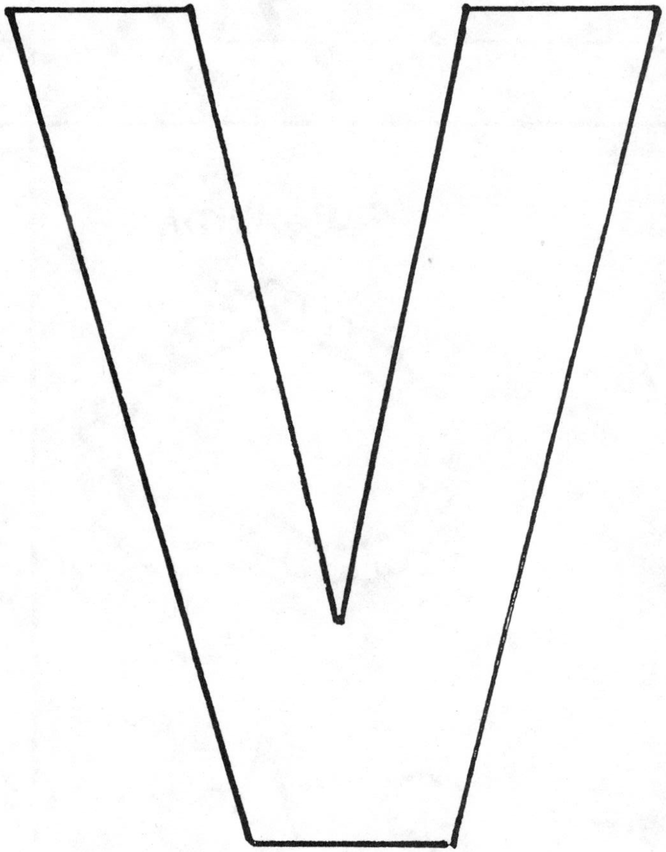

valentine

REVIEW

39

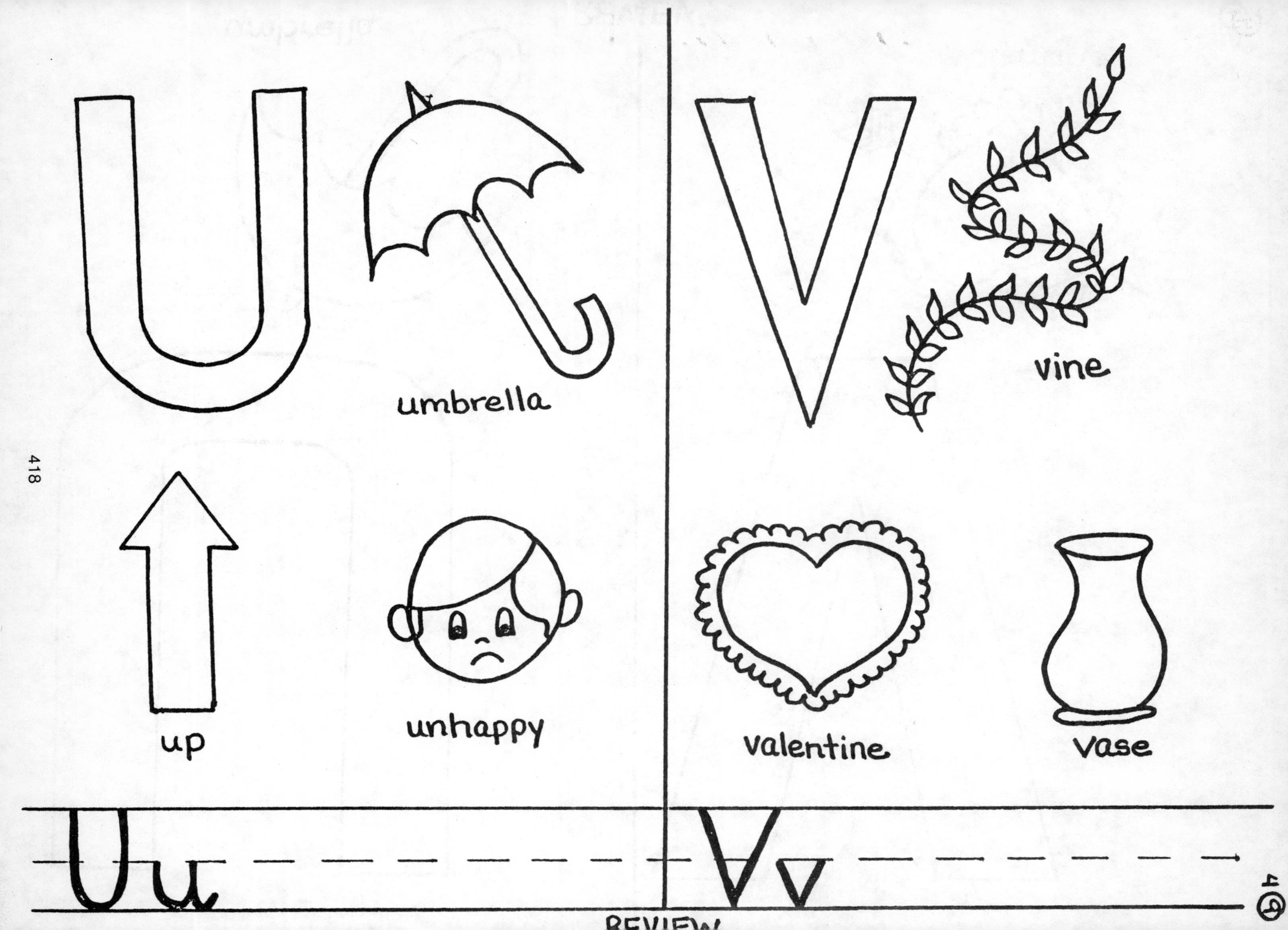
U
umbrella
up
unhappy
V
vine
valentine
vase
Uu
Vv
REVIEW
4 9

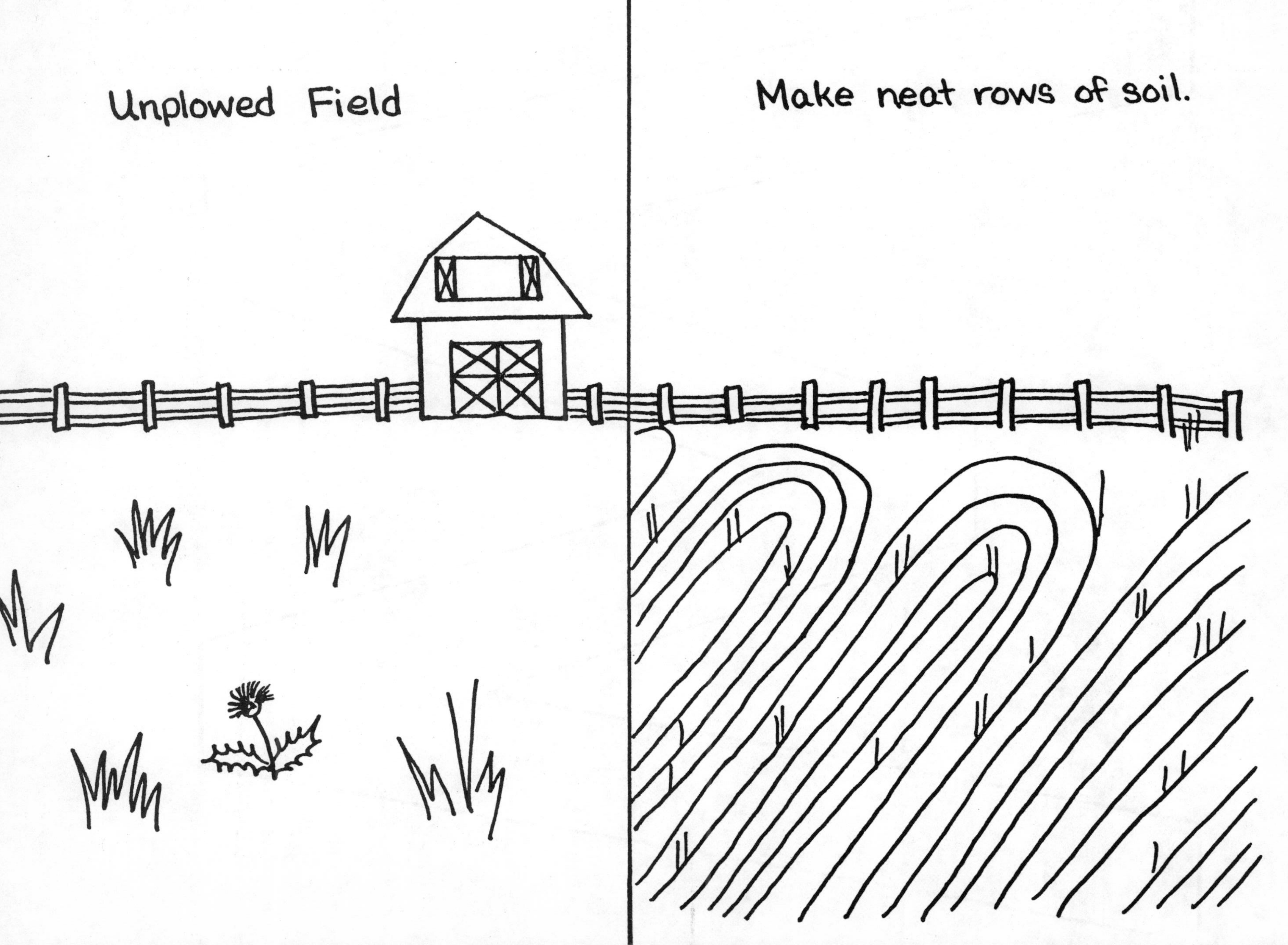
Unplowed Field
Make neat rows of soil.

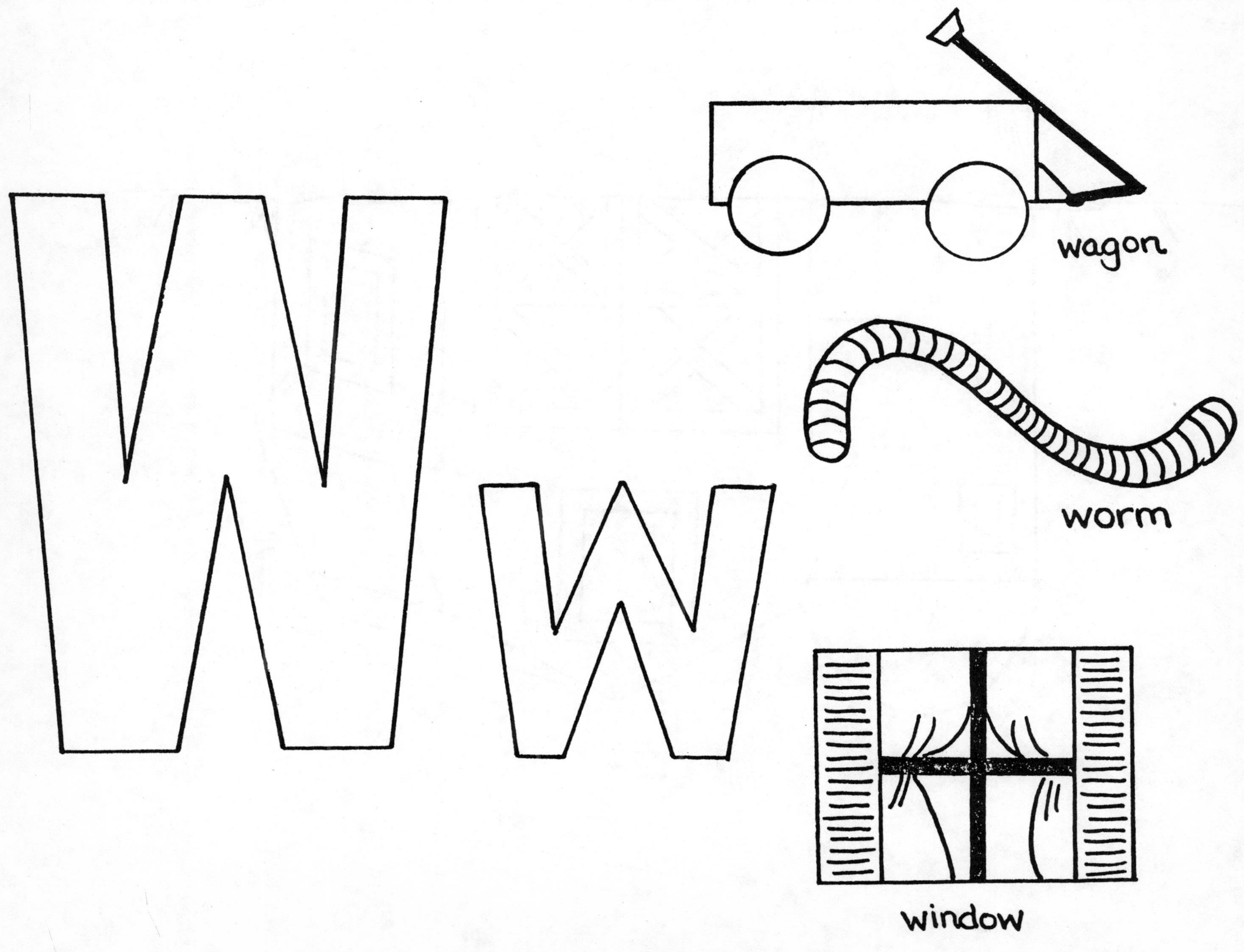
W w
wagon
worm
window

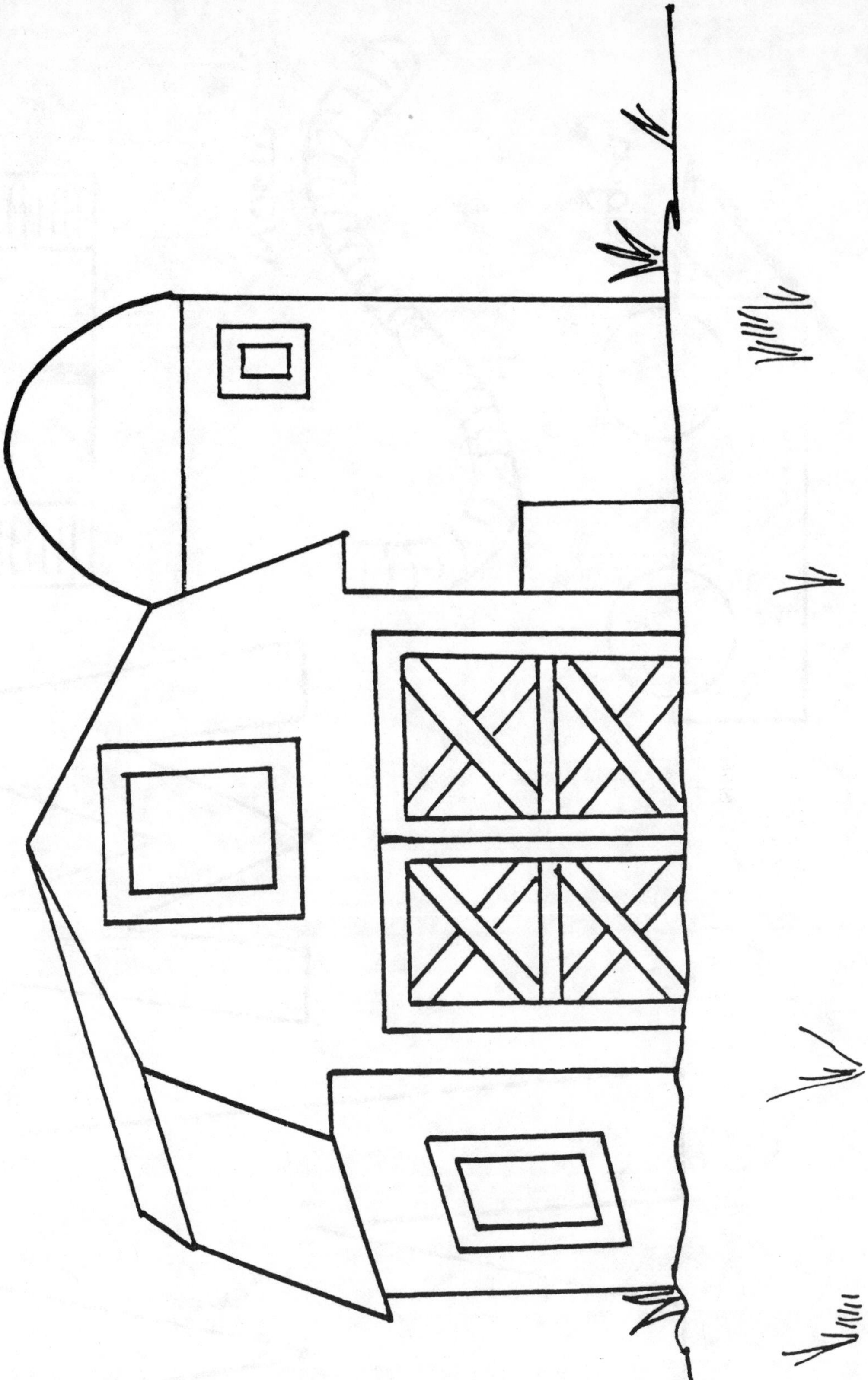

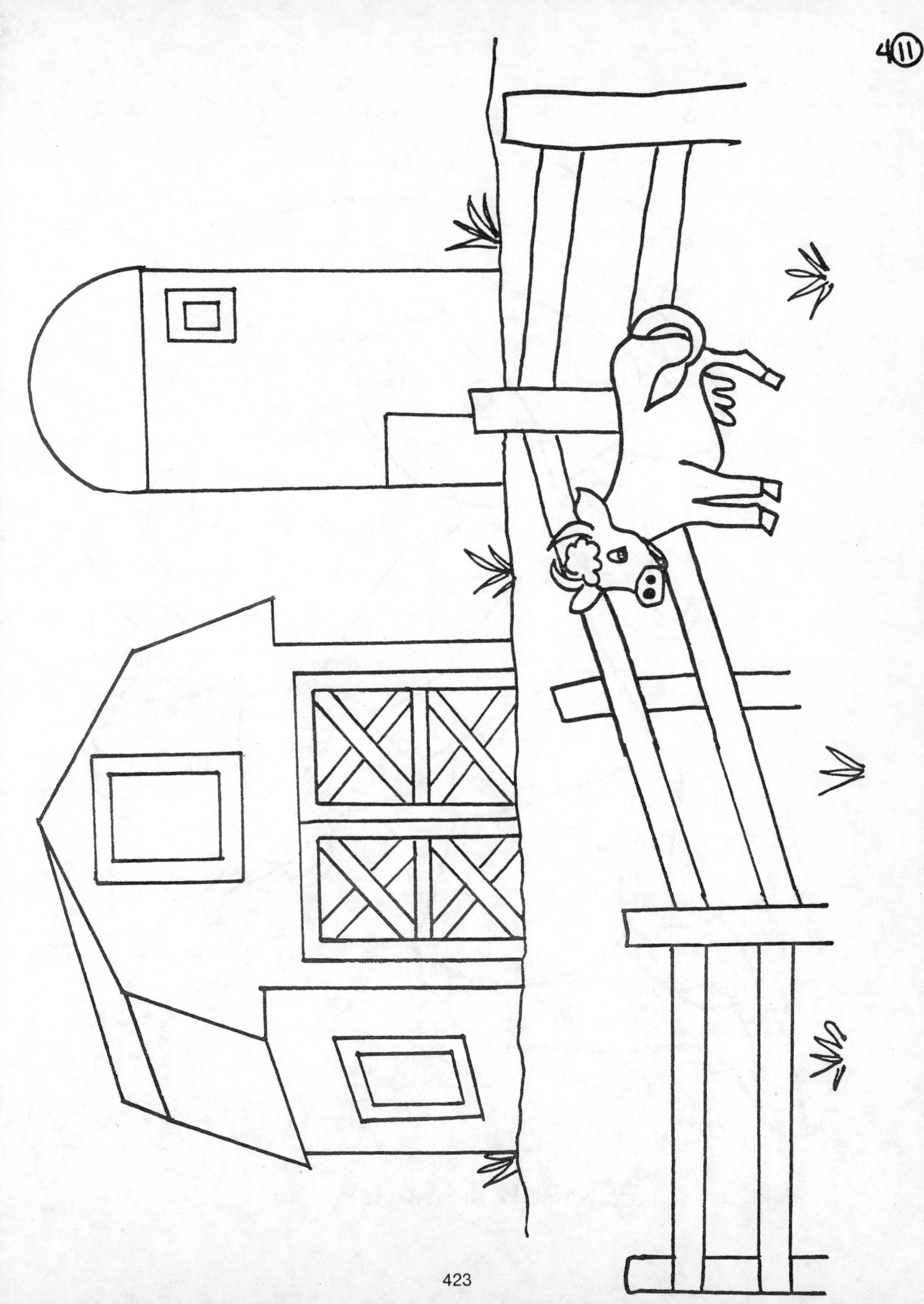

BACKYARD FARMER

BACKYARD FARMER

3 (14)

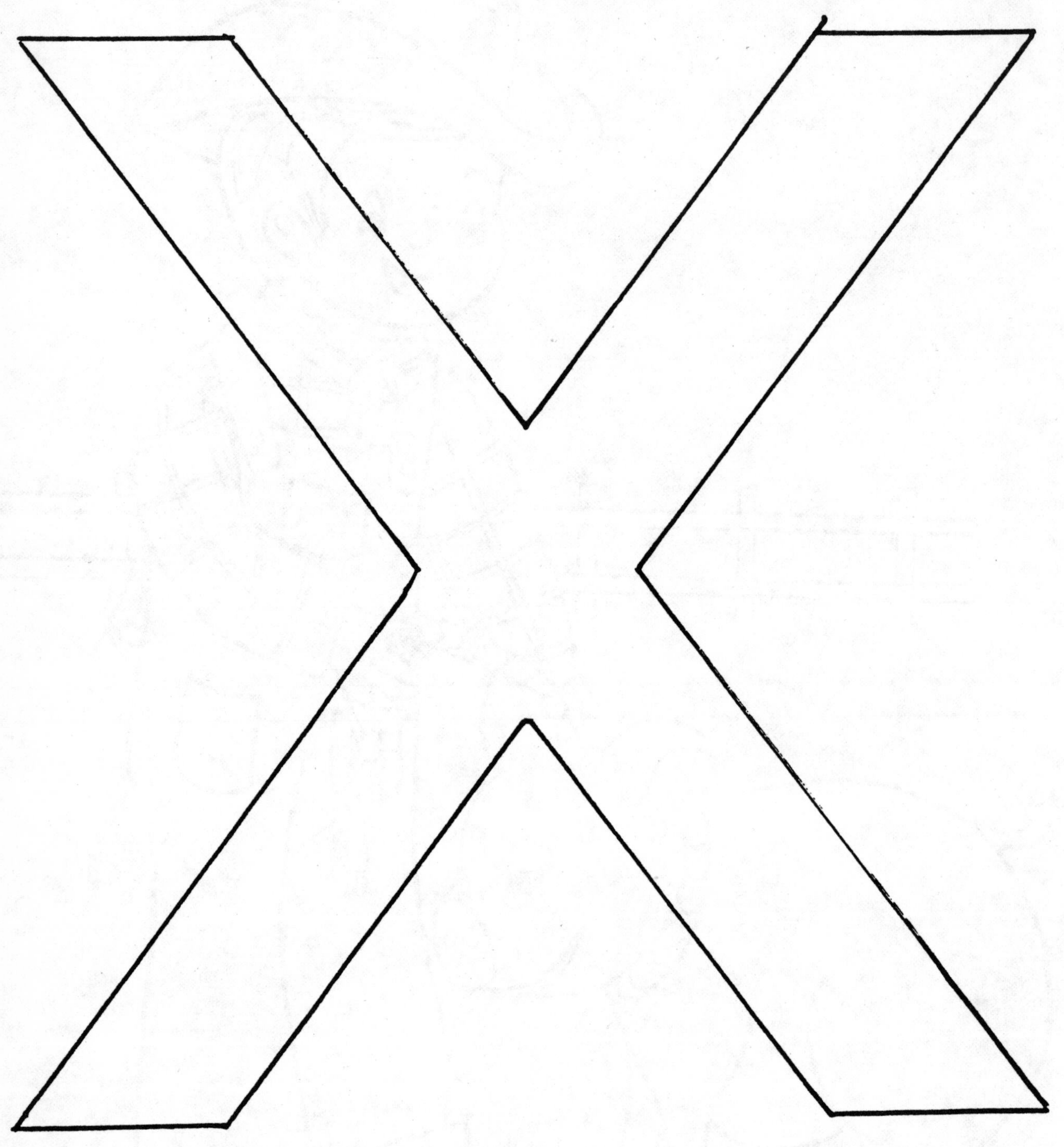

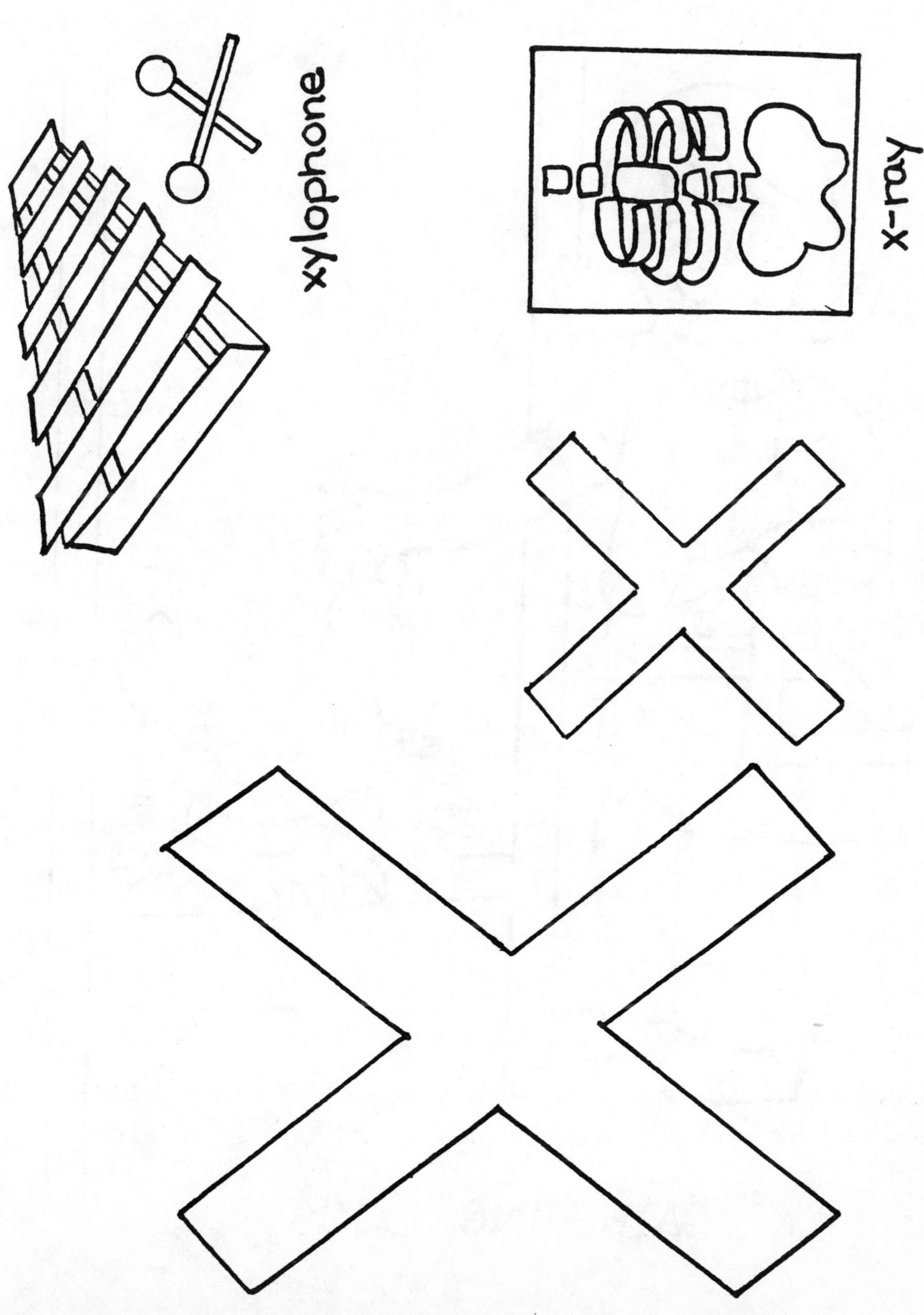
xylophone
x-ray

GATHERING EGGS

GATHERING EGGS

ACE
PRODUCE

TRAIN

Attach cotton balls for puffs of smoke.

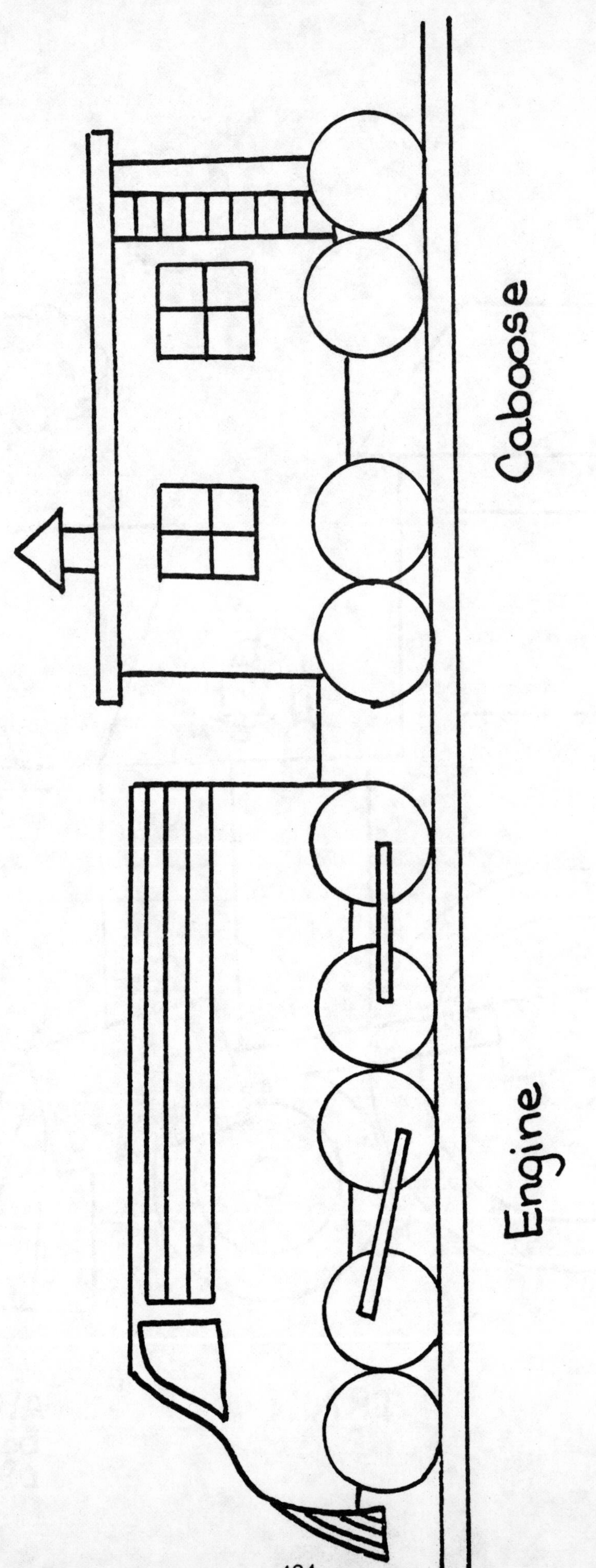

TRAIN

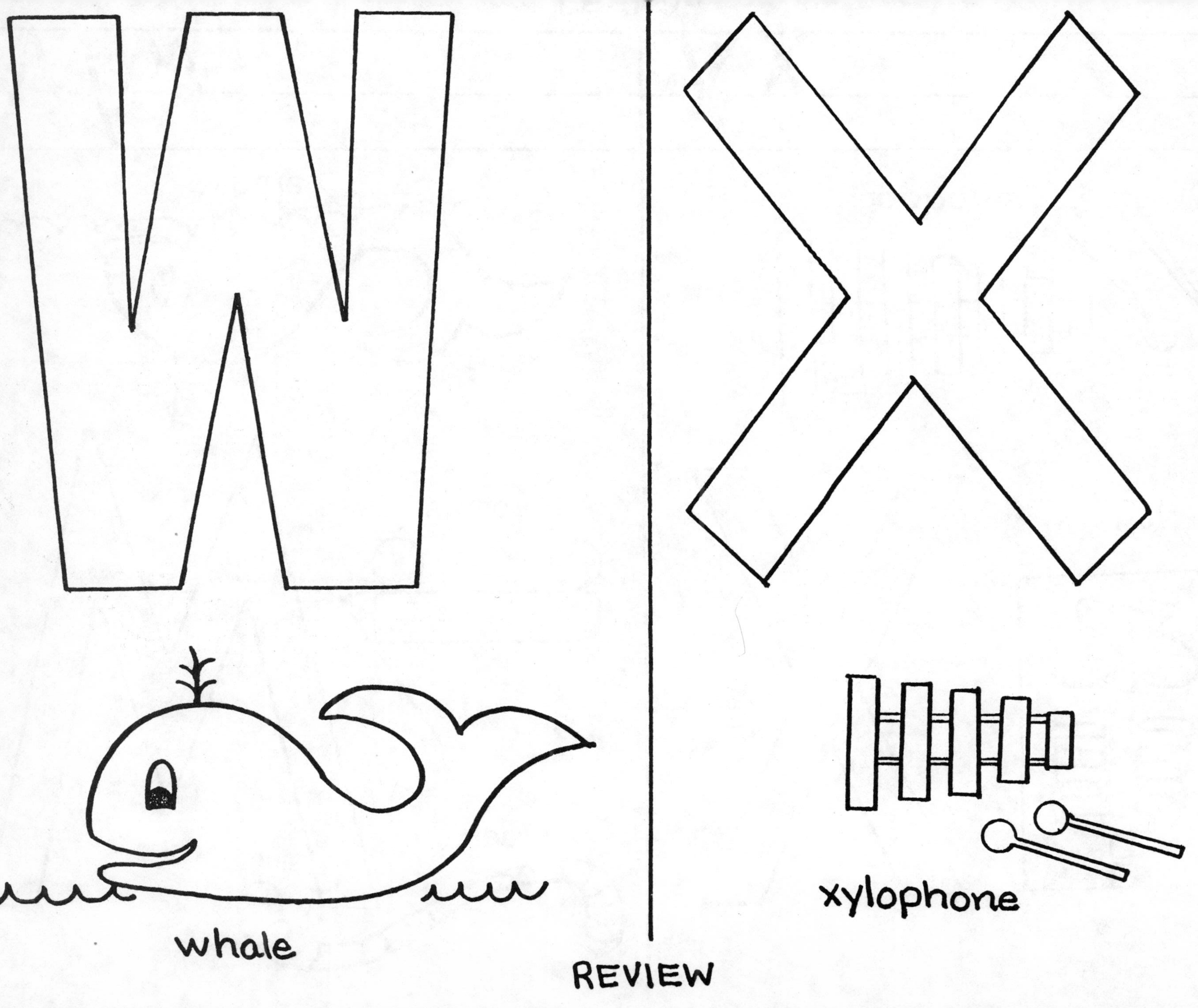

REVIEW

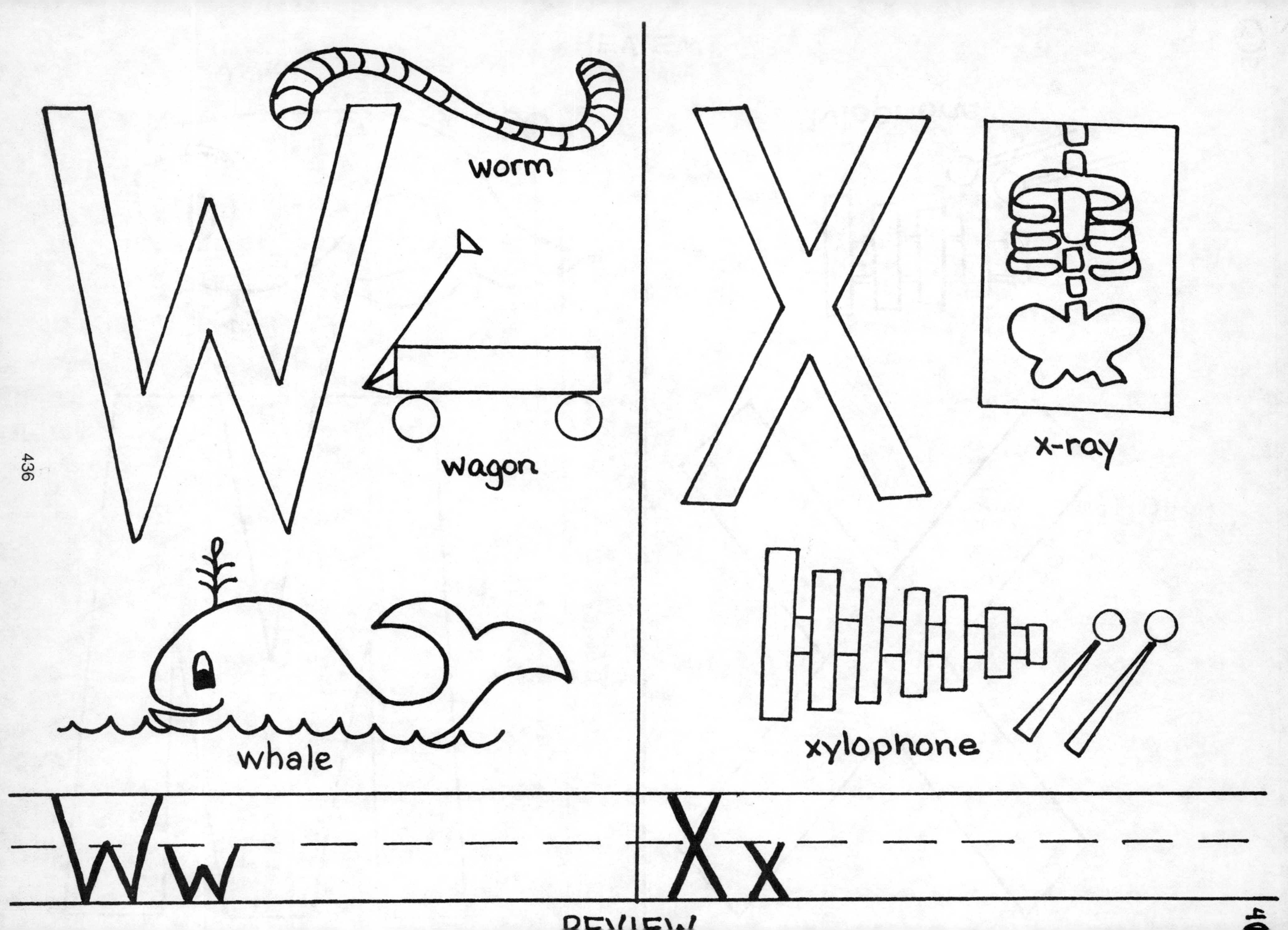

REVIEW

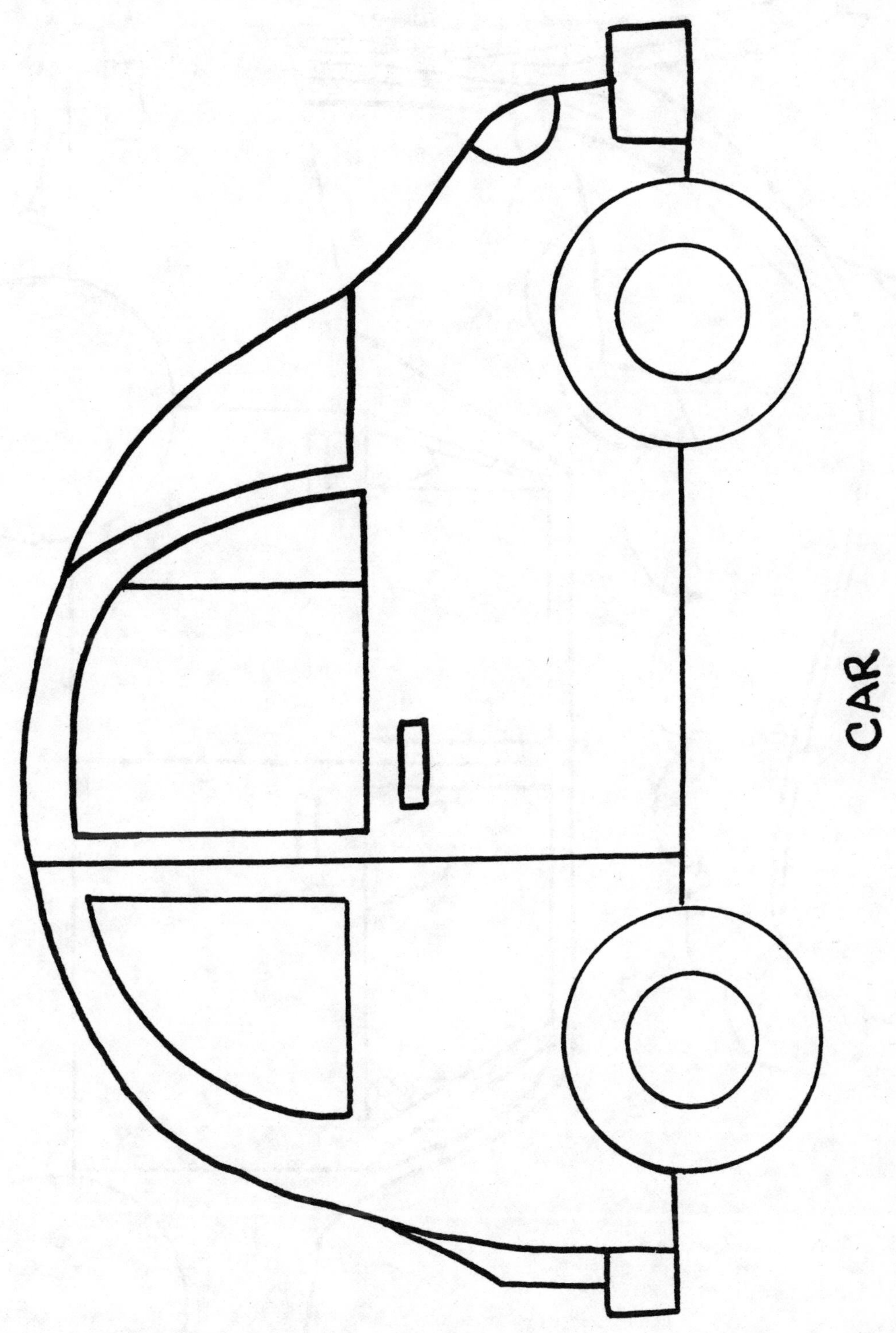
CAR

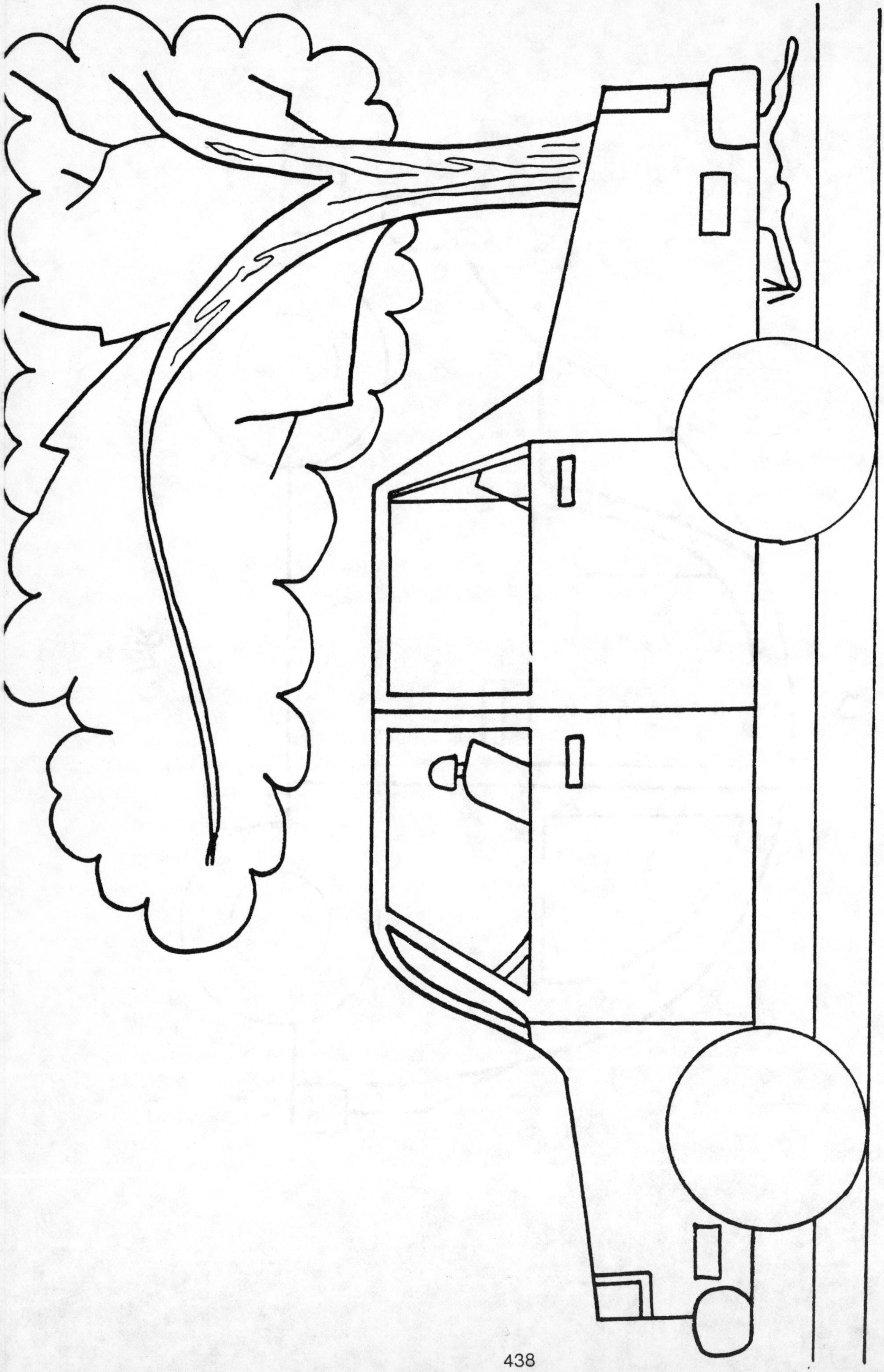

FAMILY CAR

4⑰

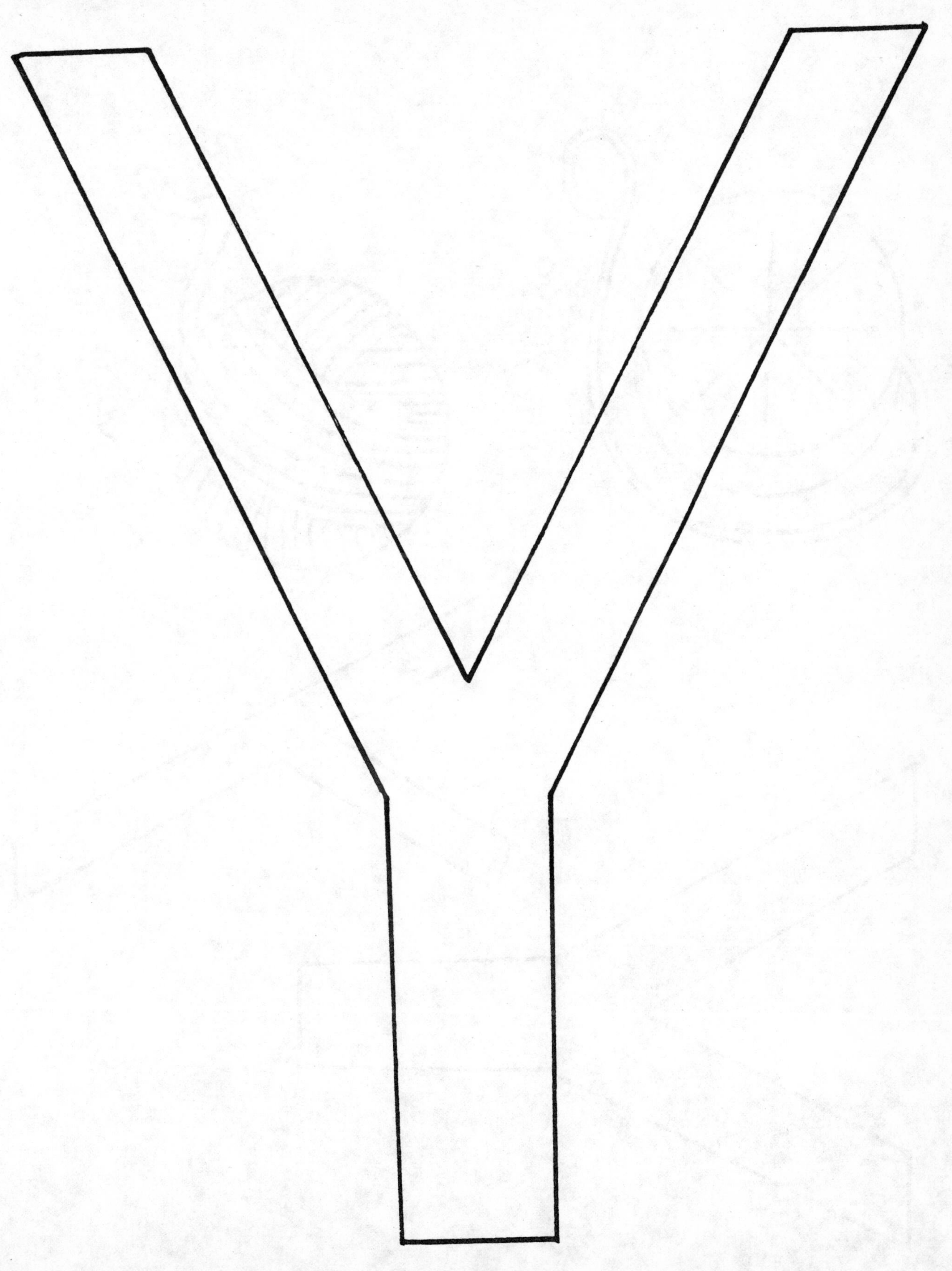

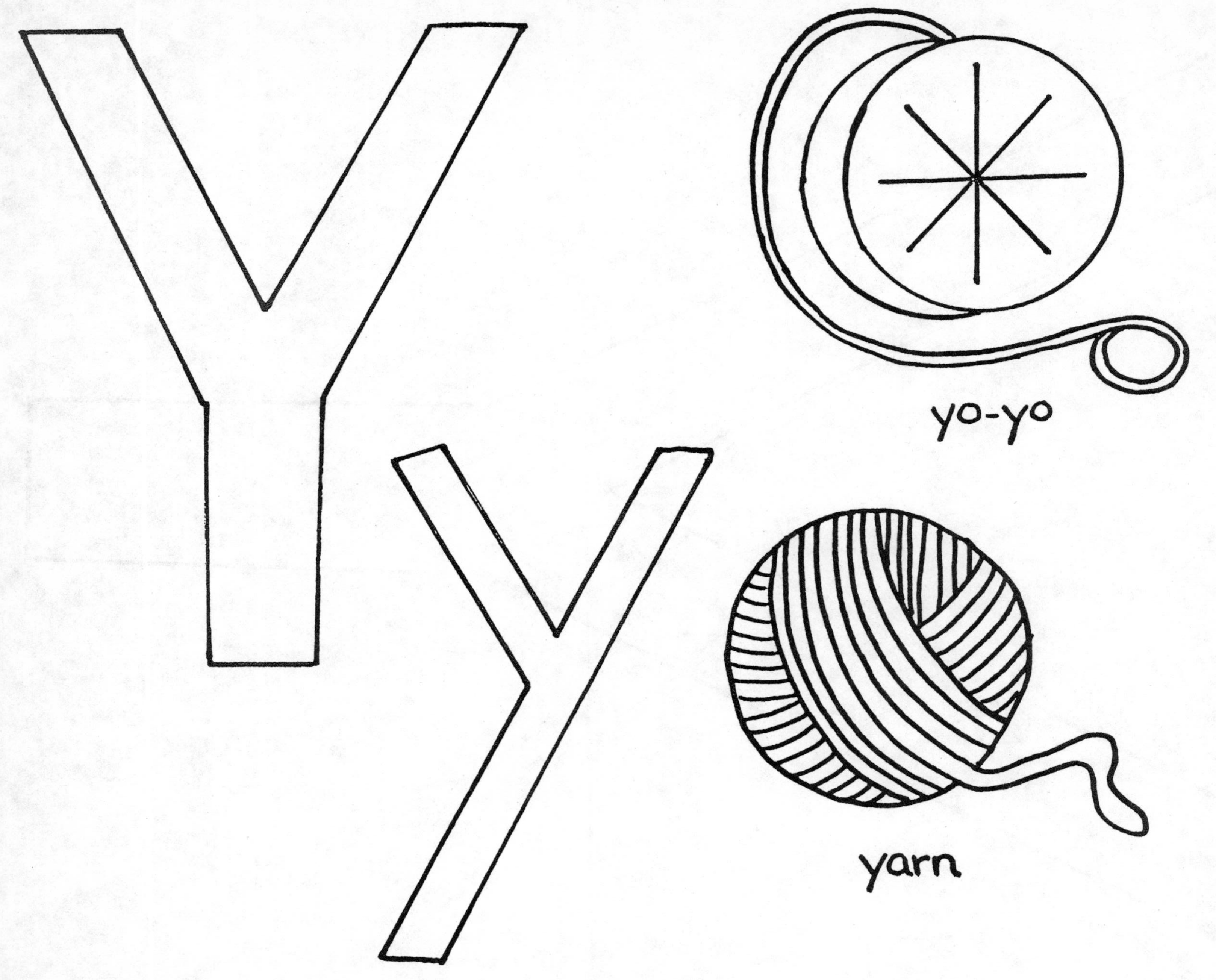
Y y
yo-yo
yarn

AIRPLANE

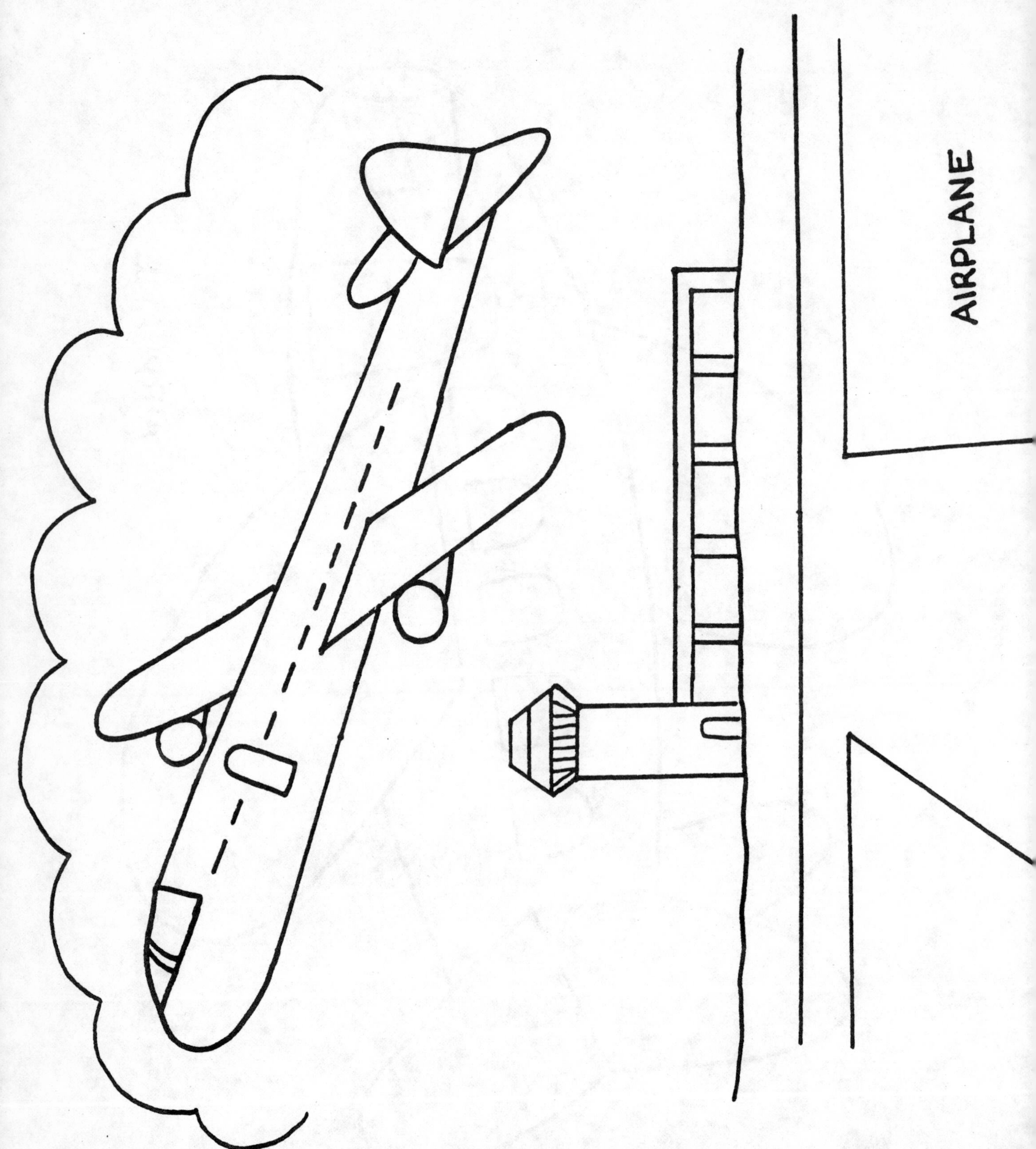
AIRPLANE

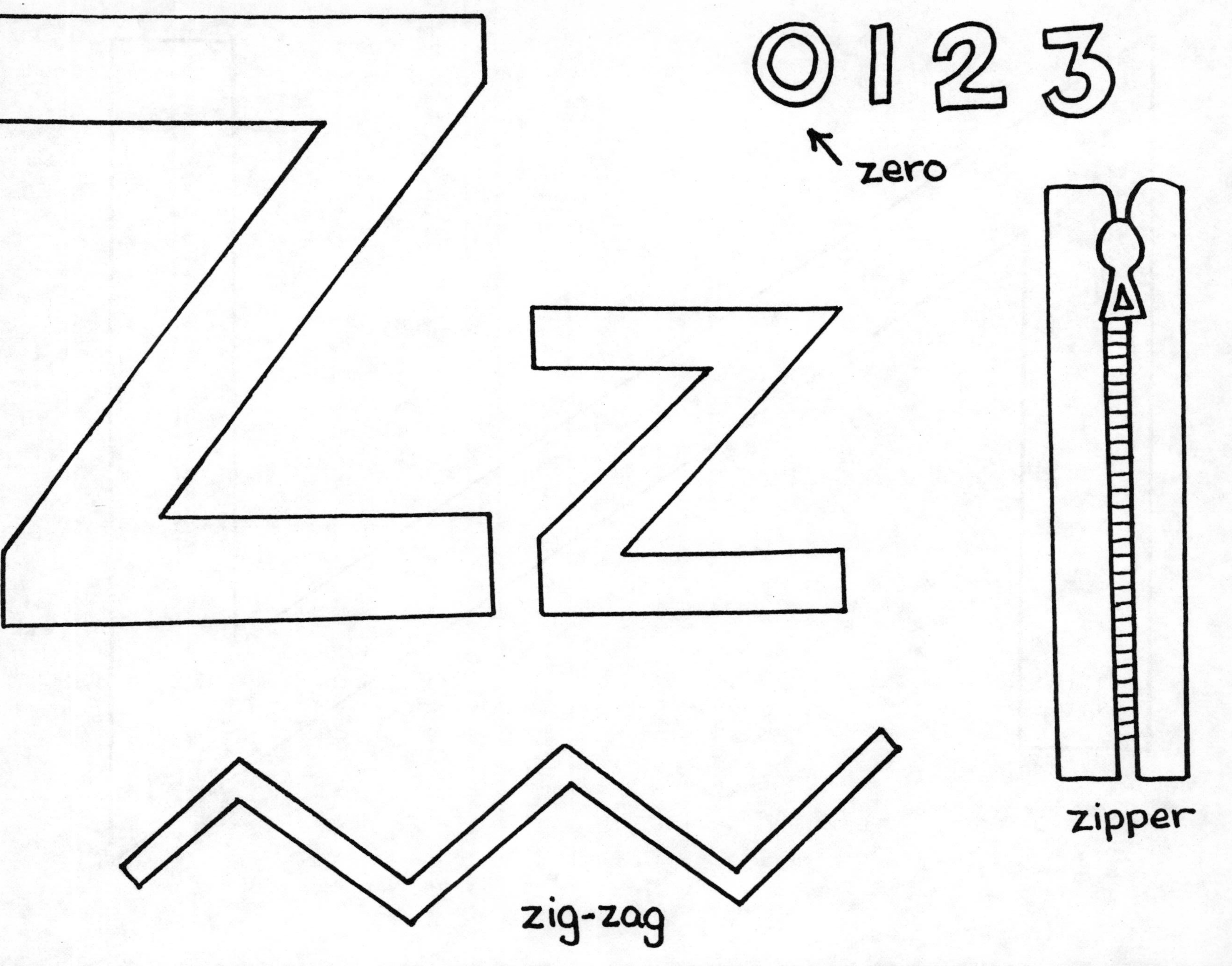
0 1 2 3
zero
zipper
zig-zag

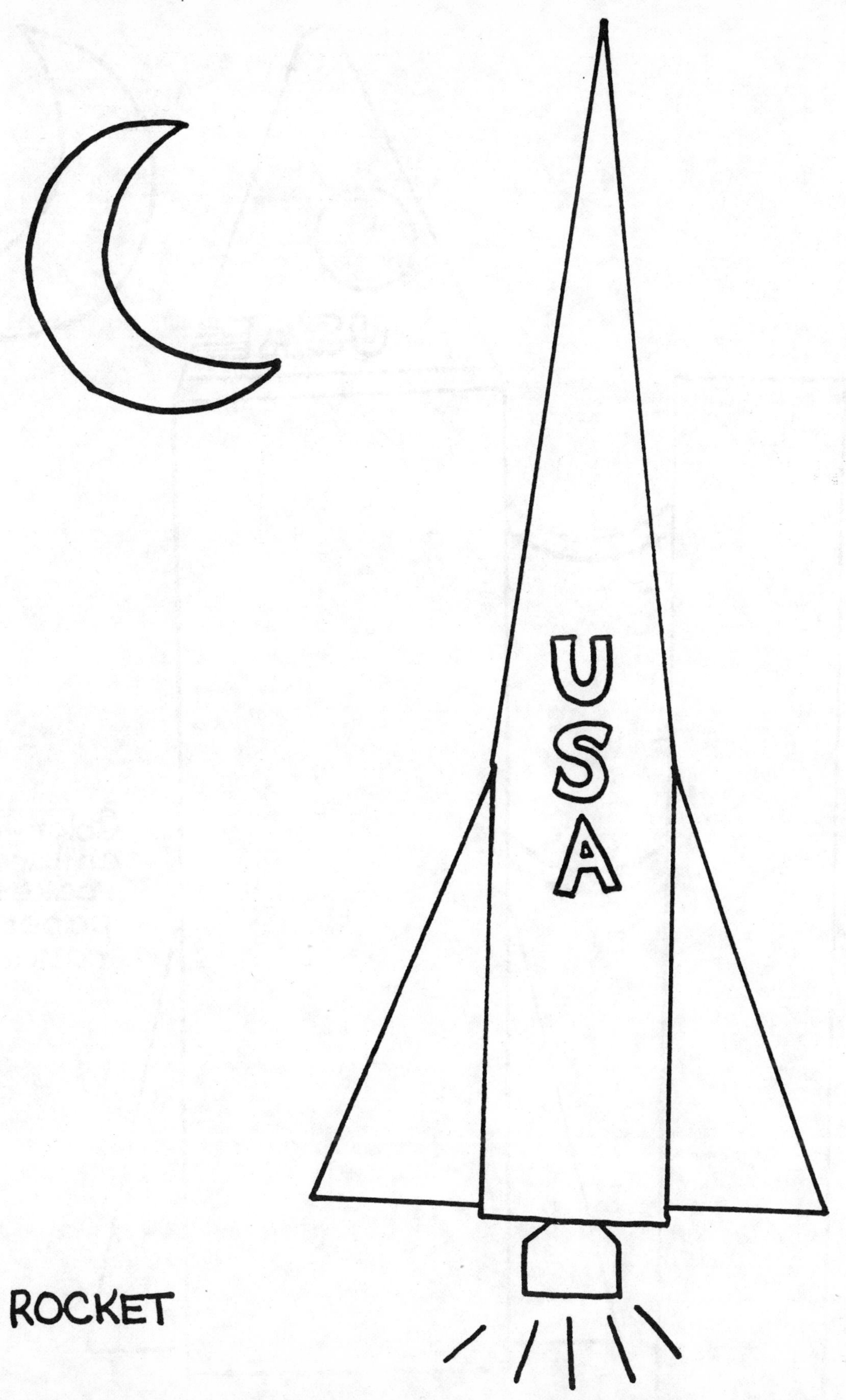
USA
ROCKET

4 (19)

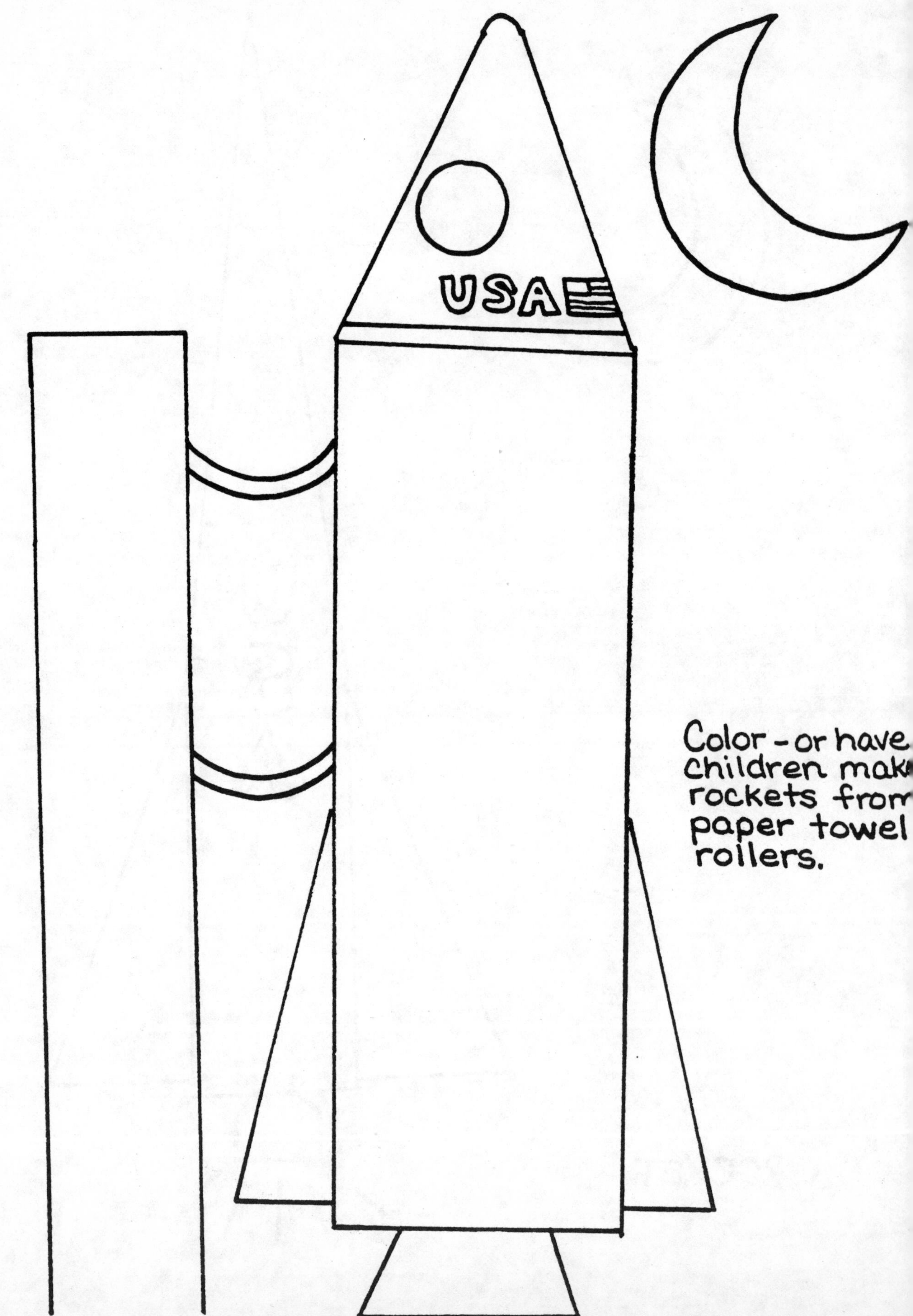
USA
Color - or have
children mak
rockets fro
paper towel
rollers.

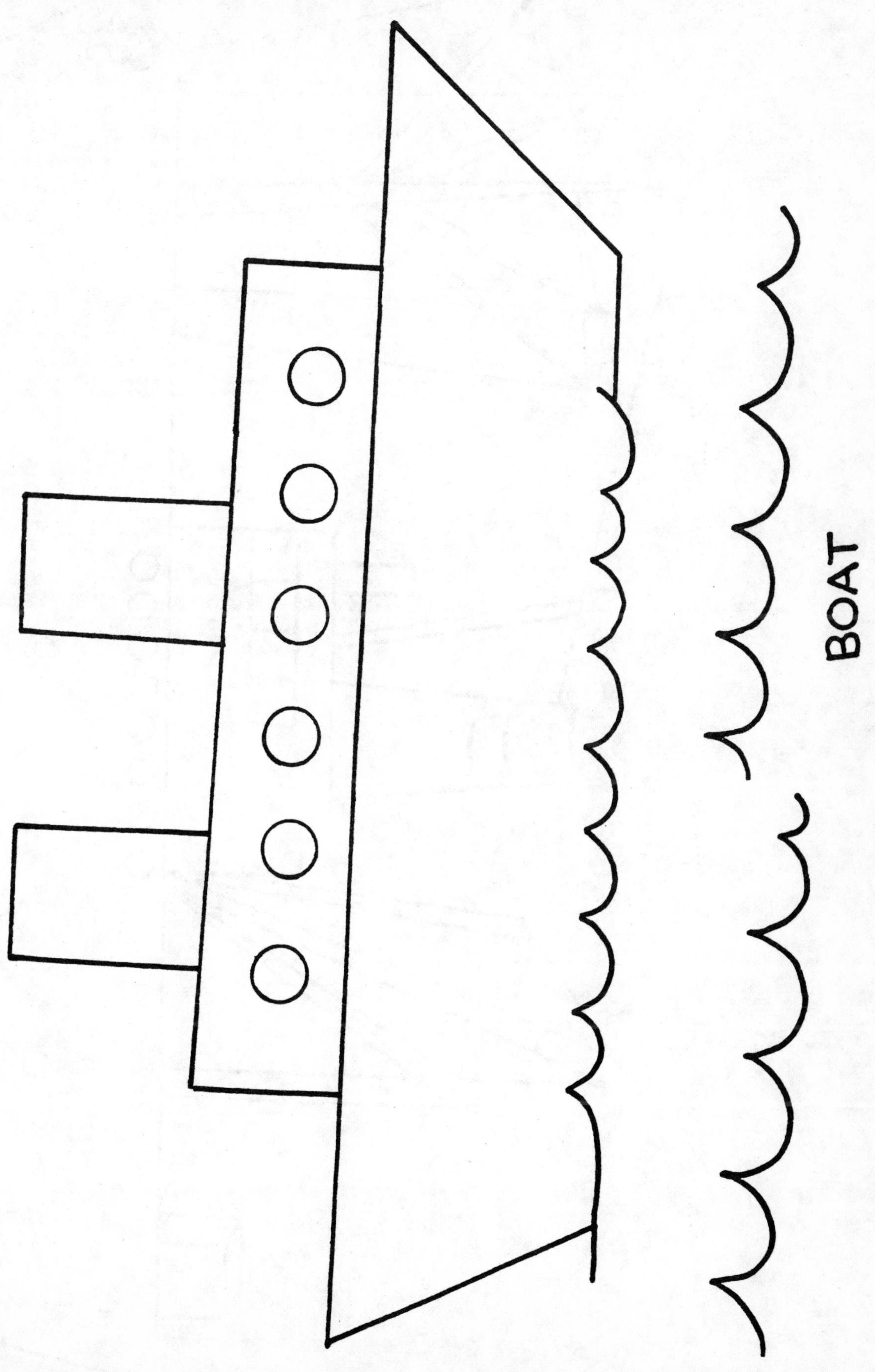
BOAT

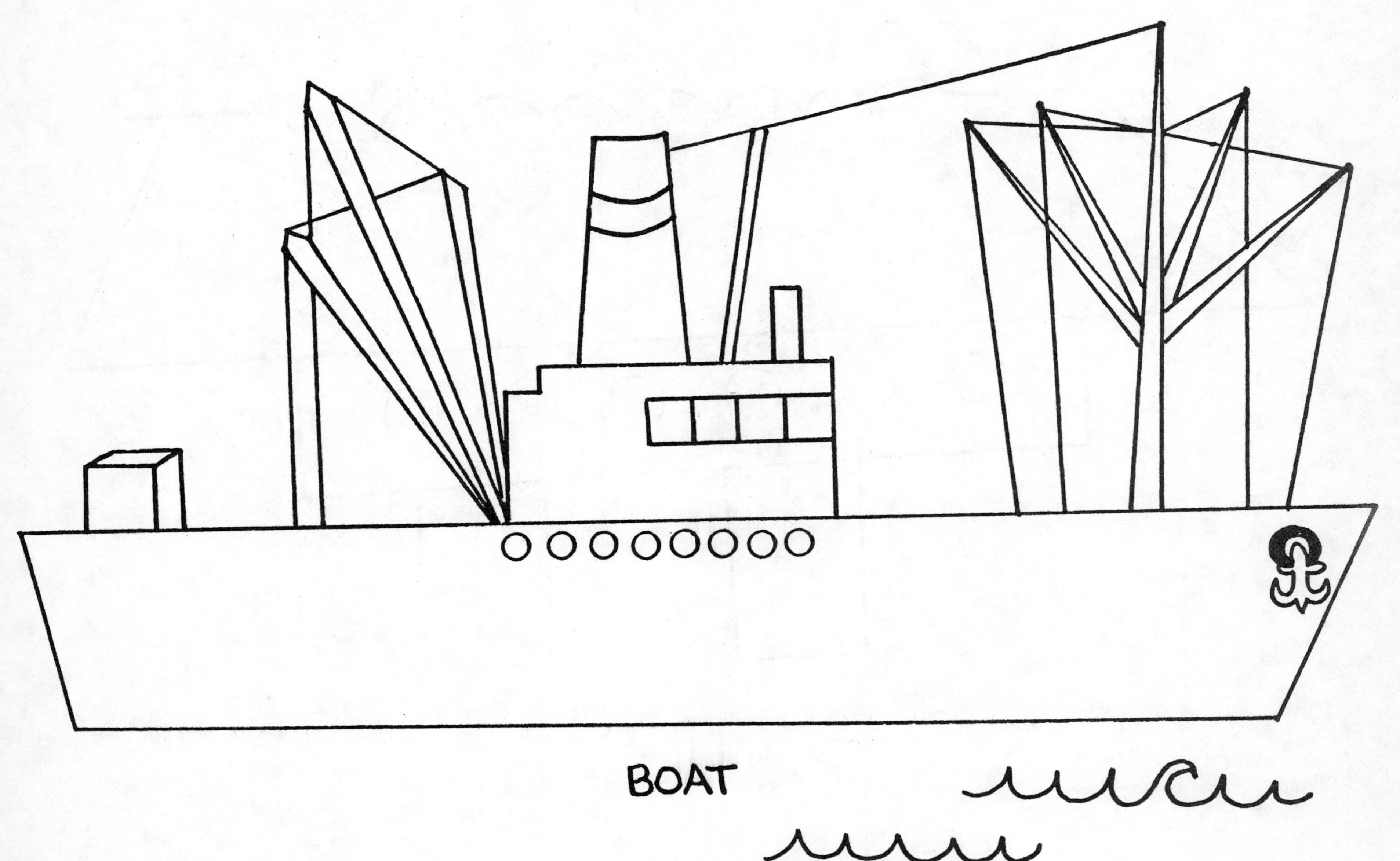
BOAT

yo-yo

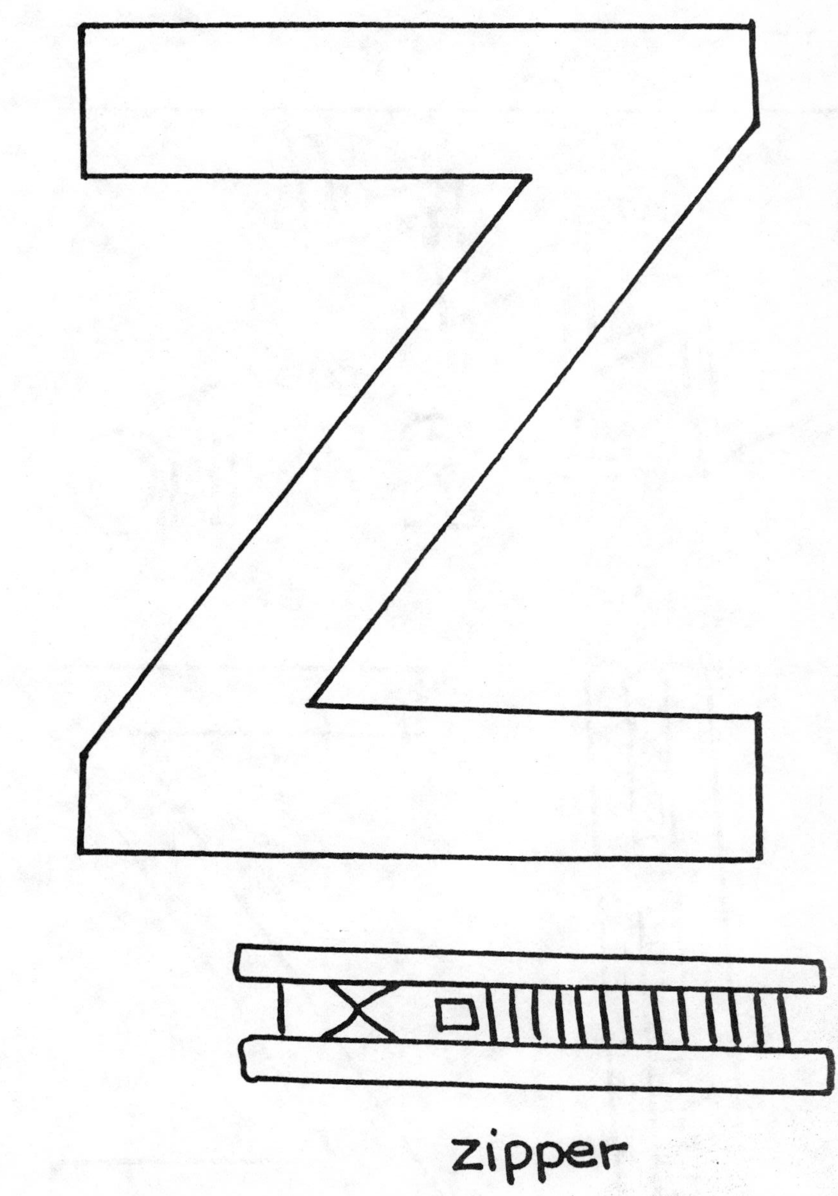
zipper

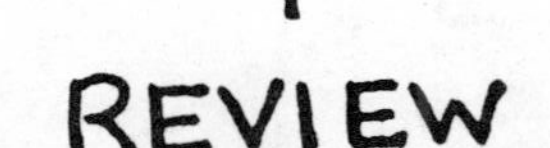
REVIEW

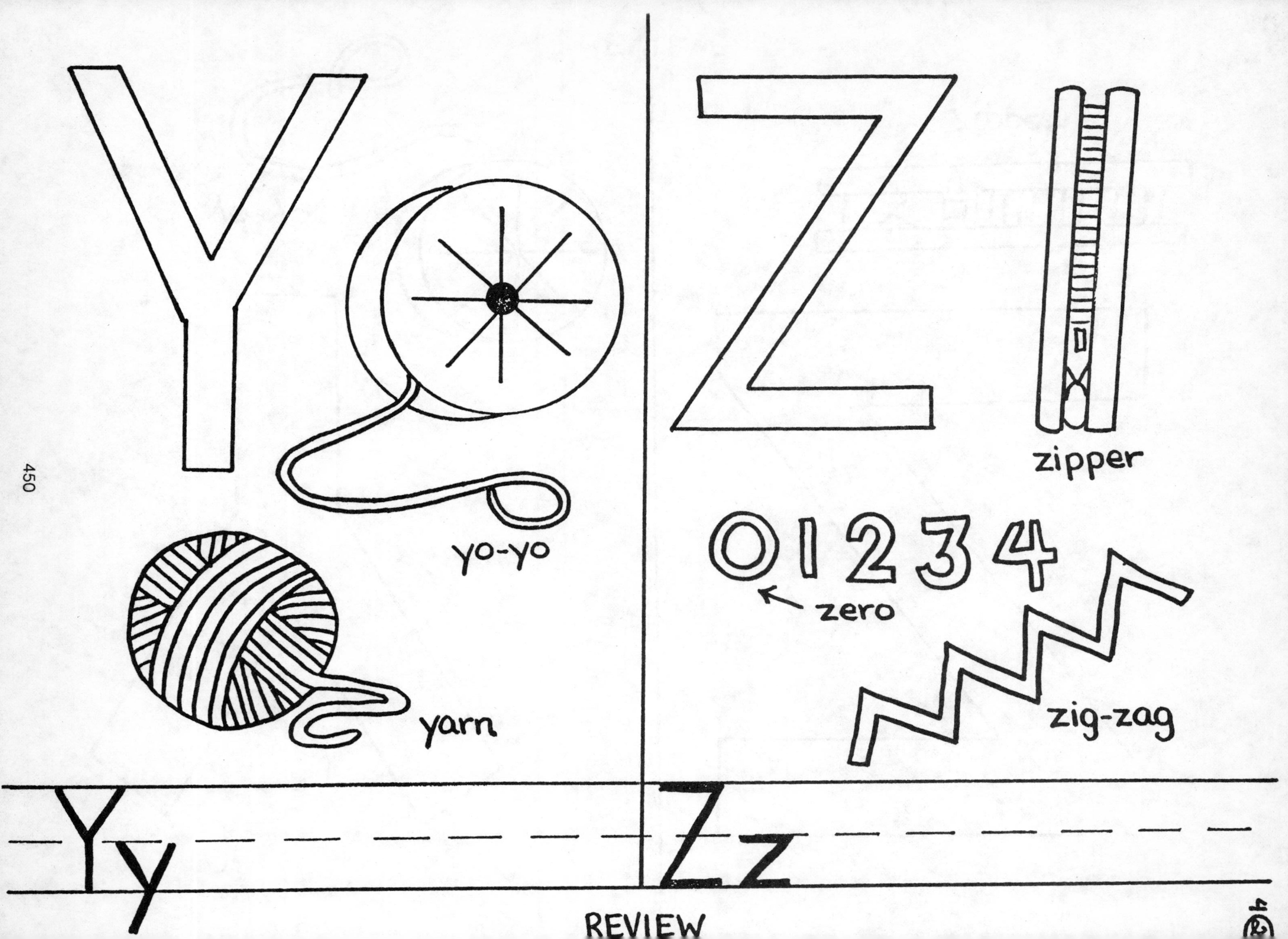
Y
Z
yo-yo
yarn
zipper
0 1 2 3 4
zero
zig-zag
Yy
Zz
REVIEW
4

MAY UNITS:

I. Color Review
- **A.** Review basic primary colors and secondary colors.
- **B.** Check for child's ability to differentiate red/green, blue/purple.
- **C.** Colors reviewed
  1. Red
  2. Yellow
  3. Blue
  4. Green
  5. Orange
  6. Purple
  7. Brown
  8. Black

II. Shape Review
- **A.** Review four basic shapes
- **B.** Shapes covered
  1. Circle
  2. Square
  3. Triangle
  4. Rectangle

III. Number Review
- **A.** Cover numbers 1-10.
- **B.** Include not only sight recognition of the numeral, but employ counting on the 4 year-old level.

IV. Alphabet Review
- **A.** This unit spans the months of May and June.
- **B.** The three year-old group reviews the alphabet once.
- **C.** The four year-old group will review the alphabet twice from different stimuli and activities.

V. Nature units
- **A.** Flowers
  1. Zinnia
  2. Rose
  3. Tulip
  4. Pansy
  5. Dandelion
- **B.** Birds
  1. Cardinal
  2. Robin
  3. Blue Jay
  4. Woodpecker
  5. Bluebird (or state bird)
- **C.** Reptiles
  1. Frog
  2. Turtle
  3. Lizard
  4. Snake
  5. Fish

D. Insects — This unit continues next month
1. Butterfly
2. Cricket

VI. Mother's Day
A. Emphasize that it is a special day to say thank you to our mothers, but that we should make every day a special one for her.
B. Age three colors a card to take home.
C. Age four makes a project for a gift and colors a card.

VII. Memorial Day
A. There is no school on this holiday, and a study of America and the flag appears in the June program.
B. A simple explanation of the holiday should be sufficient. See Appendix III for a picture to color if desired.

PROBLEM/CONCEPT	**SUGGESTED ACTIVITIES**
COLOR REVIEW:	Have children dressed in the different colors stand up when you call out the color. Point out colors in the room. Pass out pieces of construction paper and play a match up game. Make sure the children are coloring (painting) their pictures in the proper colors. Check for apparent color blindness.
SHAPE REVIEW:	Point out shapes of objects in the classroom. Match up blocks of different colors.
NUMBER REVIEW:	Sing the "10 Little Indians" song. Count fingers. Count children when passing out snacks. Sing "1, 2, Buckle My Shoe" . . .

ALPHABET REVIEW:	Sing the alphabet song. Use cut-out letters to let the children review the contours.
NATURE UNITS: Flowers	Refer back to the farm unit and explain that flowers are one of nature's crops. Even a weed can be a flower. Have the children cut out pictures of flowers in magazines to make a collage.
Birds	There are many kinds of birds in the world, but we only look at five. The cardinal is easy to see because he is bright red. Birds eat seeds that come from the flowers. They also eat insects and worms. If a child finds a baby bird, explain that he or she should leave it alone. The mother is out looking for food since baby birds eat all day long. Birds are the only animals with feathers. That makes them special. For the last day, substitute a line drawing of the state bird if you wish.
Reptiles	They feel cold when you pick them up. Bring in a snakeskin belt or purse and let the children feel the hide. Check outdoors near light fixtures to see if a frog is in residence. Encourage the children to bring in a "caged" pet lizard or frog.

Insects	They eat leaves and other insects. They provide food for other animals and help the farmer. There are good insects and bad insects (ladybug — mosquito). Try to catch a butterfly to show to the class. Encourage the children to bring a bug to class. See if they can count the six legs.

MOTHER'S DAY PROJECT - 4 Year Olds

Recipe Holder

Materials needed:

1. Plastic "dixie" type cups or small flower pots
2. Plastic picnic forks
3. Plaster of paris
4. Plastic flowers

Method:

1. Give each child a cup, flower and fork
2. Mix plaster as needed.
3. Pour plaster in cup.
4. Center fork in plastic (handle down)
5. Stick flower stem into plaster
6. Let dry.

Recipe card will fit on tines of fork.

May

MONTH: MAY

(1) Calendar Review: red, yellow Begin: FLOWERS (zinnia)	(2) Review: blue, green (rose)	(3) Review: purple, orange (tulips)	(4) Review: brown, black (pansy)	(5) Comprehensive color review (dandelion)
(6) Shape review: CIRCLE Begin: BIRDS (cardinal)	(7) SQUARE (robin)	(8) TRIANGLE (blue jay)	(9) RECTANGLE (woodpecker)	(10) Mother's Day projects (bluebird, or state bird)
(11) NUMBER REVIEW Age 3: 1,2 Age 4: connect dots, count objects	(12) Age 3: 3,4 Age 4: connect dots, count objects	(13) Age 3: 5,6 Age 4: connect dots, count objects	(14) Age 3: 7,8 Age 4: connect dots, count objects	(15) Age 3: 9,10 Age 4: connect dots, count objects
(16) Begin: REPTILES (frog) Age 3: A,B Age 4: A,B,C	(17) (turtle) Age 3: C Age 4: D,E,F	(18) (lizard) Age 3: D Age 4: G,H,I	(19) (snake) Age 3: E Age 4: J,K,L	(20) (fish) Age 3: F,G Age 4: M,N,O
(21) Begin: INSECTS (butterfly) Age 3: H Age 4: P,Q,R	(22) (cricket) Age 3: I Age 4: S,T,U.	(23) Memorial Day (See Appendix III)		

3-4 ①

MAY

SUN.	MON.	TUES.	WED.	THURS.	FRI.	SAT.

STOP
red

yellow

4①

Zinnia

blue

green

green

3-4 ②

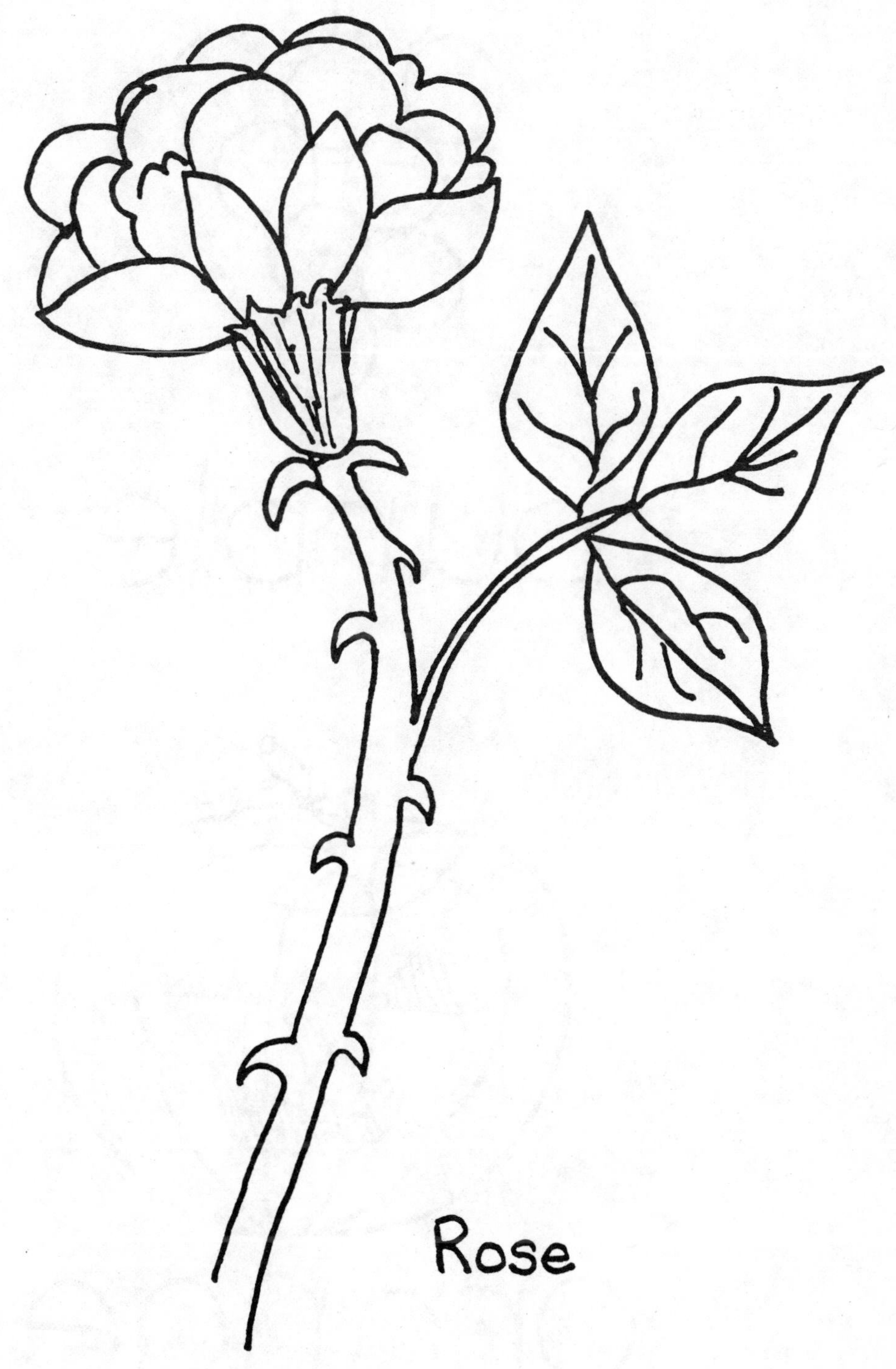

purple
orange

purple

orange

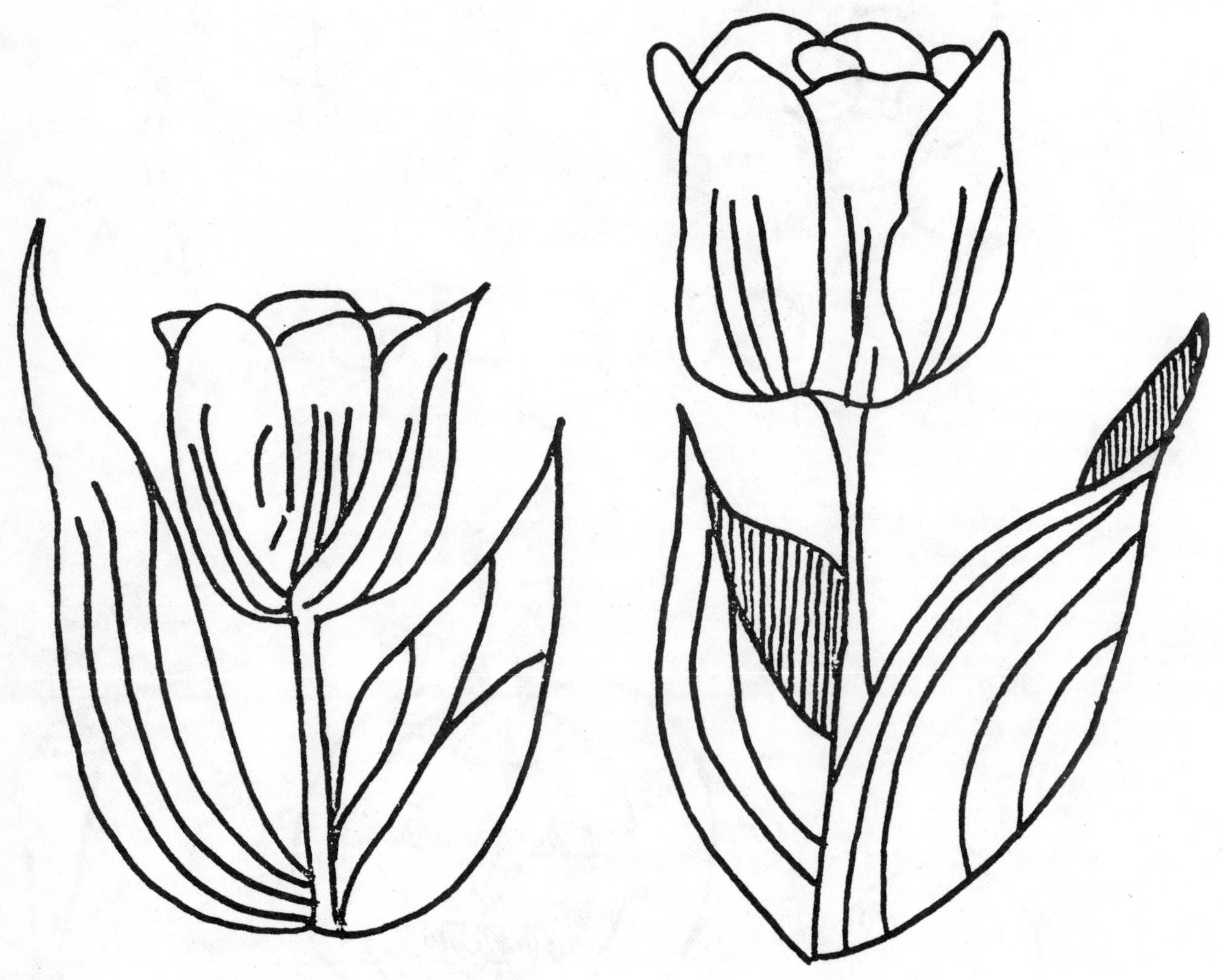

Tulips

black

brown

black

Pansy

Red
Yellow
Blue
Green
Purple
Orange
Brown
Black

Dandelion

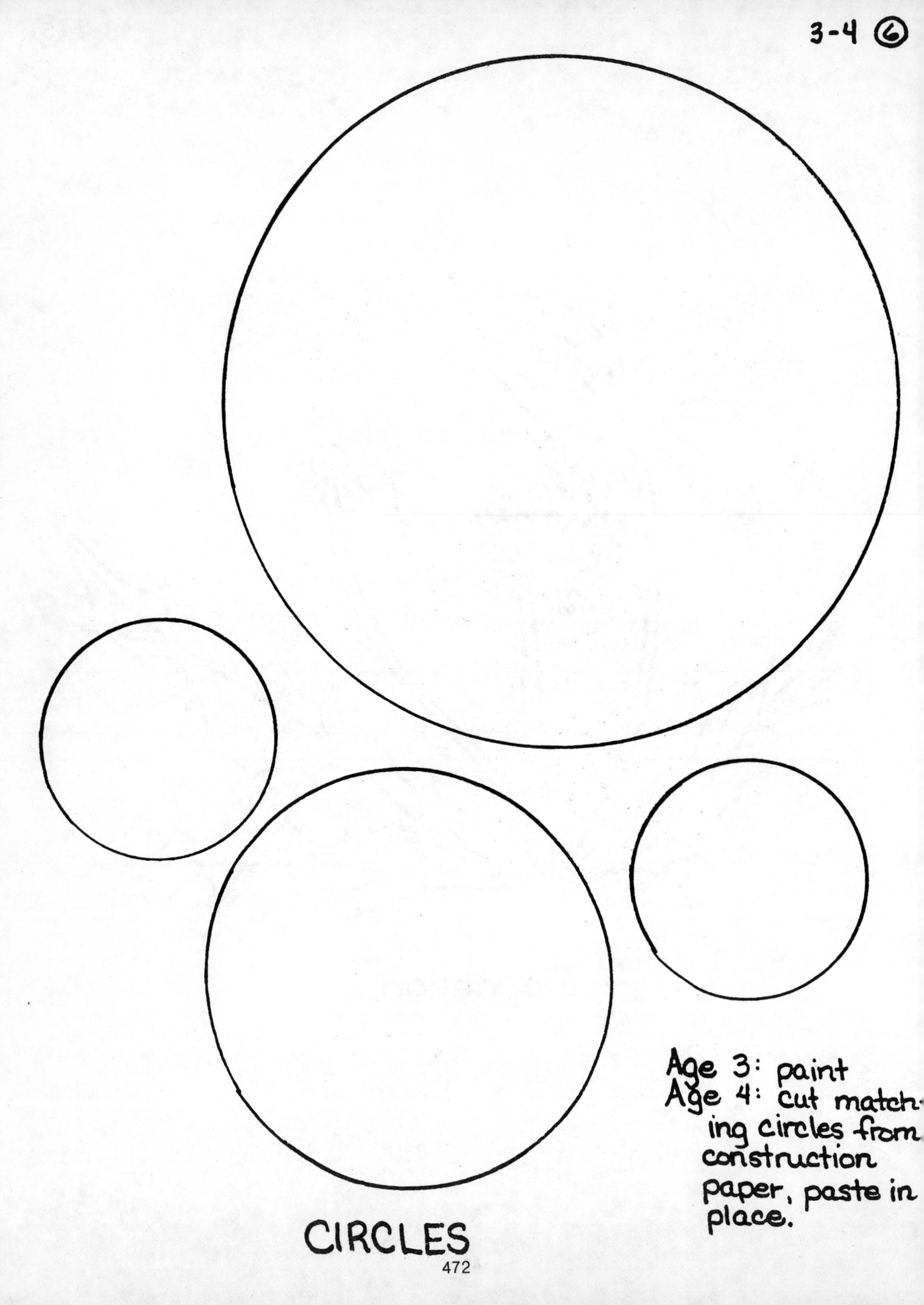
Age 3: paint
Age 4: cut matching circles from construction paper, paste in place.
CIRCLES

Cardinal

Cardinal

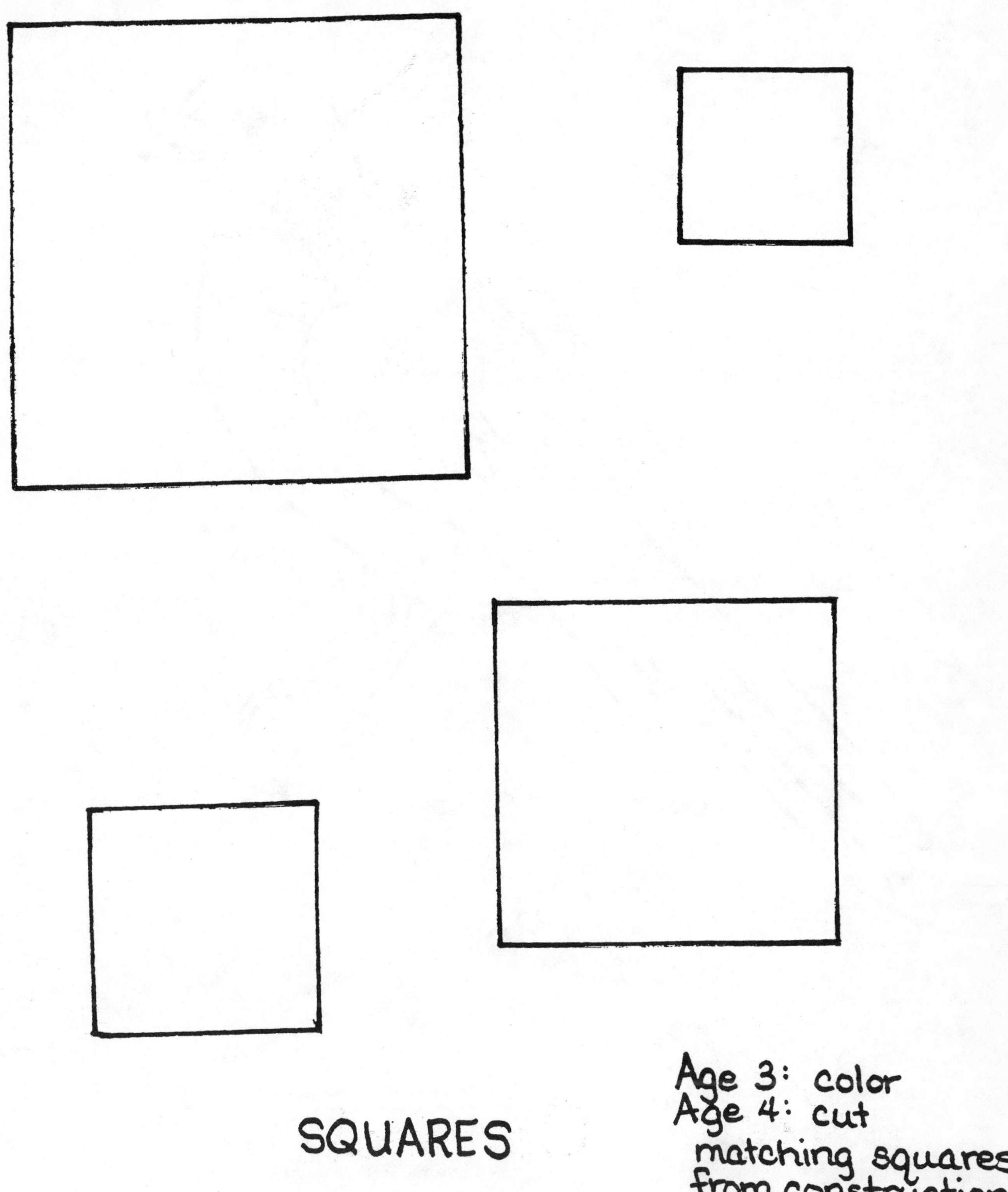

SQUARES

Age 3: color
Age 4: cut matching squares from construction paper; paste in place.

3⑦

Robin

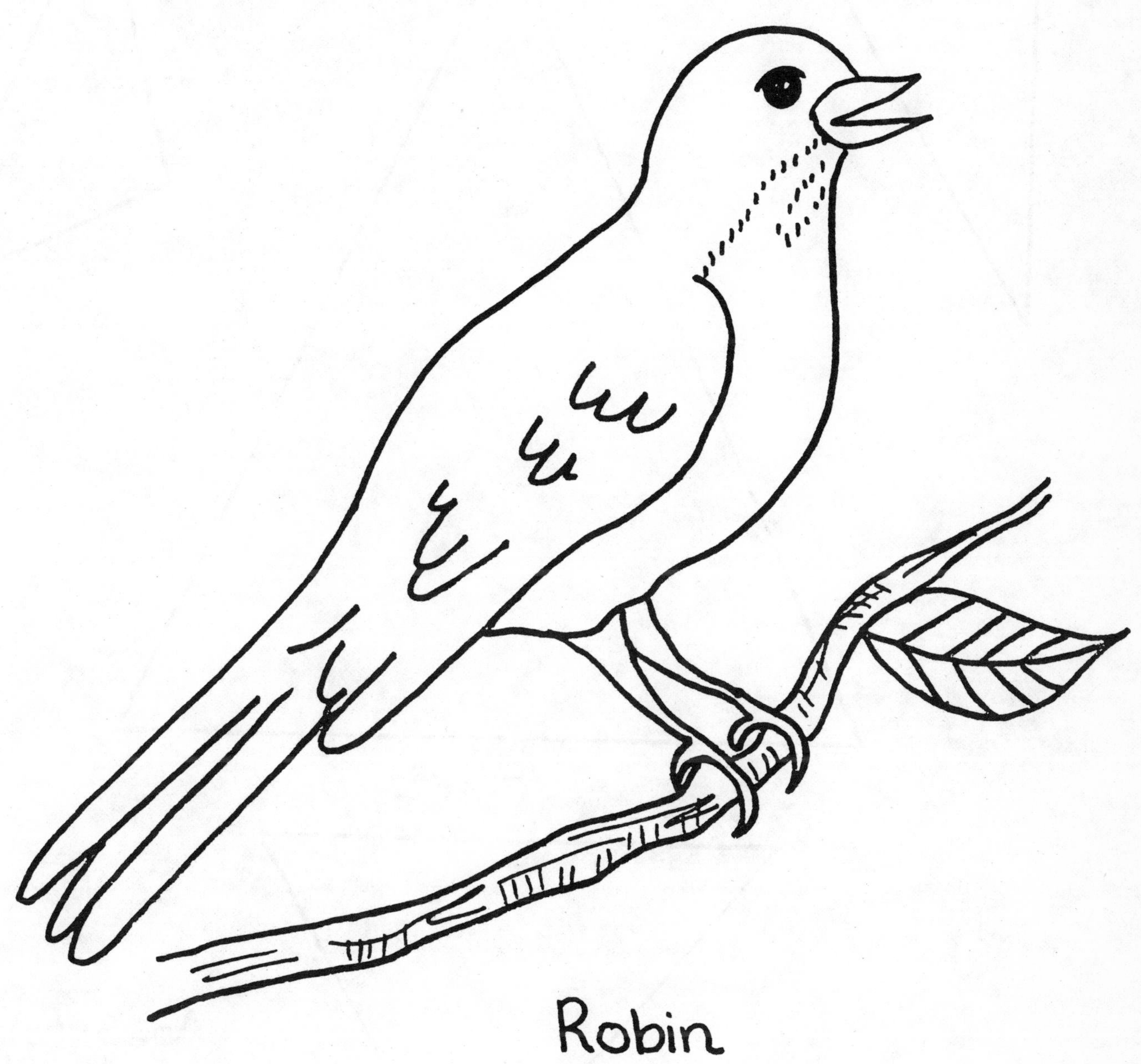

Robin

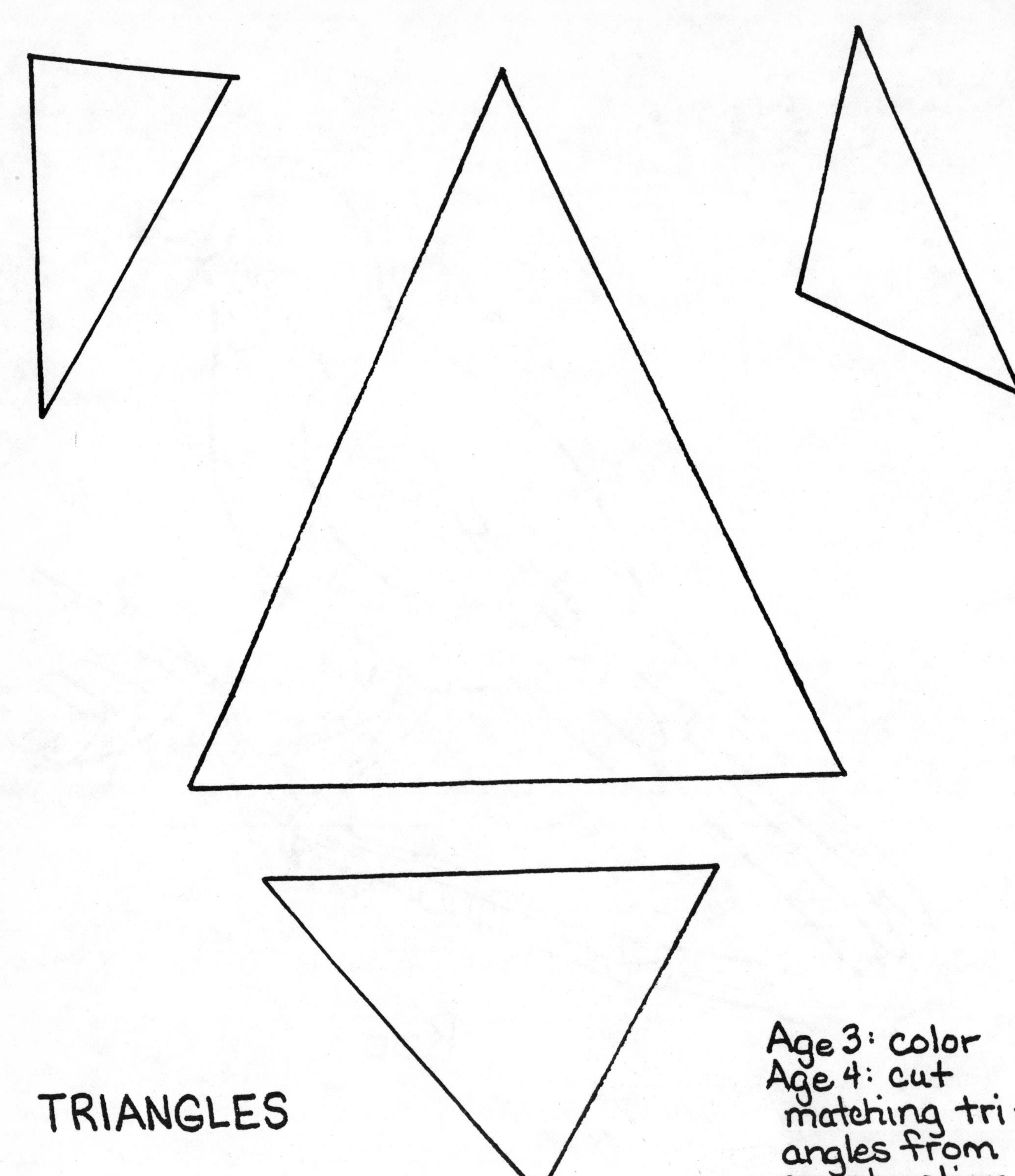

TRIANGLES

Age 3: color
Age 4: cut matching triangles from construction paper; paste in place.

Blue Jay

Blue Jay

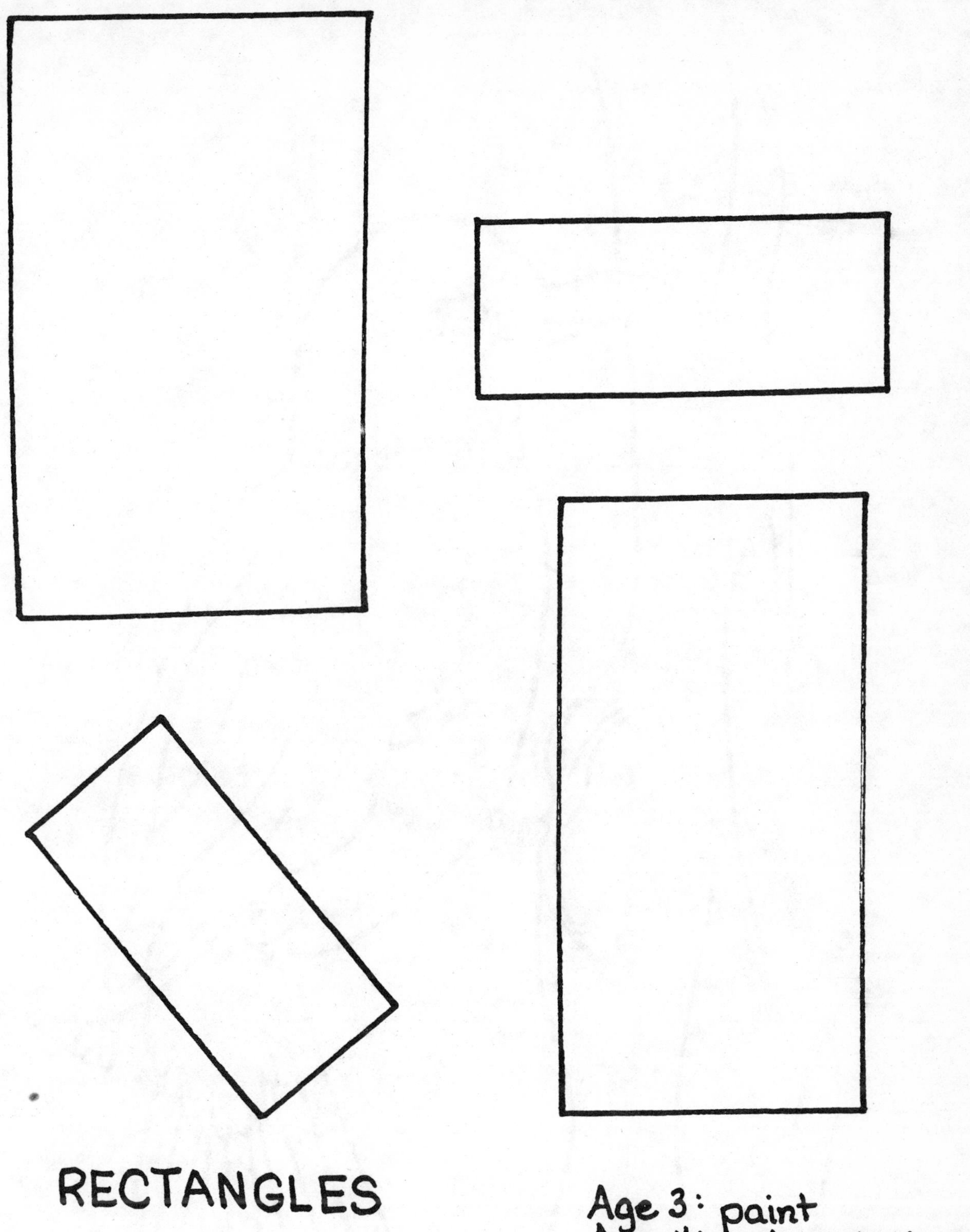

Age 3: paint
Age 4: cut matching rectangles from construction paper; paste in place.

Woodpecker

Red Headed Woodpecker

Bluebird

Teacher: Substitute picture of state bird today, if desired. Example: Florida's state bird is the Mockingbird.

Bluebird

Teacher: Substitute picture of state bird today, if desired. Example: Florida's state bird is the Mockingbird.

Though I'm just a little one,
I wanted you to know.
Today's your very special day,
And I love you so!

This flower shines with love for you
On this, your special day.
You're the best mom in the world
In every single way!

HAPPY
MOTHER'S
DAY!

NUMBER REVIEW

NUMBER REVIEW

NUMBER REVIEW

Connect the dots in order and color the picture.

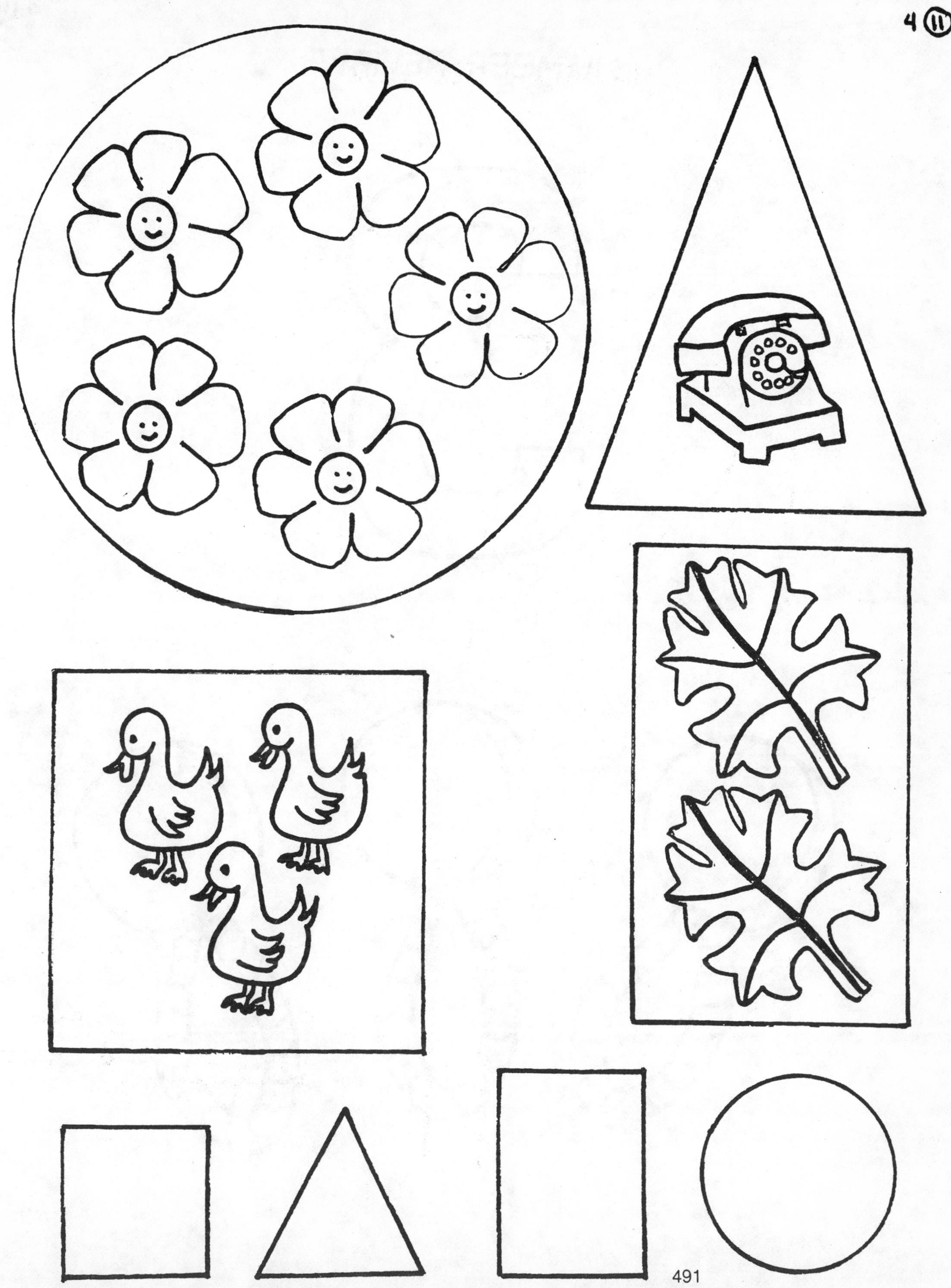

Write the correct number in the corresponding shape.

NUMBER REVIEW

NUMBER REVIEW

NUMBER REVIEW

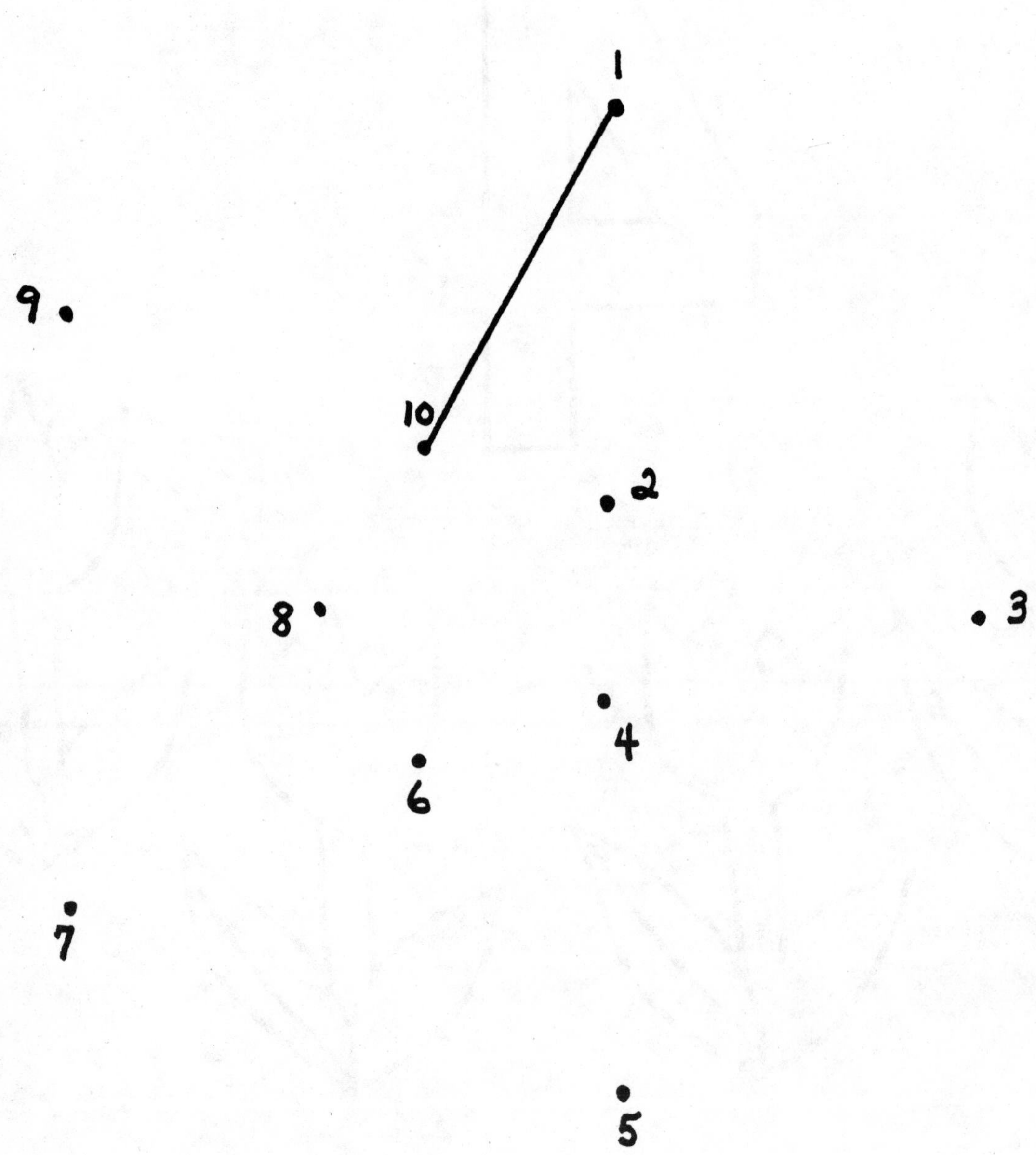

Connect the dots in order and color the picture.

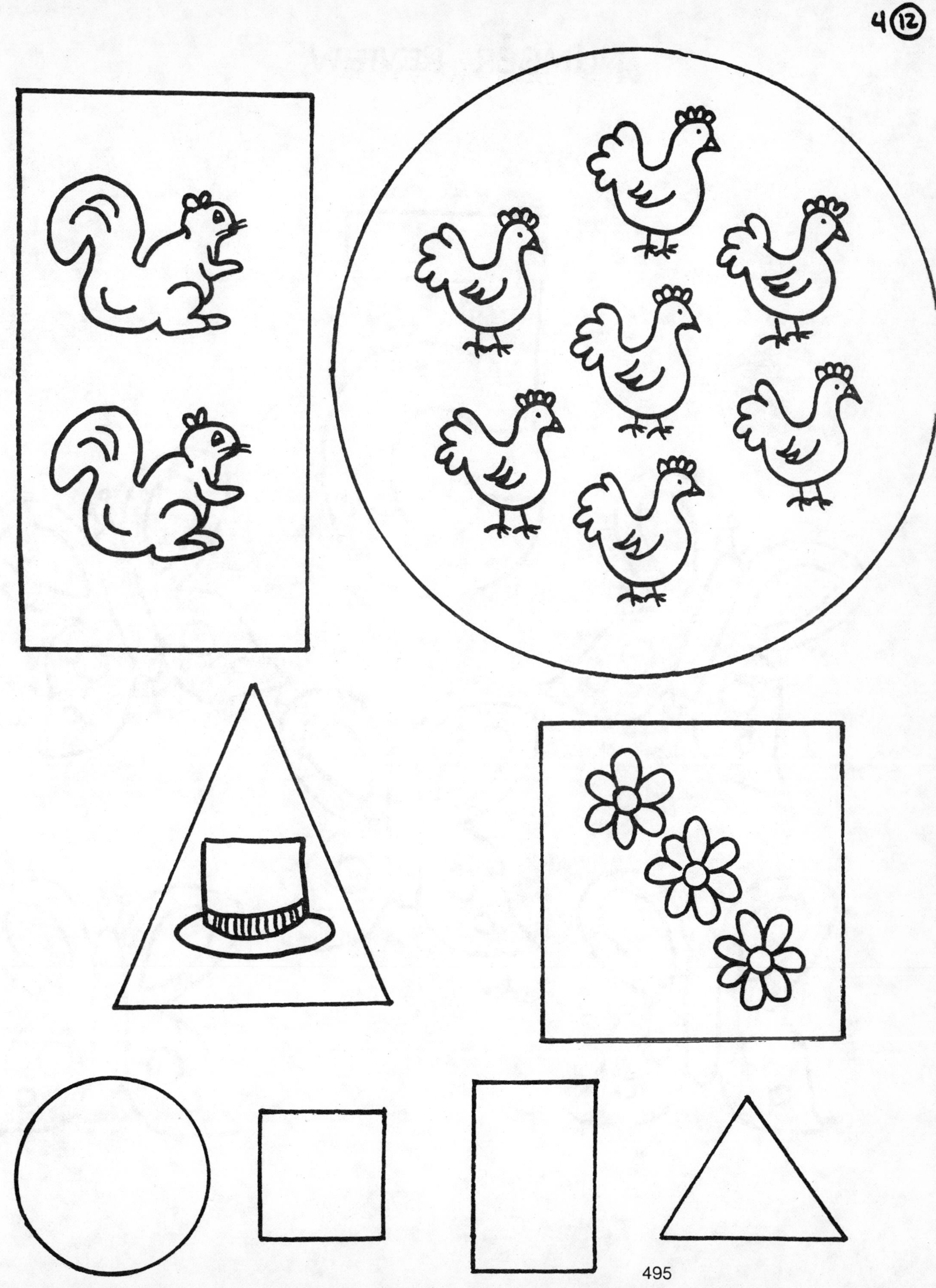

Write the correct number in the corresponding shape.

NUMBER REVIEW

NUMBER REVIEW

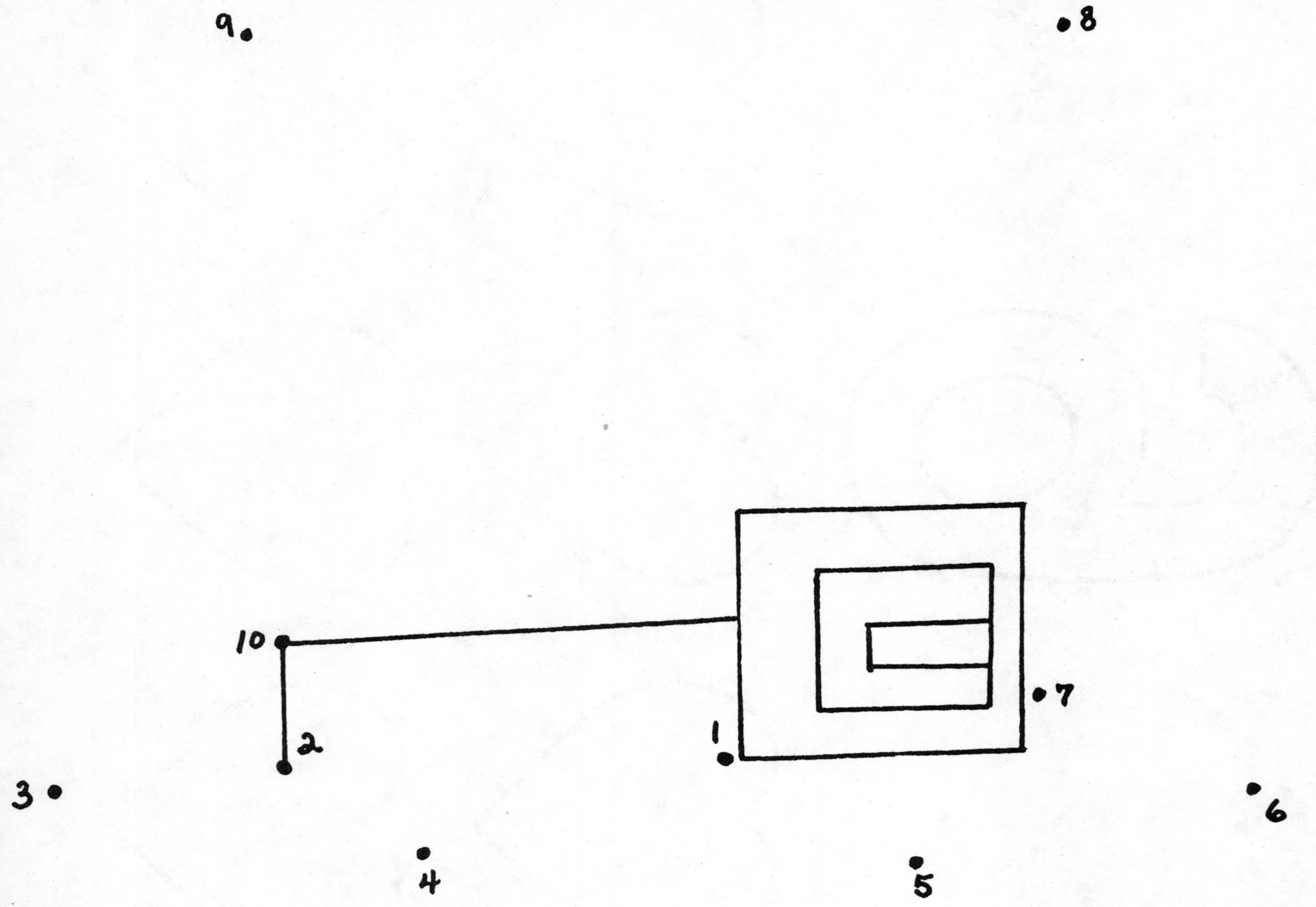

9 8

10 7

2 1

3 6

4 5

Connect the dots in order and color the picture.

Write the correct number in the corresponding shape.

NUMBER REVIEW

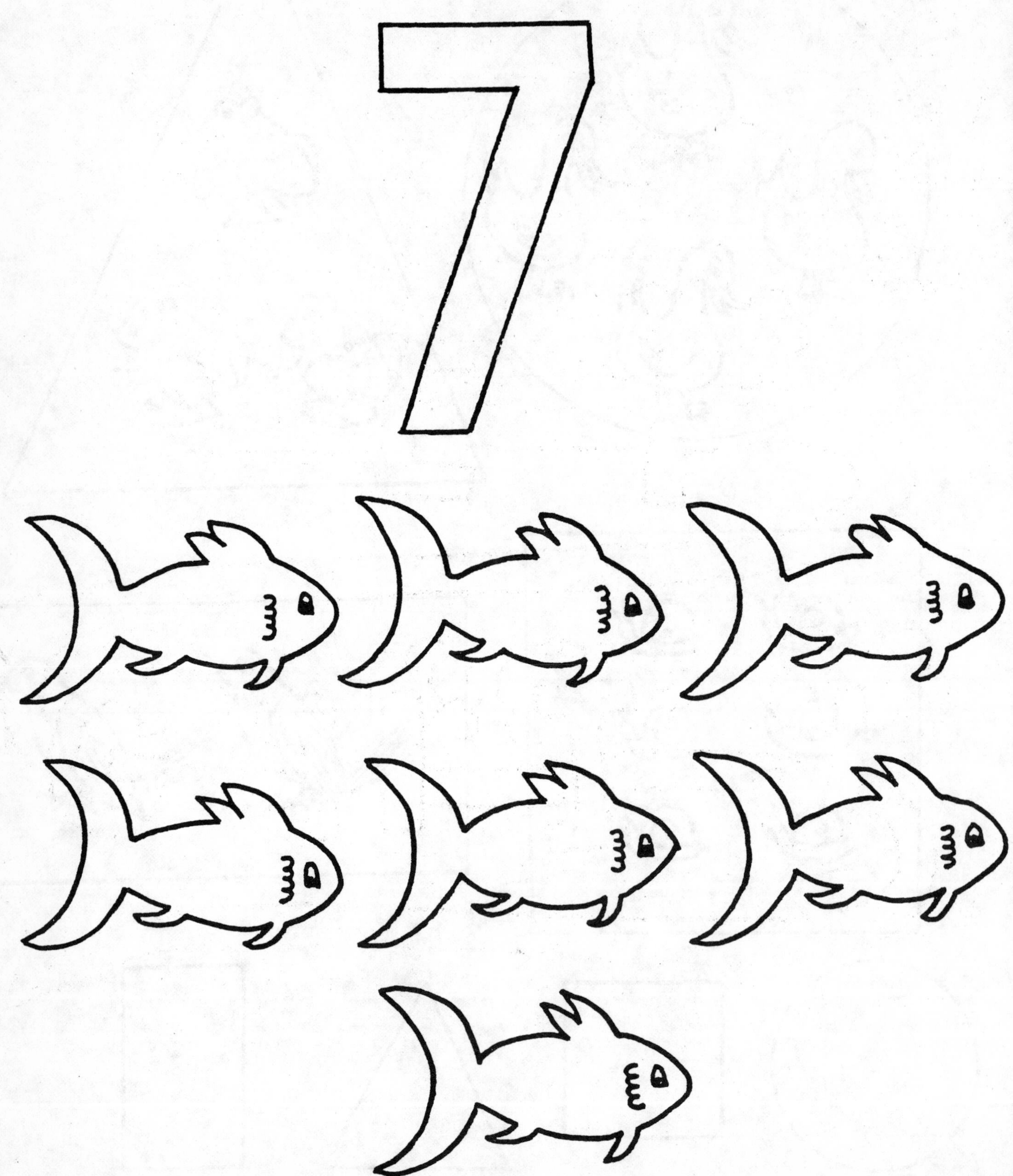

NUMBER REVIEW

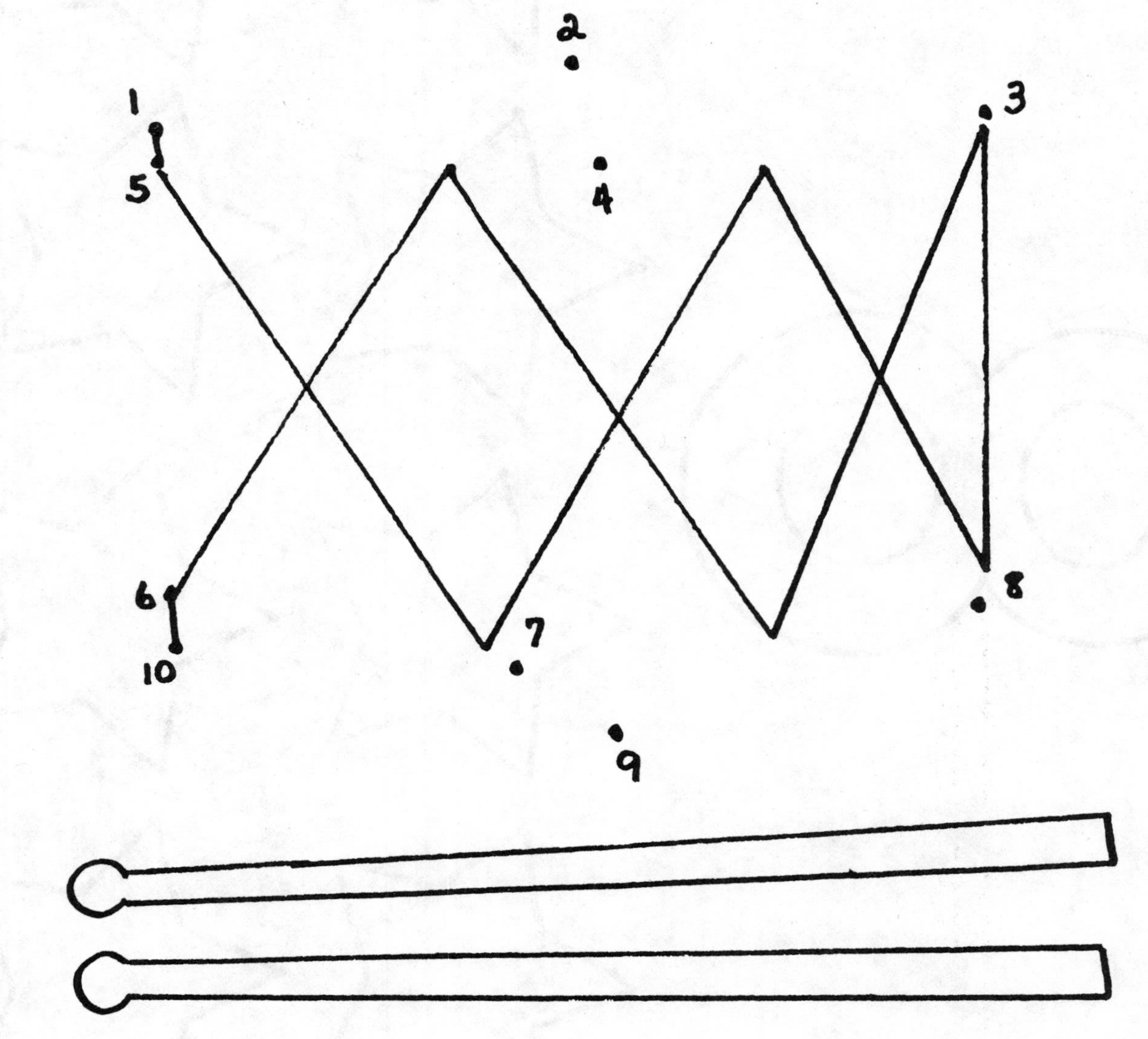

Connect the dots in order and color the picture.

4 (14)

Write the correct number in the corresponding shape.

NUMBER REVIEW

NUMBER REVIEW

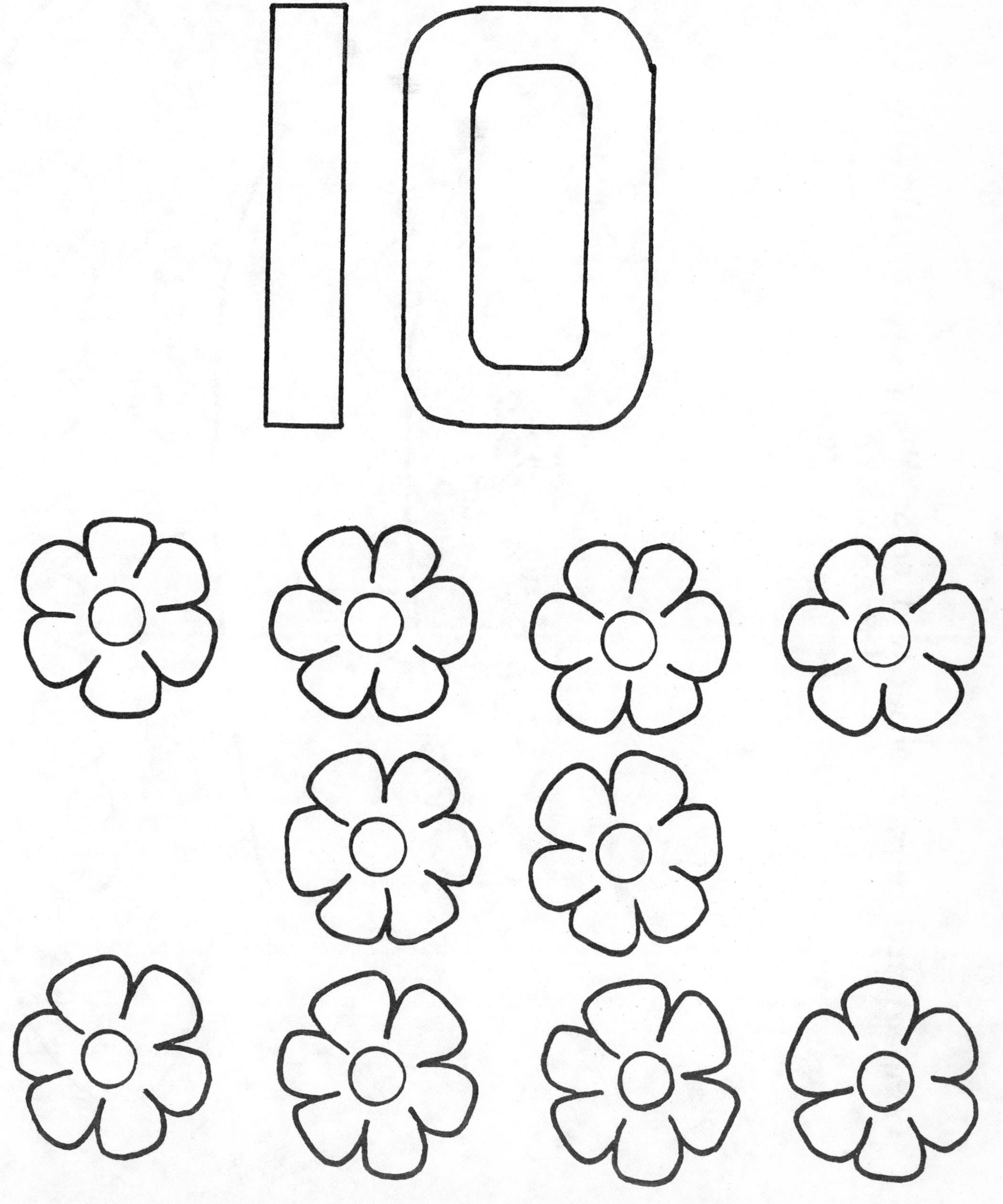

Connect the dots in order and color the picture. Draw a candle for each year.

Write the correct number in the corresponding shape.

A
apple

bear

A apple

B bear

C cat

Frog

C
cat

D dog
E egg
F fish

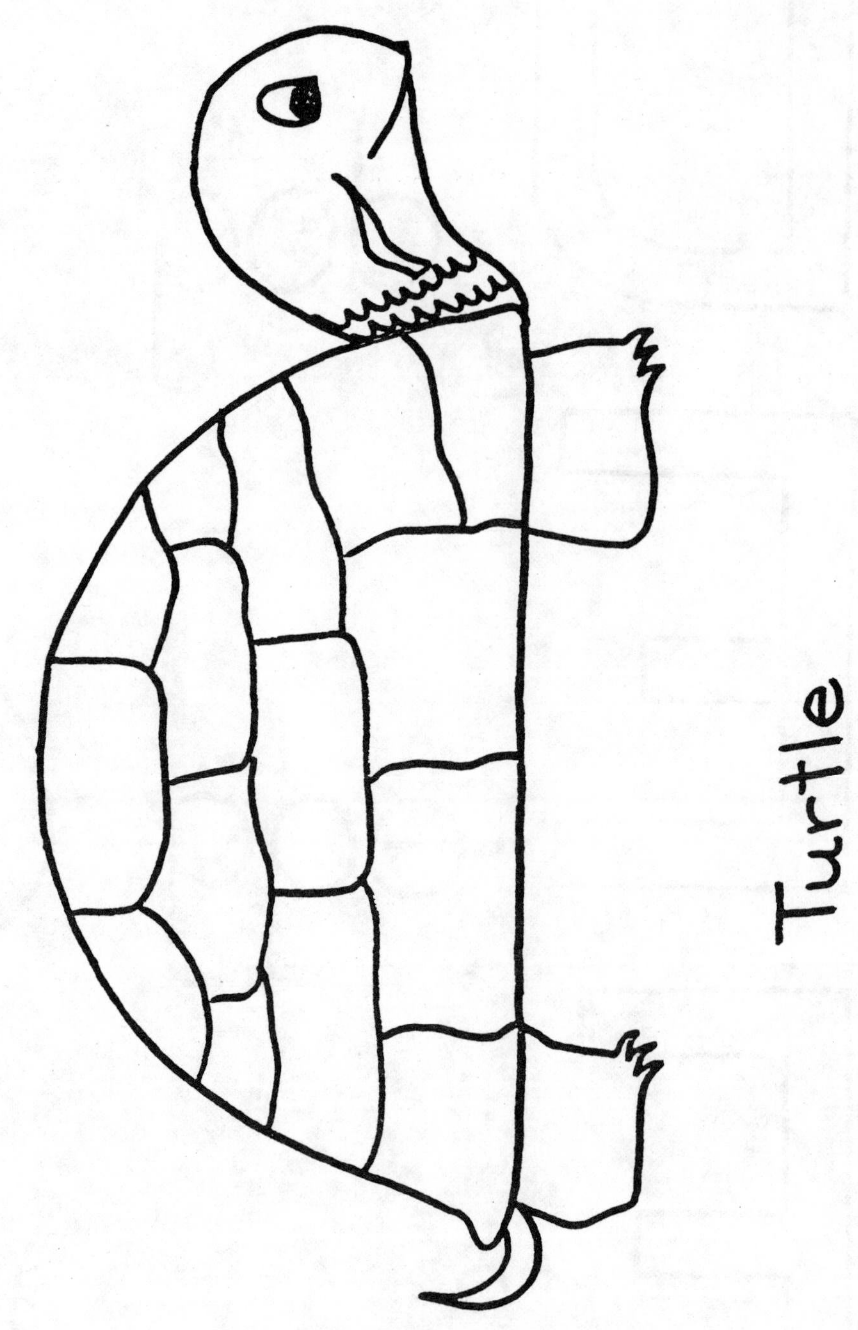
Turtle

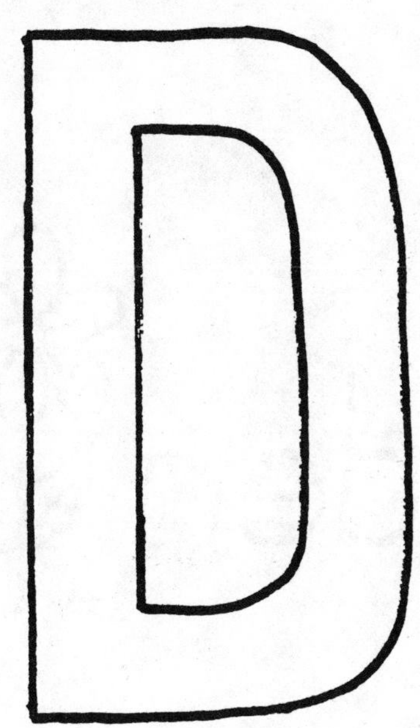

drum

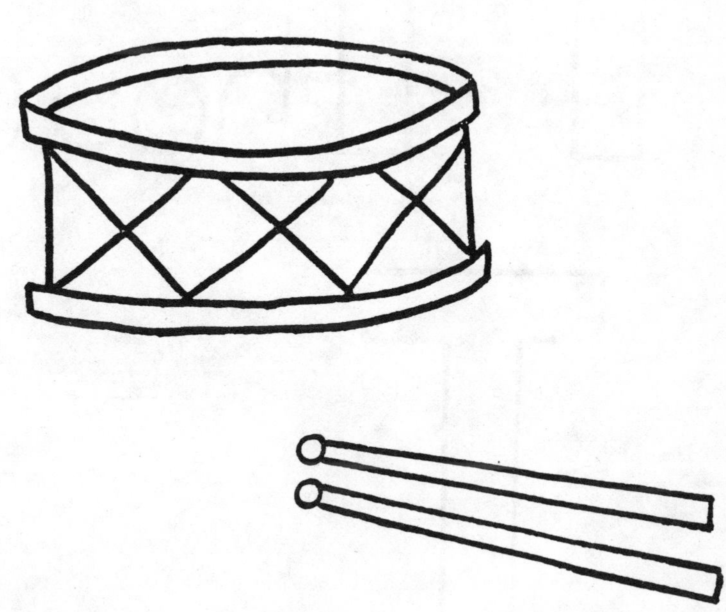

G garden
H house
I ice-cream

3-4 (18)

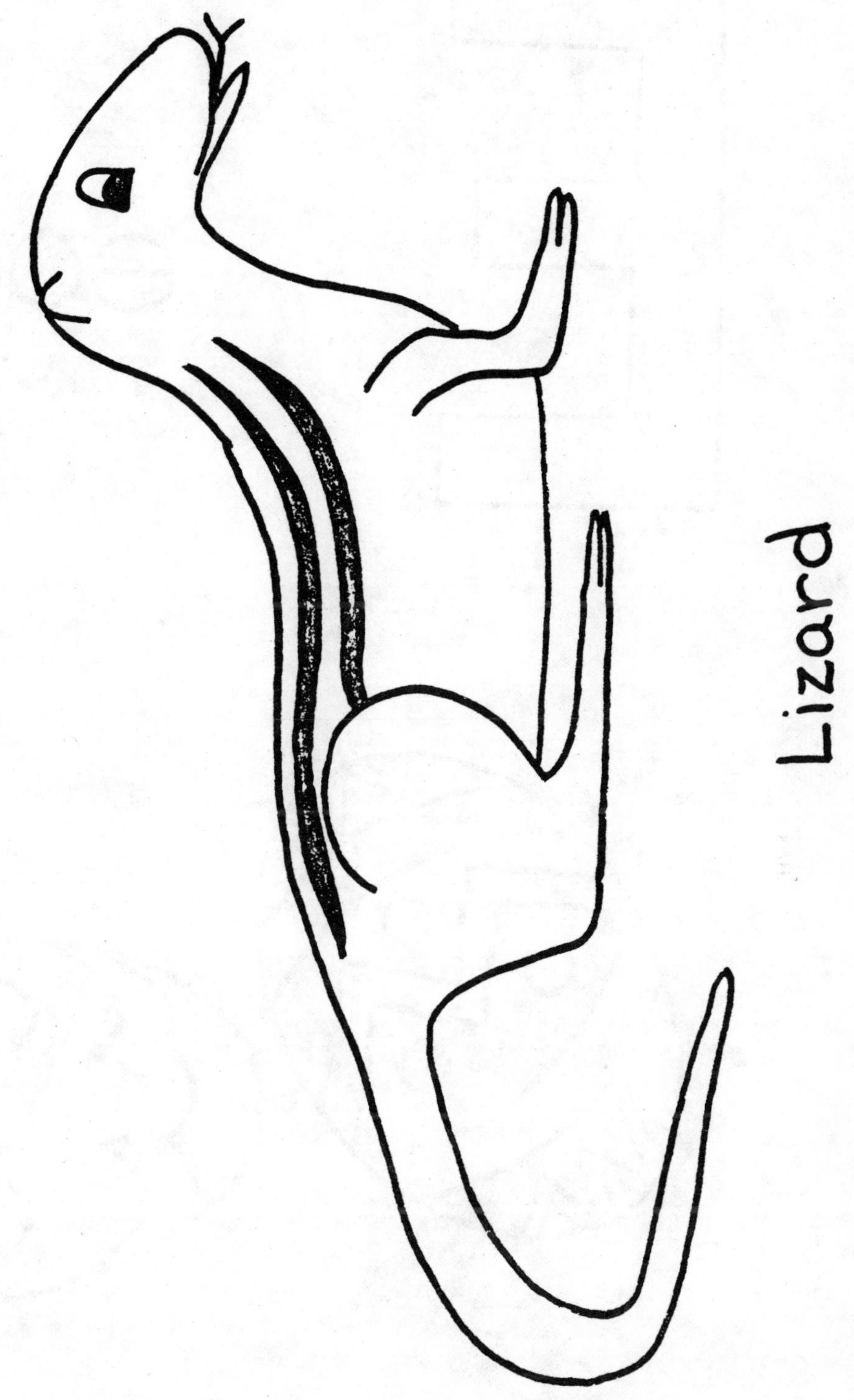

E
eggs

J
jack-in-the-box
K
kite
L
lamp

3-4 (19)

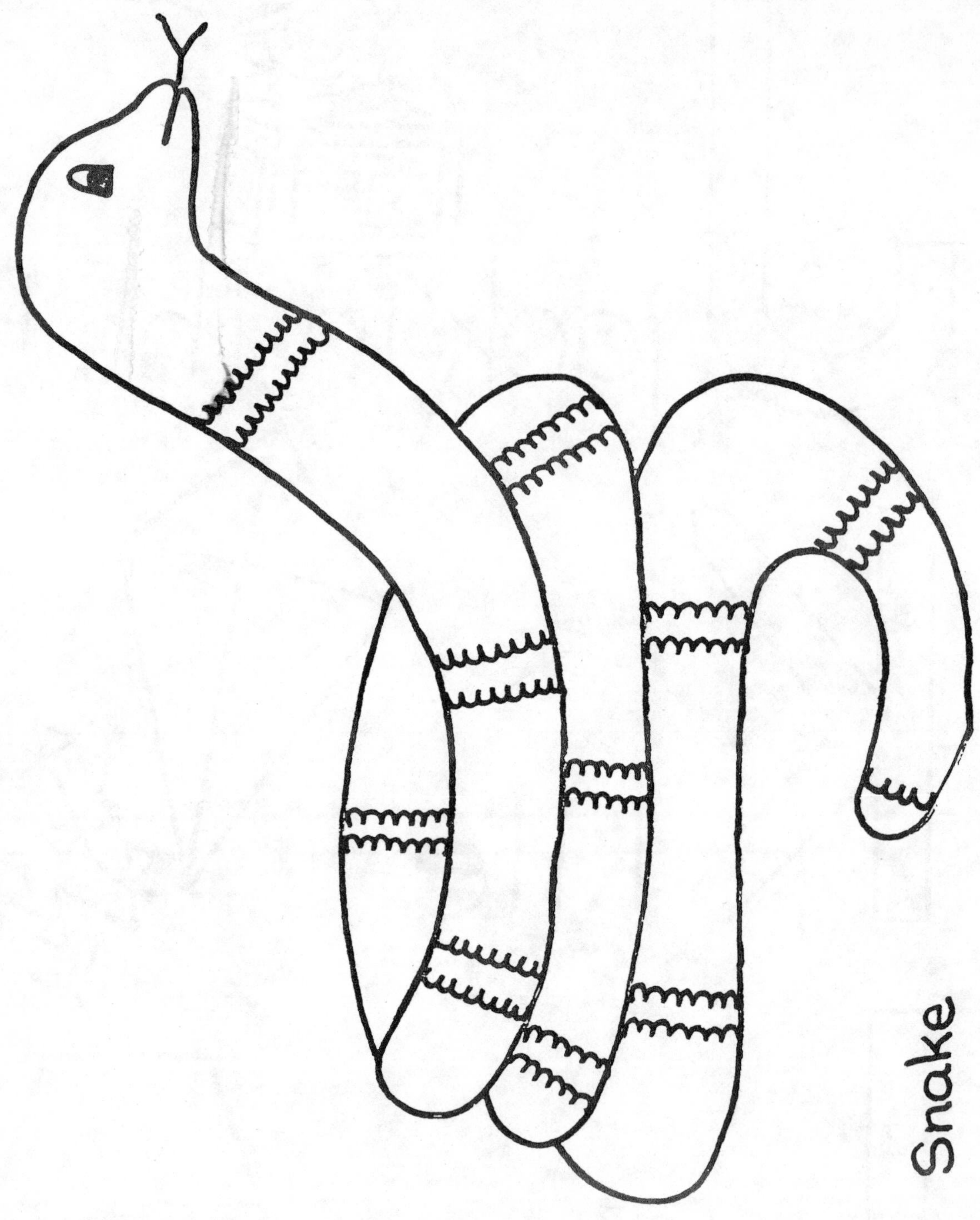

F

frog

G

goat

M moon
N necktie
O octopus

Fish

3-4 (20)

H
heart

P
pencil
Q
queen
R
roller-skate

Butterfly

I

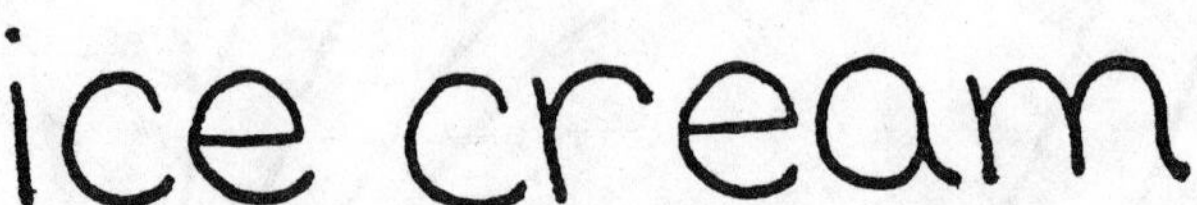

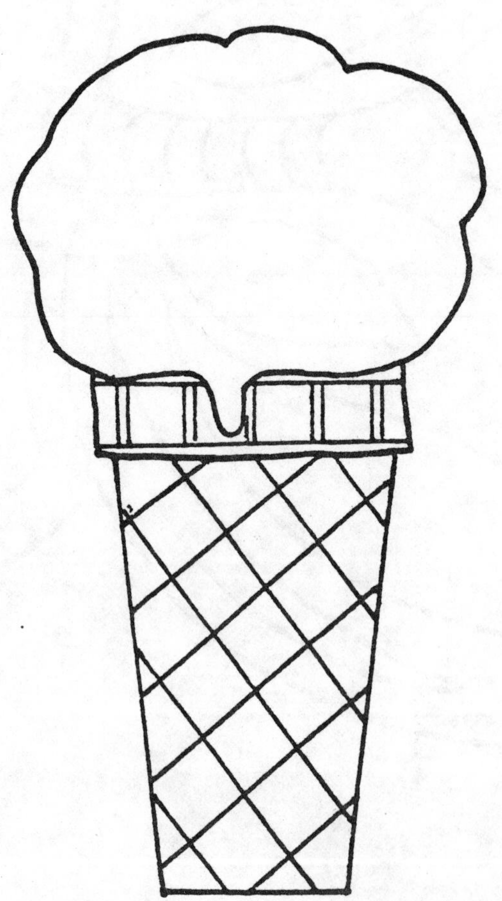

S
star
T
tree
U
umbrella

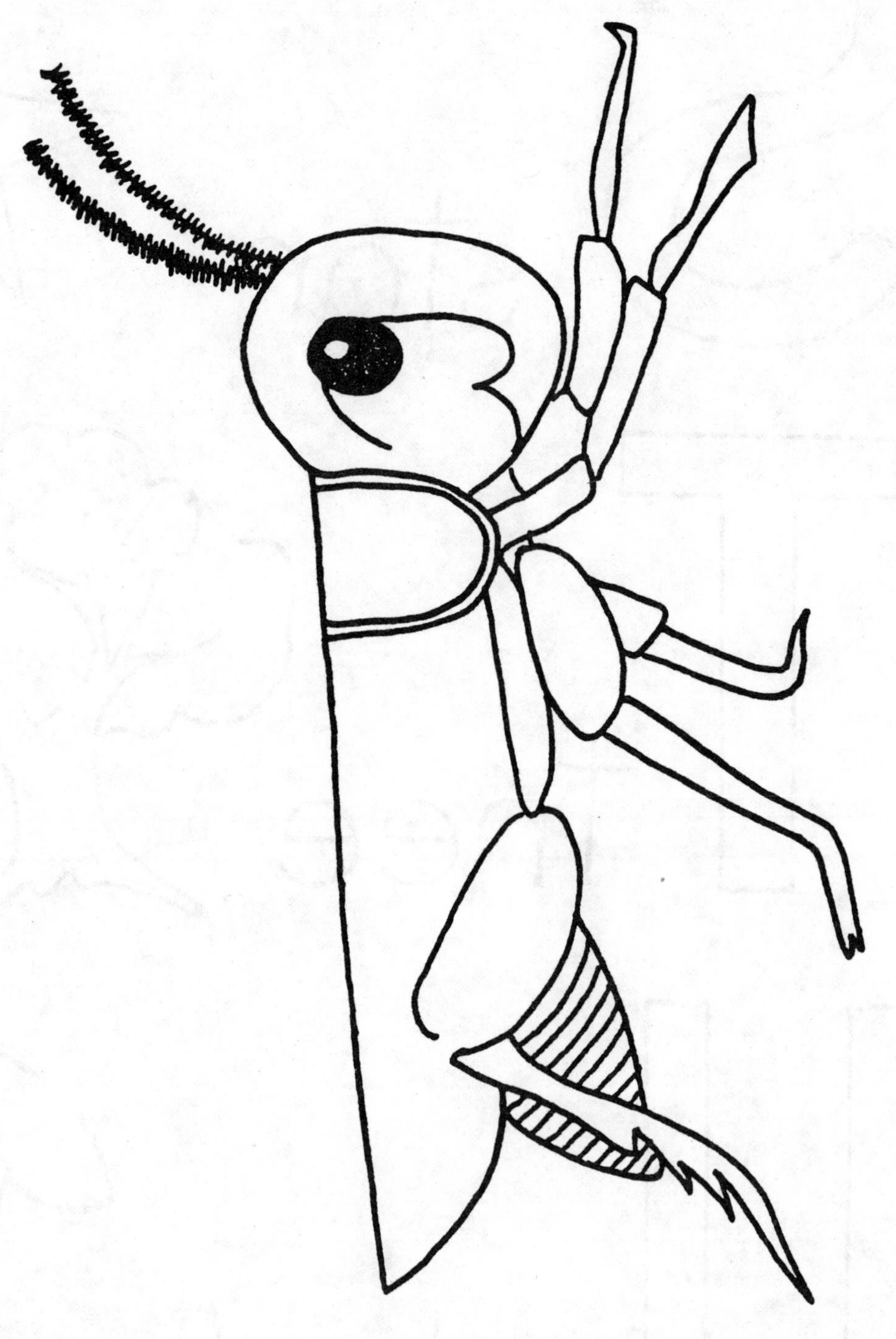

Cricket

JUNE UNITS:

I. Alphabet Review continued
   - **A.** Refer to the May syllabus.
   - **B.** The four year old class will go over the alphabet a second time. The emphasis is on printing the letters and learning the sounds they make.

II. Insect unit
   - **A.** Continued from the May unit
     1. Bee
     2. Dragonfly
   - **B.** Emphasize that insects are not all bad, but do help the flowers grow, and they are food for birds and reptiles.

III. America
   - **A.** This unit is presented the week following Memorial Day.
   - **B.** The unit emphasizes national symbols and includes some geography.
     1. American flag
        - a. Picture to color for age three
        - b. Project for age four
     2. Statue of Liberty — stress that it was given as a gift to the people of America from the people of France.
     3. Map of the United States
     4. Map of your state (Florida is used as an example)
     5. "Keep Our Country Clean" poster (civic responsibility)

IV. Other lands
   - **A.** A different country is presented each day of the week.
   - **B.** Briefly discuss the customs of the people and their language.
     1. Mexico
     2. India
     3. Holland
     4. Poland
     5. Japan

V. Father's Day projects
   - **A.** To show appreciation for what our fathers do for us
   - **B.** Cards
     1. Age 3: color or paint
     2. Age 4: color or paint and attach to gift
   - **C.** Age 4 class makes a paper weight as a gift.

PROBLEM/CONCEPT	**SUGGESTED ACTIVITIES**
ALPHABET REVIEW:	See May syllabus.
INSECTS:	See May syllabus.

AMERICA:	Say the Pledge of Allegiance.
Flag	Talk about the history of the flag. 1. 13 stripes for the original colonies 2. 50 stars, one for each state
Statue of Liberty	France gave this statue to the people of America as a gift. It is the first sight a ship sees when coming to New York. Explain that it is so big that people can go inside and up to the observation windows in the torch. It is a symbol of freedom.
Maps	The United States is a large country and has two states that don't touch the rest of the country. Bring in a globe and show the children where our country is. Try to locate your state on the big map. Substitute a map of your state as the line drawing. Locate the state capitol and any other interesting place that the children may be familiar with. Sing "America the Beautiful". Try to promote pride in our country, our state and our town. Review the community helpers unit from September. Discuss litter and responsibilities when using public areas.
OTHER LANDS:	Introduce a picture of the flag of the country for the day. Tell what language the people speak. Explain some of the more colorful customs.

Read a story about a child living in that country.

Talk about the kind of clothes the people wear.

Explain any interesting features of the country
Example -
Holland: Tulips and Windmills

Japan: Islands

Mexico: Neighbor

India: Largest democracy in the world

FATHER'S DAY PROJECT - 4 Year Olds:

Paperweight

Materials needed:

1. photo of each child
2. clear plastic caster cups
3. Elmer's glue
4. Plaster of paris
5. Felt

Method:

1. Trim picture to fit inside cup
2. Squeeze glue into cup
3. Place picture on top of glue, face side down
4. Let dry overnight or longer - until glue turns clear.
5. Fill cup with plaster, let dry
6. Cut felt to fit
7. Glue felt to plaster.

June

① Calendar Age 3: K, J Age 4: V, W, X (bee)	② Age 3: L Age 4: Y, Z (dragonfly)	③ Begin: America unit (flag) Age 3: M Age 4: A, B, C	④ (statue of liberty) Age 3: N, O Age 4: D, E, F	⑤ (map of. U.S.) Age 3: P Age 4: G, H, I
⑥ (state map) Age 3: Q, R Age 4: J, K, L	⑦ (keep our country clean) Age 3: S Age 4: M, N, O	⑧ Begin: other lands unit (Mexico) Age 3: T, U Age 4: P, Q, R	⑨ (India) Age 3: V Age 4: S, T, U	⑩ (Holland) Age 3: W, X Age 4: V, W, X
⑪ (Poland) Age 3: Y, Z Age 4: Y, Z	⑫ (Japan) Father's Day cards			
		Craft items: plastic straws See special sheet for Father's day gift materials.		

JUNE

SUN.	MON.	TUES.	WED.	THURS.	FRI.	SAT.

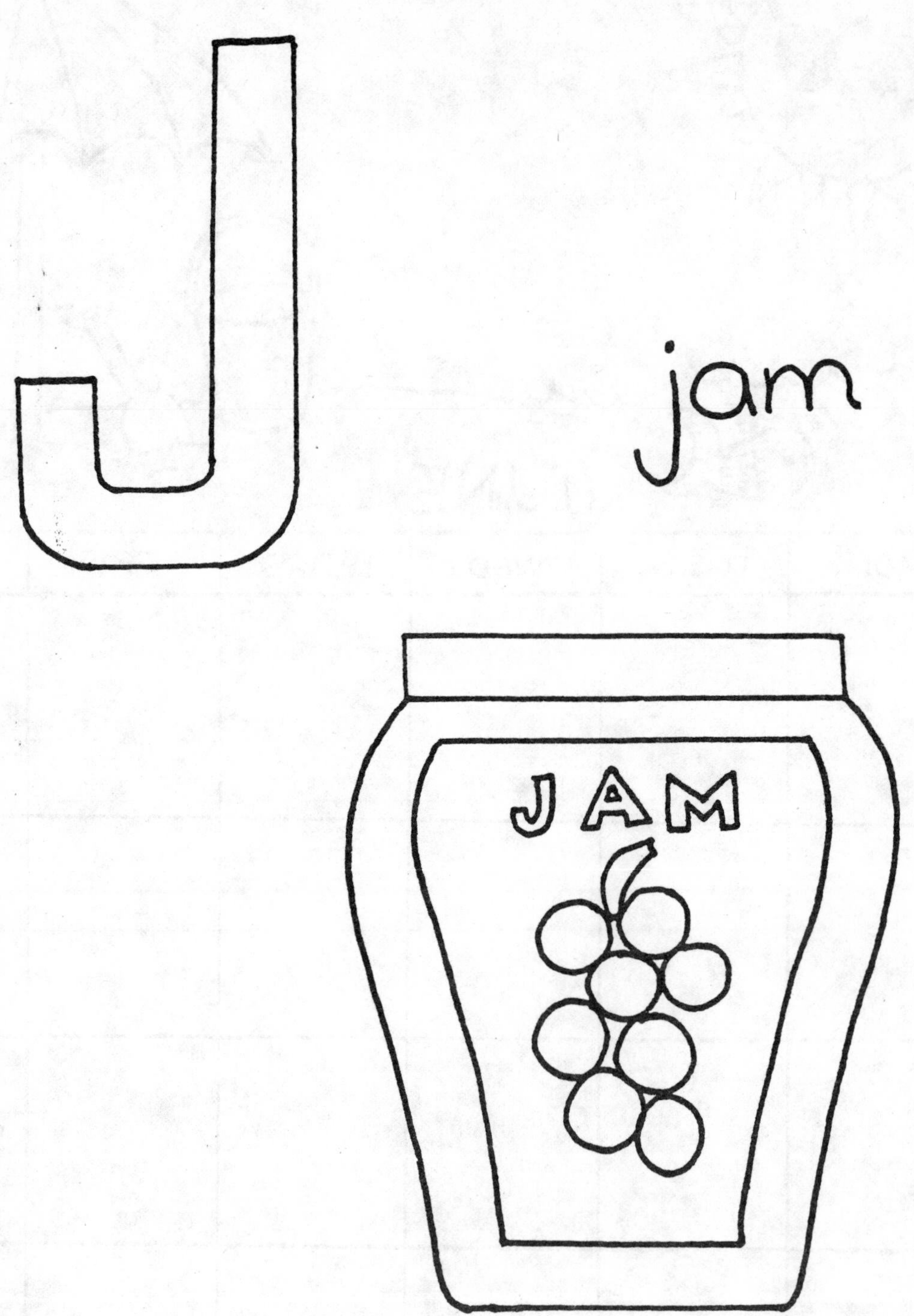
jam
JAM

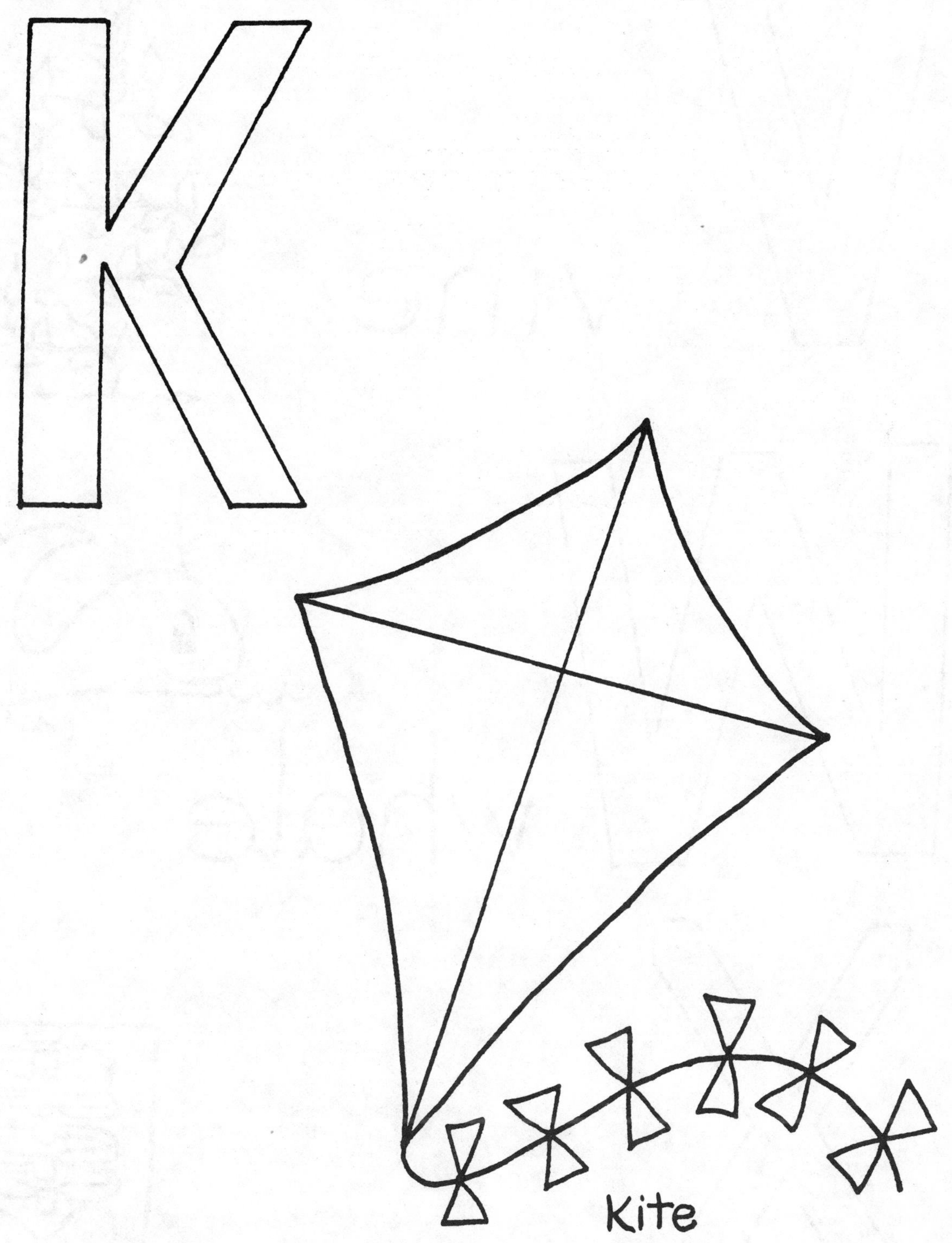
K
Kite

V
vine
W
whale
X
x-ray

Bee

L
lamp

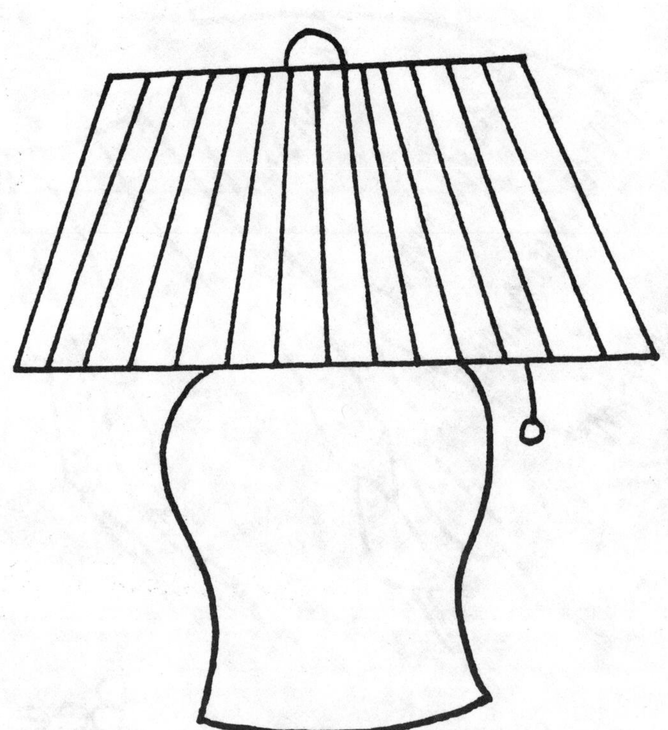

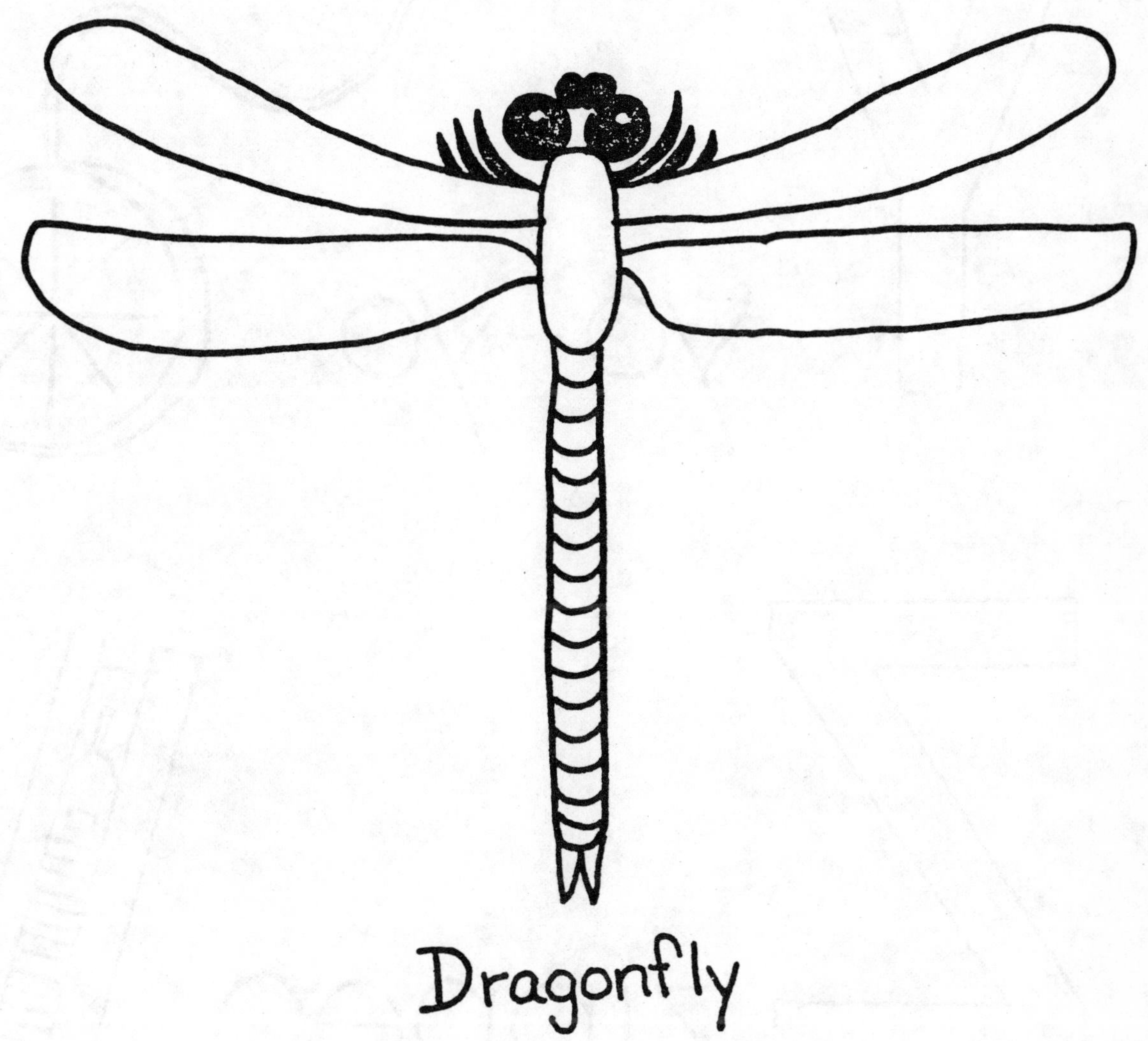
Dragonfly

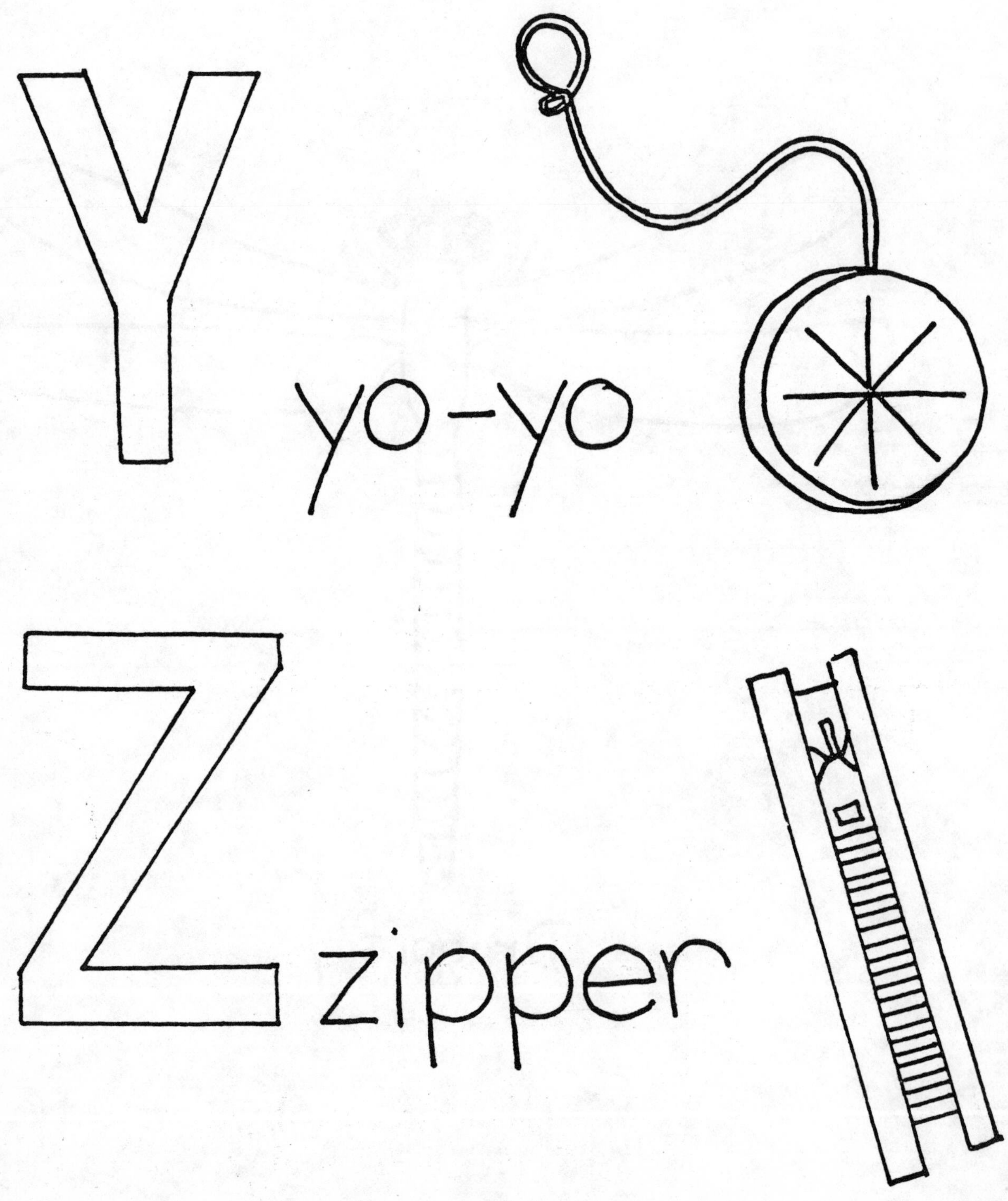
Y
yo-yo
Z
zipper

M
mouse

Aa

Aa

Bb

Bb

Cc

Cc

3 ③

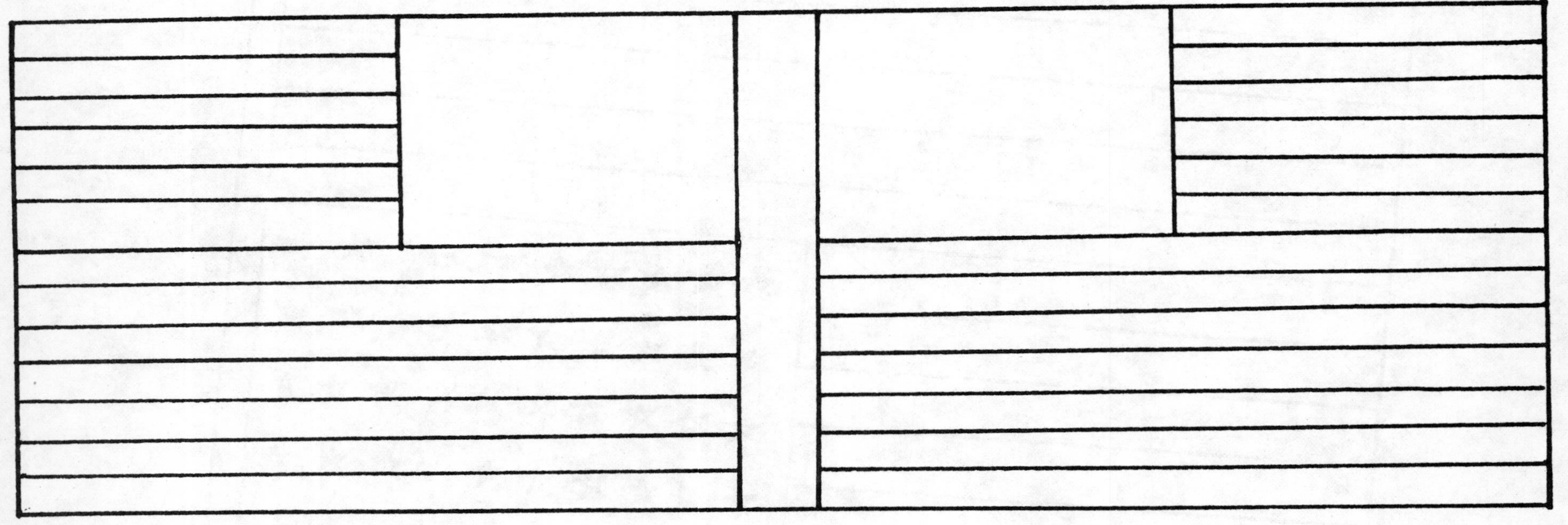

1. Color flag
2. Cut out in one piece
3. Paste sides together around drinking straw.

4③

N
nut

3 ④

Dd
Dd
Ee
Ee
Ff
Ff

P
penguin

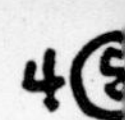

Gg

G g

Hh

H h

Ii

I i

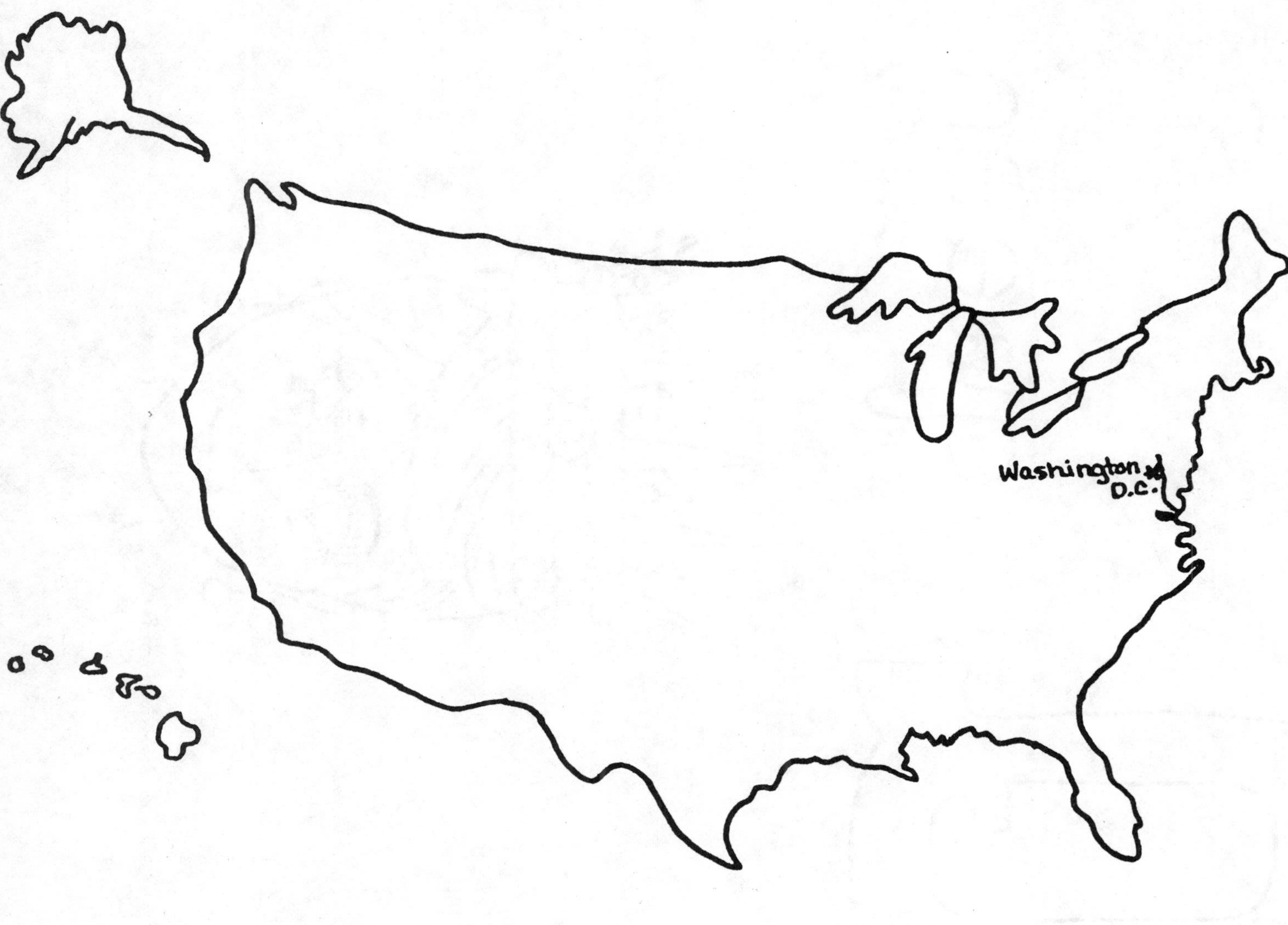

THE UNITED STATES OF AMERICA

Q

queen

R
rabbit

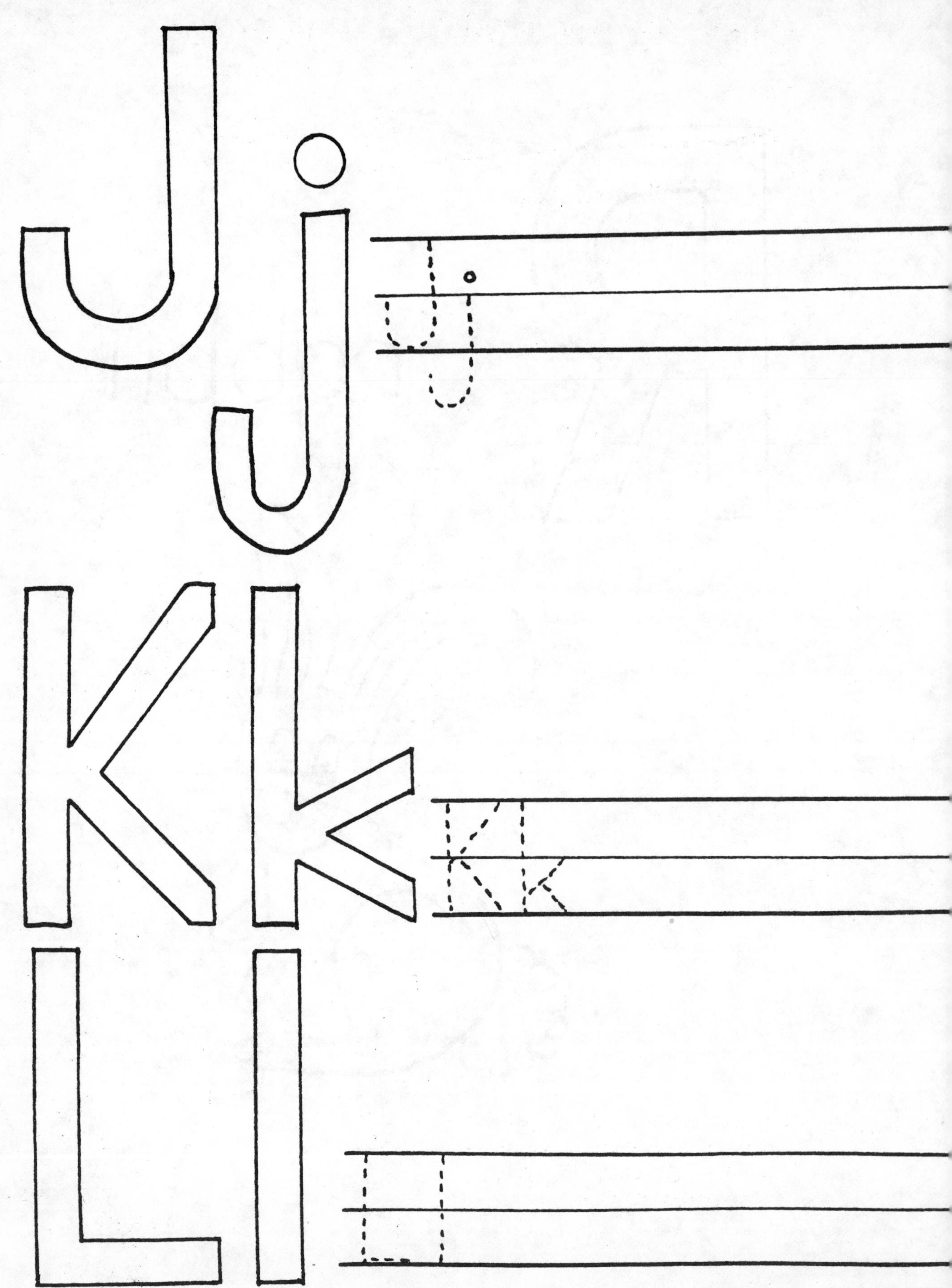

MAP OF MY STATE: FLORIDA

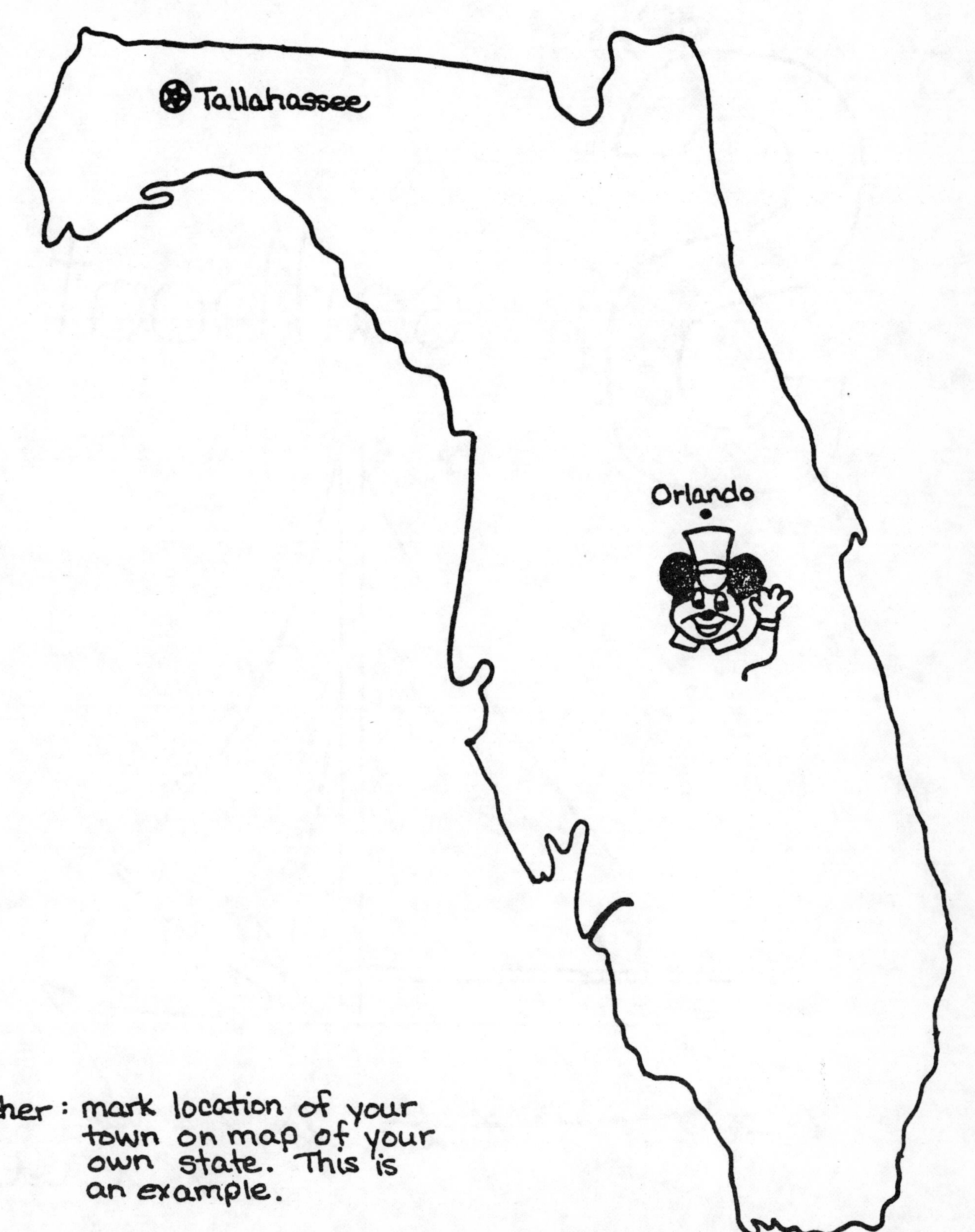

Teacher: mark location of your town on map of your own state. This is an example.

S
sailboat

Mm
Mm
Nn
Nn
Oo
Oo

PITCH IN

T
toothbrush

U
umbrella

P p
Q q
R r

MEXICO

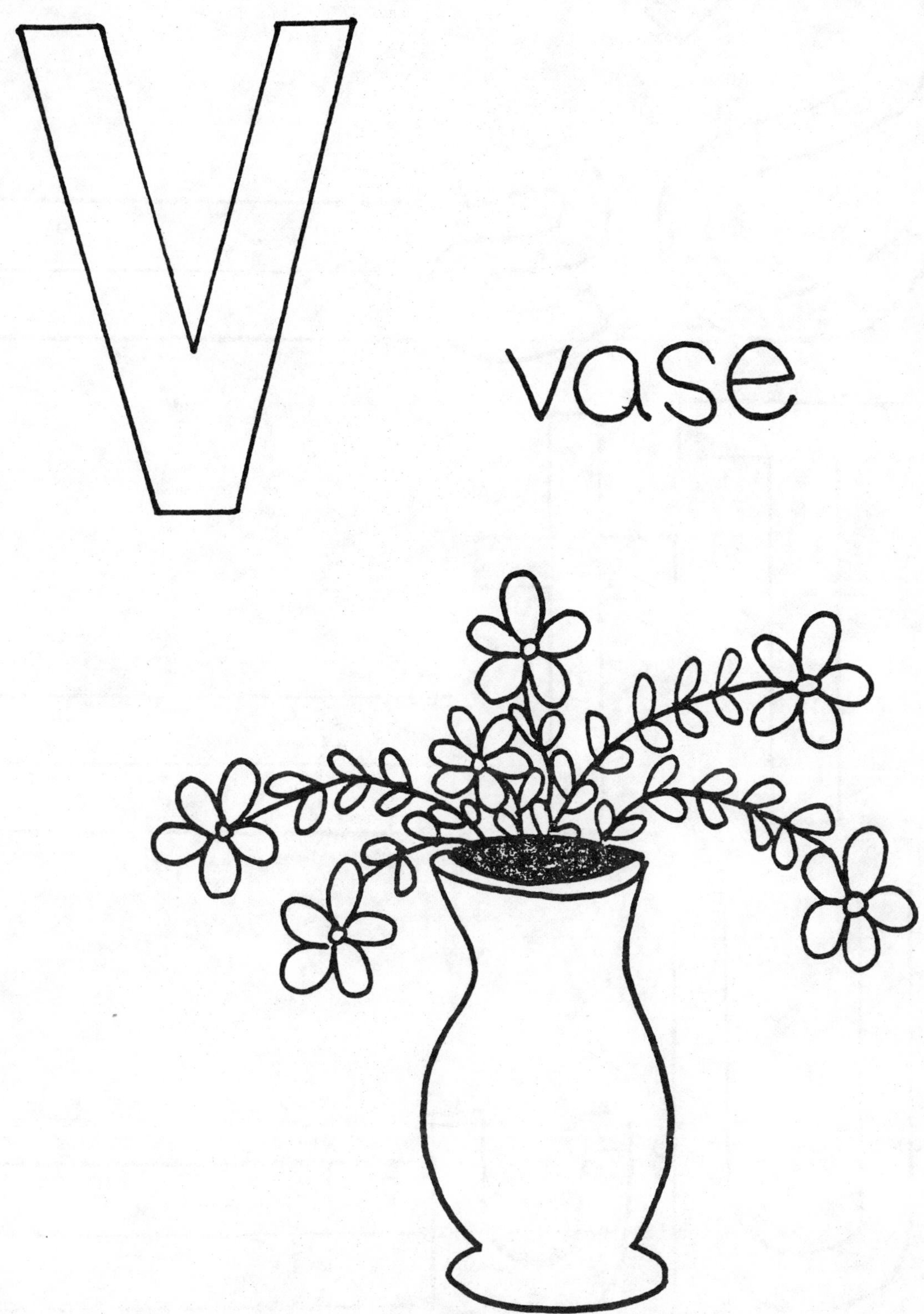
V
vase

INDIA

W
whale

3 ⑩

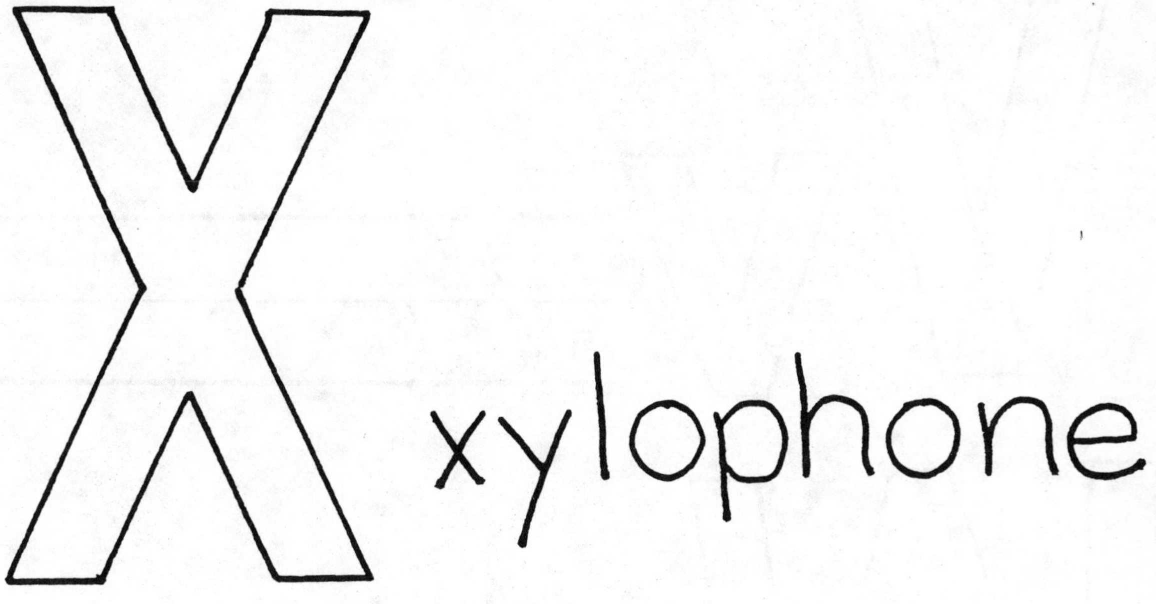

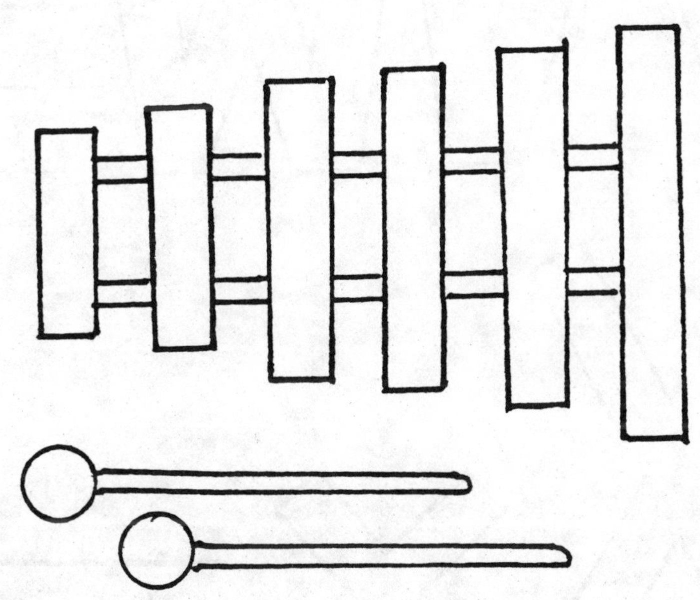

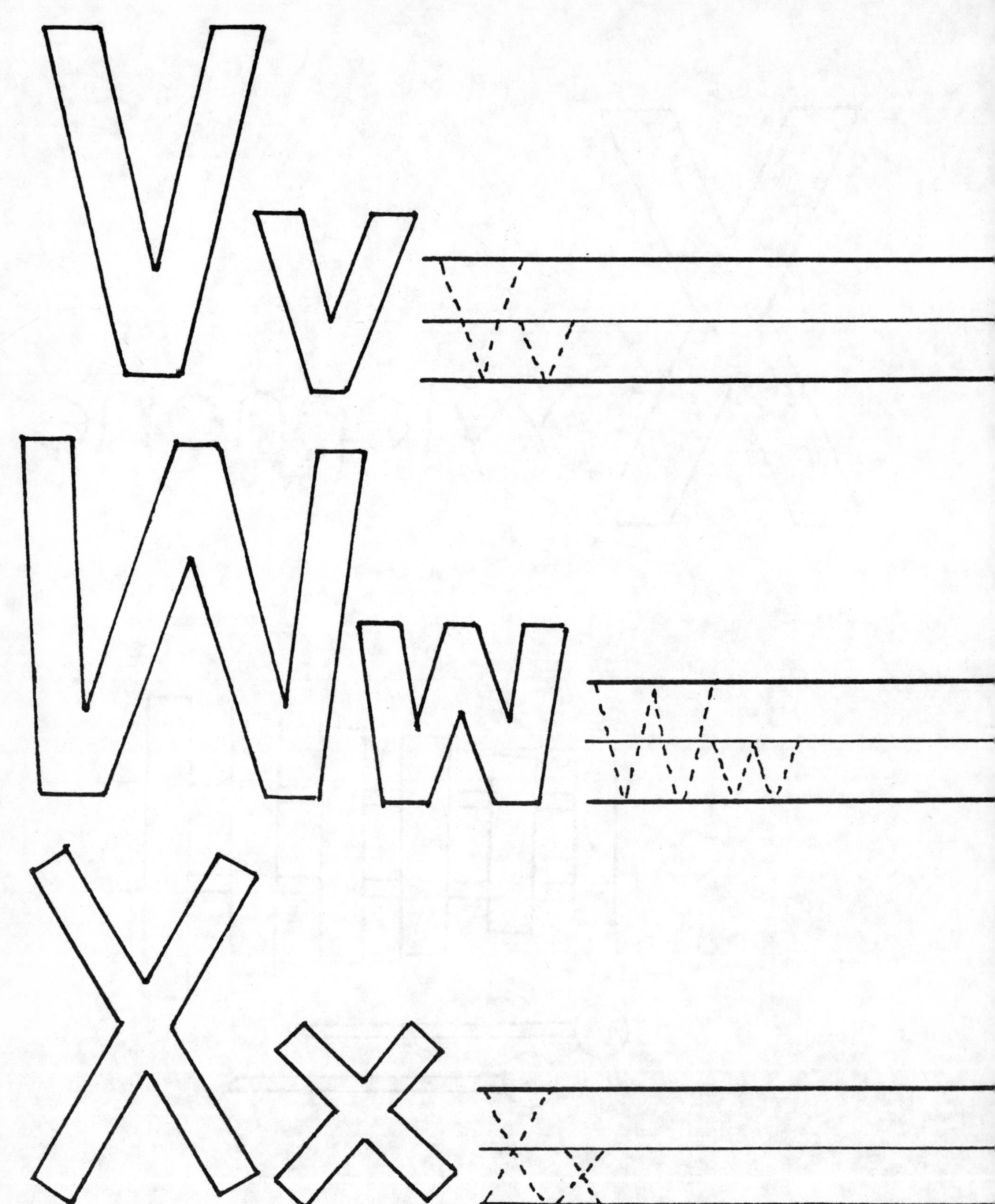
Vv
Ww
Xx

HOLLAND

HOLLAND

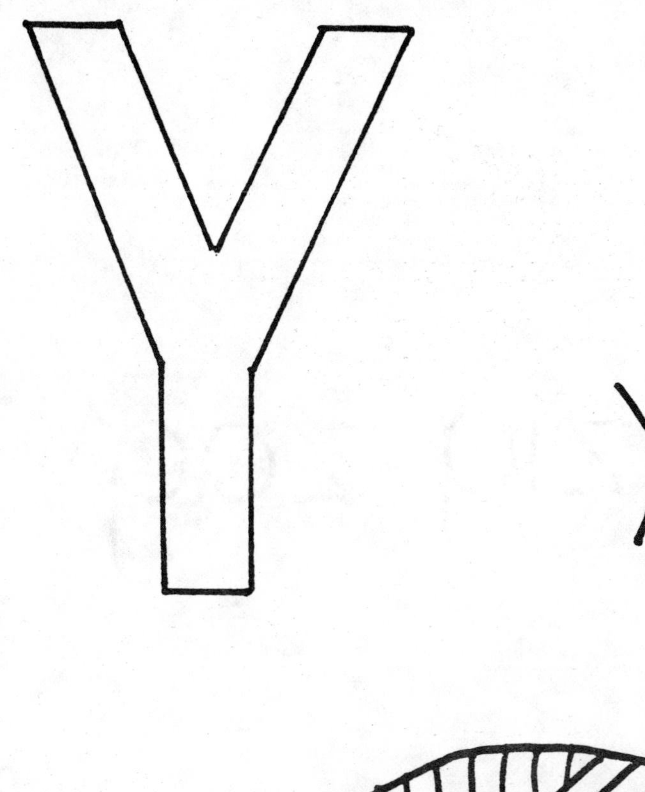

yarn

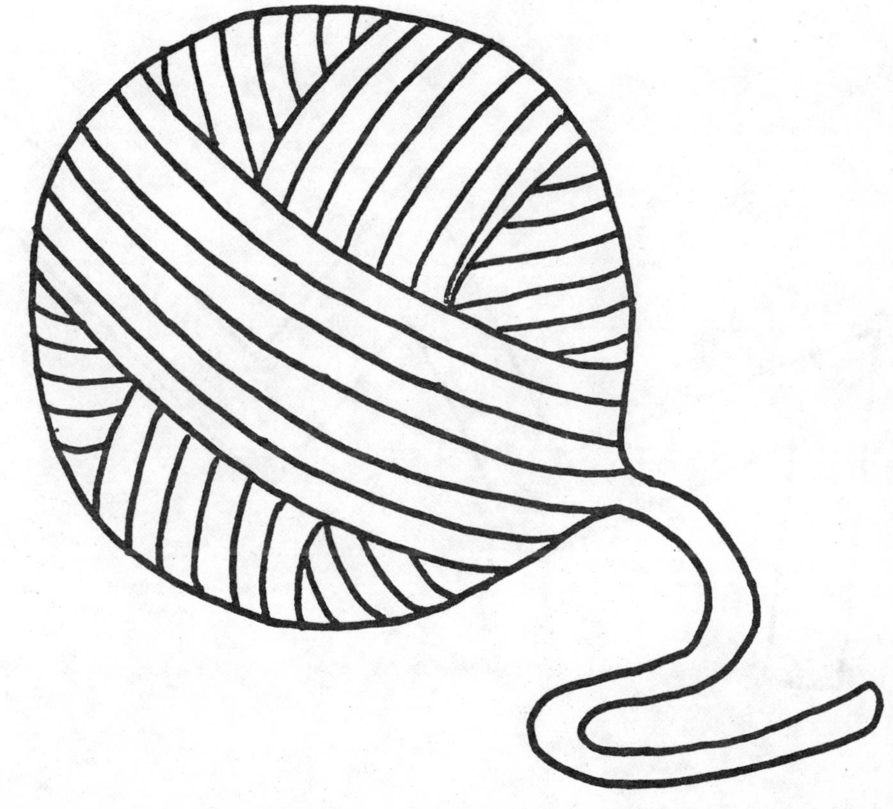

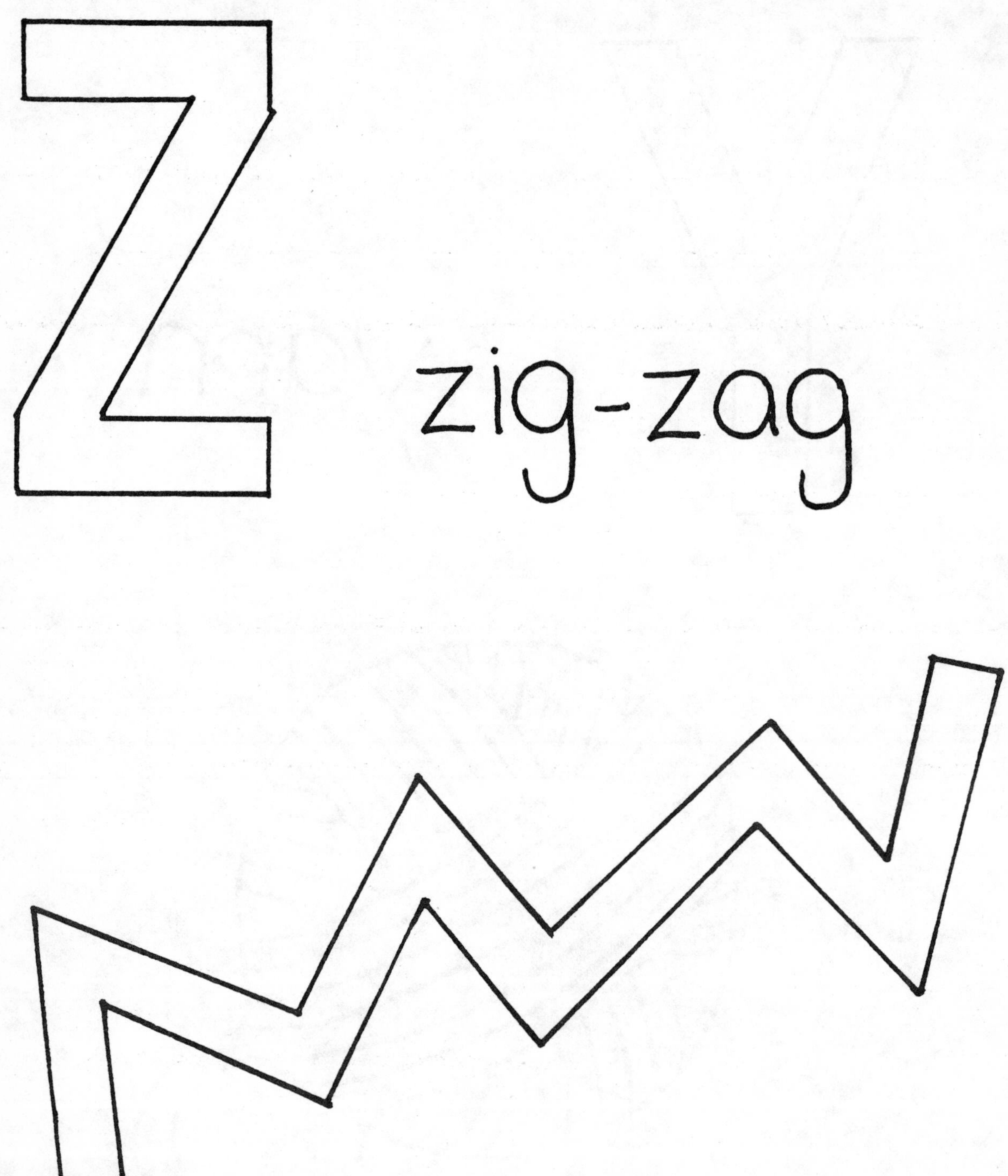
Z
zig-zag

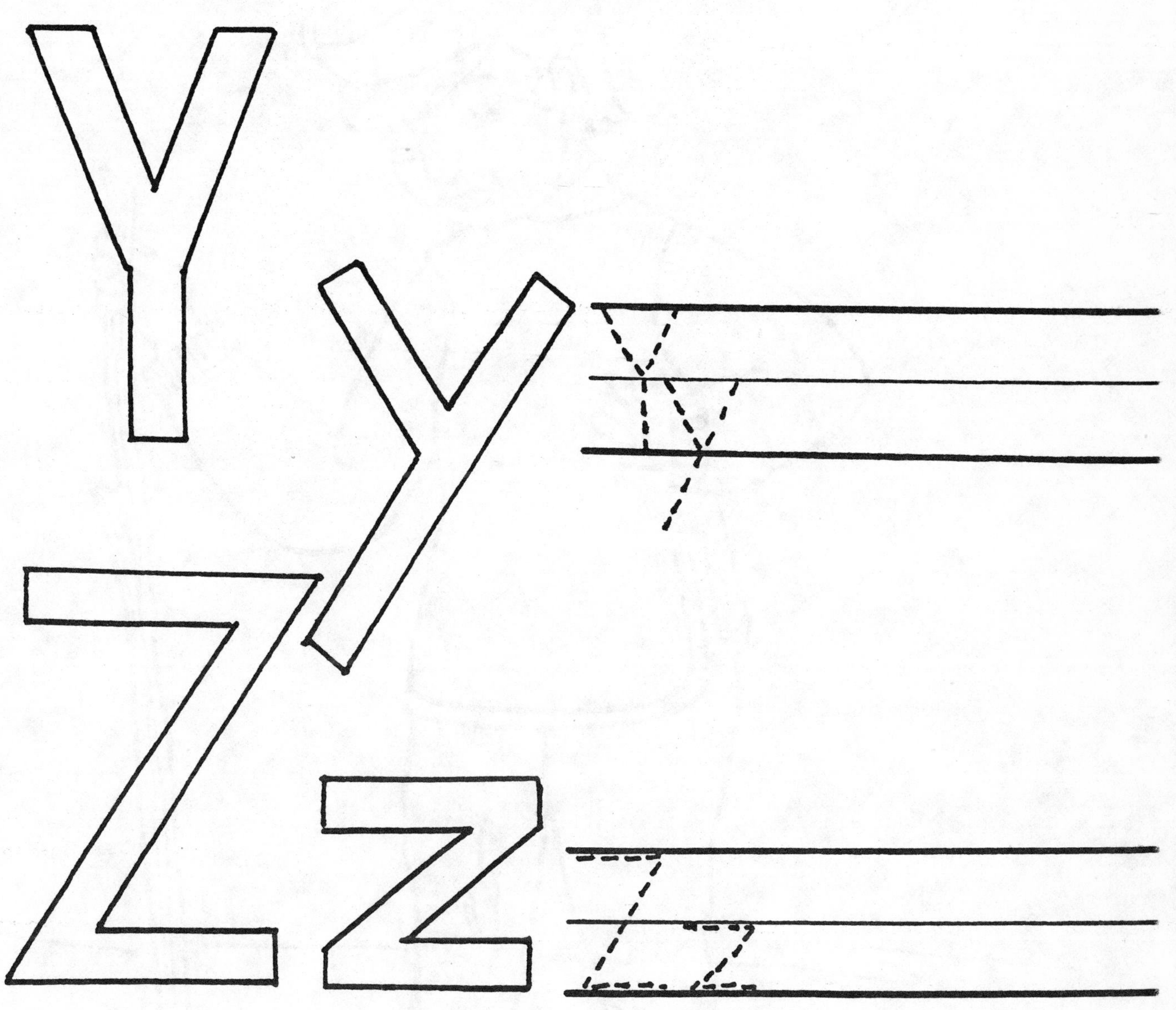

POLAND

JAPAN

3-4 (12)

Though I'm just a little one,
I am so very glad
To tell you that I love you so -
My very special Dad.

Today's your very special day,
And I wanted you to know:
You're the best in all the world,
And I love you so!

Appendix I

(Color Book)

MY COLOR BOOK

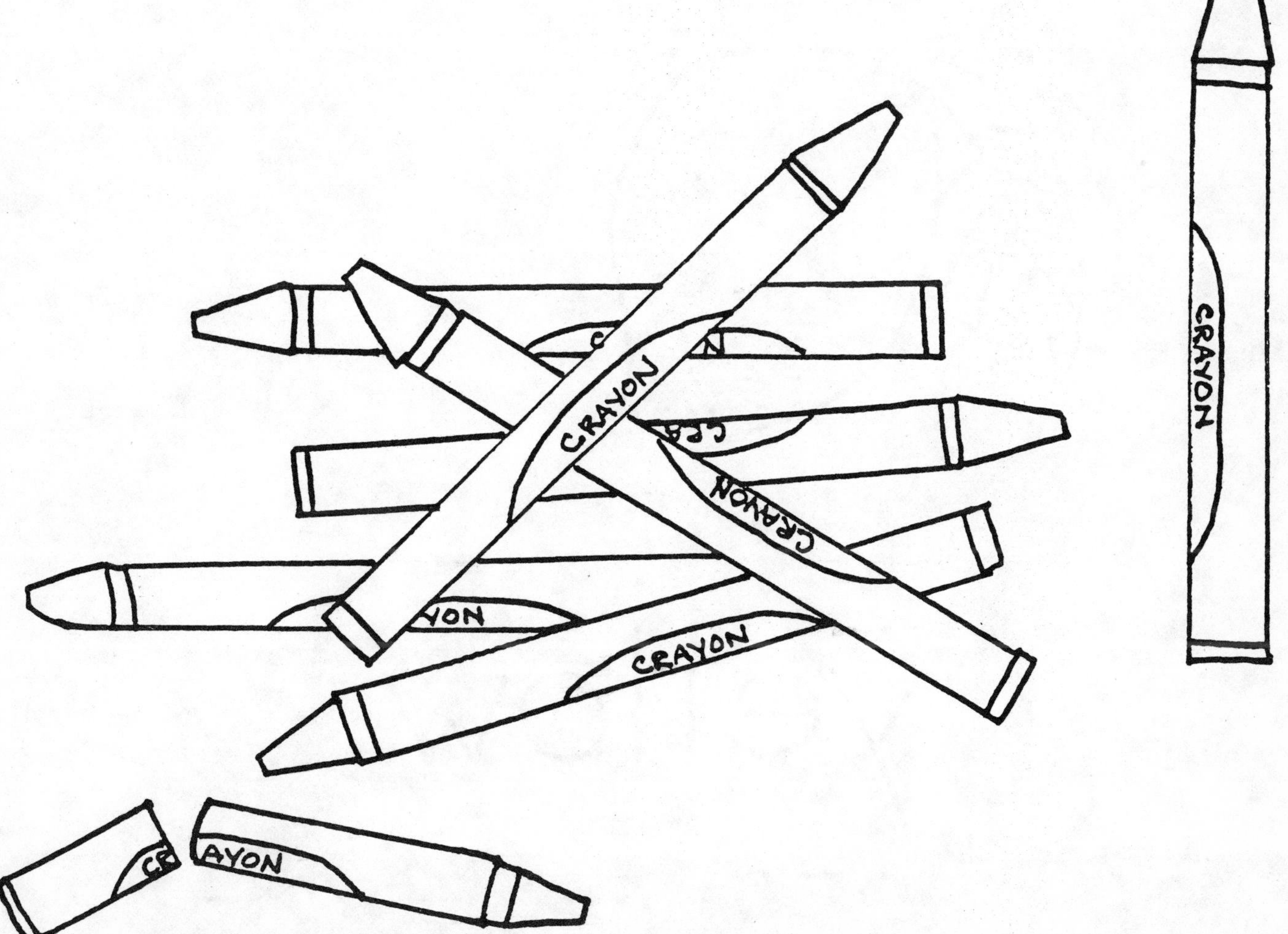

yellow

STOP
red

brown

orange

blue

green

purple

black

Appendix II
(Alphabet Book)

MY OWN ALPHABET BOOK

NAME: ______________________________

A	B

C	D	E

F	G	H	I	J	K

L	M	N	O	P	Q	R

S	T	U	V	W	X	Y	Z

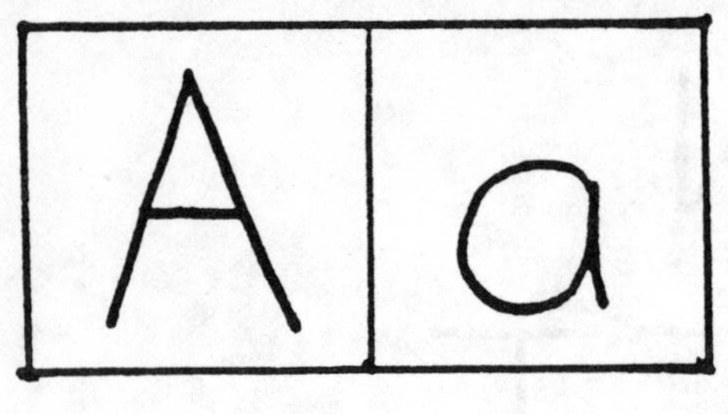

apple

automobile

anchor

A					
a					

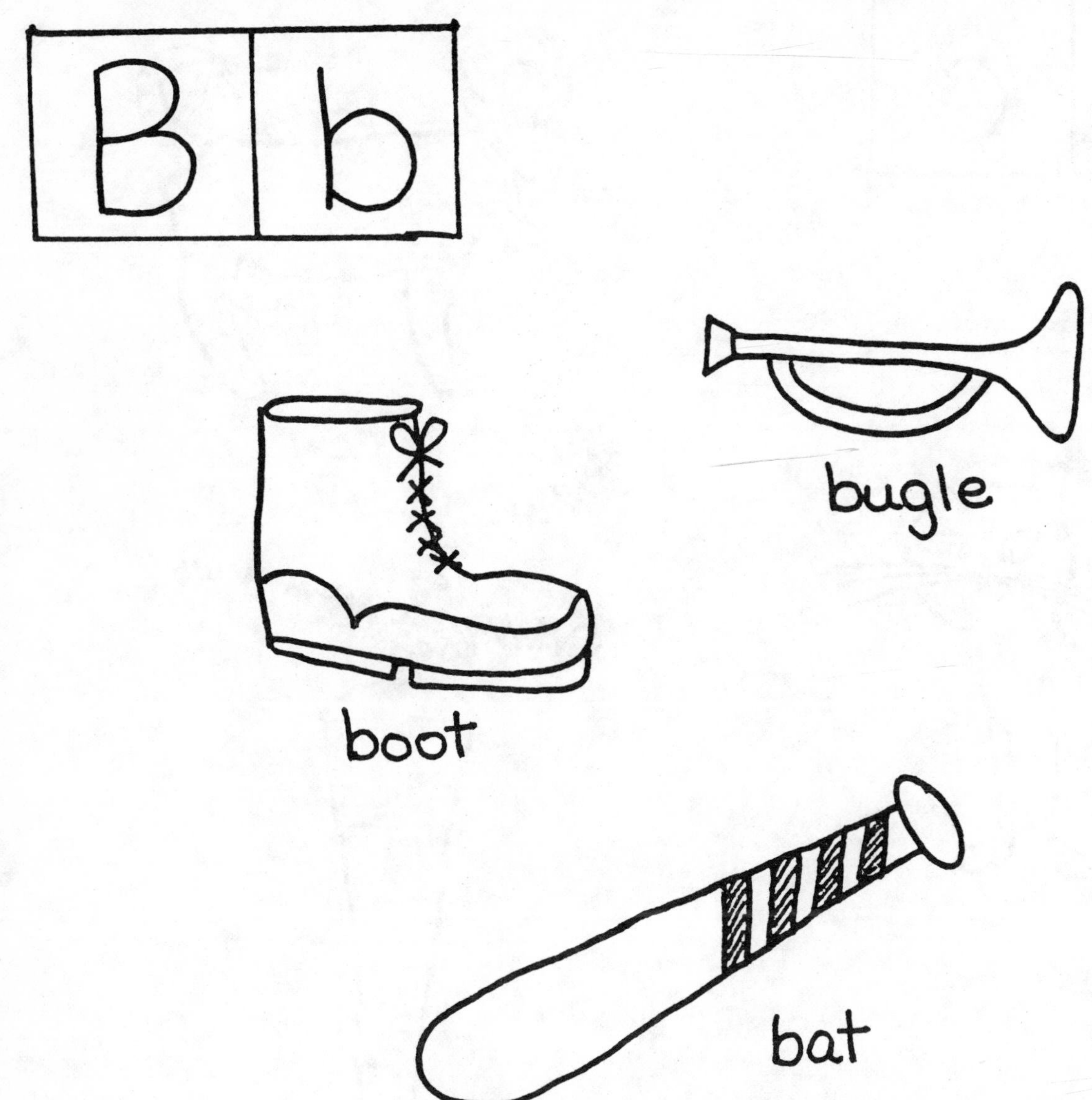

B					
b					

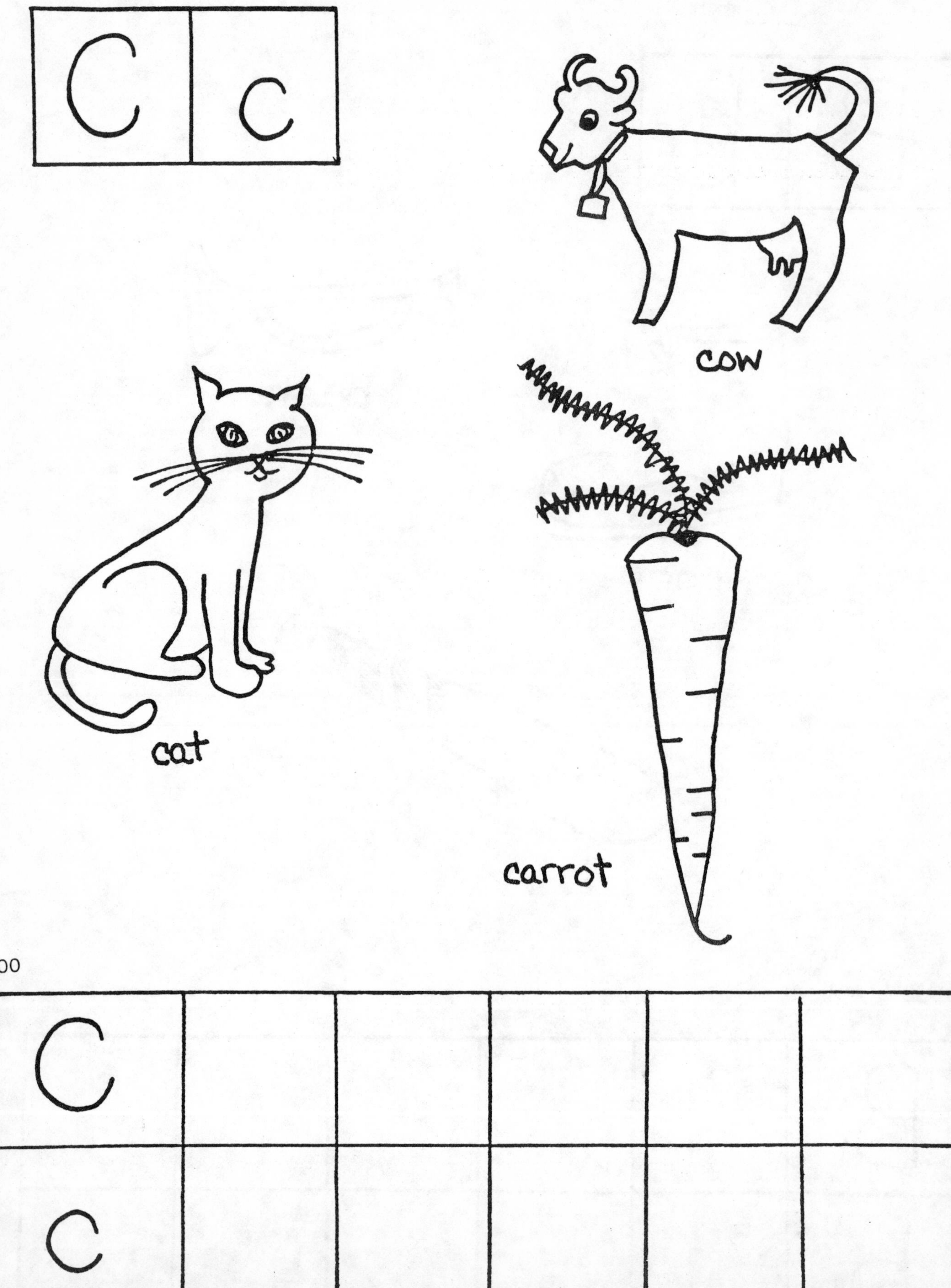
C c
cow
cat
carrot
C
c

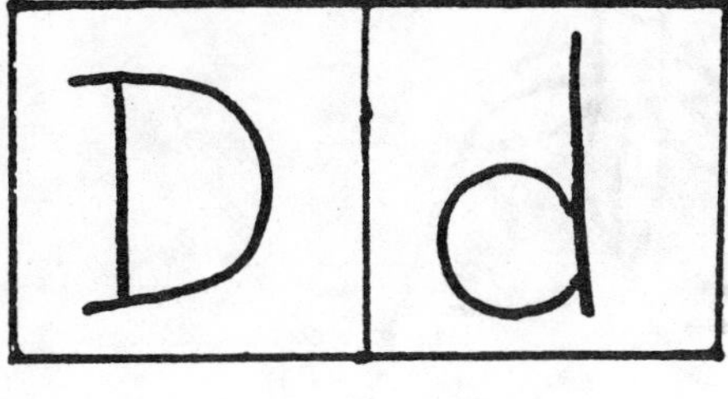

donkey

drum

dog

D					
d					

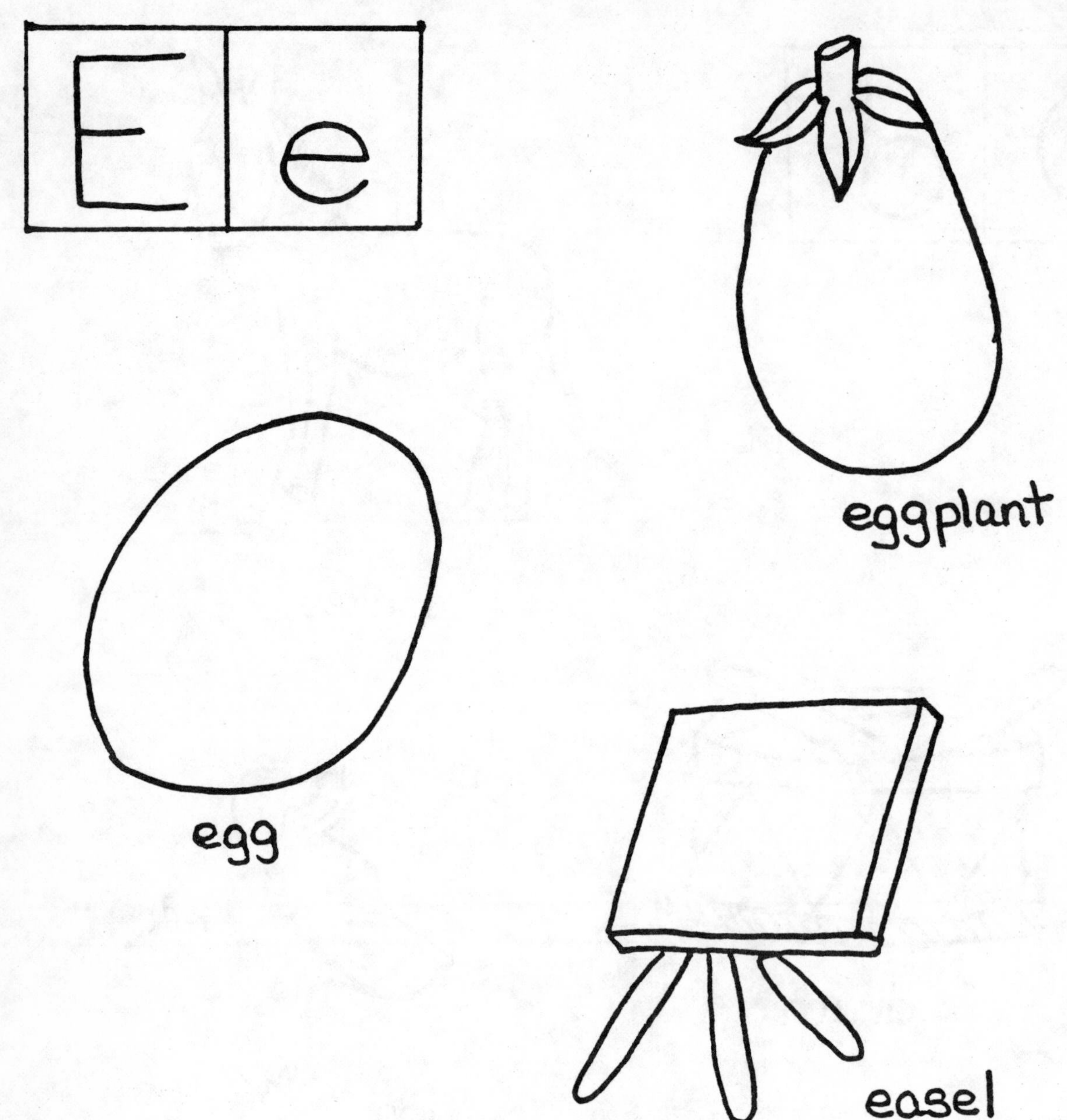

E					
e					

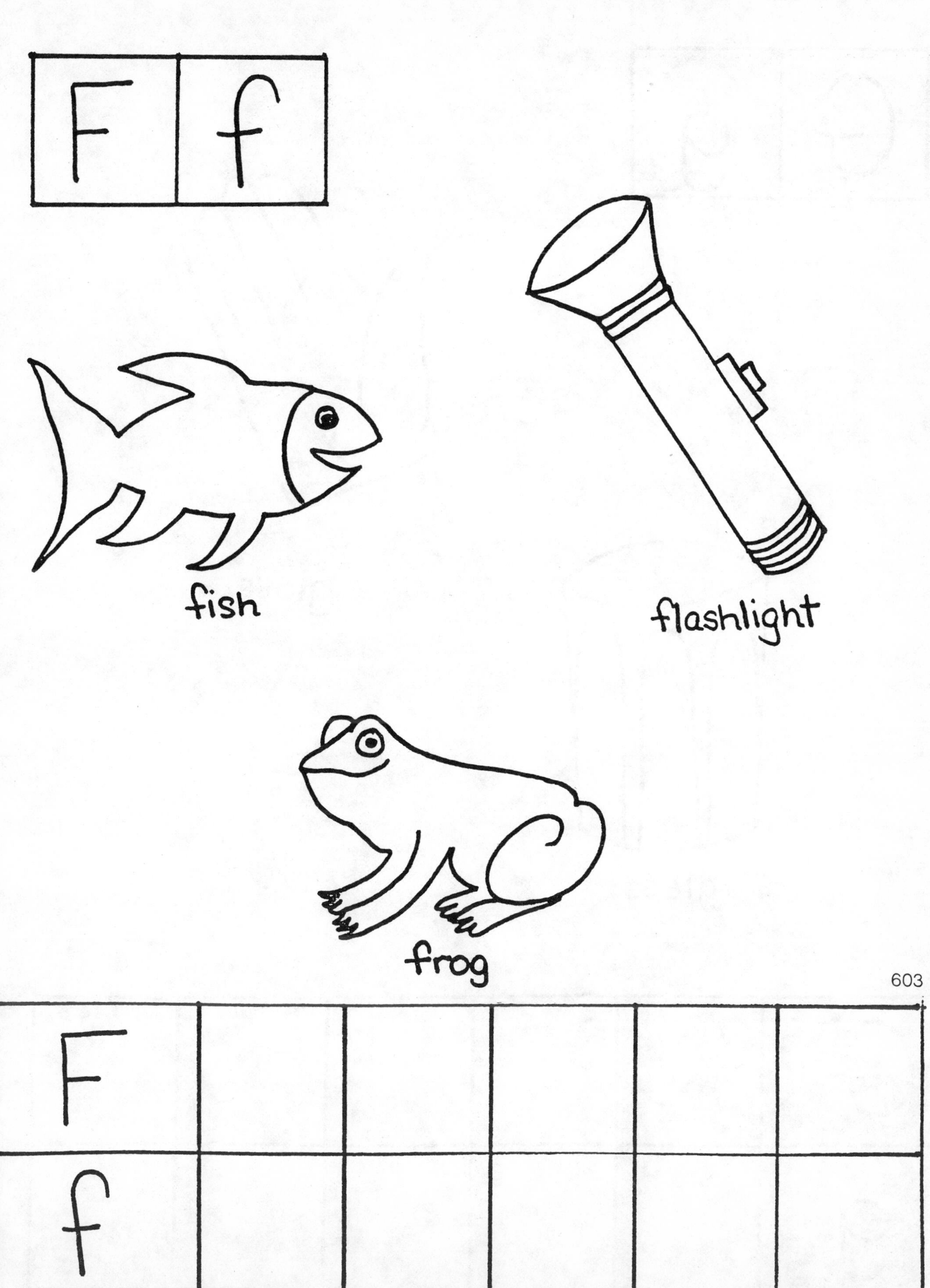
F f
fish
flashlight
frog
F
f

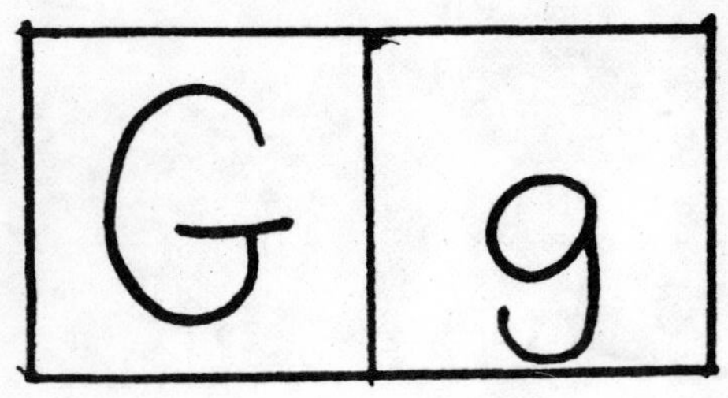

glove

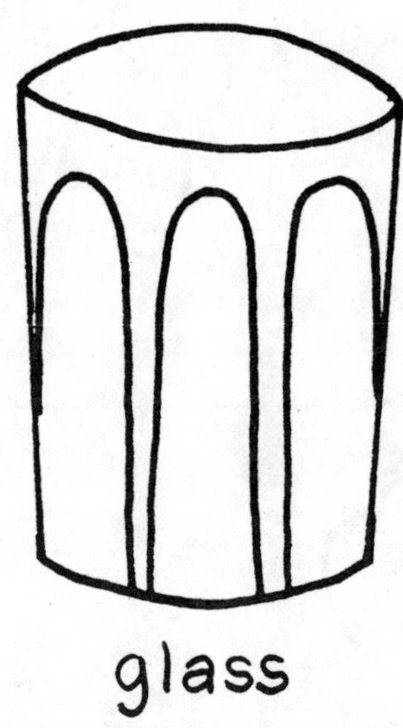

glass

G					
g					

heart

hat

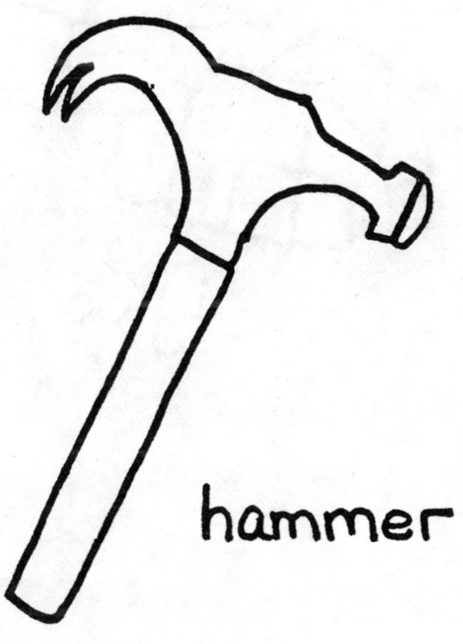
hammer

H					
h					

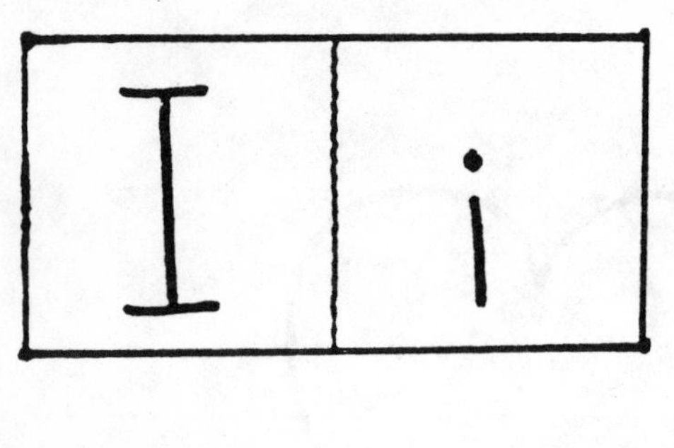

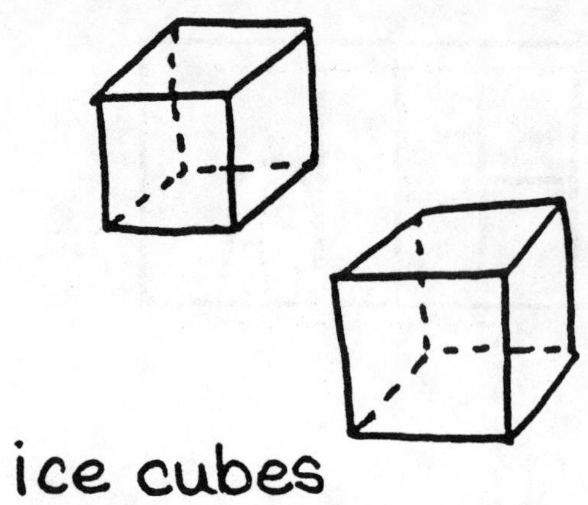

ice cubes

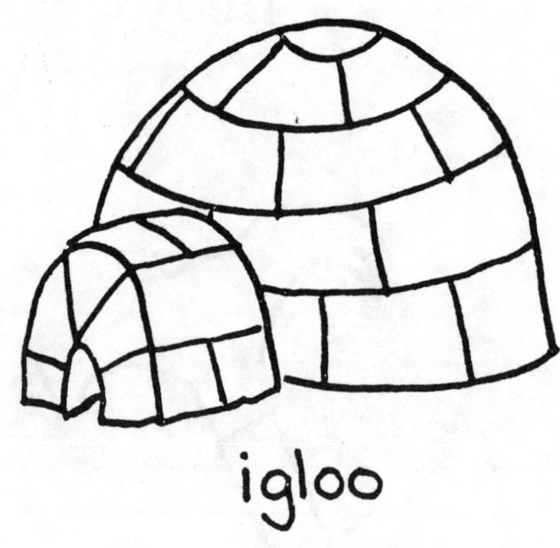

igloo

ice cream cone

I					
i					

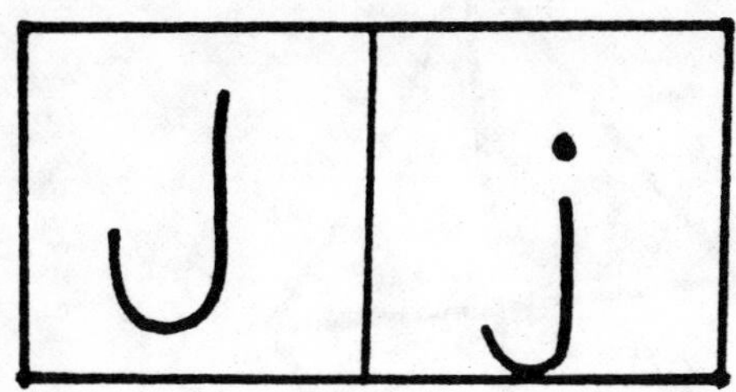

J					
j					

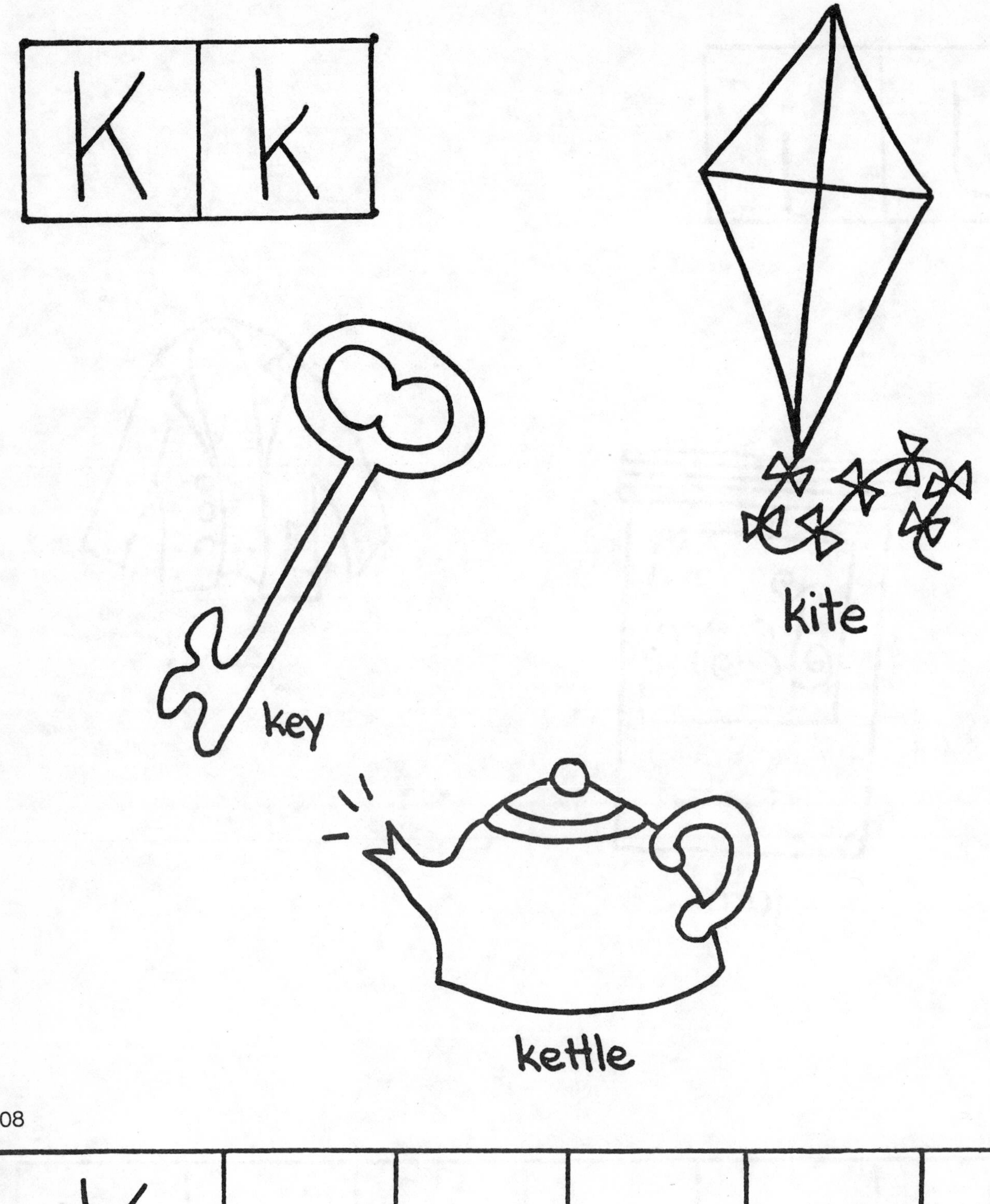

K					
k					

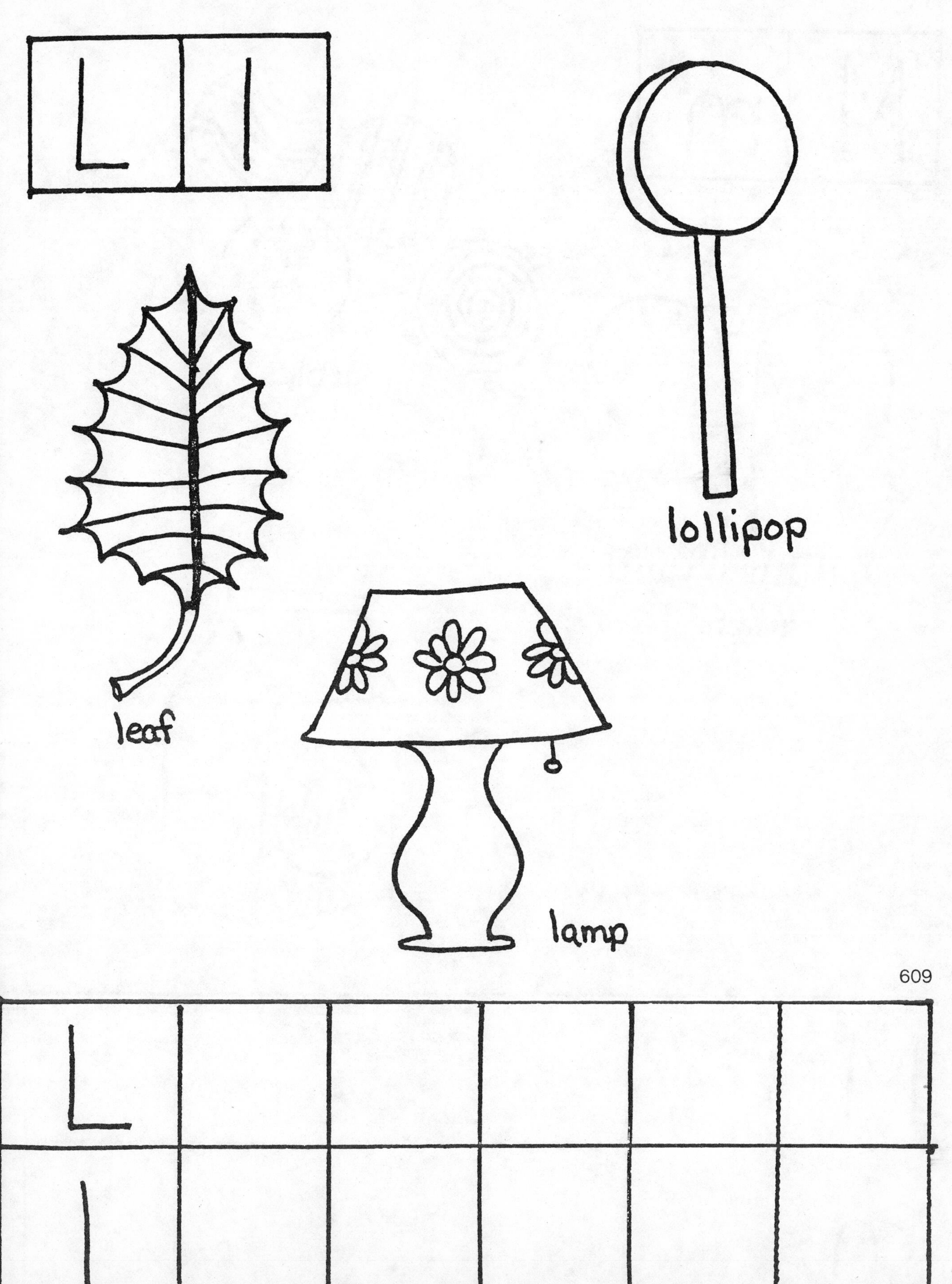
L l
lollipop
leaf
lamp
L
l

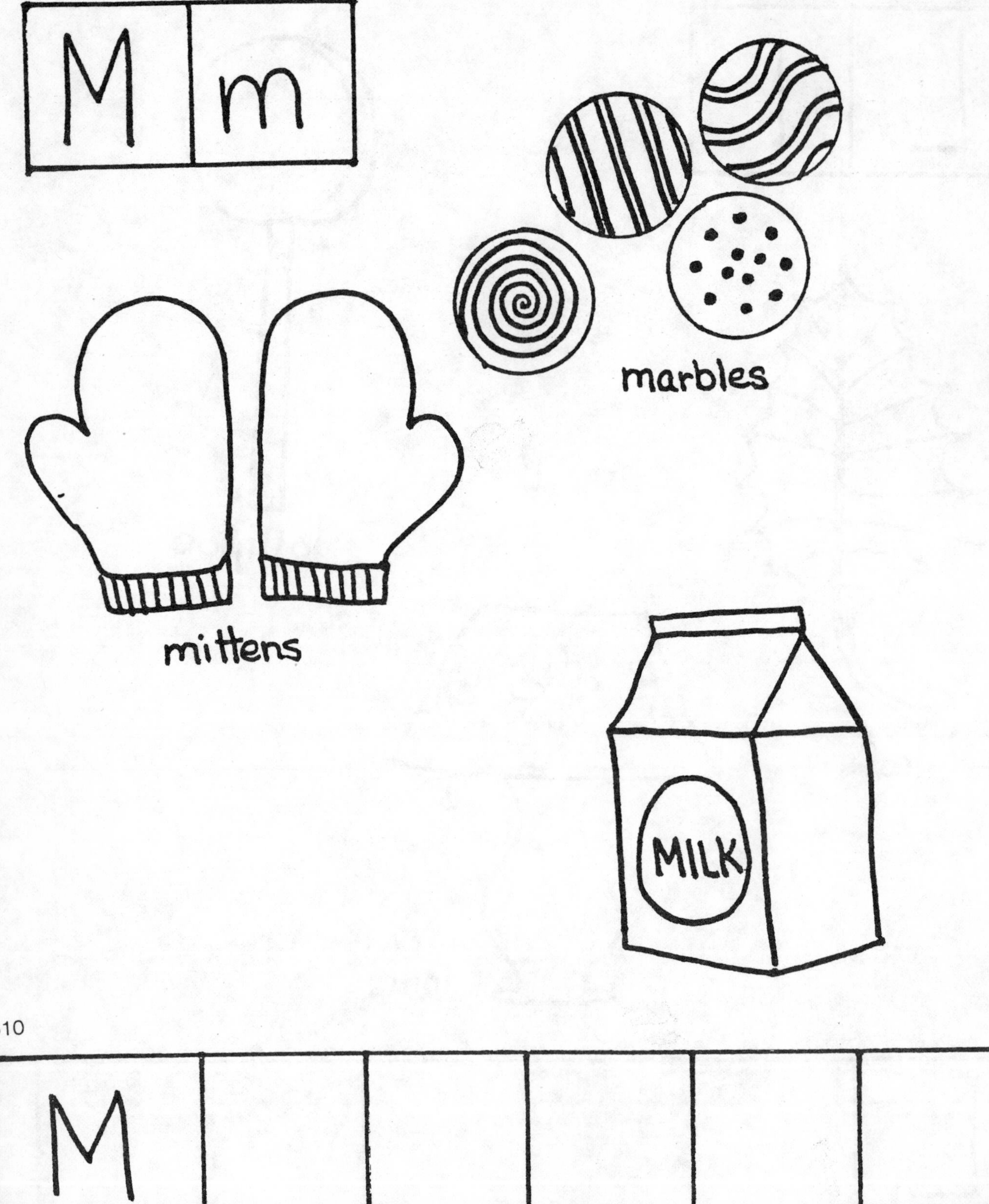

M					
m					

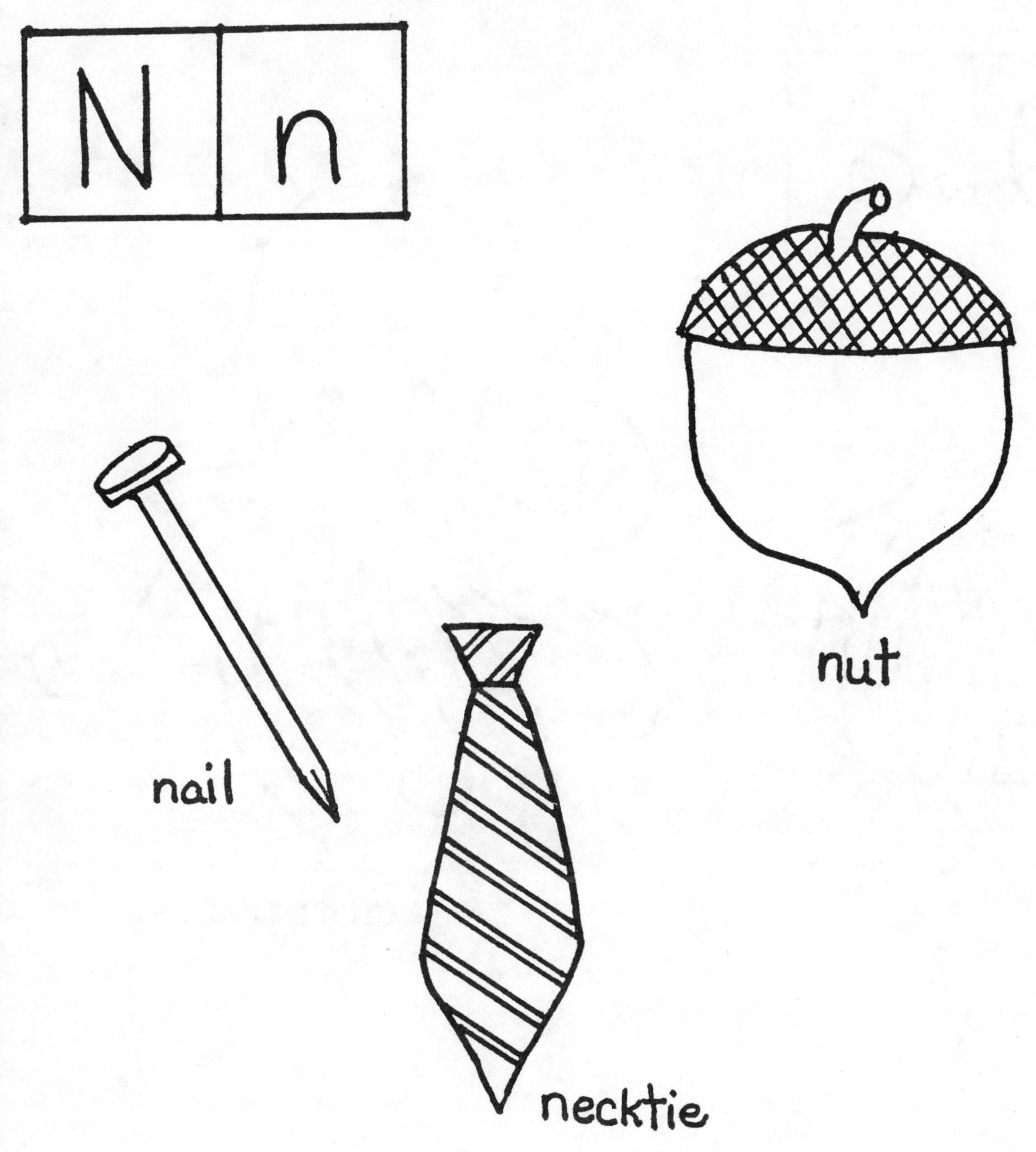

N					
n					

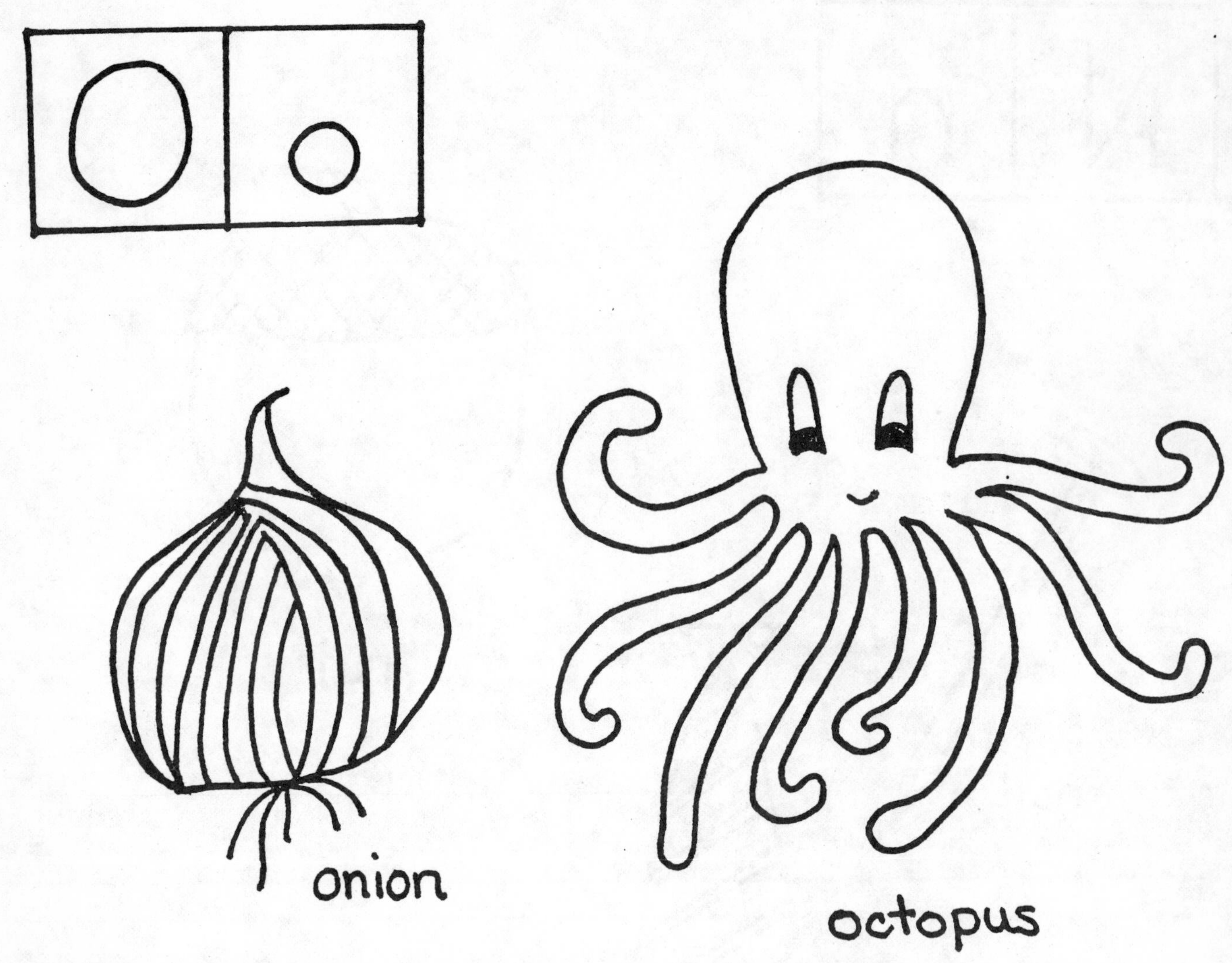

O					
o					

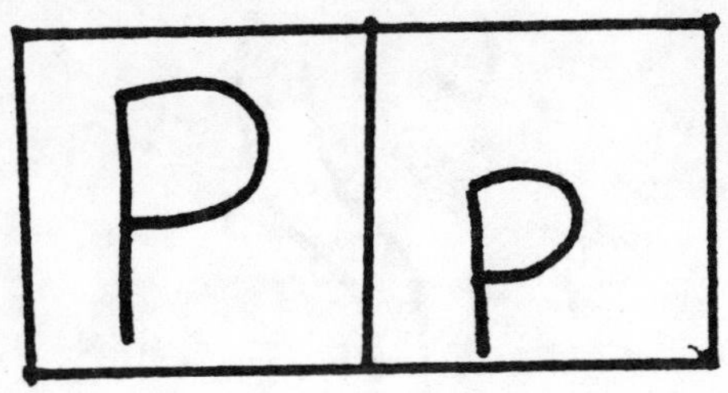

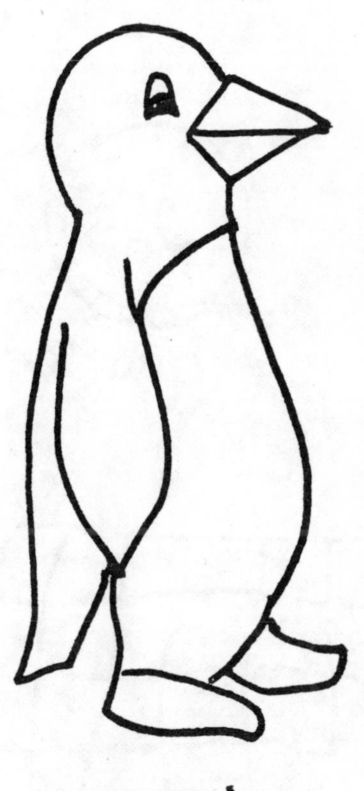

P					
p					

Q q
question
25¢
quarter
queen
quilt
Q
q

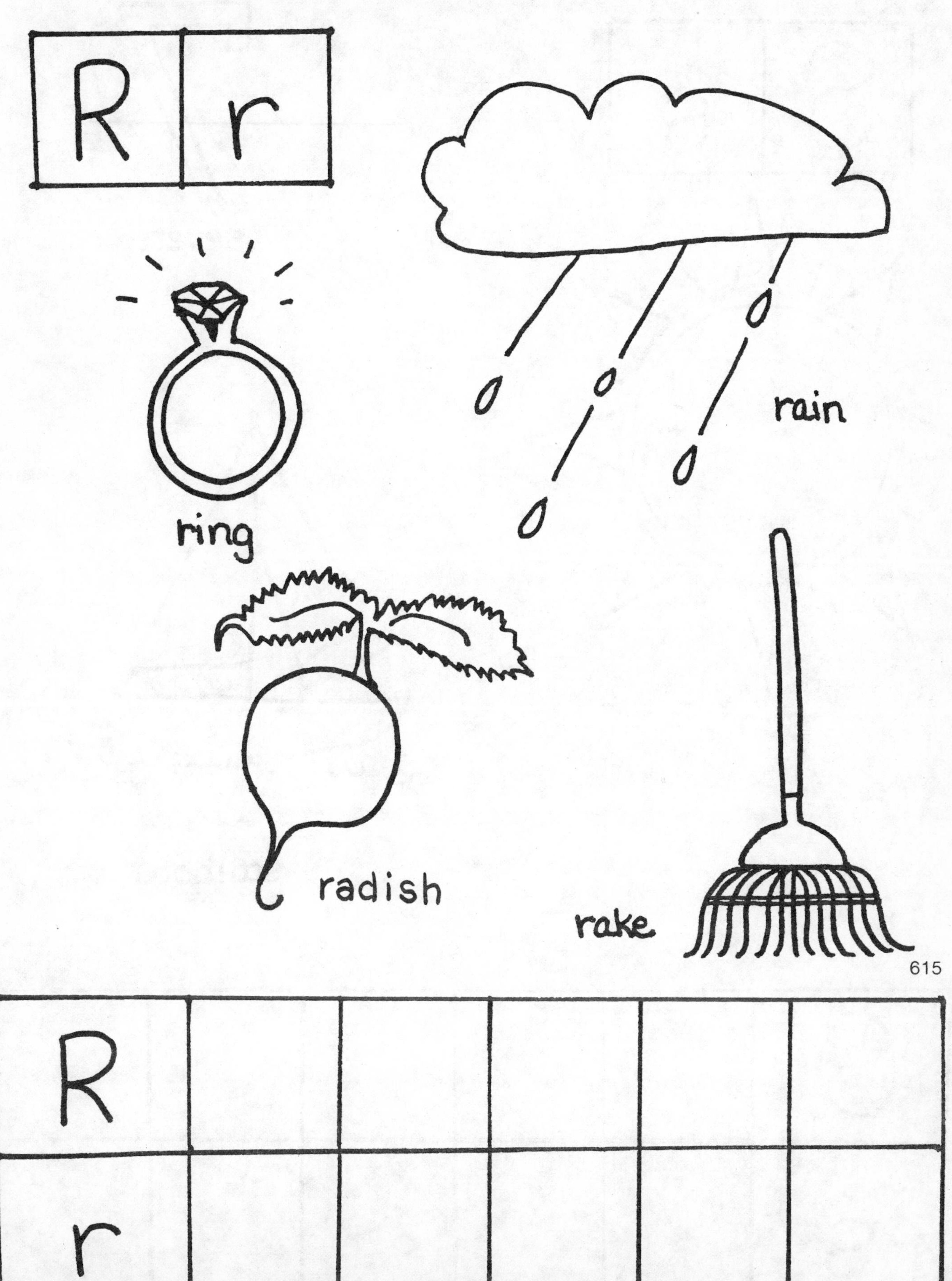
R r
rain
ring
radish
rake
R
r

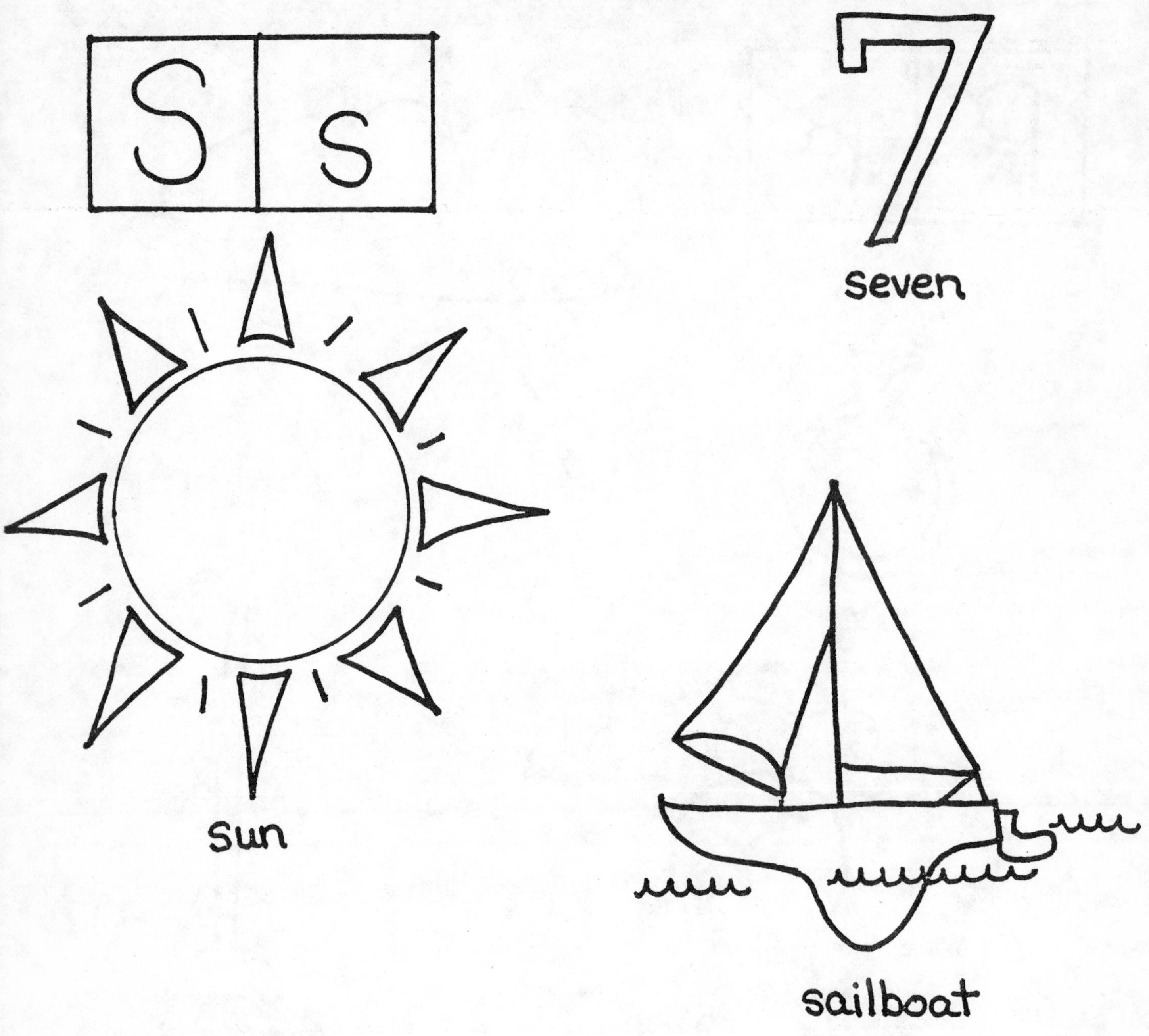

S					
s					

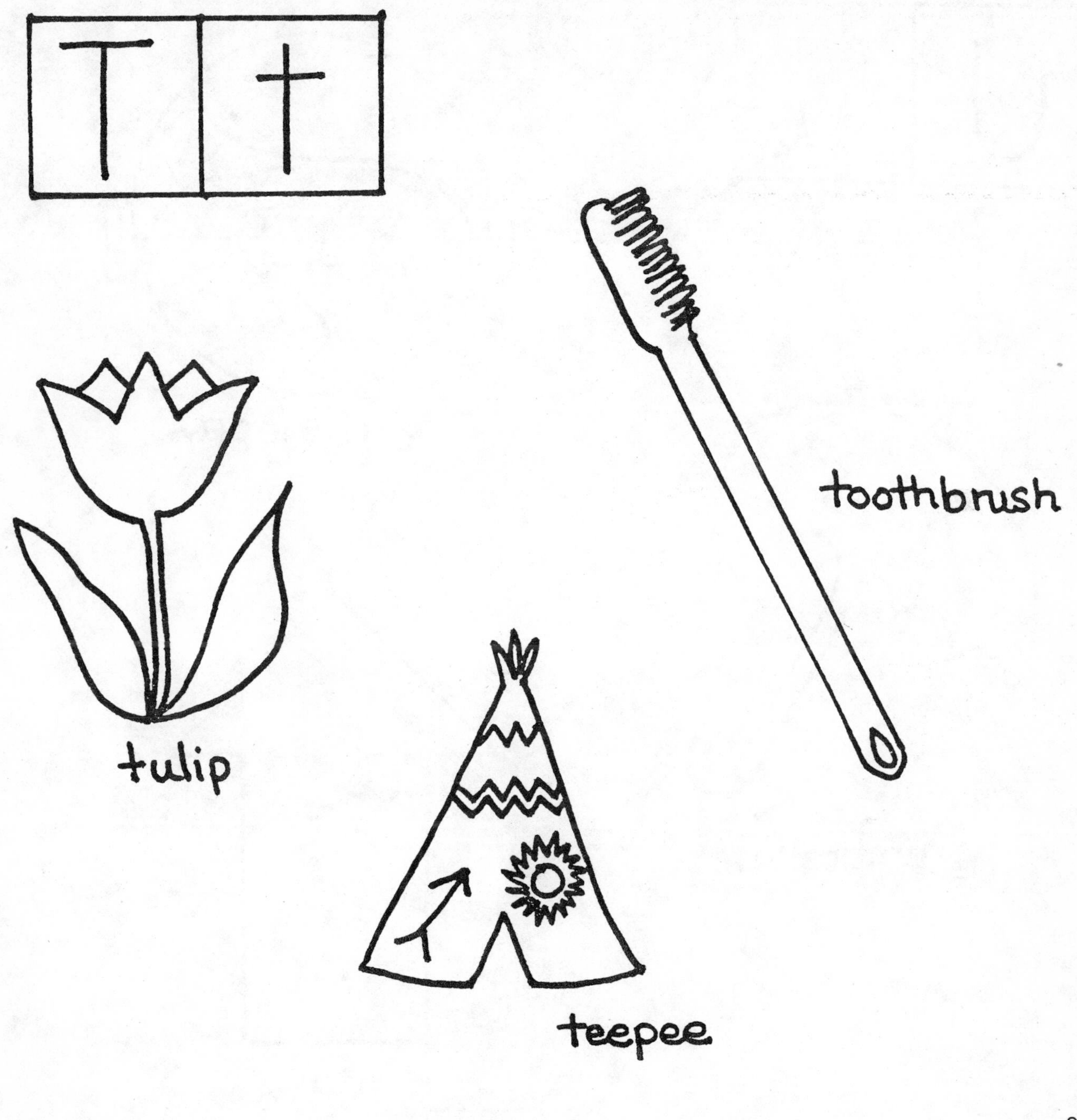

T					
t					

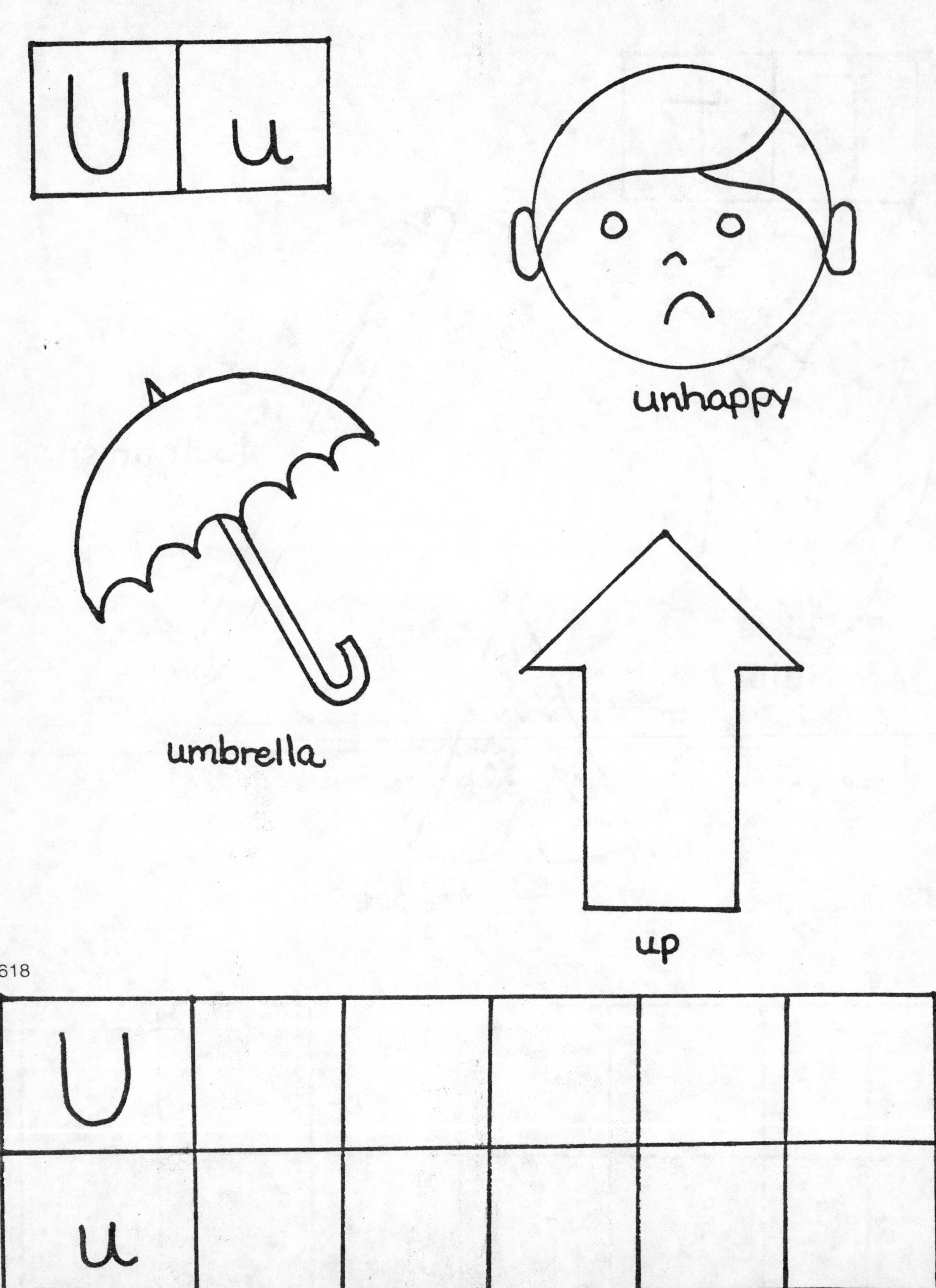

618

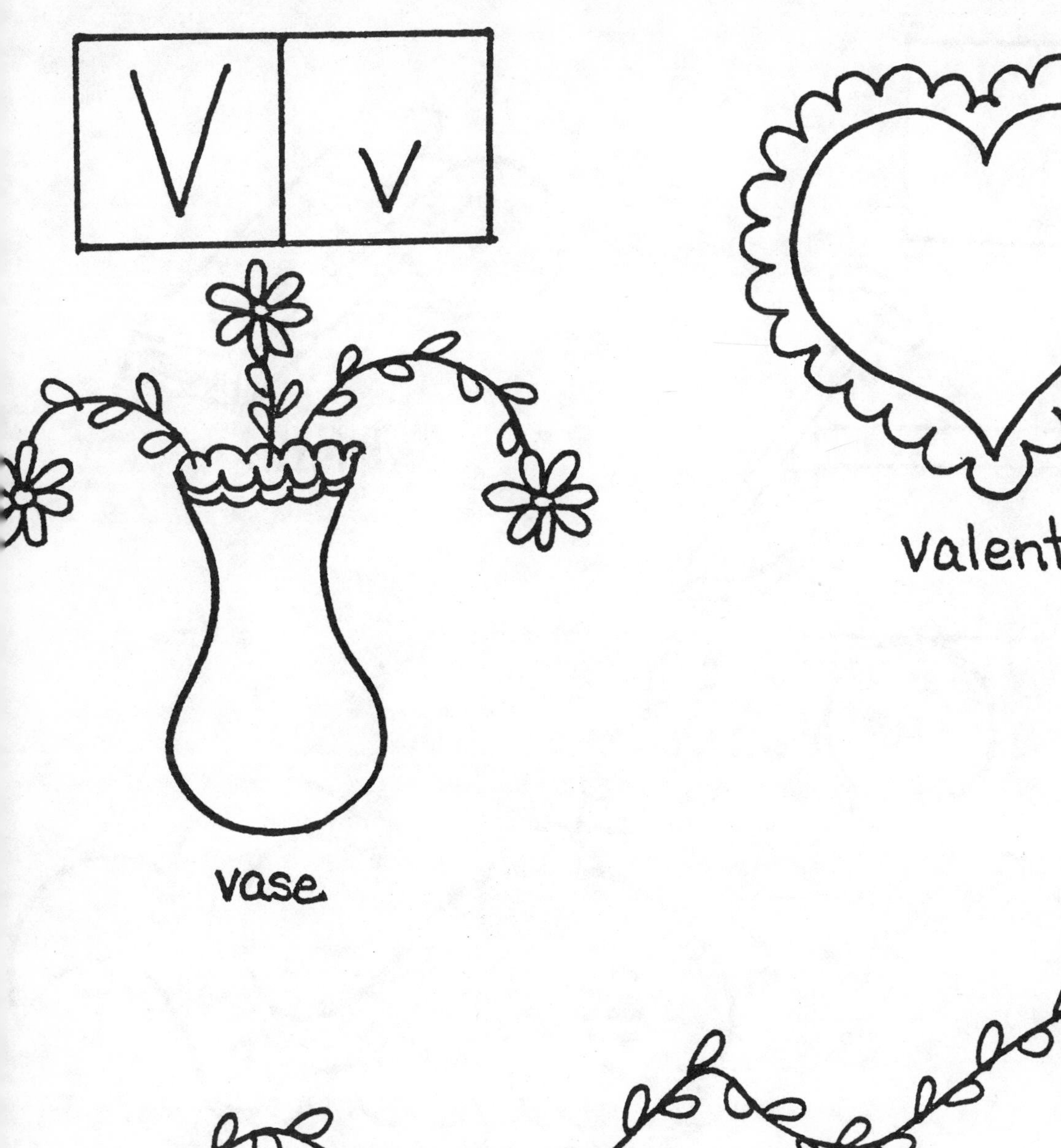

619

V					
v					

W w
whistle
wagon
whale
W
w

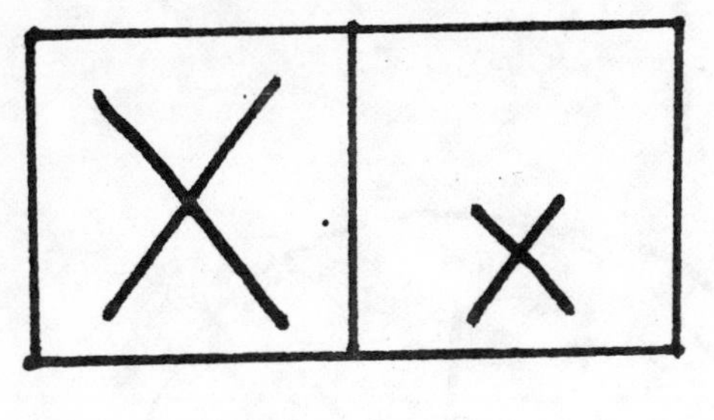

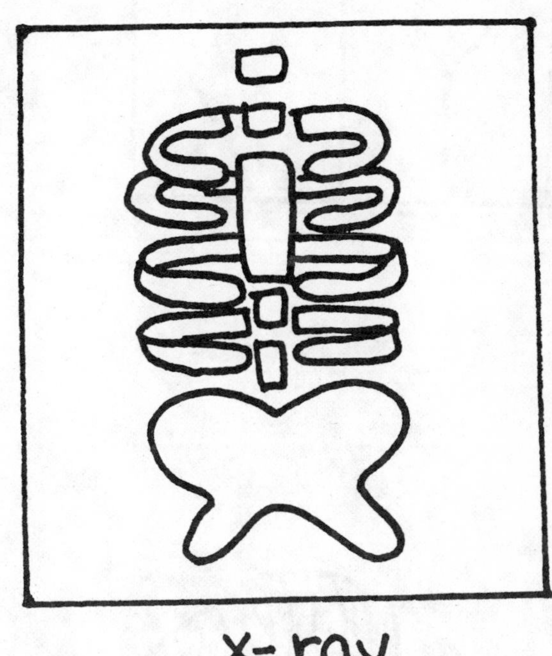

x-ray

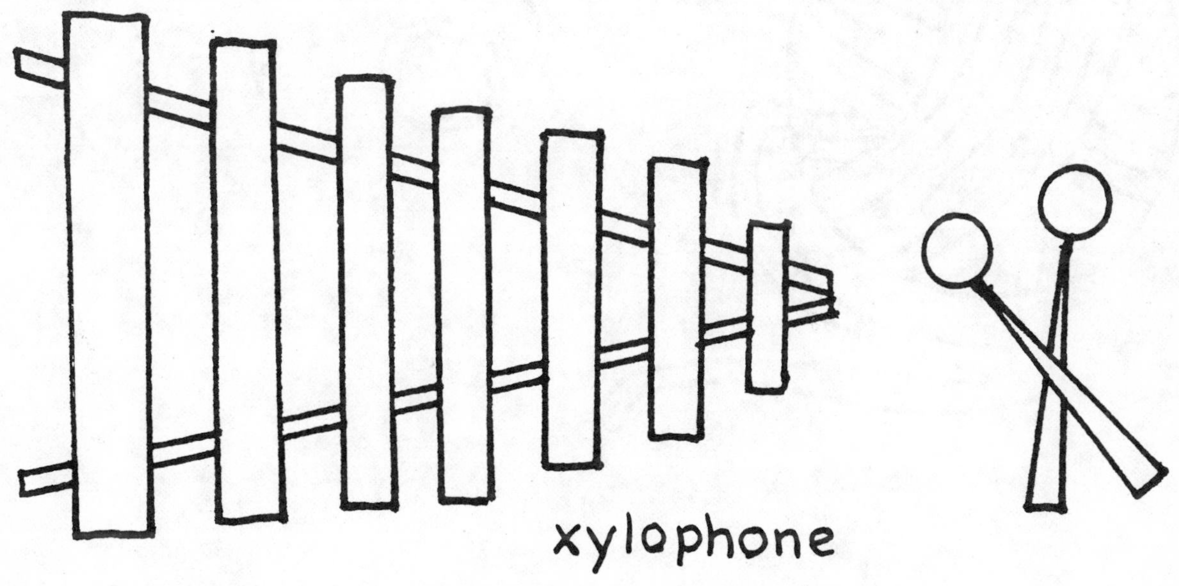

xylophone

X					
x					

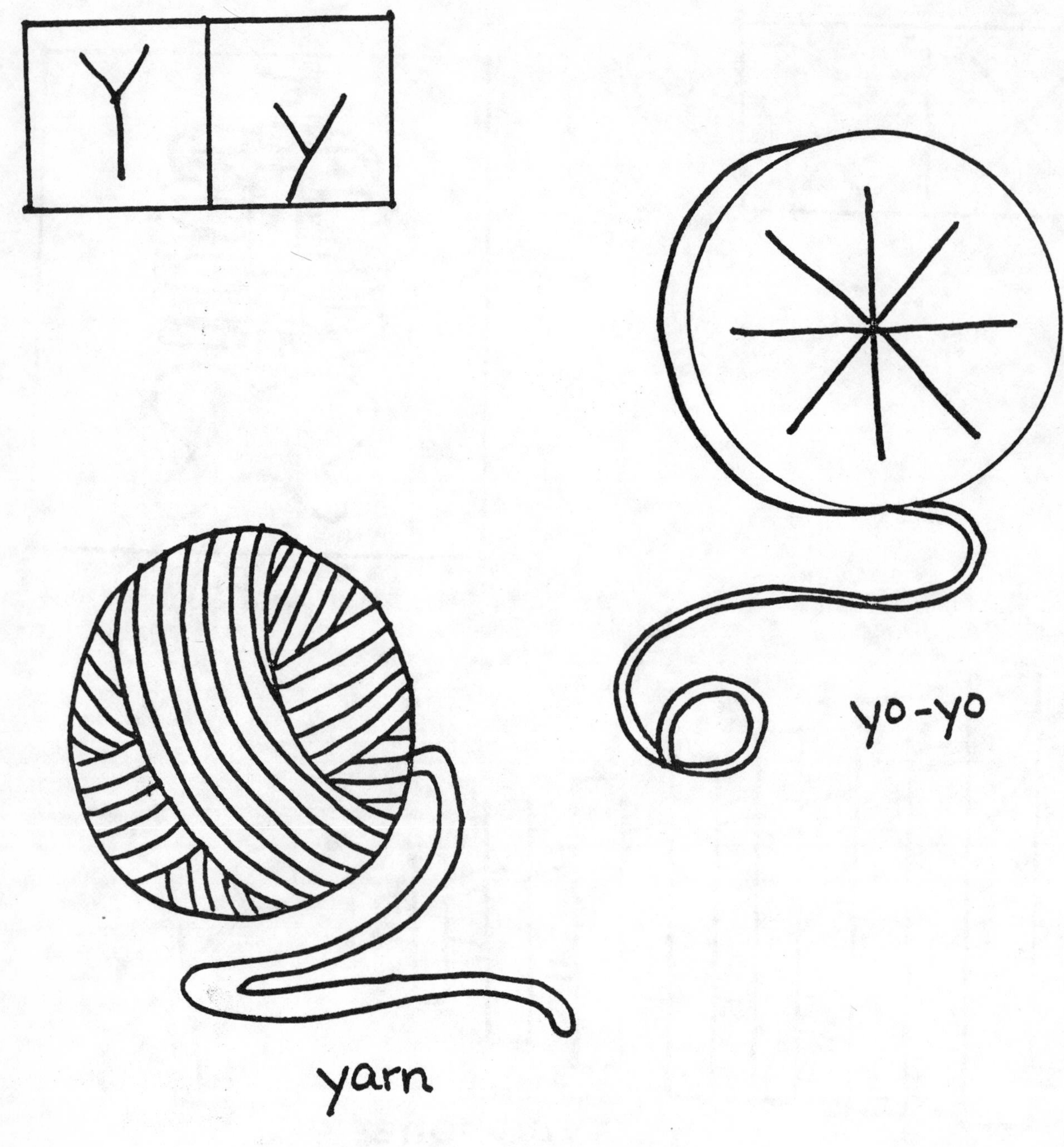

Y					
y					

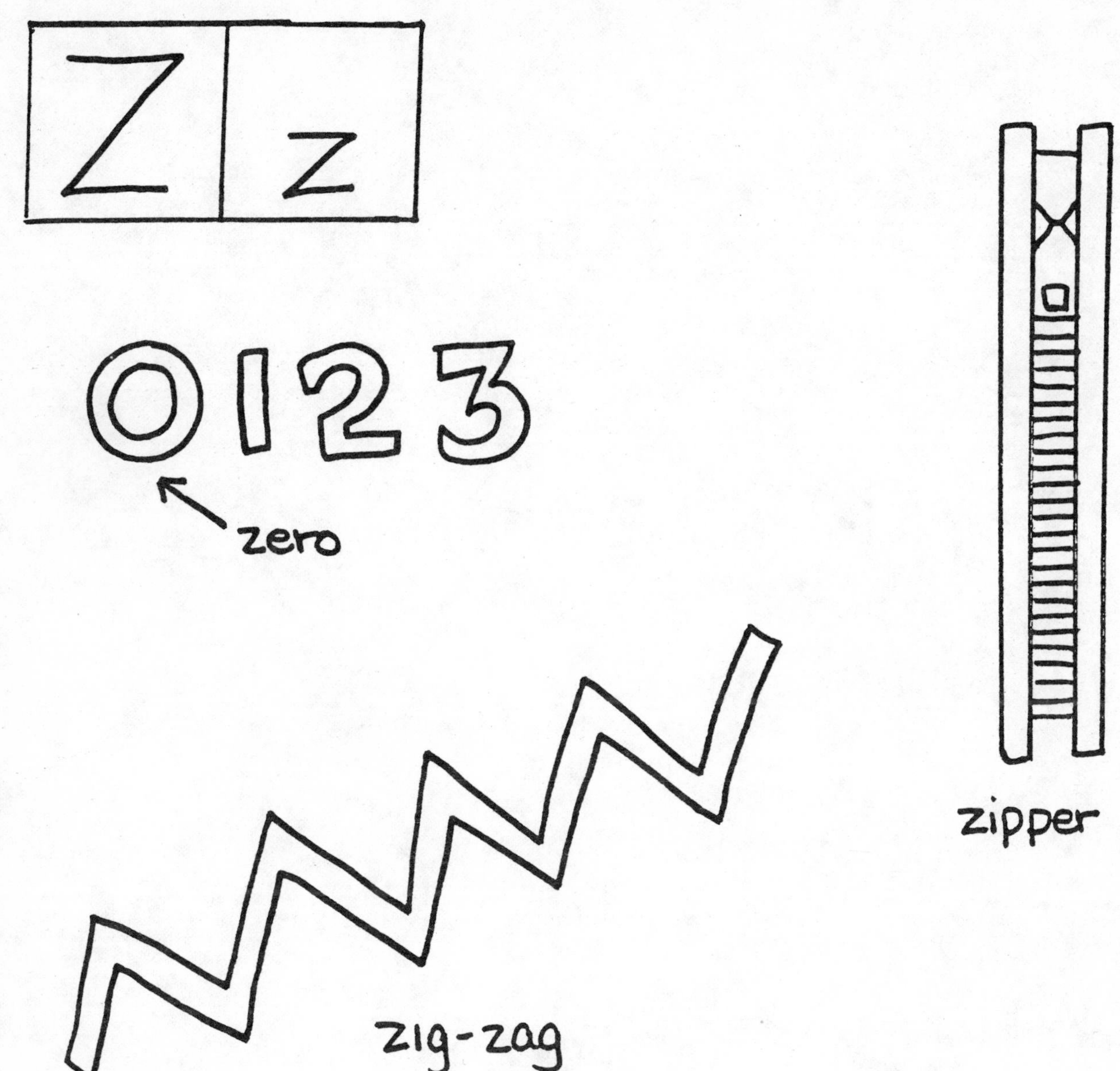

Z					
z					

Appendix III

(Holidays)

HALLOWEEN

This holiday is celebrated on the evening of October 31, and is possibly the most fun of all. Long ago though, it was a scary time. The Celtic people of northern England made huge bonfires on the hills to scare away the evil spirits that the winter would bring. They wore masks and costumes to scare away the devils and witches. They thought this would keep the evil ones away, and began the custom of wearing costumes.

1. Make sure the children understand this is a fun holiday.
2. Help them to differentiate between fantasy and reality.
3. Teach the safety rules for Halloween fun.

POEMS

"Five Little Pumpkins"

Five little pumpkins sitting on a fence
The first one said, "My it's getting late."
The second one said, "There's witches in the air."
The third one said, "We don't care."
The fourth one said, "It's only Halloween fun."
The fifth one said, "Let's run, run, run!"

(Blow) Swoosh went the wind
(Clap) Out went the lights!
5 little pumpkins rolled out of sight!

This is a finger play poem. Have the children hold up their fingers for each pumpkin sitting on the gate, then close their fist when the pumpkins roll away.

"The Friendly Pumpkin"

I made a little pumpkin man
To shine for Halloween
I cut out eyes and nose and mouth
The widest ever seen.
I think I'll be a pumpkin man,
Pretend I have a light
I'll turn it on and always smile
At everyone in sight.

A Halloween friend for company

COLUMBUS DAY

In 1492 on this day, Christopher Columbus found the New World. The United States is part of the land that he saw. We now believe that he was not the first explorer to find our land, but settlement began after his voyage. He had three ships in his company, the Nina, the Pinta and the Santa Maria. It took 72 days to journey to an island named El Salvador which is southeast of Florida.

POEM

"Columbus"

In fourteen hundred and ninety-two
Columbus sailed the ocean blue.
For seventy two days he headed west
Then new land was sighted from the crow's nest.
Long years ago he showed he was brave.
On this special day, his memory we save.

Set up three napping mats or pillows on the floor (ocean). Let three of the children sit on each mat, and pretend they are having an ocean voyage. You can pretend storms, hot days, and days with no wind to move the ships. Let your imagination run free and have fun with your children.

NINA
PINTA
SANTA MARIA

4 year olds make a boat:

Use ½ egg carton for each.
Put popsicle stick through center,
paste or tape square sail to stick

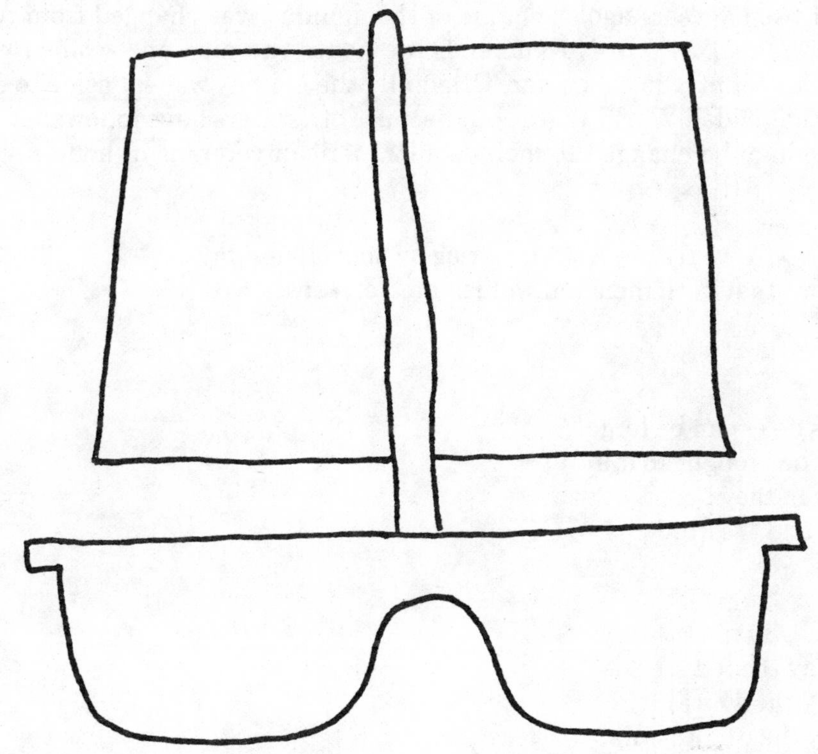

VETERAN'S DAY

More than twenty years ago the name of this holiday was changed from Armistice Day to Veteran's Day. On November 11 we honor the men and women who have fought for our country in every war. Originally the holiday was set aside to celebrate the peace that ended World War I, but because other wars have followed it is logical that the holiday be changed to include all American veterans in honoring ceremonies.

1. Explain why we fly the American flag on special holidays.
2. Point out that both men and women are veterans.

POEMS:

Our heroes ne'er can be forgot
They'll all be brought to mind!
Oh never can they be forgot,
The noble and the kind.

Our Flag

Be brave say the red stripes
Be pure say the white,
Be true say the bright stars,
And stand for the right.

VETERAN'S DAY

THANKSGIVING

Our first Thanksgiving took place with a small group of settlers living at Plymouth, Massachussetts. The colonists had had a hard year in the new land and half of them had died. The people left had planted corn and reaped a good harvest. They built shelters for the coming winter and had been successful hunting wild game. They were very thankful in their hearts. In 1621 they set aside a time to be thankful and invited their Indian friends to share in a feast with them. Today we celebrate Thanksgiving on the fourth Thursday in November.

1. Help the children understand who the Pilgrims were and the reasons they came to the New World.
2. Create an appreciation for what the Indians and early colonists did for our country.
3. Develop an awareness for things to be thankful for.

POEMS:

Thanksgiving Day will soon be here;
It comes around but once a year
If I could only have my way
We'd have Thanksgiving everyday.

"America"

Oh beautiful, for spacious skies,
For amber waves of grain,
For purple mountains majesties,
Above the fruited plain.
America, America,
God shed his grace on thee,
And crown thy good with brotherhood
From sea to shining sea.

Happy Thanksgiving

CHANUKAH (HANUKKAH)

This is the Jewish holiday known as the Feast of Lights. This happy eight day celebration comes in the winter and is a time of presents and parties. Long ago, when a foreign king and his army took over Palestine and the temple there, the Jews fought their enemy for three years and at last they won. Lights were always kept burning inside the temple, but finally there was only enough oil left for one more day. Then the great miracle occurred. The light burned for eight days and nights, giving the Jews enough time to prepare more oil. Ever since then, Jews around the world celebrate Chanukah by lighting one candle each night of the eight nights until all are lit on the last day of the holiday.

The menorah is a special nine-branched candelabra and is used for this holiday. One candle is used each night and the ninth branch holds an extra candle from which the other candles are lighted.

1. Develop an understanding of the holiday.
2. What Christian holiday is celebrated around this time?
3. Name other Jewish holidays — Christian holidays.

POEMS

Chanukah, Chanukah begins this way,
By lighting a candle for every day.
Until all eight are lighted this way
To celebrate the holiday.

Eight little candles
All in a line
Eight little candles
Glitter and shine.

Eight little candles
Each little flame
Whispers a legend
Of honor and fame.

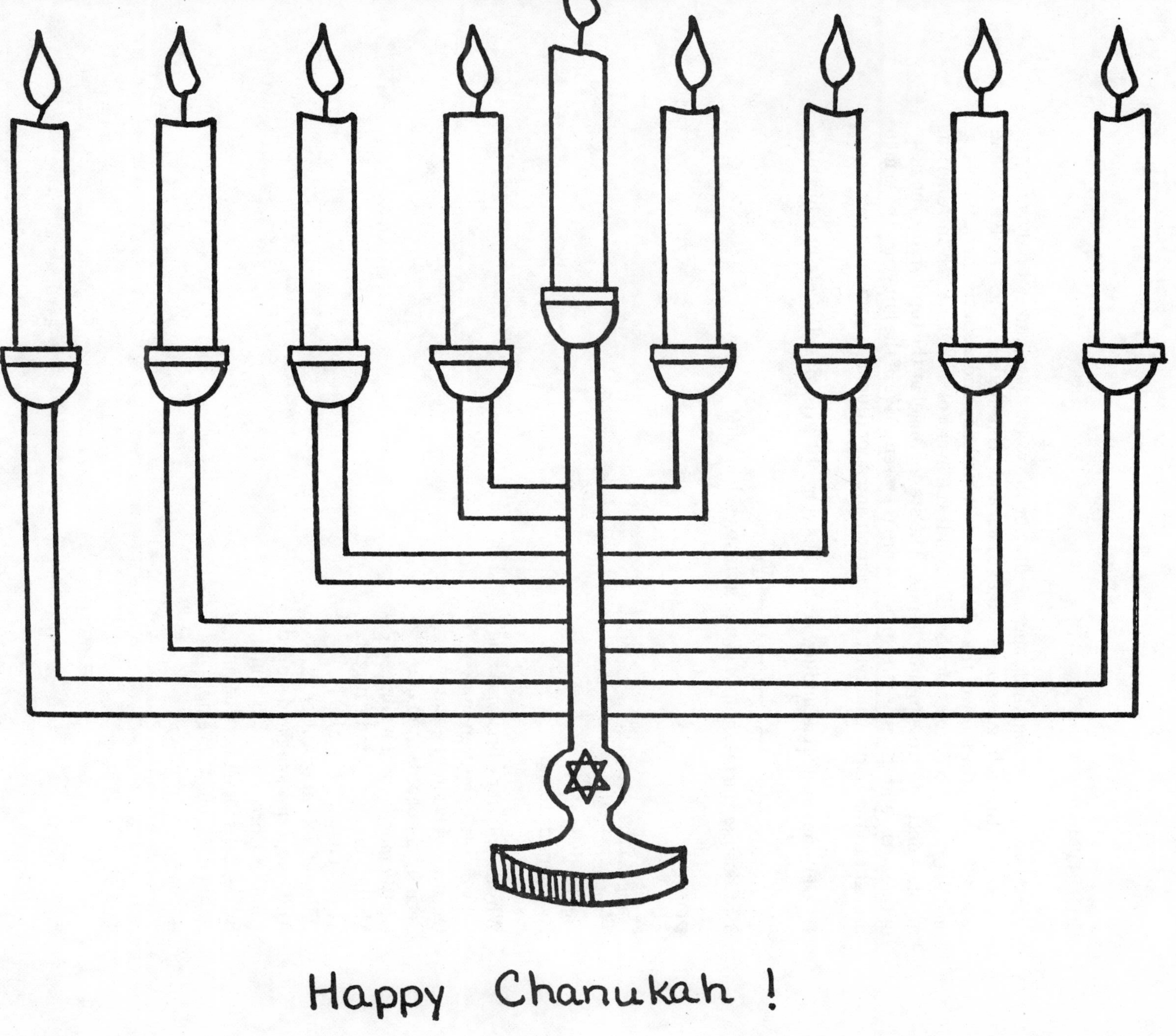
Happy Chanukah!

CHRISTMAS

Christmas means something special all over the world. It means not only a Christmas tree with bright glass balls, silver tinsel and bright lights, songs, holly, ivy, and Santa; but also the story of the Christ Child's birthday and a special hope for peace on Earth, good will toward men. To recall the event of Christ's birth in America, families decorate trees in their homes. The star or angel at the top heralds the news of the birth, and the gifts strewn below are representative of the gifts three wise men brought to the Christ Child in appreciation and adoration of His presence.

1. Develop an understanding of the meaning of Christmas. It's really a birthday party for Christ.
2. Tell about celebrations in other lands.
3. Consider the meaning of giving gifts to each other.

POEMS:

Hang up the stockings
Turn out the light.
Get ready for Santa
He's coming tonight.

Why do bells for Christmas ring?
Why do little children sing?
Once a lovely shining star
Seen by shepherds from afar
Gently moved until its light
Made a manger's cradle bright.
There a darling baby lay
Pillowed soft upon the hay,
And its mother sang and smiled
"This is Christ, the Holy Child."
So the bells for Christmas ring,
So the little children sing.

Merry Christmas!

MARTIN LUTHER KING DAY

This is a new holiday on January 15, established to honor a great American black leader who practiced peaceful demonstration for equal rights. Martin Luther King was born in the South and grew up to become a Baptist minister. His work for equal rights was supported by people of all races, and he was given many awards for his efforts. Unfortunately, he was shot and killed on April 4, 1968 in Memphis, Tennessee, and our whole country lost a great leader.

1. Correlate equal rights to sharing toys and taking turns.
2. Explain how discussion and cooperation (peaceful means of problem solving) are more effective than fighting and violence.
3. Color the picture. Tell the children that King's most famous speech talked about his dream of equality and brotherhood for all people in the future.

POEMS:

A man named Martin Luther King
Gave us a new song to sing.
A black man, a minister's son
Told us we could overcome.
Equality will be our right,
And brotherhood will shine its light.

Martin Luther King stepped out;
Told us how, without a doubt.
Equality would march on through
With brotherhood for me and you.

Martin Luther King Day

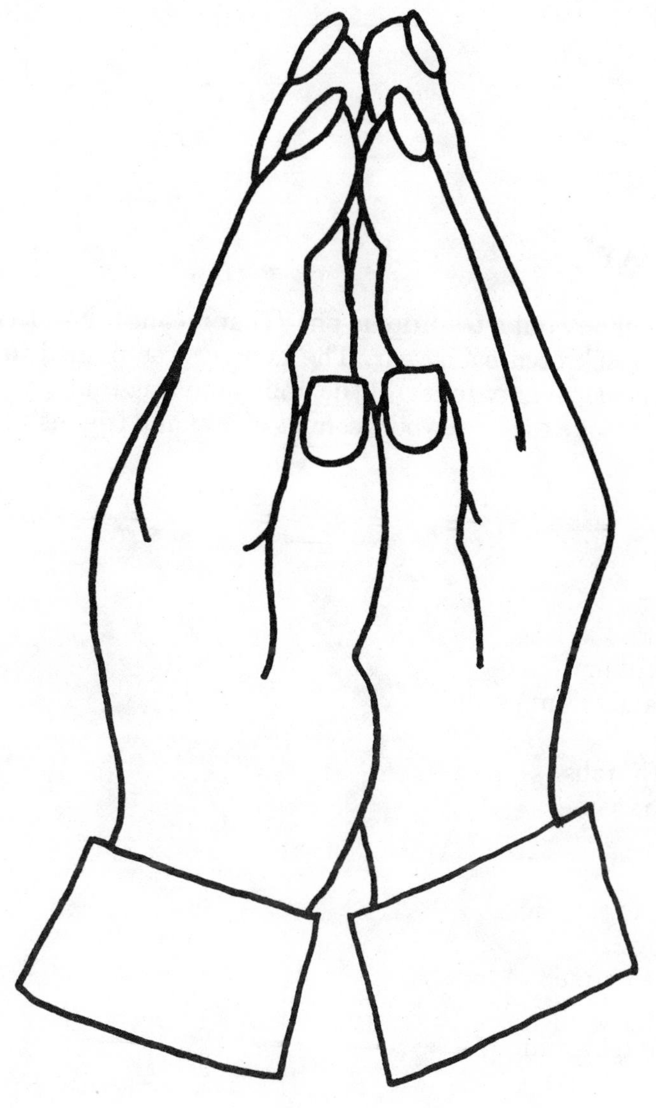

He had a dream and
worked for equal rights.

VALENTINE'S DAY

This is not a legal holiday but a traditional one. That means it has become a custom handed down and celebrated each year. The holiday was named in honor of two saints named Valentine. We try to instill the understanding that Valentine's Day is a special holiday set aside to express our feelings of love and friendship for others.

POEMS:

To My Valentine

If apples were pears
And peaches were plums
And the rose had a different name,
If tigers were bears
And fingers were thumbs
I'd love you just the same.

Valentine

Valentine, valentine
Who will be my valentine?
Valentine, valentine,
I'll be yours, if you'll be mine.

HAPPY VALENTINE'S
DAY!

HAPPY
VALENTINE'S
DAY
Make a mobile :

PRESIDENT'S DAY

In most states the third Monday in February is called President's Day and it celebrates Washington's birthday and Lincoln's birthday. Sometimes it is called Washington-Lincoln Day. On June 24, 1968 a law was passed which went into effect in 1971, approving four Monday holidays for all federal employees in order that they could enjoy a three day weekend. President's Day is included under this law.

POEMS:

When Lincoln was a little boy
He worked hard everyday.
He learned to read and took up law
Then was President one day.

He helped us in a time of strife
When south and north were split.
Let freedom ring for everyone
Go on and never quit.

When Washington was only five
As it was told to me
He took his shiny hatchet
And he chopped a cherry tree.

The tree was new and very small
Beside a bigger one
And thoughtless George just cut it down
Because he thought it fun.

His father walking out that day
Was cross to find it gone;
And sternly spoke to little George
"Come here to me, my son."

"Do you know why this little tree
Is lying on the ground?"
"Oh yes, sir. It was I who made
My hatchet cut it down."

"How sad!" his father said to him,
"And now it cannot grow.
"But though you did a foolish thing,
You told the truth, I know."

Happy President's Day!

ST. PATRICK'S DAY

This is a happy holiday in March that celebrates the myth of St. Patrick in Ireland. We celebrate this day on March 17. Tell the myth of St. Patrick chasing the snakes out of Ireland to bring good luck to the people there. Explain Ireland's legend of the little people and the good luck that follows them. Their pot of gold is found at the end of the rainbow, if anyone can ever get there before the rainbow fades.

1. The day before this holiday, ask the children to wear green to school the next day.
2. Color the shamrock green.

POEM:

Shamrocks, shamrocks,
On Ireland's hills,
Greenest of green
Over rocks and rills.

Good luck they do bring,
For one and all,
On St. Patricks's Day
We can see them call.

ST. PAT'S
DAY!
HAPPY

EASTER

This holiday comes on a different day each year, sometimes in March and sometimes in April. For Christians it is a day of great gladness, but for all people it is a happy time of rebirth and the coming of spring. Stress the re-birth of things to the children. Have an egg hunt in the classroom with eggs made out of colored paper. Four year-olds can make Easter baskets for a special project.

Two drawings are included for this holiday because the children enjoy preparing for it. Space the projects over a week period immediately preceding Easter Sunday.

POEM

Bunnies, bunnies,
Everywhere.
Bunnies, bunnies
Here and there.

Hiding colored eggs
Under chair legs
Heralding spring,
Having a fling.

Bunnies, bunnies,
Here and there,
Bunnies, bunnies
Everywhere!

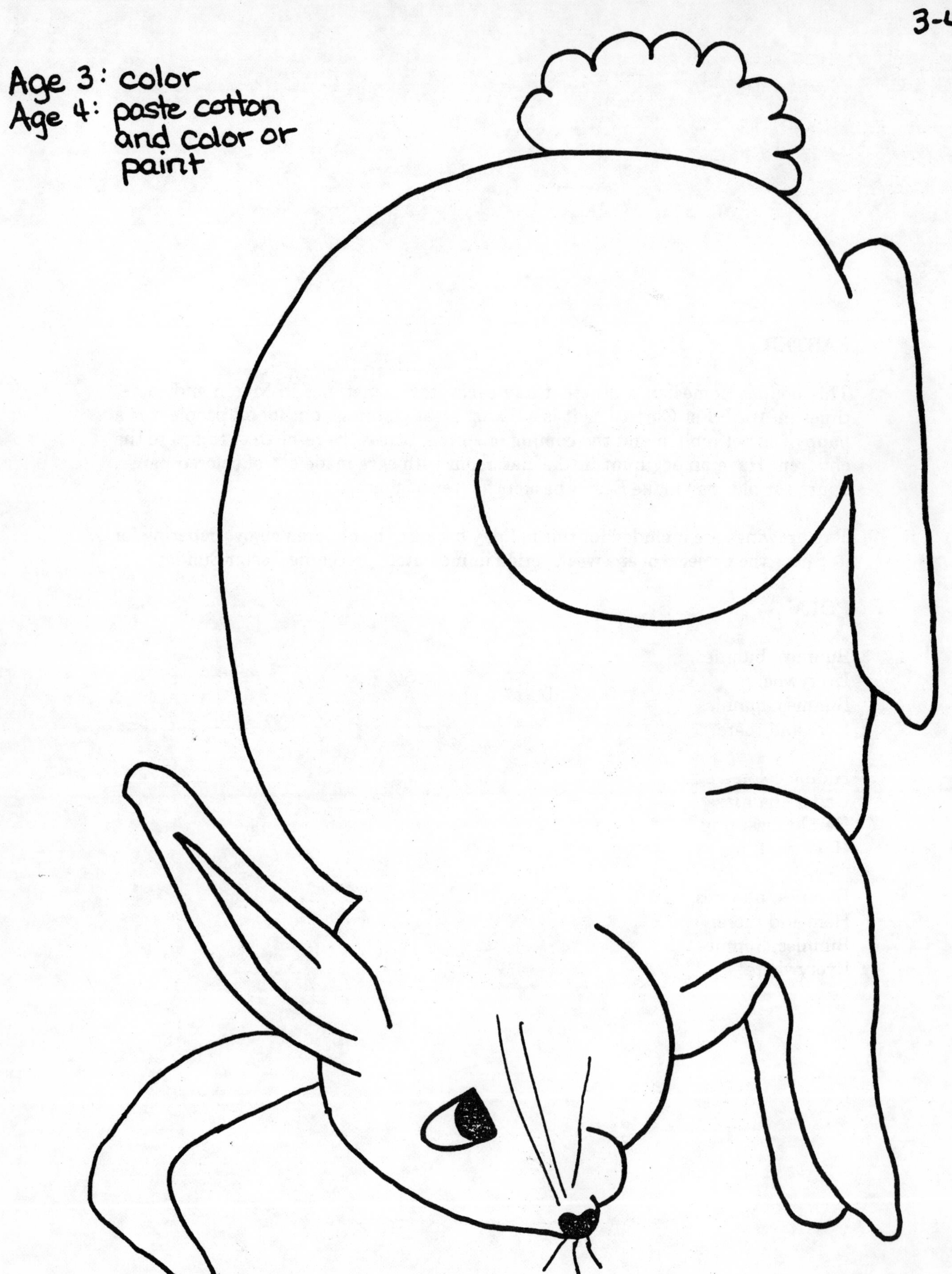
3-4
Age 3: color
Age 4: paste cotton
and color or
paint

Age 3: color
Age 4: paste pieces of egg carton to basket, color or paint eggs.

EASTER BASKET

EASTER PROJECT : 4 Year Old

Basket

Materials needed :

Colored egg cartons
Pipe cleaners (long)
Easter grass
Jelly beans

Method:

1. Cut egg cartons into 3 parts, with 4 sections in each:

2. Attach pipe cleaners to opposite corners for basket handle. If pipe cleaners are unavailable, cut strip from top of carton. Staple in place.

3. Add grass and a few jelly beans.

MEMORIAL DAY

May 30th is a sad day for our country for it is this day that we remember the hundreds of thousands of men and women who have been killed in the wars our country has fought. This is another holiday which used to have another name (Decoration Day). Families and friends used to go to the graves of loved ones who were killed in the wars and decorate them with flowers and flags.

1. Display the flag.
2. Explain fighting for our country to keep us safe.
3. Have a parade in the classroom.

POEMS:

(See syllabus for Veteran's Day)

MEMORIAL DAY